MODERNISM IN WONDERLAND

MODERNISM IN WONDERLAND

Legacies of Lewis Carroll

Edited by Michelle Witen and John D. Morgenstern

BLOOMSBURY ACADEMIC
LONDON • NEW YORK • OXFORD • NEW DELHI • SYDNEY

BLOOMSBURY ACADEMIC
Bloomsbury Publishing Plc
50 Bedford Square, London, WC1B 3DP, UK
1385 Broadway, New York, NY 10018, USA
29 Earlsfort Terrace, Dublin 2, Ireland

BLOOMSBURY, BLOOMSBURY ACADEMIC and the Diana logo
are trademarks of Bloomsbury Publishing Plc

First published in Great Britain 2024

Cover design: Eleanor Rose

A catalogue record for this book is available from the British Library.

Library of Congress Cataloging-in-Publication Data
Names: Witen, Michelle L. (Michelle Lynn), editor. | Morgenstern,
John D. (John David), 1980- editor.
Title: Modernism in Wonderland : legacies of Lewis Carroll / edited by
Michelle Witen and John D. Morgenstern.
Description: London ; New York : Bloomsbury Academic, 2024. |
Series: Historicizing modernism ; vol 46 | Includes bibliographical references and index.
Identifiers: LCCN 2023030710 (print) | LCCN 2023030711 (ebook) |
ISBN 9781350248717 (hardback) | ISBN 9781350248755 (paperback) |
ISBN 9781350248724 (pdf) | ISBN 9781350248731 (ebook)
Subjects: LCSH: Carroll, Lewis, 1832–1898–Influence. | Modernism (Literature) |
Fiction–20th century–History and criticism.
Classification: LCC PR4612 .M54 2024 (print) | LCC PR4612 (ebook) |
DDC 823/.8–dc23/eng/20230719
LC record available at https://lccn.loc.gov/2023030710
LC ebook record available at https://lccn.loc.gov/2023030711

ISBN: HB: 978-1-3502-4871-7
         ePDF: 978-1-3502-4872-4
        eBook: 978-1-3502-4873-1

Series: Historicizing Modernism

Typeset by Integra Software Services Pvt. Ltd.

To find out more about our authors and books visit www.bloomsbury.com
and sign up for our newsletters.

CONTENTS

FIGURES

NOTES ON CONTRIBUTORS

David Conlon is Lecturer at Maynooth University, where he teaches courses on the short story in Latin America, crime and popular culture in Latin America, Latin American crime cinema, and translation. His main research interests lie in Latin American Literature and film, with a particular focus on political, ecocritical and crime narratives. He has published articles and book chapters on Antonio Di Benedetto, Ricardo Piglia, Rodolfo Walsh, and Kleber Mendonça Filho, and has publications forthcoming on Norah Lange, ecological crime narratives, and Latin American crime fiction on screen.

Paul Fagan is Irish Research Council Fellow at Maynooth University, a co-founder of the International Flann O'Brien Society, a founding general editor of the *Journal of Flann O'Brien Studies*, and an elected member of the International James Joyce Foundation Board of Trustees. Paul is the co-editor of *Irish Modernisms: Gaps, Conjectures, Possibilities* (2021) and *Stage Irish: Performance, Identity, Cultural Circulation* (2021), as well as four edited volumes on Flann O'Brien. He is currently finalizing monographs on Irish literary hoaxes and celibacy in Irish women's writing, 1860s–1950s and edited collections on the nonhuman in Flann O'Brien and *Finnegans Wake*.

Yaeli Greenblatt received her PhD from The Hebrew University of Jerusalem. Her research interests include the materiality of the modernist image, typography, illustrations, and graphic-novels, alongside non-human and digital theatre. Her articles and reviews have appeared in *The Parish Review*, *James Joyce Quarterly*, and the *European Joyce Studies* special collection on Joyce and the arts. She has also published on the body as costume in *Flann O'Brien: Gallows Humour* (2020) and on animal vulnerability in *An Béal Bocht* in *Flann O'Brien and the Nonhuman* (2024). Greenblatt teaches English literature at Bar-Ilan University and theater studies at The Jerusalem Academy of Music and Dance.

Alexandra Lukes is Assistant Professor of French and Translation Studies at Trinity College Dublin. She works on the relationship between sound, sense, and nonsense, and on experimental literary translation. She is the editor of the special issue 'Nonsense, Madness, and The Limits of Translation' (*Translation Studies*, 2019) and *Avant-Garde Translation* (2023), and has published articles in *MLN*, *Modernism/modernity*, *Revue d'Histoire Littéraire de la France*, *Romanic Review*, *Translation and Literature*, *Translation Ireland*, and *Translation Studies*. She has contributed chapters to *Modernism and Non-Translation* (2019), *Prismatic Translation* (2019), and *The Edinburgh Companion to Nonsense* (2021).

Céline Mansanti is Assistant Professor of American Studies at the University of Picardie Jules Verne in Amiens, France. She works on the cultural history of the United States, mostly from a transnational perspective, with a focus on early twentieth-century periodicals. She is the author of a book on the American exile magazine *transition* (Paris, 1927–38) and she coedited collective works on modernist magazines, transatlantic intellectual networks (1914–64), and American surrealist literary experiments of the first half of the twentieth century.

Ann Martin is Associate Professor in the Department of English at the University of Saskatchewan. Her areas of interest include Anglo-American and Canadian modernisms, the dynamics of intertextuality, and the relationship between cultural studies and new materialism. Her current project is *Modernity Must Drive,* an essay collection on motor cars and car culture in interwar British fiction, which she is coediting with Christopher Townsend.

Jessica R. McCort is Associate Professor in the Literature, Culture, and Society Department at Point Park University, as well as the Director of the Honors Program. She earned her PhD in English and American literature from Washington University in St. Louis, specializing in American literature and women's writing. McCort's scholarship focuses largely on the appropriation of children's literature, particularly Grimm's and Andersen's fairy tales and Lewis Carroll's *Alice* books, by American women writers. She was also the editor of a compilation of essays concerning the intersection of the horror genre and children's and young adult literature and culture, titled *Reading in the Dark: Horror in Children's Literature and Culture.*

Michelle E. Moore is Professor of English at the College of Dupage. She is the author of *Chicago and the Making of American Modernism: Cather, Hemingway, Faulkner, and Fitzgerald in Conflict* (Bloomsbury 2019) and co-editor of *Refocus: The Films of Paul Schrader* (2020). She has published articles in *Faulkner Journal, Literature/Film Quarterly* and *Cather Studies 9 and 11.* In addition she has published chapters in the collections: *Rape in Art Cinema, Teaching Henry James,* and *Hemingway in the Digital Age.*

John D. Morgenstern is a scholar of twentieth-century literature and the arts who has taught in England, Germany, and the United States. He now serves as Associate Librarian at Emory University. John is the co-editor of *The Edinburgh Companion to T. S. Eliot and the Arts* (2016) and the founding editor of *The T. S. Eliot Studies Annual.* He is currently revising a book manuscript tentatively titled *T. S. Eliot: Controversialist,* which reconstructs the French periodical debates that he encountered as a student in Paris and later reformulated in his early, influential criticism.

Lisa Mullen is Senior Teaching Associate at the University of Cambridge, and Fellow of Fitzwilliam College. Her research is in modern and contemporary literature, film, and critical theory, with a particular interest in phenomenological and materialist approaches to embodiment, environment, and toxicity. Her first monograph, *Midcentury Gothic* (2019), was on the uncanny agency of the non-human in post–Second World War literature and culture; her next will be on Orwell and illness. She edited the Oxford World Classics edition of Orwell's *Homage to Catalonia* (2021), and her *Very Short Introduction to Ecocriticism* is forthcoming.

Allan Pero is Associate Professor of English and Core Faculty at The Centre for the Study of Theory and Criticism at the University of Western Ontario, Canada. He is also Editor-in-Chief of *English Studies in Canada*. He is co-editor of and contributor to *The Many Façades of Edith Sitwell* (2017). Recent publications include articles on Camp, Denton Welch, Lynda Barry, Wyndham Lewis, Katherine Mansfield, Jacques Lacan and the Posthuman, Ford Madox Ford, and Brigid Brophy. He is currently working on an edition of Lewis's *The Childermass* and book-length projects on Camp and Modernism and Wyndham Lewis.

Teresa Prudente is Associate Professor of English Literature at the University of Turin, Italy. She has authored a monograph on Woolf's temporalities (*A Specially Tender Piece of Eternity: Virginia Woolf and the Experience of Time*, 2009), a book on Woolf, Joyce, and science (*To Saturate Every Atom: Letteratura e Scienza in Woolf e Joyce*, 2012), and edited and translated into Italian Shakespeare's *The Two Noble Kinsmen* (2015). Her research focuses on interdisciplinary investigations connecting literature with linguistics, epistemology, and, more recently, the cognitive sciences.

James Williams is Senior Lecturer in Nineteenth-Century Literature and Culture at the University of York. He wrote his PhD on Victorian nonsense writing and *Finnegans Wake*. His publications include *Edward Lear and the Play of Poetry* (2016, co-edited with Matthew Bevis), *History Is Our Mother: Three Libretti* by Alice Goodman (2017, introduction and notes), *Edward Lear* (2018), *The Edinburgh Companion to Nonsense* (2022, co-edited with Anna Barton), and articles and chapters on writers from Tennyson, Carroll, and Darwin to Samuel Beckett and Dorothy Parker. He is an editor of the OUP journal *Cambridge Quarterly*.

Michelle Witen is Junior Professor of English and Irish Literature at the Europa-Universität Flensburg as well as Director of the EUF Centre for Irish Studies. She obtained her DPhil from the University of Oxford and is the author of *James Joyce and Absolute Music* (2018). Recent publications include articles on *Darby O'Gill and the Little People* and stage Irishness, the Ladybird books and Brexit, *Dracula* and the Irish question, and a special edition of the *James Joyce Quarterly* on 'Joyce and the Nonhuman'. Her current research interests include nineteenth- and twentieth-century British and Irish literature, particularly within the contexts of music, interdisciplinarity, intermediality, serialization, and genetic criticism.

SERIES EDITORS' PREFACE TO *HISTORICIZING MODERNISM*

This book series is devoted to the analysis of late nineteenth- to twentieth-century literary modernism within its historical contexts. *Historicizing Modernism* therefore stresses empirical accuracy and the value of primary sources (such as letters, diaries, notes, drafts, marginalia, or other archival materials) in developing monographs and edited collections on modernist literature. This may take a number of forms, such as manuscript study and genetic criticism, documenting interrelated historical contexts and ideas, and exploring biographical information. To date, no book series has fully laid claim to this interdisciplinary, source-based territory for modern literature. While the series addresses itself to a range of key authors, it also highlights the importance of non-canonical writers with a view to establishing broader intellectual genealogies of modernism. Furthermore, while the series is weighted towards the English-speaking world, studies of non-Anglophone modernists whose writings are open to fresh historical exploration are also included.

A key aim of the series is to reach beyond the familiar rhetoric of intellectual and artistic 'autonomy' employed by many modernists and their critical commentators. Such rhetorical moves can and should themselves be historically situated and reintegrated into the complex continuum of individual literary practices. It is our intent that the series' emphasis upon the contested self-definitions of modernist writers, thinkers, and critics may, in turn, prompt various reconsiderations of the boundaries delimiting the concept 'modernism' itself. Indeed, the concept of 'historicizing' is itself debated across its volumes, and the series by no means discourages more theoretically informed approaches. On the contrary, the editors hope that the historical specificity encouraged by *Historicizing Modernism* may inspire a range of fundamental critiques along the way.

Matthew Feldman
Erik Tonning

ACKNOWLEDGEMENTS

In addition to our wonderful authors, we wish to thank those who have contributed through their time, expertise, and support. First, our editors at Bloomsbury, especially David Avital, Ben Doyle, Rachel Walker, and Laura Cope, who supported and encouraged this project. We would also like to thank the *Historicizing Modernism* series editors, Matthew Feldman and Erik Tonning, for including this volume among their titles. We are grateful to Derek Gottlieb for his indexing magic and to the production work of Integra, especially Kaveya Saravanan.

We would also like to thank Ronald Bush, Ina Habermann, and Nils Langer for the inspiration of their examples and encouragement; Katherine Ebury, for her advice and support; Frances Dickey, for her generous suggestions on the Eliot chapter; Sam Slote, for his input on the violet ink of the Joyce chapter; and Kathrin Behrends, for her hard work as a student assistant. We also wish to thank our institutions – the Europa-Universität Flensburg, Exeter College (Oxford), the University of Basel, Clemson University, and Emory University – who provided support and the resources essential to the conception and realization of this volume at various points during its composition. Finally, and most importantly, we thank our families, especially Michael, Stew, and Danny, without whose support and patience the volume certainly would not have reached completion.

Chapter 1

INTRODUCTION: TWENTIETH-CENTURY WONDERLANDS

Michelle Witen

The Queen of Hearts shouting 'off with their heads'; the chasing of the perpetually late, waist-coated White Rabbit down the Rabbit Hole; food labelled 'DRINK ME' and 'EAT ME'; a game of croquet with a flamingo as a mallet; a convoluted conversation with Humpty Dumpty and/or a hookah-smoking Caterpillar; asking directions from a grinning, disappearing Cheshire Cat; talking flowers; a Mad Tea Party with the Mad Hatter, the March Hare, and a dormouse; Alice's blue dress and white pinafore; the concept of the un-birthday; roses being painted red to placate an unreasonable queen; absurd trial scenes involving tarts; body parts that grow and shrink almost uncontrollably; playing cards and chess pieces that have come to life; the concept of a topsy-turvy wonderland or an inverted world that can be accessed through the looking-glass; etc. These references to Lewis Carroll's novels, *Alice's Adventures in Wonderland* and *Through the Looking-Glass and What Alice Found There*, are so embedded in cultural memory that they have the capacity to evoke images at their mere mention, even for those who have not read the texts. Whether filtered through the novels' afterlives in film, drama, music, caricatures, illustrations, language, or parody, these images have lasted long past the respective publication dates of 1865 and 1871.[1] John Tenniel's iconic illustrations – which also informed all subsequent film productions, including the 1951 Disney film – have played a particularly large role in the longevity of the *Alice* books[2]: critics such as Ahmet Süner have argued that the illustrations exist outside of the novels, supplementing Carroll's text 'by drawing out and depicting the nonsensical references and odd creatures of Wonderland that may be overlooked or ignored by the reader' and even 'reinforc[ing] the effect of nonsense' that might 'otherwise remain buried'.[3] In this way, Alice and her entourage of characters become immediately recognizable, whether one has read the text or not. This is part of the text's immortality as well as proof that the *Alice* books are 'not just one writer's imaginary universe' but, in the words of Robert Douglas-Fairhurst, 'something more like a cultural multiverse, a loose network of real places and intangible ideas where the line that divided the actual from the possible could be stretched and blurred'.[4]

When it first appeared in 1865, *Alice's Adventures in Wonderland* was hailed by magazines, such as *Aunt Judy's Magazine*, as an 'exquisitely wild, fantastic, impossible, yet most natural history' that nevertheless should not be considered as 'knowledge in disguise',[5] but rather as 'one long dream of sheer nonsense'.[6] In other words, for the Victorian child reader, under no circumstances should Alice's adventures be taken as educational, a sentiment voiced by Lewis Carroll himself: 'I can guarantee that the books have no religious teaching whatever in them – in fact they do not teach anything at all'.[7] Instead, the *Alice* books contain situations that defy child-friendly contexts. For example, Alice falls to the temptation of drinking substances out of bottles that do not delineate their contents, despite knowing the fates of preceding children doing the same: 'for she had read several nice little stories about children who had got burnt, and eaten up by wild beasts […] all because they *would* not remember the simple rules their friends had taught them […] and she had never forgotten that, if you drink much from a bottle marked "poison", it is almost certain to disagree with you, sooner or later'.[8] Since the bottle is not marked 'poison', Alice assumes it is safe to drink, disregarding that during the Victorian period, many dangerous substances and 'toxic ingredients, like carbolic acid, were contained in bottles and packages that were indistinguishable from other household products', causing numerous accidental deaths.[9] In fact, it was not until 1902 that the necessity for differentiated packaging between dangerous and safe liquids was legislated through the Pharmacy Act.[10] Alice soon learns that even though it does not have a label marking it as poison, the 'DRINK ME' bottle nevertheless causes her to undergo significant physical transformation and discomfort, causing the same fate to befall her as those who had come before. As such, despite *Alice* not being an overtly instructive tale – often quite the opposite, where bad behaviour is rewarded or goes unpunished – it does conform with some elements of eighteenth- and nineteenth-century children's literature, evincing the Victorian-specific messaging that matches moral tales about harmful consumption.

Notwithstanding these instances, as a novel – one that was particularly read by modernist authors (during their childhood and after) – *Alice* opened the possibility of children's literature moving beyond didactic considerations. Until the nineteenth century, British children's literature was moral and pedagogical. It was intended to be used for 'whatever ethical message was then in fashion, whether it be that hard work always leads to improvement in one's financial and social position […], or that idle and thoughtless children would soon die an unpleasant death and then suffer everlasting torment in Hell'.[11] However, as a protagonist, Alice grows beyond the 'model child' of the eighteenth century, who was a 'perfect imitation adul[t] […] under the tutelage of adults',[12] demonstrating the changing perception of the Victorian child. As Hugh Haughton states in his introduction to his edition of *Alice's Adventures in Wonderland* and *Through the Looking-Glass*, 'The publication of the Alice books marks a watershed in the literature about childhood as well as children's literature. For all their originality, they are a product of a culture with a huge and developing investment in the idea of childhood.'[13]

In conjunction with literature geared towards children, Humphrey Carpenter writes in *Secret Gardens: A Study of the Golden Age of Literature* that the most popular reading for children prior to the nineteenth century was *Aesop's Fables*, abridged versions of Jonathan Swift's *Gulliver's Travels*, and Daniel Defoe's *Robinson Crusoe*, as they 'managed to combine excitement with some sort of moral message', balancing 'tale and message'.[14] However, with Alice, no longer was the child being conditioned by fairy tales or cajoled by moral stories into good and proper behaviour; no longer were adventures things that only happened to adults like Lemuel Gulliver or Robinson Crusoe, who were allegedly better equipped to handle the challenges of alterity. Instead, Alice, like both men, is permitted adventures outside of the everyday, enquiries that are uncomfortable but not permanently life-threatening – at least not for her: the other inhabitants in Wonderland and Looking-Glass country appear to be continually endangered – and to exist in nonsense and misremembered lessons. Alice becomes the authority and the rebel, continually questioning the rules that govern these topsy-turvy worlds. In fact, as Ann Lawson Lucas writes in 'Enquiring Mind, Rebellious Spirit: Alice and Pinocchio as Nonmodel Children': 'by ordinary social standards, Alice is often rude and shows no acknowledgment of her elders also being her betters, especially in the intellectual domain',[15] and she considers herself to be both authority and arbiter of justice in Wonderland and Looking-Glass country, despite the presence of authority figures (superficially) more qualified than herself. Similarly, from an educational standpoint, while Alice is continually doubting herself as a student based on her inaccurate recitations of lessons learned in school – 'the words did not come the same as they used to do [...] I'm sure those are not the right words'[16] – she also adopts the role of educator, for example trying to teach the Duchess 'figures', playing the social worker who should remove the pig-baby from the Duchess's custody lest it be murdered, and instructing the pig-baby in manners, saying that its grunting is 'not at all a proper way of expressing yourself'.[17]

This crux of instructor and instructed is one of the reasons the place of the *Alice* books in the genre of children's literature has been so deeply problematized. As Roger Henkle puts it, the texts

> have been impossible to integrate into the development of the novel, and thus we have had to place them in separate categories: fantasy, or children's literature. Yet they do not sit easily in those genres either, for they contain a great deal of overt social criticism of social manners, of Victorian morality, of Darwinism, and of ideas about time, language, and logic that one normally does not find in such literature.[18]

Henkle pinpoints the problems of *Alice* as rooted in the overt critique of Victorian historical, political, linguistic, cultural, educational, scientific, moral, and social contexts. While social problem novels existed, they were not generally geared towards children, who were meant to benefit from the socializing lessons of these stories. *Alice* was the first of its kind to celebrate childishness and childhood. Thus, in many ways, the *Alice* books prompted a shift in the way these exact contexts were represented: childhood, girlhood, morality, and selfhood were in a state of flux. As Aihong Ren states, Alice overcomes the 'power imbalance between adults and children' by struggling against the 'mad and disorderly world of adults' in Wonderland who seek to 'dominate [...] and infantilize' her.[19] In so doing, she 'subverts the fixed hierarchical structure of adults and children' of the Victorian period.[20]

From the perspective of a coming-of-age narrative, the *Alice* books also contain interesting messages that fit within the genre of travel writing about the dangers of women travelling alone, a thread of criticism that is also taken up in this collection. Whether travelling by water, by foot, or by train, Alice continually encounters obstacles. Over the course of her adventures, Alice nearly drowns, albeit in a pool of her own tears;[21] is nearly dismembered and burned to death when she enters an unknown house;[22] is caught travelling without a train ticket, resulting in her being subjected to the gaze of a 'telescope', 'microscope', and 'opera glass', before moving from stationary observed object to moving subject as a postage package labelled 'Lass with care', then a 'telegraph message'.[23] Eventually she even becomes a beast of burden, instructed to 'draw the train herself the rest of the way'.[24] She is lost in the wood and cannot remember her own name or identity,[25] and there are ubiquitous dangers in all the terrains of the looking-glass checkerboard. While she is ultimately safe and conquers these dangers (unlike the inhabitants), they nevertheless contain elements of the cautionary tale, both for the child and for the girl/woman travelling alone.

In addition to engaging with coming-of-age narratives, travel writing, and prompting trends in Victorian children's literature – all of which would be formative to the consciousness of the modernist authors discussed in this collection – the *Alice* books also participated in contemporary debates of the time in interesting and fruitful ways. This has been shown by Gillian Beer in *Alice in Space*, which is entirely devoted to uncovering the insights the *Alice* books provide into many of the artistic debates taking place from mid- to late nineteenth century.[26] Similarly, Anna Kerchy also demonstrates how Carroll engages with contemporaneous debates concerning animal rights and anti-vivisectionists.[27]

Nevertheless, the question remains: how exactly does one go about categorizing these novels which seem to defy categorization? Should they be seen as fairy tales? Folktales? Fantasy? Are they even novels at all? Or are they simply nonsense? Turning to the text, Lewis Carroll himself sets the tone for the reading of *Alice* as a fairy tale in his prefatory poem 'Christmas-Greetings [from a fairy to a child]', which was attached to *Alice's Adventures in Wonderland* in the facsimile MS of *Alice's Adventures Under Ground* (1864).[28] However, writing in 1959, J. R. R. Tolkien very clearly rejects the by-then typical reading of *Alice* as fairy tale in his effort to define the term 'fairy story':

> But since the fairy-story deals with 'marvels', it cannot tolerate any frame or machinery suggesting that the whole story in which they occur is a figment or illusion. The tale itself may, of course, be so good that one can ignore the frame. Or it may be successful and amusing as a dream-story. So are Lewis Carroll's Alice stories, with their dream-frame and dream-transitions. For this (and other reasons) they are not fairy-stories.[29]

According to Tolkien, because of the dream-framing device and Alice's ability to disengage from Wonderland/Looking-Glass country by waking up, the stories lack the full immersion in the faerie realm that Tolkien deems necessary for the classification of fairy tale or fairy story. Instead, for Tolkien, the *Alice* books come closer to fantasy because of Carroll's use of language. Carroll's 'combining [of] nouns and redistributing [of] adjectives' is part of the novels' charm: 'For creative Fantasy is founded upon the hard recognition that things are so in the world as it appears under the sun; on a recognition of fact, but not a slavery to it. So upon logic was founded the nonsense that displays itself in the tales and rhymes of Lewis Carroll.'[30]

Tolkien is certainly not the first to seek to classify *Alice's Adventures in Wonderland* and *Through the Looking-Glass* via its use of language and nonsense. Writing in 1902, G. K. Chesterton even goes so far as to claim that 'nonsense is a new literature (we might almost say a new sense).'[31] This 'literature of the future' is a genre in its own right:

> If, therefore, nonsense is really to be the literature of the future, it must have its own version of the Cosmos to offer; the world must not only be the tragic, romantic, and religious, it must be nonsensical also […] Viewed from that other side, a bird is a blossom broken loose from its chain of stalk, a man a quadruped bagging on its hind legs, a house a gigantesque hat to cover a man from the sun, a chair an apparatus of four wooden legs for a cripple with only two.[32]

Related to this altered perception of the world, Chesterton, like Tolkien, pinpoints an insincerity in Carroll's writing: the world presented is only temporary and thus so is its version of the 'Cosmos'. Unlike Edward Lear's rhymes, whose writing Chesterton prefers, Carroll's works display an escapist reversal of daily Oxford life that is a holiday not a state of being: 'His Wonderland is a country populated by insane mathematicians. We feel the whole is an escape into a world of masquerade; we feel that if we could pierce their disguises, we might discover that Humpty Dumpty and the March Hare were Professors and Doctors of Divinity enjoying a mental holiday.'[33] This same disorientation aligns with Alice's own experience of Wonderland, where she also wakes from 'a wonderful dream' in *Alice's Adventures in Wonderland*.[34] In the case of *Through the Looking-Glass*, Alice even identifies how the kittens and chess pieces around her morphed into their dream associations and eventually cannot dissociate herself from the aura of those objects: the Red King 'was part of my dream, of course – but then I was part of his dream too! *Was* it the Red King, Kitty? You were his wife, my dear, you should know.'[35]

Although the *Alice* novels sparked many fields of criticism and have been approached through a variety of lenses – from Marxism, to economics, to feminism, to didactics, to food studies, to animal studies, to postcolonialism, to psychoanalysis, to nonsense and language studies, to discussions of its afterlives, etc. – this collection hones in on a very specific method with reference to the novels: namely, how and in what ways the influence of the novels can be detected in writings produced by modernists. This topic has been touched upon by a variety of scholars, with the most well-known studies being produced by critics of the 1950s and 1960s, such as J. S. Atherton and Ann McGarrity Buki (on James Joyce), Jeffrey Stern (on surrealism), Michael Holquist (on nonsense), and Elizabeth Sewell (on T. S. Eliot).[36] More recent texts include Juliet Dusinberre's *Alice to the Lighthouse: Children's Books and Radical Experiments* as well as the above-mentioned Gillian Beer and Robert Douglas-Fairhurst texts.[37] As these critics have argued, the experimentalism of the text proved to be a fertile playground for fin-de-siècle and early twentieth-century writers, and authors such as Woolf, Eliot, and Joyce have all been connected in terms of their indebtedness to Carroll's works. As Haughton writes: 'Translated by Nabokov into Russian, adopted by the Surrealists as proto-surrealist dream books in France, taken up by T. S. Eliot, Virginia Woolf, James Joyce, W. H. Auden and more recently Peter Ackroyd as models, the Alice books have been taken to prefigure modernism at its most experimental as well as children's writing at its most elemental.'[38] While critics have identified that the two *Alice* books are 'forerunners of the modernist novels,'[39] with the character of Alice being 'simultaneously Victorian and modern, old and young [...] belong[ing] everywhere and nowhere,'[40] it is arguably the texts' 'eerie perfection of the literary sphinx,'[41] and the possibilities offered in terms of navigating 'whether being modern meant abandoning the past or merely adapting it in more original ways' that most appealed to modernist authors.[42] This collection advances this earlier work on Carroll and individual modernists, and is the first to curate a diverse constellation of modernist writers and thus explore the extent of modernism's debt to Carroll at large.

Modernism in Wonderland retraces the steps of a surprising array of twentieth-century writers who ventured into the fantastical, topsy-turvy world of Lewis Carroll's fictions and discovered there the quintessence of their own modernity. Testing the authority of language and mediation through extensive word-play and genre-bending, the *Alice* books undoubtedly prefigure literary modernism at its most experimental. Yet, as this book also demonstrates, Carroll's influence extended far beyond literary style, pervading all aspects of modern life from commercial culture to politics, to childhood studies, to philosophy/epistemology, to globalism. This book challenges the tendency to view experimental modernism as a break with the past, instead highlighting the common denominator of indebtedness to Carroll's texts in a more capacious conception of modernism.

The collection is organized both chronologically and thematically. It draws out and expands upon established and less-established threads that extend from Carroll's world into modernist literature, starting with nineteenth-century French and early influences, and moving through themes, genres, and devices such as travel writing, femininity and coming-of-age, the development of creative identity, philosophies of language, time and space, fragmentedness, intertextuality, nonsense, and absurdity. Ending with chapters on later modernist texts from all over the globe, this collection seeks to engage with notions of global modernism and redefine its limits by exploring how the works and ideas of Carroll's *Alice* books are handled in a similar fashion by an unexpectedly broad cross-section of modernist writers. As such, *Modernism in Wonderland* demonstrates that even within the broader geographic definition of modernism, there remains a common antecedent, attitude, and approach(es) based on the prolific imaginary world of Lewis Carroll.

The volume opens in the nineteenth century, with Alexandra Lukes writing on 'Carroll's French and Mallarmé's English'. Lukes pays close attention to Lewis Carroll's and Stéphane Mallarmé's reverence for language to demonstrate that both engage with comparative philology and contemporaneous discussions concerning the historical relationships between languages. Converging around notions of pedagogy, Lukes demonstrates that both Carroll and Mallarmé seek parallel 'purifications' of English: Mallarmé through the uncovering of ancient French words in the English language as a vestige of the Norman invasion, Carroll through the defamiliarization of English to create nonsense.

As a contemporary of Lewis Carroll, Mallarmé had a comparably far-reaching influence on many of the authors discussed in this volume. This French connection has been well established, and thus the next two chapters by Céline Mansanti and John D. Morgenstern acknowledge the modernist indebtedness to French Symbolists and French surrealists, but rework Lewis Carroll into this conversation as well. For example, Morgenstern's piece, 'T. S. Eliot's Adventures in Wonderland', examines Eliot's *Inventions of the March Hare* and his earliest juvenilia – the fourteen issues of his little magazine, *Fireside* – to show how Eliot's early weaving of Carroll's poetry, characters, and literary nonsense with French Symbolism was instrumental in the formation of his later poetics. Mansanti also highlights chronological indebtedness in 'Fantastic Surrealism: The Influence of Lewis Carroll's Wonderland on *transition* Magazine's American Surrealist Literary Experiments'. Here again, the influence of Carroll's characters, dream world, and personifications in the formation of 'American superrealism', as seen in *transition* issues of the late 1920s and 1930s, predates French surrealist interest. This influence becomes a defining factor in the differentiation of an American, fantastic form of surrealism (i.e., in the works of Andrews, Burnett, Coates, Emory, Godwin, Hoffman, Tracy, and Whitsett), and its broader reception by an American audience, as opposed to its French counterpart. It also paves the way for the appearance of Joyce's 'Work in Progress' (*Finnegans Wake*) in *transition* from 1927 to 1938.

The American audience is similarly important to Michelle Moore's 'Alice and the Expansion of the American West: Modernism, the NPR's Wonderland Route, and Kate Chopin's *The Awakening*'. Following a feminist line of thought, Moore shows that the North Pacific Railroad's Wonderland Route's propaganda—featuring images of an intrepid, touristic Alice—positions her between Victorian and modernist ideals of womanhood. These images and metaphors are then replicated by Kate Chopin in *The Awakening*'s travel writing, which presents an adult, curious, travelling, exploratory Alice.

By contrast, in '"Open Alice's Door": Lewis Carroll's Influence on Elizabeth Bishop and Sylvia Plath', Jessica McCort demonstrates the opposite of the development of a grown-up Alice, focusing instead on how Plath and Bishop overcome the childhood narrative and feminine expectations of Wonderland to forge their own creative identities. In a parallel vein, Teresa Prudente's 'Becoming a Child: Lewis Carroll and Virginia Woolf's Poetics of Fluidity and Permanence' also focuses on the relationship between childhood, perception, and language. In this case, Prudente contrasts the integrity of Carroll's child-narrative with Woolf's preservation of Carrollian child-like linguistic fluidity in *The Waves*, as seen through the lens of Deleuze's philosophies of language and becoming.

Next in the collection is Lisa Mullen's '"Reeling and Writing" in Benjamin's *Arcades*: The Curious Case of the Girl who Wasn't There', which also explores the realms of subjectivity and capitalism. Benjamin's familiarity with Carroll, Mullen writes, was based on attempts at reading a few pages in the original English, but also through the mechanical reproductions of the text (i.e., film and Carroll's 1889 Wonderland Postage-Stamp Case). Mullen provides a kaleidoscopic reading of Carroll and Benjamin's *Arcades Project*, with Alice as ideal child-consumer who can be detected through Benjamin's unfinished work.

Completing the triad on philosophical standpoints, Allan Pero's '"These Tautomeric Changes": The Figures of Alice and Humpty Dumpty in the Work of W. H. Auden' layers Heidegger and Lacan onto Auden's prose and poetry. Navigating through language, desire, consciousness, unconsciousness, meaning, nonsense, and arbitrariness, Pero presents a new reading, particularly of Auden's very early 'Humpty Dumpty', that converges around the notion of secondary worlds.

Chronologically, the collection then moves into the 1930s, segueing into David Conlon's 'Nightmares of History: Modernism and Colonialism in Lewis Carroll and Jorge Luis Borges'. While the link between *Alice* and magic realism has long been a point of conversation, Conlon offers a new and rich reading of Latin American modernist mediation of colonial spaces through Carroll's ethnographic gaze. Focusing on elements such as time, space, perspective, and situatedness, Conlon repositions pivotal moments in the *Alice* novels in the texts of García Márquez, González Echevarría, and, more considerably, Borges to demonstrate how the authors navigate analogous relationships – such as imperialism, ethnography, political consciousness, and colonial violence – between Anglophone and Latin American modernisms.

Yaeli Greenblatt addresses a different form of violence, reading fragmented bodies in Nabokov as a distortion of Carrollian decapitation in '"Sentence First Verdict Afterwards": Carroll, Nabokov, and the Fragmented Body'. Nabokov's *Invitation to a Beheading* is read in conjunction with both *Alice* texts, where the significance of being under constant threat of decapitation destabilizes and unravels the nature of language. Greenblatt demonstrates how Carroll's nonsense, absurdity, and wordplay are reiterated as intertexts in Cincinnatus C.'s phantasmagoria, highlighting the arbitrariness of justice and violence and thereby providing a stark contrast between the two texts' use of execution.

Intertextuality is also an important component of Ann Martin's '"You're nothing but a pack of cards!": Carrollian Intertextuality and the Detective Fiction of Dorothy L. Sayers'. Here again, the focus is on later modernism, with Sayers's Wimsey novels (*Whose Body?* [1923], *Strong Poison* [1930], *Busman Honeymoon* [1937], and *The Wimsey Papers* [1939–40]), demonstrating parallels between detective fiction and the modernist subject. Converging around ideas of class, culture, socio-economic background, inhabited space, and playfulness, Martin highlights how explicit allusions to characters, the playing cards, and the chessboard of the *Alice* novels become the cultural landscape of Sayers's detective genre fiction as well as a moment of rupture between Victorian tradition and late modernism.

Martin's reading of play transitions into an exploration of James Joyce's *Finnegans Wake*, where James Williams's understanding of play extends from playhouse to playroom to wordplay to children's games in "'The Mime of Nick, Mick and the Maggies"; or, "Alice" on the Stage'. Williams presents a close reading of the Carrollian allusions and associations of Book II, Chapter 1 of the *Wake* as well as the preceding 'Anna Livia Plurabelle' chapter (I.8), which provides the setting of Carroll's famous 'golden afternoon' boat trip.[43] Together, these form what he refers to as an appropriated Carrollian mythos of the stage.

The final chapter of the collection returns full circle to its starting point – Carrollian nonsense – but now with a particular focus on how absurdity and time contribute to the notion. Paul Fagan's 'Wasting Timelessness: Lewis Carroll, Flann O'Brien, and Modernist Temporality' centres on time, Derridean *limitrophy*, excess, and waste in Flann O'Brien's *Irish Times* columns (published as Myles na gCopaleen) and *The Third Policeman*. Fagan enlarges on the concept of Wonderland time – with an emphasis on the Mad Tea-Party – as an unexplored trope in O'Brien's writing that can be politicized to show views on labour, politics, and dark comedy. Thus, the collection ends as it began, with reiterations of nonsense from the nineteenth to the twentieth centuries that have been refashioned into something new and modern.

Modernism in Wonderland: Legacies of Lewis Carroll, in brief, invites you down the Rabbit Hole, or perhaps it is through the looking-glass, to uncover twentieth-century modernist wonderlands. Drawing upon all the permutations and associations with this Carrollian construct, it brings together literary criticism on authors who are conventionally regarded as central and on the periphery of modernist studies and renders these distinctions topsy-turvy. In so doing, it problematizes and counters reductive ways of looking at modernism via engagement with the *Alice* novels. Examining how these authors converge around Lewis Carroll's works allows us to see lateral and linear parallels between the authors and their contemporaries as well as uncover unexpected discoveries regarding Carroll's influence on these authors. In so doing, a new conversation emerges concerning the narrative of rupture and rejection that has defined the relationship between literary modernism and the nineteenth century as well as individual indebtedness to Carroll's *Alice* books.

Notes

1   For an in-depth study of the transmedial afterlives of the *Alice* books, especially through the lens of the novels' 'generic hybridity' (4–5), see Anna Kerchy, *Alice in Transmedia Wonderland: Curiouser and Curiouser New Forms of a Children's Classic* (Jefferson: McFarland, 2016).

2   See Michael Hancher, *Tenniel's Illustrations to the Alice Books* (Columbus: Ohio University Press, 1985) for a more in-depth study of the relationship between Tenniel's illustrations, Victorian parody (especially *Punch* magazine), and the *Alice* books. For the afterlife of Tenniel's *Alice* illustrations in *Punch* magazine, see Frances Sarzano, *Sir John Tenniel* (London: Art and Technics, 1948) and Michael Hancher, '*Punch* and *Alice*: Through Tenniel's Looking-Glass', in *Lewis Carroll: A Celebration, Essays on the Occasion of the 150th Anniversary of the Birth of Charles Lutwidge Dodgson*, ed. Edward Guiliano (New York: Clarkson N. Potter, 1982), 26–49. For the collaboration between Tenniel and Carroll during the illustration process, see Richard Kelly, '"If you don't know what a Gryphon is": Text and Illustration in *Alice's Adventures in Wonderland*', in *Lewis Carroll: A Celebration*, 62–74; Janis Lull, 'The Appliances of Art: the Carroll-Tenniel Collaboration in *Through the Looking-Glass*', in *Lewis Carroll: A Celebration*, 101–11; and Robert Dupree, 'The White Knight's Whiskers and the Wasp's Wig in *Through the Looking-Glass*', in *Lewis Carroll: A Celebration*, 112–22.

3   Ahmet Süner, 'On the Contribution of Tenniel's Illustrations to the Reading of the Alice Books', *Children's Literature in Education* 51 (2020): 43.

4   Robert Douglas-Fairhurst, *The Story of Alice: Lewis Carroll and the Secret History of Wonderland* (Boston: Harvard University Press, 2015), 336.

5   An excerpt from a first review in *Aunt Judy's Magazine*. According to Gillian Avery, this was likely penned by Mrs Gatty (Gillian Avery, 'Fairy Tales with a Purpose; Fairy Tales for Pleasure', in *Alice in Wonderland, Norton Critical Edition*, ed. Donald J. Gray [New York: W. W. Norton & Company, 1992], 326–7). For the original review, see also 'Reviews: *Alice's Adventures in Wonderland*. By Lewis Carroll: with Forty-two Illustrations by John Tenniel', *Aunt Judy's Magazine* 1, no. 2 (1 June 1866): 129, https:// www.bl.uk/collection-items/review-of-alices-adventures-in-wonderland.

6   Charlotte Yonge, quoted in Avery, 'Fairy Tales', 327.

7   Michael Holquist, 'What is a Boojum? Nonsense and Modernism', *Yale French Studies* 43 (1969), reproduced in *Yale French Studies: 50 Years of Yale French Studies, A Commemorative Anthology* 96 (1999), quoting Lancelyn, 109.

8   Lewis Carroll, *Alice's Adventures in Wonderland* and *Through the Looking-Glass*, ed. Hugh Haughton (London: Penguin, 1998), 13.

9   'Ten Dangerous Things in Victorian and Edwardian Homes', https://www.bbc.com/ news/uk-25259505, n.p.

10   Ibid.

11   Humphrey Carpenter, *Secret Gardens: A Study of the Golden Age of Literature* (London: George Allen and Unwin, 1985), 2. It should be noted that Carpenter identifies Catherine Sinclair's *Holiday House* (1839) as the first work of fiction that elevates the naughty child, and that this was gifted by Carroll to the Liddells shortly before the infamous boat-trip down the Isis (9).

12   Ann Lawson Lucas, 'Enquiring Mind, Rebellious Spirit: Alice and Pinocchio as Nonmodel Children', *Children's Literature in Education* 30, no. 3 (1999): 158.

13   Hugh Haughton, 'Introduction', in *Alice's Adventures in Wonderland* and *Through the Looking-Glass*, ed. Hugh Haughton (London: Penguin, 1998), lviii.

14   Ibid., 3. John Bunyan's *The Pilgrim's Progress* was also extremely popular with younger readers (3).

15   Lucas, 'Enquiring Mind', 160.

16   Carroll, *Alice*, 19.

17   Ibid., 54.

18   Roger B. Henkle, 'Carroll's Narratives Underground: "Modernism" and Form', in
      Lewis Carroll: A Celebration, 89.
19   Aihong Ren, 'Power Struggle between the Adult and Child in *Alice's Adventures in
      Wonderland*', *Theory and Practice in Language Studies* 5, no. 8 (2015): 1659.
20   Ibid., 1663.
21   Carroll, *Alice,* 21.
22   Ibid., 35–6.
23   Ibid., 146–7.
24   Ibid.
25   Ibid., 153.
26   See Gillian Beer, *Alice in Space: The Sideways Victorian World of Lewis Carroll*
      (Chicago: Chicago University Press, 2018), where she covers themes such as
      mathematics, space, language, philosophy, pedagogy, identity politics, and
      consumerism.
27   See Anna Kerchy, 'Alice's Non-Anthropocentric Ethics: Lewis Carroll as a Defender
      of Animal Rights', *Cahiers victoriens et édouardiens* 88 (Fall 2018), http://journals.
      openedition.org/cve/3909.
28   Lewis Carroll, 'Christmas-Greetings [from a Fairy to a Child]', in *Alice in Wonderland,
      Norton Critical Edition*.
29   J. R. R. Tolkien, 'On Fairy Stories' https://coolcalvary.files.wordpress.com/2018/10/on-
      fairy-stories1.pdf, n.p.
30   Ibid., n.p. See also Avery, 'Fairy Tales', 321–7.
31   G. K. Chesterton, 'A Defence of Nonsense', in *A Defence of Nonsense and Other Essays*
      (New York: Dodd, Mead and Co., 1911), 8.
32   Ibid., 9–10.
33   Ibid., 5.
34   Carroll, *Alice,* 109.
35   Ibid., 240.
36   See J. S. Atherton, 'Carroll: The Unforeseen Precursor', in *The Books at the Wake:
      A Study of Literary Allusions in James Joyce's* Finnegans Wake (New York: Viking,
      1960), 124–35 and Ann McGarrity Buki, 'Lewis Carroll in *Finnegans Wake*', in
      Lewis Carroll: A Celebration, 154–66; Jeffrey Stern, 'Lewis Carroll the Surrealist', in
      Lewis Carroll: A Celebration, 132–53; Michael Holquist, 'What is a Boojum? Nonsense
      and Modernism'; and Elizabeth Sewell, 'Lewis Carroll and T. S. Eliot as Nonsense
      Poets', in *T. S. Eliot, A Symposium for His Seventieth Birthday*, ed. Neville Braybrooke
      (London: Rupert Hart-Davis Ltd., 1959), 49–56.
37   See Juliet Dusinberre, *Alice to the Lighthouse: Children's Books and Radical
      Experiments in Art* (Basingstoke and London: Palgrave Macmillan, 1999) and Beer,
      Alice in Space.
38   Haughton, 'Introduction', xii.
39   Henkle, 'Carroll's Narratives Underground', 90.
40   Douglas-Fairhurst, *Story of Alice,* 391.
41   Haughton, 'Introduction', xii.
42   Ibid., 372.
43   Carroll, *Alice,* 5.

Chapter 2

'SPEAK IN FRENCH WHEN YOU CA'N'T THINK OF THE ENGLISH': CARROLL'S FRENCH AND MALLARMÉ'S ENGLISH

Alexandra Lukes

When discussing the relationship between Lewis Carroll and French literature, one typically thinks of the surrealists. This is because Carroll's influence on the group was extensive and explicit: not only did André Breton reclaim Carroll as one of the group's numerous forefathers, describing him as 'surrealist [...] in nonsense',[1] but Carroll's books also generated a number of translations, adaptations, and interpretations across different media. For instance, Henri Parisot translated the *Alice* books and Louis Aragon translated the *Hunting of the Snark*, Antonin Artaud produced an idiosyncratic version of Alice's encounter with Humpty Dumpty, and Salvador Dalí and Max Ernst created illustrations for Alice's adventures.[2] Yet this direct link has overshadowed, within the scholarship, another indirect link between Carroll and his contemporaries across the Channel. The limited scholarly interest in this connection is striking when we observe that the surrealists point out a strong tie between Carroll's work and the poetic innovations that were happening in France at the same time, in the 1860s and 1870s, in the writings of Lautréamont, Arthur Rimbaud, and Stéphane Mallarmé. Breton establishes this link in noting that these four writers, from both sides of the Channel, were reacting vigorously against what he calls 'the depreciation of language', creating new forms of writing that had profound effects on modern literary practice.[3] The poet Paul Éluard, while also mentioning the same four authors together, narrows the focus of the connection to Mallarmé and Carroll, underscoring the significance of this cross-Channel relationship for the development of the modern literary tradition to which the surrealists claimed to belong.[4]

The only comparative monograph on Carroll and Mallarmé to date is Elizabeth Sewell's posthumously published *Lewis Carroll: Voices from France*. In the book, Sewell notes, however, that the two authors 'turn up together in the literature all the time', albeit fleetingly, for instance in works by W. H. Auden, Jean-Paul Sartre, Jacques Derrida, and Gilles Deleuze.[5] This predominantly French interest is not surprising, given the wealth of French criticism on Carroll within the theoretical and philosophical landscape of the second half of the twentieth century – in particular,

Jacques Lacan's 1966 radio broadcast, 'Homage to Lewis Carroll';[6] Deleuze's 1969 analysis of Carroll's nonsense, *The Logic of Sense*;[7] and the 1971 *Cahier de l'Herne* devoted to Carroll, with contributions from Hélène Cixous, Jean Gattégno, Jean-Jacques Lecercle, Henri Parisot, and Raymond Queneau, among others.[8] Echoing these 'French voices',[9] Sewell outlines her own interest in Carroll and Mallarmé by retracing her scholarly career, from the almost synchronous publication of two early monographs – *The Structure of Poetry* in 1951 on Mallarmé and *The Field of Nonsense* in 1952 on Carroll – to her aforementioned final comparative study of the two.[10] The latter sets up the discussion by highlighting many points of convergence between the two authors: beyond the coincidental fact that they both died in the same year (1898) and that they were both teachers by profession (Carroll taught mathematics at Oxford and Mallarmé taught English to lycée students across France), Sewell explores their respective fascination with nothingness, a 'devotion to logic and intellect',[11] and the proliferation of game-playing: 'each man produces a long poem about a voyage or quest; each is haunted by mirrors; each turns to games for the partial structuring of one, two, three masterpieces, Carroll conjuring with cards and chess, Mallarmé with dice; each is a methodologist as well as a practitioner of his own art'.[12]

The connection between Carroll and Mallarmé is indeed evocative, but it appears at first glance to be somewhat tenuous. The former's childlike play has little of the forbidding nature of the latter's purported hermeticism, and Carroll's word games relish in muddying the relationship between words and their referents that Mallarmé's verse aims to clarify. However, a closer inspection reveals a correspondence between Carroll's literary nonsense and Mallarmé's poetry that emerges precisely through the very act of bringing these two authors into dialogue with each other. Sewell opens the way for such an investigation by framing her analysis with a suggestive sentence inspired by Walter de la Mare: 'Nonsense is how the English choose to take their *Poésie pure*', that is, pure poetry.[13] While the unfinished nature of her book prevents a full development of the analysis,[14] Sewell's argument follows Breton's suggestion that both authors emerge as complementary modes of engaging with the fin-de-siècle crisis of language. Thus, the book links Carroll to Mallarmé by foregrounding their common programme to redefine the role of poetry and their aspiration to 'purity': Mallarmé's 'pure work', which implies the 'disappearance' of the poetic voice,[15] and Carroll's self-sustaining fictional universe for a '[c]hild of the pure unclouded brow',[16] which would also be '[a] perfect and absolute blank'.[17] Beyond the differences inherent in these notions of 'purity', in highlighting the parallel, Sewell accounts for what she calls 'the modern preoccupation with Nothingness',[18] which she ascribes to a heightened awareness of the arbitrary relationship between language and the world and to which she attributes the distinctively modern concern with meaning and its absence, with its corollary self-reflexive and obscure writing practices.

While the discussion of notions such as obscurity and hermeticism has become a staple of modernist scholarship, Sewell's argument can be taken in a different direction, namely, to focus on the ways in which Carroll's and Mallarmé's writings bring languages into dialogue with one another. Indeed, given the attention that both authors pay to their respective languages and to language as such, a comparative study of Carroll's English and Mallarmé's French invites us to ask whether there may be a productive relationship between the two languages within the works themselves. Such a line of inquiry develops Sewell's comparative study of Carroll and Mallarmé into an examination of the comparative approach itself; and it does so by bringing into play the discipline of comparative philology. The rationale for this approach lies in the fact that both Carroll's and Mallarmé's works engage, directly and indirectly, with comparative philology and with discussions that were taking place at the time about the historical relationships between languages. In particular, both writers were familiar with the work of the philologist Max Müller, who popularized the discipline in the 1850s via his publications and his renowned lecture series at Oxford. Carroll most likely attended Müller's lectures, and aspects of his nonsense literature can be read as responses to philological debates of the day.[19] And Mallarmé, after envisaging a doctorate in comparative linguistics, not only published a philological study of the English language, *Les Mots anglais* (1877) (*English Words*), but also translated into French a book based on Müller's theories on myth, *Les Dieux antiques* (1879) (*The Ancient Gods*), as part of a series of pedagogical texts written to supplement his profession as an English-language teacher.[20]

This chapter explores the connection between Carroll and Mallarmé by examining the relationship between French and English in their works, with a view to understanding the broader implications for modern literary practice. The analysis emphasizes pedagogy, which both writers considered to be the point of convergence between philology and poetics. In Mallarmé's case, this concerns primarily the texts he wrote for teaching English to French students; for Carroll, it means examining how the *Alice* books, as representative of the genre of literary nonsense, stage the process of learning language, whether it be English, French, or indeed nonsense.

Let us begin with Mallarmé. The poet's relationship with English is well known. As an English-language teacher, Mallarmé was vocal in his complaints about his chosen profession. Many were the difficulties he encountered in the classroom, documented not only in his letters, but also in comments by former students and in the less-than-glowing reports by school inspectors.[21] However, Mallarmé wrote a series of pedagogical texts, the number and variety of which suggest that perhaps, while ostensibly written for 'pecuniary purposes',[22] the poet might have enjoyed writing them more than it would initially appear. In addition to the two aforementioned texts, *Les Mots anglais* and *Les Dieux antiques*, Mallarmé produced English-French translation manuals (*Thèmes anglais pour toutes les grammaires* [*English Translations For All Grammars*] and *Recueil de 'Nursery Rhymes'* [*Collection of 'Nursery Rhymes'*]), a literary anthology of English texts (*Beautés de l'Anglais* [*Beauties of English*]), and a practical toy for individual language learning (*L'Anglais récréatif* [*Recreational English*]). These texts are not only playful and creative in their form, but, in terms of content, they reveal a serious preoccupation with language, not dissimilar from the concerns Mallarmé addresses elsewhere in his poetry and prose writings. Indeed, Paul Valéry notes that *Les Mots anglais* may well be the most revealing document of Mallarmé's 'intimate work';[23] and the poet Léopold Dauphin recounts in his memoirs that Mallarmé expressed a long-lasting elation about his project *L'Anglais récréatif* that went well beyond its short-term financial benefits.[24]

Les Mots anglais and *Les Dieux antiques* stand out among the pedagogical works because Mallarmé mentions them in what is commonly referred to as his 'autobiographical' letter to Paul Verlaine, written in 1885 for the influential series *Hommes d'aujourd'hui* (*Men of Today*). However, while mentioning these texts, Mallarmé also dismisses them, claiming that they were written merely to supplement his income, and suggesting that they be relegated to oblivion.[25] Bertrand Marchal characterizes this dismissal as a 'preterition', insofar as Mallarmé was aware of the implications of naming these texts in the letter that was to become the cornerstone of his own legend.[26] Significantly, in explaining this incongruity, Marchal mentions Max Müller: he notes that the dismissed pedagogical texts, *Les Mots anglais* and *Les Dieux antiques*, find a point of contact with the new poetics presented in Mallarmé's letter to Verlaine precisely in the figure of Müller, insofar as the philologist incarnates the connection between linguistics and mythology. In this context, Marchal discusses Müller's theory of myths, according to which myths are formed by linguistic oblivion, as the origins of words are forgotten and expressions used to designate natural phenomena, such as sunrise and sunset, are transformed into mythical stories. The implication of Marchal's comment is that Mallarmé's understanding of Müller's theory of linguistic amnesia underpins both his pedagogical texts and his 'pure poetry'.

Les Mots anglais explicitly connects philology with mythology: as Mallarmé notes, 'Mythology as well as Philology'.[27] In the book, which was initially intended to be a comparative study of Indo-Germanic languages, Mallarmé examines the origins of English and, in doing so, discusses the development of French. Mallarmé observes that, given that English originates in part from the Franco-Norman invasion of 1066, it is to a large extent made up of French words. More precisely, it conserves French words that would otherwise have become obsolete in their original language. Echoing Müller's notion of the forgetfulness of languages, Mallarmé discusses English as a repository of words that are lost in French: 'Many old and good words, forever lost or so distant that contemporary speech ignores even their meaning, survive in the neighbouring tongue.'[28] Learning English then becomes a way for French speakers to recover linguistic memory, finding words that the language once possessed. Mallarmé refers to this practice as a purifying 're-immersion' into the foreign source that connects French to its forgotten origins.[29] Examples of words that are lost in French but that 'survive' in English are, among many, 'esmer' ('aim'), 'desgouziller' ('to guzzle'), and 'subduzer' ('to subdue').[30]

By framing the study of English words as a way for French to recover its lost memory, Mallarmé also engages with contemporaneous studies in comparative philology that were investigating the common origins of Indo-European languages. These origins were traced back to 'a primordial "Aryan" language that predated ancient Greek and Sanskrit',[31] in the search for an original language. In his studies on the topic, Müller identifies three linguistic branches that, together, 'clearly show a convergence towards one common source'.[32] These 'three mighty arms'[33] are the Aryan (or Indo-European), the Semitic and the Turanian – the latter being a controversial category that included a variety of nomadic dialects (Mongolic, Turkic, Finnic, etc.), later dismissed by linguists as one of Müller's unscientific inventions. In *Les Mots anglais*, Mallarmé adopts all three of Müller's linguistic categories, but, as Jacques Michon notes, he did not fully ascribe to Müller's theories of original language.[34] Instead, Michon claims, Mallarmé focused on the role of poetics in language development. This difference can be seen in the ways in which Müller and Mallarmé discuss etymology and myth, in particular, the question of word formation in onomatopoeias.[35] For Müller onomatopoeia is linguistically of minor interest because words derived in this way do not have a historical etymology that can be traced;[36] conversely, for Mallarmé, onomatopoeias reveal a poetic dimension of language, in that they show mankind's attempts to create a connection via sounds between words and things.

This leads to a second aspect of Mallarmé's characterization of the English language. English provides Mallarmé with a counterpoint for examining how the sounds of words relate to the reality that the words represent. Despite some minor reservations, Mallarmé views English as being more suited than French for representing the world – in other words, more Cratylistic: 'yes, **sneer** is an *evil smile* and **snake** is a perverse animal, the *serpent*, *SN* thus affects the reader of English like a sinister digraph'.[37] Thus, English makes up for the inadequacy of the French language, which contains what Mallarmé sees as a 'perverse' sound-sense reversal that allows, for instance, the word for day, 'jour', to sound dark when compared to the bright-sounding word for night, 'nuit'.[38] In this way, English comes closer than French to approximating the ideal of a 'pure language', one that would be transparent to the world it represents.[39]

Carroll circles around similar notions, but he does so by inverting the two languages. While Carroll's interest in French was not as developed as Mallarmé's investment in English, references to French recur, sporadically, throughout the *Alice* books in ways that suggest a reversed yet similar appreciation of the need to turn to the corresponding foreign language. The first Carrollian reference to French comes towards the beginning of *Alice's Adventures in Wonderland*, in the context of Alice's first attempt to converse with an inhabitant of the new realm into which she has fallen, a mouse. Having unsuccessfully addressed the Mouse in English, she wonders whether it might not be best to speak to it in French:

'Perhaps it doesn't understand English,' thought Alice. 'I daresay it's a French mouse, come over with William the Conqueror.' (For, with all her knowledge of history, Alice had no very clear notion how long ago anything had happened.) So she began again: 'Où est ma chatte?', which was the first sentence in her French lesson-book. The Mouse gave a sudden leap out of the water, and seemed to quiver all over with fright. 'Oh, I beg your pardon!' cried Alice hastily, afraid that she had hurt the poor animal's feelings. 'I quite forgot you didn't like cats.'

'Not like cats!' cried the Mouse in a shrill, passionate voice. 'Would *you* like cats, if you were me?'[40]

The reference to the Norman invasion of England, which brought with it the French language, indirectly recalls the origins of English.[41] This suggests that there may be a correspondence between entering into the dream-world, on the one hand, and recovering the origins of a language, on the other. This correspondence occurs in conjunction with Alice's progressive loss of mastery of English insofar as, before her encounter with the Mouse, Alice 'quite forgot how to speak good English', surprising herself with the erroneous exclamation 'Curiouser and curiouser!'[42] Recovering the origins of English thus seems to come at the price of losing her mastery of that very language.

While the dream-world may affect Alice's ability to speak English, her utterance in French elicits a response from the Mouse that her initial use of English did not: French jolts the Mouse into action, producing an intense physical response to the perceived threat of a predatory cat. The French language, here, initiates an interaction that is based on confrontation and laden with violent undertones, at odds with the polite conversation that Alice attempts to establish. This tone is typical of the majority of the exchanges that occur between the characters in Carroll's dream-land, testifying to a world that predates socialization.[43] Thus, French not only puts into question Alice's mastery of English to begin with, but it also sets in motion the conversation between her and the Mouse, thereafter held in English. Given that the Mouse is the first inhabitant of Wonderland with whom Alice interacts (her failed attempt at engaging the Rabbit in conversation notwithstanding), her use of French is perhaps more significant than it might initially seem. The type of conversation established here sets the tone for the rest of Alice's interactions in Wonderland, where the English language is often a source of befuddlement – such as in the following example: 'Alice felt dreadfully puzzled. The Hatter's remark seemed to her to have no sort of meaning in it, and yet it was certainly English. "I don't quite understand you," she said, as politely as she could.'[44]

Alice's ostensible loss of mastery over words can be understood in the context of Carroll's reworking of Müller's theories of language. James Williams explains that Müller's notion of 'organic' language, whereby 'Language [...] seems almost to think for man',[45] generated 'a loss of popular faith in speakers' control of their own words'.[46] One of the examples that Williams cites in this context is helpful for our discussion. The episode takes place just before Alice's encounter with the Mouse, when, having fallen into the strange topsy-turvy world of Wonderland, Alice forgets who she is. In order to recover her sense of self, she tries to recall the things she used to know, by reciting her lessons: '"I'll try and say 'How doth the little –"', and she crossed her hands on her lap as if she were saying lessons, and began to repeat it, but her voice sounded hoarse and strange, and the words did not come the same way as they used to do.'[47] Alice's fear of becoming someone else turns into reality when she hears a strange-sounding voice coming out of her mouth. Not only does her voice sound peculiar, but the words belong to someone else – as Williams notes, Alice 'finds herself uttering a sophisticated parody which is not of her own invention'.[48]

This example, Williams argues, shows Carroll's direct engagement with Victorian comparative philology, in that he transforms the anxiety caused by 'the autonomous language of the philologists' into humour.[49] This anxiety goes beyond an individual's concerns about their identity, as in this instance of Alice fearing that she has become her friend Mabel; rather, the anxiety to which Carroll gives voice reveals the relationship between 'the developing "science of language" and questions of collective history, culture, and self-definition'.[50] In this context of widespread anxiety about collective identity, Anglo-Saxon takes on a significant role. Williams notes that the Victorians' interest in the study of Anglo-Saxon was paralleled by the commonly held view that the development of English constituted 'decay from a previous state of purity',[51] and led philologists and poets to resort to archaisms, in a bid to find terms that would 'rejuvenate' the language.[52] Thus, while Mallarmé was turning to English to 'purify' French by finding ancient French words that were no longer in use, the Victorians were looking at Anglo-Saxon to 'purify' the corrupted English language diachronically. In both cases, there is a recognition of the presence of the other language, whether it is considered a safeguard of linguistic treasures or a catalyst of corruption.

A second example from Carroll's *Through the Looking-Glass* develops and complicates these reflections. In a conversation with the Red Queen, Alice is given the following injunction: 'Speak in French when you ca'n't think of the English for a thing – turn out your toes as you walk – and remember who you are!'[53] These instructions are significant on many levels: in the absence of a word for a thing in English, the order is to turn to French, thereby suggesting that the French language is more readily suited to represent the world (not unlike what Mallarmé proposes for English). Moreover, the act of turning to the foreign language is illustrated by the image of turning one's toes out when walking, depicting a counterintuitive movement that seemingly prevents linear progress, but one that, in pointing towards the outside and, by implication, the foreign, allows for the possible recovery of one's memory and identity. In a narrative steeped in questions surrounding identity and fears of memory loss, it is significant that the ability to retain both (identity and memory) is associated with the capacity to speak French. This appears to be at odds with what Carroll takes from Müller's aforementioned conception of the purity of Anglo-Saxon compared to English, which assumes that the introduction of French is partly responsible for the language's decay and subsequent challenges to collective identity. However, it does suggest a recognition on Carroll's part that, in order to establish one's identity as an English-language speaker, one must become aware of the foreign elements that English contains.

Here we can draw a parallel with Mallarmé's views on English. Speaking English is considered a way for his French students to recover the memory of the French language by uttering words that do not belong to their everyday usage, because these words were transplanted onto English soil and were subsequently lost in French. This practice generates in the speakers what Mallarmé calls 'a delicate enchantment', which allows them instantaneously to bridge centuries of lost time through a simple utterance.[54] For Mallarmé's French students, then, speaking English has a beneficial, and fundamentally physical effect: as if through incantation, the French speaker of English is somehow 'purified', via the immersion into the English repository of French linguistic memory. Analogously, Carroll's

Alice, in speaking French, accesses a direct connection with the world around her, and doing so implies that she will regain the memory of who she is.

We might note at this point that there is a difference in medium through which the exploration of the foreign language occurs. On the one hand, there are Mallarmé's generically unclassifiable works, in-between pedagogical manual, linguistics treatise, and expression of poetics; on the other, Carroll's fictional land of wonder and the topsy-turvy domain beyond the looking-glass, both of which are framed by the narrative device of the dream. The first identifies a filiation between languages and proposes a way of recovering linguistic memory; the second illustrates that such a recovery constitutes a form of unconscious knowledge.

The point of contact between the two lies in the value they each place on language-learning processes. Both authors underscore the complexities inherent in language acquisition, whether it be a child learning language for the first time or a foreign-language student navigating the intricacies of two different language systems. Indeed, in relation to nonsense literature, Jean-Jacques Lecercle observes that 'nonsense as a genre is a modern version of the great Romantic myth of the child', but rather than focusing on the child's soul, the modernity of the myth lies in its focus on the child's language and on the learning process: 'The essential childishness of the child, as nonsense pictures it, lies in the fact that she is a language-learner: the important thing for Alice is not that she goes through the looking-glass, but that she undergoes the mirror stage, and lives up to all the linguistic consequences of this.'[55]

Accordingly, lessons abound in the *Alice* books. We have already seen Alice recite her lessons in order to try to remember who she is; equally, in her interaction with the Mouse, the question that she asks, 'Où est ma chatte?' (where is my cat?), is described as 'the first sentence in her French lesson-book'.[56] However, as we have seen, both lessons produce the opposite effect of what was intended: in the first instance, reciting the poem 'How doth the little crocodile' serves to reinforce the fear that Alice is indeed someone else – 'I must be Mabel after all';[57] and speaking to the Mouse in French causes it to recoil from her in fear. But, in both examples there is a 'lesson' for the readers: the first, as we saw, diffuses through humour the 'anxiety' produced by the notion of 'autonomous language';[58] the second teaches us about the importance of context in language use.[59]

Elsewhere, in a passage replete with wordplay on the topic of school lessons, Alice tells the Mock Turtle that she learnt 'French and music'.[60] Alice's statement prompts the Mock Turtle to launch into an array of puns where English words are replaced by similar sounding ones: 'Reeling and Writhing' for reading and writing; 'Ambition, Distraction, Uglification, and Derision' for addition, subtraction, multiplication, and division; 'Mystery' and 'Seaography' for history and geography; 'Drawling, Stretching, and Fainting in Coils' for drawing, sketching, and painting in oils; and finally, 'Laughing and Grief' for Latin and Greek.[61] The game here relies on the fact that the Mock Turtle's words sound similar to the ones they supposedly replace, but have different meanings, so that readers can hear the intended original subjects behind the Mock Turtle's words, while also revelling in the humorous substitutions.

While puns were commonly used in works of the period,[62] the technique adopted here is familiar to nonsense literature, which emphasizes sounds over meaning – a poetics that can be summed up in the expression 'take care of the sounds, and the sense will take care of itself'. This is an inverted rewording of the Duchess's moral 'take care of the sense, and the sounds will take care of themselves',[63] itself a rewriting of the proverb 'Take care of the pence, and the pounds will take care of themselves'. Carroll's version of the proverb exploits sonic similarities between words, by replacing 'pence' with 'sense' and 'pounds' with 'sounds', thereby tricking readers into thinking there is an analogy between the two sentences. Yet, while we may not be surprised by the ensuing notion of language as currency, Carroll's rewording displaces sense in favour of sound, because sense does not accrue to sound in the same way that pence accrue to pounds. The reversal of Carroll's sentence, then, highlights Carroll's method by insisting on sounds over meaning, while also drawing attention to what happens when words are replaced by similar sounding ones – a practice also known as homophonic translation.

Homophonic translation has a long and rich history.[64] It occurs not only across languages, such as in the case of Luis d'Antin van Rooten's *Mots d'Heures: Gousses, Rames*, where a beloved nursery rhyme character such as 'Humpty Dumpty' becomes the French 'Un petit d'un petit' (literally, 'A little of a little') who, instead of sitting on a wall, marvels at the famous Parisian market Les Halles ('s'étonne aux Halles' replaces 'sat on a wall').[65] Homophonic translation also occurs within one language, as for example in Howard Chace's *Anguish Languish*, where an English nursery rhyme such as 'Sing a song of sixpence' is transformed into a 'noisier ram' written in 'Anguish', by the title 'Sinker Sucker Socks Pants',[66] or where the popular song 'For he's a jolly good fellow' becomes a 'thong' entitled 'Fur Hazy Jelly Gut Furlough'.[67] It is not insignificant that Alice mentions French in conjunction with music, because doing so underscores the sonorous qualities of the language, and, more broadly, the notion that sound takes precedence over meaningful content.[68]

In addition to this implicit use of homophonic translation, Carroll explicitly mentions translation to make a point about language learning and identity. Towards the end of *Through the Looking-Glass*, the Red Queen and the White Queen ask Alice a series of questions, in order to test her qualifications before she is allowed to become Queen.

> 'Do you know Languages? What's the French for fiddle-de-dee?'
> 'Fiddle-de-dee's not English,' Alice replied gravely.
> 'Who ever said it was?' said the Red Queen.
> Alice thought she saw a way out of the difficulty, this time. 'If you'll tell me what language "fiddle-de-dee" is, I'll tell you the French for it!' she exclaimed triumphantly.
> But the Red Queen drew herself up rather stiffly, and said 'Queens never make bargains.'[69]

In this exchange, Alice is asked to perform an act of translation, but her difficulty lies in the fact that she does not know the original language. Seemingly, however, her knowledge of French is not put into question: Alice claims that, once the language of the original has been identified, she will be able to produce a translation into French. Here, French acts as a language into which all languages can be translated, insofar as it constitutes an unconscious linguistic memory, as we saw above, more immediate for Alice than the English spoken in the reversed world of the looking-glass.

Notably, the word in question, 'fiddle-de-dee', is typically used as a synonym for 'nonsense'.[70] Thus, Alice's inability to translate the term would imply that she is at a loss in trying to find the French equivalent for English nonsense. This not only raises the question of whether the term 'nonsense' can be translated, but also the extent to which nonsense itself can be translated.[71] The term 'nonsense' appears as a 'philosophical untranslatable' in Barbara Cassin's *Vocabulaire européen des philosophies: dictionnaire des intraduisibles*.[72] This book, translated into English as *Dictionary of Untranslatables: A Philosophical Lexicon*,[73] explores some of the most commonly mistranslated, or over-translated, philosophical terms (such as 'logos', 'sense', and 'subject'). The entry on nonsense is primarily dedicated to the term's philosophical meanings, but it also mentions its literary uses, with references to Carroll. In the French text, the entry opens by placing the English term in a relation of untranslatability with respect to the French: 'NONSENSE (anglais) – fr. *non-sens, absurdité*'.[74] While we may assume that the first term, 'non-sens', is the most straightforward and neutral translation of the English, the entry itself begins by putting that assumption into question: 'Why is it generally difficult to translate "nonsense" as the French expression *non-sens*?'[75]

Indeed, not only does 'non-sens' not translate to 'nonsense', but it also raises particular questions about the very practice of translation and the function of mistranslations. The term 'non-sens' appears in the French pedagogical marking scheme to indicate serious misunderstandings of a source text.[76] But, significantly, mistranslations play a crucial role in language development and foreign-language learning. Indeed, they are central to Mallarmé's conception of the relationship between philology and mythology, in the context of Müller's theory that myths occur when words lose the memory of their original meanings. In *Les Mots anglais*, Mallarmé addresses such questions when discussing the English origins of the expression 'The Cat and the Fiddle'. Mallarmé retraces the expression to the French 'Le chat fidèle' (the faithful cat), which, he notes, was a common name used for taverns during the French conquest, and he implies that the mistranslation from French to English is the result of a felicitous play on words.[77] The transformation of 'faithful' ('fidèle') into 'fiddle' is anything but a faithful translation; finding the French for 'fiddle-de-dee', then, as requested by the Red Queen, is bound to be as faithful a translation as the one that equates the French term 'non-sens' with the English 'nonsense'.

Mistranslations and mistakes are common in Mallarmé's teaching materials. While many of them may simply be the result of inattention, their cumulative effect is revealing. Of particular note is a mistake concerning the pronunciation of English words in *L'Anglais récréatif*, given the significance that Mallarmé ascribes to speaking English in light of the 'delicate enchantment' that doing so supposedly produces in French speakers. The text, also referred to as *Boîte pour apprendre l'Anglais en jouant et seul* (*Box for learning English by playing and alone*), is a device designed to help students learn English in a series of lessons: it is comprised of fourteen cards, with coloured illustrations, handwritten instructions and tables, in both English and French, complete with leavers, movable parts, and a bag of tokens, all covering a variety of grammar topics. From the outset, the cards present a number of difficulties, beginning with the instructions that are not only sometimes difficult to decipher in Mallarmé's small and compact handwriting, but also occasionally incomplete if not outright incorrect. Furthermore, Mallarmé's use of different colours to distinguish between French and English (French in black ink, English in purple) is not strictly maintained, so that, in some instances, it can be unclear at first which language is which.

The card in question (Figure 2.1) teaches students how to pronounce the English 'th', which, in *Les Mots anglais*, Mallarmé describes as 'an absolutely new sound' for French speakers.[78] The card contains a colourful drawing of a male figure, with bright blond hair and eyebrows, dressed in a blue jacket, with green and orange tweed trousers, yellow gloves, a cane, and a top hat. The most eye-catching feature, however, is the man's long red tongue, which is retractable via the activation of a lever at the bottom of the page. At the top of the page, students are instructed to place their tongue between their teeth and make one of two sounds: 'ç when the th is soft', followed by the examples 'the, this, that, these, those'; and 'z when the th is hard', represented by the words 'thumb, thick, thorn, mouth'.[79] These instructions are accompanied by indications of how to imitate the figure, by either bringing the tongue inwards or sticking it out, as students are invited to either pull or push the lever that activates the figure's tongue.

This card raises a series of problems, the most glaring being the inaccuracy of the instructions. Mallarmé seems to have reversed the examples of soft (or voiceless) sounds and hard (or voiced) sounds, insofar as 'the, this, that, these, those' are voiced and 'thumb, thick, thorn, mouth' are voiceless, contrary to Mallarmé's indications on the card. Furthermore, it is not clear from the instructions how the French sounds 'ç' and 'z' relate to the two English sounds 'th' (represented in the International Phonetic Alphabet as /θ/ for the voiced 'th' and /ð/ for the voiceless 'th') because the student is being given two alternatives: either produce the sound 'ç' or pull the tongue in; either produce the sound 'z' or push the tongue out.[80] Trying to obey these instructions produces English words heavily calqued on French sounds: if we follow Mallarmé's rules, we produce something like 'çe, çis, çat, çese, çose' or 'zum, zick, zorn, mouz', or, if we rectify Mallarmé's mistake by flipping the voiced examples for the voiceless ones, we say 'ze, zis, zat, zese, zose' and 'çumb, çick, çorn, mouç'. In both cases, Mallarmé does not explain that 'ç' and 'z' are simply ways to differentiate between voiceless and voiced sounds, rather than correct ways of pronouncing the 'th' sounds in English.[81] We are thus invited to speak English as though it were French, a practice akin to van Rooten's 'Un petit d'un petit' mentioned above, where French words sound like English spoken with a French accent. While the latter may be an amusing game for bilingual English-French speakers, it is doubtless a questionable pedagogical method for learning a foreign language.

Figure 2.1 Stéphane Mallarmé, *L'Anglais récréatif* (from Bertrand Marchal and Marie-Pierre Pouly, *Mallarmé et L'Anglais récréatif. Le Poète pédagogue* [Paris: Cohen & Cohen, 2014], 62). ©Cohen&Cohen éditeurs.

Yet, Mallarmé's practice of blurring the boundaries between the two languages is more significant than it may seem.[82] In another pedagogical text, Mallarmé's translations of English nursery rhymes, published posthumously in 1964, the poet-pedagogue offers examples of French superimposed on English. Here, we find ungrammatical fragments of sentences in French that look grammatically and syntactically like word-for-word translations of English: for instance, 'comme profondément vous êtes dormant' is a word for word translation of 'how deeply you are sleeping' and 'combien contente elle doit avoir été' literally translates 'how happy she must have been'.[83] While the pedagogical function of these ungrammatical phrases serves ostensibly to facilitate retranslation into English, in that students are required only to replace the French words with English ones without changing their order, the presence of such phrases is nonetheless striking. These incorrect French expressions, calqued on English syntax, induce in readers the uneasy feeling of sliding between the two languages, with the end result of losing French idiom.[84] While this effect may be pedagogically dubious, it has an important role in the development of Mallarmé's poetics of purity: by playing on the relationship between sound and meaning – as Mallarmé writes in 'Crise de vers' 'Crisis of verse', 'alternating re-immersion in sense and sound'[85] – the poet also separates between the ordinary language of idiomatic expression ('parole brute'), on the one hand, and the essential language of poetry ('parole essentielle'), on the other.[86]

These considerations return us to the initial comparative discussion of Carroll's 'nonsense' and Mallarmé's 'pure poetry'. Both authors not only explore the relationship between sounds and sense in their respective languages, but in doing so, they also position themselves as scholars of language. This chapter has focused primarily on the relationship between French and English in their works within the pedagogical context. However, the implications for the development of modernist poetics are significant, if we conceive of such poetics as an exploration of the inner working of language, founded upon a self-conscious play with the sounds and meanings of words within and across languages. A comment made by van Rooten in the foreword of *Mots d'Heures: Gousses, Rames* offers some final thoughts that can be clarifying, in that, as we have observed, his homophonic translations of English nursery rhymes share a number of characteristics found in both Carroll's and Mallarmé's approaches. In describing his invented French poems, van Rooten claims that they 'may be the creations of some Gothic cultural link midway between François Rabelais on the one hand and James Joyce on the other'.[87] By choosing to highlight a French author whom Antoine Compagnon identifies as the incarnation of the French lineage of literary nonsense,[88] and an Irish writer whose work is widely considered to exhaust the resources of English-language modernism – having reached, as he claims 'the end of English'[89] – van Rooten indicates that his homophonic translations belong to a Franco-English literary tradition that plays with sound as much as it does with meaning. Both Carroll and Mallarmé participate in this literary trajectory, as linguists, pedagogues, and poets, attentive to the history of their respective languages and the interactions between them, as well as to the ways in which that history influences the development of poetics and the understanding of language itself.

Notes

1   André Breton, 'Surrealism: Yesterday, Today and Tomorrow', *This Quarter* 5, no. 1
     (1932): 7–44, 17.

2   For more details, see Marie Hélène Inglin-Routisseau, *Lewis Carroll dans l'imaginaire
     français: la nouvelle Alice* (Paris: L'Harmattan, 2006); Michel Remy, 'Surrealice? Lewis
     Carroll et les surréalistes', *Europe* 68, no. 736–7 (1990): 123–33; Elizabeth Sewell,
     Lewis Carroll: Voices from France (New York: The Lewis Carroll Society of North
     America, 2008); and Jeffrey Stern, 'Lewis Carroll The Surrealist', in *Lewis Carroll, A
     Celebration: Essays on the Occasion of the 150th Anniversary of the Birth of Charles
     Lutwidge Dodgson*, ed. Edward Guiliano (New York: C. M. Potter, 1982), 132–53.

3   'This need to counteract ruthlessly the depreciation of language, a need which was felt
     in France by Lautréamont, Rimbaud, Mallarmé, and at the same time in England by
     Lewis Carroll, has not ceased to be just as imperative since that time' (André Breton,
     Manifestoes of Surrealism [Ann Arbor: University of Michigan Press, 1972], 297–8).

4   'C'est entre 1866 et 1875 que les poètes entreprirent de réunir systématiquement ce
     qui semblait à tout jamais séparé […] C'est l'époque où Mallarmé écrit *Igitur*, cette
     dernière nuit sans lune d'un fantôme qu'*Un Coup de dés* […] viendra, trente ans
     après, dissiper; l'époque à laquelle Lewis Carroll chasse le Snark *avec une obligation
     de chemin de fer, avec des sourires et du savon*, avec l'authentique sens poétique
     que, par humour, il baptise non-sens. L'intelligence poétique voyait enfin ses
     frontières détruites et redonnait son unité au monde' (Paul Éluard, *Donner à voir*
     [Paris: Gallimard, 1939], 125–6). (It was between 1866 and 1875 that poets began
     systematically bringing together what seemed to be forever separate […] It was
     then that Mallarmé wrote *Igitur*, a phantom's last moonless night that, thirty years
     later, would be dissipated by *Un coup de dés* […]; at the same time, Lewis Carroll
     was hunting the Snark *with a railway-share, with smiles and soap*, with the authentic
     poetic sense that, with humour, he baptized nonsense. Poetic intelligence finally
     destroyed its limits and returned its unity to the world.) Unless otherwise indicated,
     all translations are my own.

5   Sewell, *Lewis Carroll*, 2.

6   Jacques Lacan, 'Hommage à Lewis Carroll', 1966. Available online: https://radiolacan.
     com/es/topic/208/2.

7   Gilles Deleuze, *Logique du sens* (Paris: Les Éditions de Minuit, 1969).

8   Henri Parisot, ed., *Cahier de l'Herne 17: Lewis Carroll* (Paris: Éditions de l'Herne,
     1971).

9   Sewell, *Lewis Carroll*, 4.

10   Elizabeth Sewell, *The Structure of Poetry* (London: Routledge & Kegan Paul, 1951) and
     The Field of Nonsense (London: Chatto and Windus, 1952).

11   Sewell, *Lewis Carroll*, 160.

12   Ibid., 3. It is not known whether Carroll and Mallarmé knew each other's work. Sewell
     notes that, according to Deleuze, Mallarmé did not read Carroll (ibid., 80), but she
     suggests that there might have been an indirect link through a friend of Carroll's, John
     Earle, whose philological work was known to Mallarmé (ibid., 175). It is also worth
     noting that Mallarmé gave a lecture at Oxford in 1894, 'La Musique et les Lettres'
     ('Music and Letters'): while there is no evidence that Carroll was in the audience, it is
     compelling to think that he might have been.

13 Ibid., 1. Elsewhere, Sewell writes: 'Mr. De La Mare puts these two, Nonsense and pure poetry, side by side in his work on Carroll, and that is interesting, for they are near contemporaries, and it is possible that Carroll is the English manifestation of the French logic and rigour which produced the work of Mallarmé, also labelled nonsense in its time' (Sewell, *Field of Nonsense*, 21).

14 The editor describes the book as 'virtually complete at the time of her death' (Sewell, *Lewis Carroll*, vii).

15 See Mallarmé's essay 'Crise de vers' (Stéphane Mallarmé, *Œuvres complètes*, vol. II [Paris: Gallimard, 2003], 211): 'L'oeuvre pure implique la disparition élocutoire du poète' ('the pure work of art implies the elocutionary disappearance of the poet' [Stéphane Mallarmé, 'Crise de vers', in *Mallarmé: The Poet and His Circle*, ed. Rosemary Lloyd (Ithaca: Cornell University Press, 1999), 232]).

16 From the preface to *Through the Looking-Glass* in Lewis Carroll, *Alice's Adventures in Wonderland* and *Through the Looking-Glass*, ed. Hugh Haughton (London: Penguin, 1998), 117.

17 From *The Hunting of the Snark* in Lewis Carroll, *Alice in Wonderland*, ed. Donald J. Gray (London: W. W. Norton & Company, 1992), 223. For a discussion of this poem as representative of the self-reflexive world created by nonsense, see Michael Holquist, 'What is a Boojum? Nonsense and Modernism', *Yale French Studies* 96 (1999): 100–17.

18 Sewell, *Lewis Carroll*, 19.

19 See James Williams, 'Lewis Carroll and the Private Life of Words', *The Review of English Studies* 64, no. 266 (2013): 651–71, for a discussion of Müller's influence on Carroll. See also Davis and Nicholls's presentation of Müller's influence on different aspects of Victorian culture, in light of 'his prominence as a public intellectual and his copious correspondence with leading thinkers and figures of the day' (John R. Davis and Angus Nicholls, 'Friedrich Max Müller: The Career and Intellectual Trajectory of a German Philologist in Victorian Britain', *Publications of the English Goethe Society* 85, nos. 2–3 [2016]: 67–97).

20 Both works are included in Mallarmé's *Œuvres complètes*, vol. II, in a section entitled 'Ouvrages pédagogiques' ('Pedagogical Works'). The text that served as the basis for *Les Dieux antiques* is George William Cox's *A Manual of Mythology in the Form of Question and Answer* (London: Longman, Green and Co., 1867), written to divulge Müller's theories.

21 For more details about Mallarmé's teaching career, see Bertrand Marchal and Marie-Pierre Pouly, *Mallarmé et L'Anglais récréatif. Le Poète pédagogue* (Paris: Cohen & Cohen, 2014).

22 Stéphane Mallarmé, *Œuvres complètes*, vol. I (Paris: Gallimard, 1998), 789.

23 Stéphane Mallarmé, *Thèmes anglais pour toutes les grammaires* (Paris: Gallimard, 1937), 17.

24 'Deux mois après, à Valvins, sa joie n'était pas encore calmée alors qu'il me racontait cette histoire. C'est, je crois, le seul moment de sa vie où il n'eut pas à regretter d'être professeur d'anglais' (qt. in Marchal and Pouly, *Mallarmé et L'Anglais récréatif*, 59). (Two months later, in Valvins, his joy had not yet abated as he told me this story. I think it was the only time in his life that he did not regret being an English teacher.)

25 Mallarmé, *Œuvres I*, 789.

26 Mallarmé, *Œuvres II*, 1812–13.

27 'Mythologie, autant que Philologie' (*Œuvres II*, 1046).

28 'Beaucoup de vieux et bons vocables, à jamais perdus ou si lointains que le parler
     actuel en ignore ici jusqu'au sens, se survivent dans l'idiome voisin' (ibid., 1046).
29 Mallarmé uses the term 'retrempe' (ibid., 1061).
30 Ibid., 1048, 1050, 1054.
31 Davis and Nicholls, 'Friedrich Max Müller', 87.
32 Max Müller, *Lectures on the Science of Language* (London: Longman, Green, and
     Roberts, 1862), 33.
33 Ibid.
34 Jacques Michon, *Mallarmé et* Les Mots anglais (Montréal: Les Presses de l'Université
     de Montréal, 1978), 99.
35 Ibid., 133–6.
36 See Davis and Nicholls for a more detailed discussion of Müller's position on
     onomatopoeia and its relationship with Darwin's theories of evolution ('Friedrich
     Max Müller', 90–5).
37 'oui, **sneer** est un *mauvais sourire* et **snake** un animal pervers, le *serpent*, SN
     impressionne donc un lecteur de l'Anglais comme un sinistre digramme' (*Œuvres II*,
     968; emphasis in the original).
38 Ibid., 208.
39 Gérard Genette refers to this as the Cratylistic dream, which is projected onto the
     foreign language, independently of which language that may be: 'the English-French
     relation could ultimately be reversed, the supreme language always being, for every
     natural language, the one facing or opposite it' (Gérard Genette, *Mimologics* [Lincoln:
     University of Nebraska Press, 1995], 214).
40 Carroll, *Alice's Adventures*, 21; emphasis in the original.
41 The Mouse later recounts the story of the Conquest, describing it as 'the driest
     thing I know' (ibid., 25). The Mouse's narrative is a direct quotation from Haviland
     Chepmell's *Short Course of History* (see Carroll, *Alice in Wonderland*, note 1, 22).
     Williams mentions this passage as one of the many indications of Carroll's interest in
     Anglo-Saxon history ('Lewis Carroll', 669).
42 Carroll, *Alice's Adventures*, 16.
43 For a discussion of good manners and the lack thereof in Wonderland, see Jean-
     Jacques Lecercle, *Philosophy of Nonsense: The Intuitions of Victorian Nonsense
     Literature* (London: Routledge, 1994), 69–114.
44 Carroll, *Alice's Adventures*, 62.
45 Qt. in Williams, 'Lewis Carroll', 651.
46 Ibid., 656. Williams draws out the literary and theoretical implications of Müller's
     theory: he notes that the anxiety it produced 'anticipates the spiritualists' belief in
     automatic writing' (ibid., 657), and connects it to Roland Barthes's 'view of language,
     not authors, as the origin of texts' (ibid.). We can equally draw parallels with
     Mallarmé's notion of the disappearance of the poetic voice mentioned above.
47 Carroll, *Alice's Adventures*, 19.
48 Williams, 'Lewis Carroll', 659.
49 Ibid.
50 Ibid., 663.
51 Ibid.
52 Ibid., 664.
53 Carroll, *Alice's Adventures*, 144.
54 Mallarmé claims that a pleasant feeling should emerge from reading the words
     grouped together in the tables under the heading 'Vieux mots' (Old words): 'Qui

n'éprouverait autre chose qu'un charme délicat à proférer sciemment, au cours d'une récitation à haute voix ou d'une conversation en Anglais, des paroles séparées de lui par un nombre de siècles important, aurait déjà tiré quelque bénéfice de la lecture de la première moitié de chaque Table' (*Œuvres II*, 1057). (He who feels nothing but a delicate enchantment in knowingly uttering, while reading aloud or conversing in English, words separated from him by a significant number of centuries, will already have gained some benefit from reading the first half of each table.)

55   Lecercle, *Philosophy of Nonsense*, 222.

56   Carroll, *Alice's Adventures*, 21.

57   Ibid., 19.

58   Williams, 'Lewis Carroll', 659.

59   In the note accompanying Alice's encounter with the Mouse, Hugh Haughton identifies the textbook that Alice quotes from as *La Bagatelle: Intended to introduce children of three or four years old to some knowledge of the French language* (1804). He remarks that 'Alice's recourse to it during her conversation with the Mouse is a sad index of the difficulty of applying text-book French to the real world' (in Carroll, *Alice's Adventures*, 304).

60   Carroll, *Alice's Adventures*, 83.

61   Ibid., 85.

62   See Carroll, *Alice in Wonderland*, note 5, 75.

63   Carroll, *Alice's Adventures*, 79.

64   See Vincent Broqua and Dirk Weissmann, eds., *Sound/Writing: traduire-écrire entre le son et le sens. Homophonic translation – traducson – Oberflächenübersetzung* (Paris: Éditions des Archives Contemporaines, 2019).

65   Luis d'Antin van Rooten, *Mots d'Heures: Gousses, Rames* (New York: Grossman, 1967). 'Un petit d'un petit' is the first text in the book, which is unpaginated.

66   Howard Chace, *Anguish Languish* (Englewood Cliffs, NJ: Prentice-Hall, 1956), 37.

67   Ibid., 61.

68   Similarly, *Les Mots anglais* foregrounds the importance of sound with regard to both French and English, as we can see in Valéry's assessment of Mallarmé's intention for the book: 'S'agissant de l'anglais, il tenta d'appliquer à l'étude de cette langue le sentiment infiniment délié qu'il avait des délicatesses musicales de la nôtre' (Mallarmé, *Thèmes anglais*, 17). (When it comes to English, he tried to apply to the study of that language the infinitely unbounded feeling he had of the musical graces of our own.)

69   Carroll, *Alice's Adventures*, 223.

70   See Haughton's note to this passage (ibid., 352).

71   For a comprehensive exploration of the relationship between nonsense and translation, see Jean-Jacques Lecercle, 'Translate It, Translate It Not', *Translation Studies* 1, no. 1 (2008): 90–102 and 'Modalities of Translating Nonsense', *Translation Studies* 12, no. 1 (2019): 15–23.

72   Barbara Cassin, ed., *Vocabulaire européen des philosophies: dictionnaire des intraduisibles* (Paris: Éditions du Seuil, 2004).

73   Barbara Cassin, Emily Apter, Jacques Lezra, and Michael Wood, eds., *Dictionary of Untranslatables: A Philosophical Lexicon* (Princeton: Princeton University Press, 2014).

74   Cassin, *Vocabulaire*, 859.

75   Cassin, *Dictionary*, 715.

76   See Antoine Compagnon, 'Somebody Will Always Get It', *Art & Text* 37 (1990): 71–3, 71.

77   Mallarmé, *Œuvres II*, 1045–6.

78   Ibid., 1003.

79   Mallarmé's instructions in French are as follows: 'ç quand le th est doux' and 'z quand le th est dur' (Marchal and Pouly, *Mallarmé et L'Anglais récréatif*, 62).

80   It is worth noting that, around the same time that Mallarmé created *L'Anglais récréatif*, linguists in Paris were working on the first version of the International Phonetic Alphabet (1888), which was envisaged as a tool for teachers to help schoolchildren pronounce foreign languages correctly. In the early volumes of the *Journal of the International Phonetic Association*, then called *Le Maître Phonétique*, the pronunciation of the English 'th' is described as follows: '(θ) (ð) se prononcent en mettant la pointe de la langue contre les dents d'en haut ou entre les dents: (θ) est le *th* dur Anglais […]; (ð) le *th* dous [*sic*] Anglais' ('Extrait des statuts de l'Association phonétique des professeurs de langues vivantes', *Le Maître Phonétique: Organe de l'Association Phonétique des Professeurs de Langues vivantes* [Janvier 1893]). ([θ] [ð] are pronounced by placing the tip of the tongue against the teeth from above or between the teeth: [θ] is the hard English *th* […]; [ð] is the soft English *th*.)

81   It is not, however, uncommon for French speakers to pronounce the English /θ/ and /ð/ as /s/ and /z/; for more details, see Alain Diana, 'La phonétique dans l'enseignement de l'anglais aux spécialistes d'autres disciplines: enjeux et priorités', *Recherche et Pratiques Pédagogiques en Langues de Spécialité: Cahiers de l'APLIUT* 29, 3 (2010): 10–21.

82   This notion of blurring languages not only reflects the challenges inherent in learning a foreign language but also echoes Mallarmé's considerations in *Les Mots anglais* surrounding the complex origins of English, as we can see in his discussion of the Gothic and Anglo-Saxon components: 'Distingue-t-on au premier coup d'œil l'un et l'autre des langages fondus?' (*Œuvres II*, 941). (Can we distinguish at a first glance between the two merged languages?)

83   Mallarmé, *Œuvres II*, 1256; 1272. The correct French for these two sentences is, respectively, 'comme vous dormez profondément' and 'qu'elle a dû être contente'.

84   A similar loss of idiomatic meaning can be found in Mallarmé's literal translations of old English proverbs in *Thème anglais*, such as 'To dine with duke Humphrey', rendered as 'Dîner avec le duc Humphrey' (*Œuvres II*, 1144), which misses the phrase's meaning of 'dining alone'. For a more detailed discussion, see Alexandra Lukes, 'Mallarmé's Madness: Poetry, Pedagogy, and Translation', *Modernism/ modernity* 24, no. 1 (2017): 141–60 and 'Dictionary and Divination: Mallarmé Translating, Back-Translating, and Not Translating', *MLN* 134, no. 4 (2019): 745–63.

85   In Mallarmé's words, 'retrempe alternée en le sens et la sonorité' (*Œuvres II*, 213).

86   In 'Crise de vers', Mallarmé writes of 'le double état de la parole, brut ou immédiat ici, là essentiel' (*Œuvres II*, 212) ('the double state of the word, raw and immediate on the one hand, on the other, essential' ['Crise de vers', 233]).

87   Van Rooten, *Mots d'Heures*, Foreword.

88   Compagnon writes: 'The Renaissance, through word-plays, puns and so on, cultivated undecidability and indeterminacy of meaning. This is exactly the reason why Rabelais and Montaigne, in our late 20th century, are often seen as precursors of modernity, from surrealism to Céline, from Joyce to Burroughs' ('Somebody', 73).

89   'Je suis au bout de l'anglais' (qt. in Richard Ellmann, *James Joyce*, revised edition [New York: Oxford University Press, 1982], 546).

Chapter 3

T. S. ELIOT'S ADVENTURES IN WONDERLAND

John D. Morgenstern

The standard narrative of T. S. Eliot's early poetic formation is an oft-repeated tale of momentous discovery and near-instantaneous transformation. As a Harvard undergraduate in 1908, Eliot came across a copy of Arthur Symons's *The Symbolist Movement in Literature* (1889) and in it he made first contact with the tragicomic French poet Jules Laforgue. Symons declared Laforgue's poetry 'an art of the nerves', registering 'all the restlessness of modern life' conveyed with seeming remove through 'caprice, fear, contempt, linked together by an embracing laughter'.[1] This laughter echoes in poems such as Laforgue's 'Autobiographical Preludes', where a long meditation on fire and brimstone, Christ and Buddha, resolves in an indifferent shrug: 'Oh well, a human cry for you!'[2] Soon after his discovery in the pages of *The Symbolist Movement*, Eliot went to Schoenhof's bookstore in Cambridge and ordered a copy of Laforgue's *Oeuvres Complètes* from Paris. By 1909, so the story goes, Laforgue had transformed Eliot from a bundle of secondhand sentiments into a poet, training him in free-verse poetics and introducing him to his own idiom of speech.

Eliot's encounter with Laforgue undoubtedly catalysed a shift in his poetics from the regular, metered sentimentalism of the poems he had by then published in the *Smith Academy Record* and in the *Harvard Advocate* to more modern verses marked by a freedom of prosody, a deflating irony, and an abiding air of nonchalance. Laforgue's self-mocking resounds throughout the poems that Eliot composed in the Symbolist mode and then collected in a notebook now held in the Berg Collection of the New York Public Library.[3] Eliot refashioned Laforgue's undercutting shrug, for instance, in 'First Caprice in North Cambridge' (1909), which concludes: 'Oh, these minor considerations!'[4] The protagonist of 'Opera' (1909) asks 'We have the tragic?' and then responds 'oh no! / Life departs with a feeble smile / Into the indifferent'.[5] An homage in the subtitle of 'Humouresque' (1909), '(After J. Laforgue)', signals overt imitation of the French poet. It is no wonder that the last century of Eliot criticism has by and large placed his early poems under the exclusive sign of Laforgue.

This limiting account of Eliot's poetic development was both originated and perpetuated by the poet himself, who had built his reputation upon translating into

English the innovations of French Symbolism. The language used in most critical accounts to describe the transformation from a 'bundle of secondhand sentiments into a person' are in fact paraphrases from Eliot's own testimony.[6] Christopher Ricks and Jim McCue's 2015 landmark edition of Eliot's poems stands to reinscribe further the self-fashioned legend of Eliot's spectacular transformation: they devote four of eight pages of their editorial commentary on Eliot's early development ('A Beginner in 1908') to extracts from his statements on the discovery of Laforgue.[7] Recent criticism has, however, usefully complicated the story of Eliot's literary influences, bringing to bear his early absorption in English Aestheticism and literary Decadence.[8] This chapter writes another literary preoccupation of the late nineteenth century back into the narrative of Eliot's early poetic formation: Lewis Carroll. Carroll provided Eliot with formal models to emulate in his earliest poetry and an inventory of literary references from which he drew throughout his career. Carroll's fiction was likewise instrumental in the development of Eliot's mature poetics by suggesting to him at an early age a method for bringing together disparate sources, locating their common resonance, and sounding through them in his own poetry.

In the only full-length essay to date on Eliot's debt to nonsense literature, Elizabeth Sewell noted more than a half-century ago that references to Carroll appear conspicuously throughout Eliot's poetry and critical prose.[9] Sewell ascribes the aesthetic of *The Waste Land* to the rules of nonsense literature, which she defines as 'detachment of mind from subject matter, analysis of material, [and] manipulation of patterns of unfused images'.[10] This formula, she asserts, holds the poem together within frameworks first used by Carroll: playing cards and chess.[11] Sewell applies the pattern of nonsense to Eliot's subsequent work, up to and including his last major poem: 'He has told us that he drew from *Alice in Wonderland* that rose-garden with which the first of the *Four Quartets* opens, leading into the image of the rose which pervades and closes the last of them.'[12] As intriguing as it may be, Sewell's contention that 'Carroll is the best point of reference we have for understanding Mr. Eliot' comes across as tenuous because his verse neither resembles Carroll's highly metered ballads, limericks, and concrete poems nor embraces the extensive puns and portmanteaus that foreground word-play in the *Alice* books.[13] Other critics have noted compelling parallels between Carroll and Eliot without drawing broader conclusions as to their significance: they appear as passing references, explanatory notes, or in editorial apparatus. Grover Smith's early, magisterial study of Eliot's sources, for instance, identified several references to the *Alice* books, and numerous scholars in the 1980s returned to *Alice's Adventures in Wonderland* to contextualize further the rose garden of *Burnt Norton*.[14]

The full significance of Carroll's influence remained obscure, however, until the publication in 1996 of the aforementioned poetry notebook. The notebook bears two titles: the first recto reads 'Complete Poems of T. S. Eliot' and includes a dedication to Jean Verdenal, a close friend who perished during the Battle of the Dardanelles in 1915; the second recto bears the cancelled title, 'Inventions of the March Hare', an amalgam of the March Hare from the tea-party scene of *Alice's*

Adventures in Wonderland and the linguistic burlesque on display in Chapter VIII of *Through the Looking-Glass*, 'It's My Own Invention'.[15] Given the dedication on the first recto, added years after the dates of composition indicated throughout the notebook, it stands to reason that *Inventions* was the original title, expunged in favour of the weightier *Complete Poems*.

By the time he copied the last poem into the notebook in 1916, Eliot had settled in London indefinitely, tied himself to Britain through marriage to Vivienne Haigh-Wood, and published his first mature poem, 'The Love Song of J. Alfred Prufrock', in *Poetry* magazine. By dispensing with the title *Inventions*, Eliot effaced the clearest indication of Carroll's influence on his early work: more than echoes or isolated allusions, the notebook title had placed all of Eliot's post-1908 poetry in the world of the Alice books. Christopher Ricks and Jim McCue have usefully expanded the catalogue of echoes and allusions in the copious annotation to their edition of the full corpus of Eliot's poetry. Their edition, which includes the notebook poems, along with the publication of Eliot's *Complete Prose* and the ongoing publication of his letters, allow scholars to trace for the first time the magnitude of Eliot's debt to Carroll and to make more of the surprising number of allusions to wonderland and its characters in his work than the sum of their scattered parts.

The fuller record reveals that Carroll played an integral role in the development of Eliot's poetics; in fact, Carroll provided a model for Eliot's earliest extant verses. As an eleven-year-old, Eliot produced fourteen issues of *Fireside*, a little magazine made by hand at his parents' home from January to June 1899. *Fireside* includes advertisements remade in the image of the visual culture of St. Louis at the turn of the century, performance reviews, absurd recipes, reports from around the world (that absurdly report nothing of substance), a smattering of dialogue presented as short works of fiction, and even a gossip column. The content of *Fireside* provides a rare window into the poet's childhood imagination and shows that it was indelibly shaped by Carroll's work. The second issue, for instance, features an advertisement for 'Grand Pa's Wondersoap' produced by the 'Beaver Soap Co',[16] which at once recalls *Wonder*land and the concluding line of the first stanza of 'The Beaver's Lesson' from Carroll's long poem 'The Hunting of Snark': 'They [the hunters] charmed it [a snark] with smiles and soap'.[17] Other advertisements bring to mind the tonic that reduces Alice to mouse-size and the cake that makes her inordinately tall: 'Eat "Fat-ine" to get Fat' and 'Eat Slim-me to get Slim'.[18] Loose leaves of drawings tucked into the pages of *Fireside* feature a rabbit (darting to escape a hawk) and a swan perched to drink from a teacup. The world of the *Alice* books seeps into *Fireside*, playfully reimagined by the young Eliot in parodies that resonate with Carroll's practice of nonsense.

More overt than these subtler allusions, Carroll's 'The Mad Gardener's Song' from *Sylvie and Bruno* presides over a feature that spans throughout the entire run of *Fireside*: the 'Poet's Corner'. Each stanza of 'The Mad Gardener's Song' describes a preposterous scene following the same pattern: the first line announces 'He thought he saw'; this observation is then undercut in the third line with 'He looked again and found it was'. Carroll's original is nonsense at its best, yoking the illogical with tongue-in-cheek exclamations about the absurdity of real life, such as in the opening stanza:

> He thought he saw an Elephant,
> That practised on a fife:
> He looked again, and found it was
> A letter from his wife.
> 'At length I realise,' he said,
> 'The bitterness of Life!'[19]

Eliot followed the same essential formula in ten stanzas spread across as many issues, at times closely emulating lines from his source but with deviations that shift these verses from Carroll's world to his own.

> I thought I saw an elephant
> A-riding on a 'bus
> I looked again, and found
> Alas! 'Twas only us.[20]

The eleven-year-old's rewriting of the stanza exemplifies the quality the adult Eliot would discern in the juvenilia of William Blake: 'His early poems show what the poems of a boy of genius ought to show, immense power of assimilation.'[21] While Eliot's 'assimilation' of Carroll borders on replication in the case of several *Fireside* stanzas, his notable departures adumbrate the poetics of his more mature work. 'In one aspect', as noted by John J. Soldo, one of the first critics to report on *Fireside*, 'we have a clear case of childhood plagiarism. But we also have an early signal for Eliot's penchant, nay his very necessity, for alluding to and incorporating the lines of other poets'.[22] More recently, Robert Crawford has observed of the *Fireside* stanzas that '[s]ometimes awkwardly, Tom made ["The Mad Gardener's Song"] his own'.[23] While the *Fireside* stanzas lack the more seamless and sophisticated integration of literary texts and cultural referents that characterize Eliot's later poetics, these childhood verses already show him modernizing Carroll's poem and claiming its stanzas as his own. Eliot not only reduces the first stanza from four lines to six, but he also simplifies the diction ('A-riding' initiates a pattern of verb treatment throughout the *Fireside* verses followed by 'A-running', 'A-sailing', 'A-sitting', 'A-jumping', 'A-flinging', and 'A-crackling'[24]); introduces the detritus of the modern city ('I looked again, and found / It was a man c[r]ushin' a can'[25]); integrates characters who may well have been familiar to him in his youth (such as a baker named 'Mrs. Rogers'[26]); and consistently shifts the pronoun 'He' to 'I' as if to take ownership over both the words and their telling. By omitting the undercutting conclusion of Carroll's original stanza ('The bitterness of Life!'), Eliot also shifted the tone, though the 'letter from his wife' that prompts this exclamation may account for the whimsical dedication 'to My Wife' announced in the third issue of *Fireside* and reiterated with increased urgency in the sixth issue: 'Remember, to my Wife!'[27] While minor verses on their face, the *Fireside* stanzas seed a poetics that flowers in Eliot's later work, including the more mature poems he drafted after his discovery of Laforgue.[28]

Thematic parallels, linguistic echoes, and allusions to the *Alice* books pervade the poetry notebook first published as *Inventions of the March Hare*. Alongside the interminable tea party reminiscent of the Mad Hatter's in 'Goldfish III' (1910), 'Prufrock' (1911), 'Portrait of a Lady'(1910–11), and 'Mr. Apollinax' (1915),[29] the theme of madness runs throughout the notebook, perhaps nowhere more apparently than in 'Prufrock's Pervigilium,' where Prufrock hears his 'Madness singing.'[30] In a manner redolent of Carroll's many animal characters, Eliot anthropomorphizes an 'Apollinax' and Professor and Mrs. Channing-Cheetah. From the seaweed in the hair of the rolling head in 'Mr. Apollinax' to the 'jellyfish without repose' in 'Suite Clownesque I' (1910) to the 'pair of ragged claws / Scuttling across the floors of silent seas' in 'Prufrock', and the 'crab with a barnacle on his back' in 'Rhapsody on a Windy Night' (1911), the undersea imagery that appears in the notebook may owe something to Alice's underwater adventure in chapter 10 of *Alice's Adventures in Wonderland*, 'The Lobster Quadrille.'[31] The White Rabbit that Alice follows into Wonderland may have inspired the 'white rabbit' that hops under the table, '[t]witching his nose toward the crumbs' in the concluding lines of 'Introspection' (undated).[32]

While critics have attributed the dark comedy of Eliot's early poetry to Laforgue's self-mocking irony, specific verses in the notebook suggest the fusion of French and English source material.[33] The laughter that 'tinkled among the teacups' in 'Mr. Apollinax' recalls the Mad Hatter's parody of the popular lullaby 'Twinkle, Twinkle, Little Star' during his tea party: 'Twinkle, twinkle, little bat! / How I wonder what you're at! / Up above the world you fly, / Like a teatray in the sky.'[34] Perhaps more substantively than this verbal echo, the Cheshire-Cat's mischievous, fading grin makes more than one appearance and disappearance in the notebook poems.[35] Alice first meets the Cheshire-Cat in the kitchen at the Duchess's house, but the encounter that seems to have appealed most to Eliot occurs when the Cheshire-Cat directs Alice to the Mad Hatter and the March Hare: 'Visit either you like', he tells her, 'they're both mad.'[36] When Alice resists ('I don't want to go among mad people'), the Cat replies: 'Oh, you can't help that [...] we're all mad here. I'm mad. You're mad.'[37] Alice re-encounters the Cat in the Red Queen's garden, where he's sentenced to beheading but foils the executioners by disappearing all but his grinning face. The Cheshire-Cat's fading grin joins many other overt and subtle evocations of madness in Eliot's poems, and its specific presence implies principles underlying Carroll's nonsense: what is serious may lack in sense; what is logical may lack in meaning; what is real may be absurd. In lines quoted above from 'Opera', 'Life departs with a feeble smile / Into the indifferent'. The persona of 'First Debate between the Body and Soul' (1910) is 'devoted to the pure idea', an ideal thwarted by the reality of his own lustful imagination and bodily sensations. A smile reminiscent of the Cheshire-Cat's grin signals the young persona's failure: 'Till life evaporates into a smile / Simple and profound.'[38] The image recurs in 'Morning at the Window' (1914), a poem in which the persona experiences a sudden awareness for 'the damp souls of housemaids.'[39] Opening with the sound of 'rattling breakfast plates in basement kitchens', which recalls the chaos of the Duchess's kitchen, the poem ends with the totalizing image of 'An aimless smile that hovers in the air / And vanishes along the level of the roofs'.[40] The proximity of the Mad Hatter's tea party to the Red Queen's trial in *Alice's Adventures in Wonderland* might explain why the protagonist of 'Mr. Apollinax' searches for the guest of honour's head 'rolling under a chair / Or grinning over a screen'.[41] With similar effect to the dismissive final line of Laforgue's 'Autobiographical Preludes' ('Oh well, a human cry for you!') and the line concluding the first stanza of Carroll's 'The Mad Gardener's Song' ('The bitterness of Life!'), the vanishing smile in 'Morning at the Window' undercuts the gravity of the scene, signalling the absurdity (and futility) in the human compulsion to make sense of life. Thus, far from an adolescent preoccupation, Carroll supplied Eliot for decades with the vocabulary to reconcile the unreconcilable, to discern logic in the absurd, and to make sense of his own world of nonsense.[42]

Whereas the many allusions to the *Alice* books in Eliot's early poetry demonstrate Carroll's profound impress on his imagination throughout his formative years, the first title he devised for the notebook, *Inventions of the March Hare*, suggests a more profound influence: a model for assimilating disparate cultural and literary references into his work, imbuing his own poetry with some of the meaning of his sources but imparting on them a new resonance. The 'March Hare' refers to one of the characters assembled at the Mad Hatter's tea-party: opening the cover of the notebook, readers enter a world constructed partially from the *Alice* books. The reference also connotes the sexual dynamics operating just below the surface in many of the poems as well as the madness that pervades them. 'Inventions' is a more heavily freighted term, which Frances Dickey has partially unpacked: 'inventions' can refer to discoveries, findings or creations, but, she observes, the 'idea of invention as a finding is connected to the word "inventory"'.[43] Thus, an 'invention' refers at once to something newly created and the totality of products (inventory) resulting from the process. The dual meaning suits: it describes Eliot's creations and the collection they comprise. However, in Carroll's books, 'invention' takes on yet another meaning: the characters Alice encounters recite burlesques of conventional genres (lullabies, love songs, concrete poems) as well as lines of traditional poetry, all the while claiming them as 'their own invention'.[44]

This topos of 'invention' as *re*-creation in one's own image originates in chapter 5 of *Alice's Adventures in Wonderland*, 'Advice from a Caterpillar'. Alice recites a parody of Robert Southey's 'The Old Man's Comforts' entitled 'You Are Old Father William', without any of the piety of the original. Carroll recasts the elderly devout minister of Southey's text as Father William, a fat old man whose only concern is eating fowl whole (beak and all) and balancing an eel on the end of his nose. The Caterpillar listens to Alice's recitation and responds: '"That is not quite right." "Not *quite* right, I'm afraid," said Alice, timidly: "some of the words have got altered"'.[45]

'Invention' as a form of assimilating previously known cultural material dominates Alice's encounters on the other side of the looking-glass. A scene that appears critical to Eliot's own sense of the term occurs in chapter 8 of *Through the Looking-Glass*, 'It's My Own Invention'. Alice encounters the White Knight, who claims as his own a series of inventions, each a well-known object altered to a state of uselessness, such as a lidless box to transport clothes and sandwiches, which he 'carries upside-down, so that the rain ca'n't get in'.[46] The Knight recites and revises familiar phrases, repeatedly trying to impress upon Alice his ingenuity: 'It's a plan of my own invention', he says, followed by 'I'm a great hand at inventing things' and 'I keep inventing new things'.[47] When he notices Alice's consternation, he purports to cheer her up by singing a song that he refers to by multiple titles, depending on how it is 'called': 'Haddocks' Eyes', 'The Aged Aged Man', and 'Ways and Means'.[48] Confused, Alice presses the Knight: '"Well, what *is* the song, then?" said Alice, who was by this time completely bewildered. "I was coming to that," the Knight said. "The song really is *A-sitting On A Gate*: and the tune's my own invention".'[49] However, Alice recognizes 'the melancholy music' of the song: '"But the tune *isn't* his own invention," she said to herself: "it's '*I give thee all, I can no more*'".'[50] The Knight's 'invention' remakes Irish lyricist Thomas Moore's 'My Heart and Lute', a song/poem with the first line 'I give thee all, I can no more', by combining it with allusions to Wordsworth's 'Resolution and Independence', a lyric recounting the poet's actual encounter with a leech-gatherer in the Lake District of England. '"But the tune *isn't* his own invention"', Alice observes, before an omniscient narrator interrupts the chapter to underscore the significance of the exchange: 'Of all the strange things that Alice saw in her journey Through The Looking-Glass, this was the one that she always remembered most clearly. Years afterwards she could bring the whole scene back again, as if it had been only yesterday.'[51] As Hugh Haughton has opined in his edition of the *Alice* books, 'This sudden time-shift to a mood of anticipated retrospection indicates that this incident has an exceptional status in the text.'[52] The scene stands out principally because it elaborates the method espoused throughout Carroll's work, in which songs, poems, titles, and phrases attributable to other writers are reworked and reclaimed in a different place, time, and voice. It is a conception of literary allusion that permits a new writer to overwrite the inventions of others through assimilation and alteration in the service of making them their own. The Knight recognizes the ballad by several titles, as if it were a whole new song simply by calling it by another name. The Knight's repurposing of Wordsworth's 'Resolution and Independence' underscores the process of sieving off the life force of previous creators to remake it anew – the poem recounts an encounter with someone whose job it is to collect literal bloodsuckers.

It is no coincidence that the eleven-year-old Eliot wrote stanzas that at once appear to copy Carroll's 'The Mad Gardener's Song' but with deviations that remade them as his own. This method is on full display throughout the *Alice* books, such as when the Mad Hatter recasts 'Twinkle, Twinkle, Little Star' with wholly new lyrics suited to his purposes. Eliot's simplification of the diction in the *Fireside* verses ('A-riding', 'A-running', 'A-sailing', 'A-sitting', 'A-jumping', 'A-flinging', and 'A-crackling') subtly yet plainly recalls the Knight's method in inventing the song he ultimately called '*A-sitting On A Gate*'. Eliot practised the method of invention he learned from the White Knight in *Fireside*; honed it in the notebook poems by assimilating texts in which he had found meaning, including the *Alice* books and Laforgue's *Oeuvres Complètes*; and deployed it in his mature works, perhaps most obviously in *The Waste Land*, the opening lines of which foreground assimilation in three gerunds offset by commas: 'breeding', 'mixing', 'stirring'.[53] Eliot's many allusions to literature, painting, song, and world events in *The Waste Land* and subsequent poetry are presented as his own: the original source sounds through the revision, but, as Alice would say, 'Not *quite* right'.

Notes

1   Arthur Symons, *The Symbolist Movement in Literature* (London: Archibald Constable, 1908), 108.
2   Jules Laforgue, *Poems: Bilingual Edition*, trans. Peter Dale (London: Anvil Press, 2001), 35.
3   The notebook belongs to the T. S. Eliot papers, the Henry W. and Albert A. Berg Collection of English and American Literature, The New York Public Library, Astor, Lenox and Tilden Foundations. A facsimile edition allows readers to leaf through the notebook and encounter Eliot's compositions and cancellations as they appear in the original: *The Gloucester Notebook* (Gardena, CA: Galileo Publishers, 2021). For the dating of Eliot's early poems, see Christopher Ricks, ed., 'Chronology' in *Inventions of the March Hare: Poems 1909–1917*, T. S. Eliot (New York: Harcourt Brace & Co., 1996), xxxvii–xlii and Jayme Stayer, *Becoming T. S. Eliot: The Rhetoric of Voice and Audience* in Inventions of the March Hare (Baltimore: Johns Hopkins University Press, 2021), 291–3.
4   T. S. Eliot, *The Poems of T. S. Eliot,* vol. 1, ed. Christopher Ricks and Jim McCue (Baltimore: Johns Hopkins University Press, 2015), 235.
5   Eliot, *Poems* 1, 236.
6   T. S. Eliot, 'Reflections on Contemporary Poetry [IV]' (1919), in *Complete Prose of T. S. Eliot: The Critical Edition, vol. 2: The Perfect Critic, 1919–1926*, ed. Anthony Cuda and Ronald Schuchard (Baltimore: Johns Hopkins University Press, 2014), 66.
7   Eliot, *Poems* 1, 355.
8   For the influence of Aestheticism on Eliot, see chapter 3 of Frances Dickey, *The Modern Portrait Poem: From Dante Gabriel Rossetti to Ezra Pound* (Charlottesville and London: Virginia University Press, 2012). For the literature of Decadence, see chapter 4 of Vincent Sherry, *Modernism and the Reinvention of Decadence* (New York: Cambridge University Press, 2015).
9   Elizabeth Sewell, 'Lewis Carroll and T. S. Eliot as Nonsense Poets', in *T. S. Eliot, A Symposium for His Seventieth Birthday*, ed. Neville Braybrooke (London: Rupert Hart-Davis Ltd., 1959), reproduced in Hugh Kenner, ed. *T. S. Eliot: A Collection of Critical Essays* (Englewood Cliffs, NJ: Prentice-Hall, 1962).
10   Sewell, 'Lewis Carroll', 69.
11   Ibid., 68.
12   Ibid., 67. In an interview with the *New York Times Book Review* (29 November 1953), Eliot identified *Alice's Adventures in Wonderland* as a source of the opening lines of *Burnt Norton* ('Down the passage we did not take / Towards the door we never opened / into the rose-garden'). Eliot had visited the rose gardens at Burnt Norton in 1934 with his long-time beloved Emily Hale, with whom he rekindled what would remain largely an epistolary relationship. Eliot's half of their correspondence

survives in the Princeton University Library. In a letter from 19 March 1931 that may well allude to the instability of his feelings for Hale, Eliot told her that he discerned considerable human tragedy in the passage of *Alice's Adventures in Wonderland* where Alice is small enough to fit through the tiny door into the garden but likewise too small to reach the key. (Emily Hale Collection, Emily Hale Letters from T. S. Eliot, C0686, Manuscripts Division, Department of Special Collections, Princeton University Library.)

13 Eliot even cautioned against the creation of portmanteaus in a 1932 letter to the poet Edgar Foxall: 'The idea, of course, is not a new one, and an argument in its favour may be found in *Alice in Wonderland*. […] I think that in the verses you have shown, the composite words stand out far too conspicuously. […] My own experience has been that forcing experimentation has sometimes tended to conceal from myself a poverty of what I had to communicate, and I have destroyed a fair number of my verses for this reason' (*The Letters of T. S. Eliot*, vol. 6: 1932–3, ed. Valerie Eliot and John Haffenden [London: Faber and Faber, 2016], 80–1).

14 Grover Smith, *T. S. Eliot's Poetry and Plays: A Study in Sources and Meaning* (Chicago: Chicago University Press, 1956), 68, 260, 325. See also, for instance, chapter 10 of Ronald Bush, *T. S. Eliot: A Study in Character and Style* (New York and Oxford: Oxford University Press, 1983). Bush finds Sewell's claims to be unconvincing when applied to *The Waste Land* but more fruitful with respect to the rose garden in *Burnt Norton* (200).

15 Eliot, *The Gloucester Notebook*, 15 and 17.

16 T. S. Eliot, *Fireside*, issue 2, MS Am 1635.5. Houghton Library, Harvard University.

17 Lewis Carroll, *The Hunting of the Snark: An Agony in Eight Fits* (London: Macmillan and Co., 1876), 79.

18 T. S. Eliot, *Fireside*, issue 14, MS Am 1635.5. Houghton Library, Harvard University. Eliot's punctuation was inconsistent across the two advertisements for Fat-ine and Slim-me.

19 Lewis Carroll, *Sylvie and Bruno* (London: Macmillan, 1889), 65.

20 Eliot, *Poems 2*, 147.

21 T. S. Eliot, 'William Blake' (1920) in *Complete Prose* 2, 187. Quoted by Ricks and McCue in their headnote to the *Fireside* verses (Eliot, *Poems 2*, 147).

22 John T. Soldo, 'Jovial Juvenilia: T. S. Eliot's First Magazine', *Biography* 5, no. 1 (1982): 25–37.

23 Robert Crawford, *Young Eliot: From St. Louis to* The Waste Land (London: Jonathan Cape, 2015), 43.

24 Eliot, *Poems 2*, 147–9.

25 Ibid., 149.

26 Ibid.

27 Eliot, *Fireside*, issue 6, MS Am 1635.5. Houghton Library, Harvard University.

28 Carroll's 'The Mad Gardener's Song' remained in Eliot's mature imagination decades later, when he turned to the quatrain model of Théophile Gautier's *Émaux et Camées* in his satiric poem 'The Hippopotamus'. As Smith notes (*T. S. Eliot's Poetry and Plays*, 40), the character of the hippopotamus recalls a stanza from Carroll's poem: 'He thought he saw a Banker's Clerk / Descending from the bus: / He looked again, and found it was / A Hippopotamus. "If this should stay to dine," he said, "There won't be much for us!"' Eliot rewrote the stanza in *Fireside* as follows: 'I thought I saw a banker's clerk / A-riding on a 'bus, / I looked again and saw, / It was a hippopotamus / "If he should stay to tea," thought I, / "*What would be left for us?*"' (*Poems 2*, 148).

29 Sewell noted this parallel ('Lewis Carroll', 68) and Kate McLoughlin has more recently developed the theme in 'Prufrock, Party-Goer: Tongue-Tied at Tea', in *The Modernist Party*, ed. Kate McLoughlin (Edinburgh: Edinburgh University Press, 2013), 45–63.

30 Eliot, *Inventions*, 43; Eliot, *Poems 2*, 316.

31 Ricks and McCue observe the echo between this chapter of *Alice's Adventures in Wonderland* and 'Suite Clownesque', which is supported by the proximity of 'nose', 'jellyfish', and 'toes' in both texts. See Eliot, *Poems 1*, 1110.

32 Eliot, *Poems 1*, 273.

33 Symons initiates a critical tradition of ascribing laughter to Laforgue: 'an embracing laughter [...] more than half a sob, and shaken out of him with a deplorable gesture of the thin arms, thrown wide' (*Symbolist Movement*, 108–9).

34 Lewis Carroll, *Alice's Adventures in Wonderland* and *Through the Looking-Glass*, ed. Hugh Haughton (London: Penguin, 1998), 63.

35 Eliot famously loved felines and his most overt nonsense work, *Old Possum's Book of Practical Cats*, opens with an allusion to Carroll: 'The Naming of the Cats is a difficult matter, / It isn't just one of your holiday games; / You may think at first I'm as mad as a hatter / When I tell you, a cat must have THREE DIFFERENT NAMES' (Eliot, *Poems 2*, 5).

36 Carroll, *Alice*, 57.

37 Ibid.

38 Eliot, *Poems 1*, 241.

39 Ibid., 21.

40 Ibid. Smith associates this image with the Cheshire-Cat's grin (*T. S. Eliot's Poetry and Plays*, 31). The image of the Cheshire-Cat's smile may also be a precursor for the morbid opening quatrain of 'Whispers of Immortality': 'Webster was much possessed by death; / He saw the skull beneath the skin; / And breastless creatures underground / leaned backward with a lipless grin' (Eliot, *Poems 1*, 47).

41 Ibid., 25.

42 A select catalogue of references to Carroll from Eliot's prose easily demonstrates the long presence of the *Alice* books in his mind. References first appear in his philosophical papers, drafted during his doctoral coursework, where he refers to one theory as 'simply utilitarian jabberwocky' and better still if held up to 'the looking glass' (Eliot, *Complete Prose 1*, 155). Of the twenty-five lectures on Victorian literature he delivered in 1917, Eliot devoted one evening to 'The Laureates of Nonsense': Carroll and Edward Lear (ibid., 588). Acknowledging a critical about-face in his 1929 essay on Dante, Eliot invites his reader 'to pass through the looking-glass into a world which is just as reasonable as our own. When we have done that we begin to wonder whether the world of Dante is not both larger and more solid than our own' (Eliot, *Complete Prose 3*, 733). While visiting Emily Hale at Scripps College in 1933, Eliot lectured on obscurity in nonsense poetry, distinguishing between Lear's devotion to pure poetry (music, rhythm) and Carroll's intellectual wordplay. 'Carroll is metaphysical', he claimed, 'while Lear is romantic' (ibid., 829). He similarly emphasized Carroll's wordplay in 'The Aims of Education', collected in *To Criticize the Critic*: 'I think we can learn something about "sense words" from examining nonsense words. Lewis Carroll's "portmanteau" words, like *slithy*, *gimble*, and *wabe*, are not pure nonsense words, for he defined their meaning' (Eliot, *Complete Prose 7*, 515). When a writer in the *Times* reduced modernist art and literature to 'pedantic and deliberate obscurity [...] brought down to the level of esoteric parlor games', Eliot published a rejoinder in *Horizon* under the title 'A Message to the Fish', alluding to a missive

dispatched by Humpty Dumpty in *Through the Looking-Glass* (Eliot, *Horizon* 3, no. 15 [March 1941]: 173–5).

43   Frances Dickey, 'The Musical World of Eliot's *Inventions*', in *The Edinburgh Companion to T. S. Eliot and the Arts*, ed. Frances Dickey and John D. Morgenstern (Edinburgh: Edinburgh University Press, 2016), 115.

44   See Carroll, *Alice,* 205–19.

45   Ibid., 45.

46   Ibid., 207.

47   Ibid., 209, 211, 213.

48   Ibid., 213–14.

49   Ibid., 214.

50   Ibid.

51   Ibid.

52   Hugh Haughton, 'Notes to *Alice's Adventures in Wonderland*', in *Alice's Adventures in Wonderland* and *Through the Looking-Glass*, ed. Hugh Haughton (London: Penguin, 1998), 349.

53   Eliot, *Poems* 1, 55.

Chapter 4

FANTASTIC SURREALISM: THE INFLUENCE OF LEWIS CARROLL'S WONDERLAND ON *TRANSITION* MAGAZINE'S AMERICAN SURREALIST LITERARY EXPERIMENTS (1927–38)

Céline Mansanti

Eugene Jolas's American exile magazine *transition*, published in Paris between 1927 and 1938 – with a two-year gap between 1930 and 1932 – is well known for presenting English-speaking readers with a large body of important French surrealist works of art and literary pieces, some of which were published for the first time in French, and many of which were first translated into English for *transition*.[1] In fact, *transition* was certainly the most important venue for circulating French surrealism in the United States before the end of the 1930s.[2] The magazine is less known for publishing various American surrealist texts, an event which is particularly interesting for at least two reasons – even apart from the fact that most of these texts have received very little critical attention, if any at all. First, these American productions were published early, in the late 1920s and early 1930s, decades before an American 'Surrealist Movement' was identified in Chicago, around 1966,[3] and even before the first exhibit in the United States of some French surrealist art works.[4] Second, *transition*'s American surrealist literary experiments differed from those of the French surrealists and offered, as a whole, a form of fantastic surrealism which can be considered as a counter-proposal to French surrealism.[5]

In the first section of this chapter, I will show that some of the characteristics of *transition*'s American surrealist literary experiments can be seen as resulting from the influence of Lewis Carroll's work, a specificity which might even be considered as one of the distinctive features of this early, singular current of American surrealism, in contrast to Carroll's less defining influence on the work of the French surrealists. In fact, the French surrealists did not start to show any interest in Carroll until 1929, when Aragon translated *The Hunting of the Snark*. So why was *Alice's Adventures in Wonderland* a remarkable element in the network of interactions, exchanges, and influences that came to shape *transition*'s American surrealist experiments in the 1920s and 1930s? This is the question I will address in the second section of this chapter. We will see that looking at the cultural importance of *Alice* in the American society of the 1920s and 1930s, and more specifically, looking at its role in the American reception of both the French surrealist avant-garde and Joyce's 'Work in Progress' – the most famous literary work serialized by *transition*, and which would later be published under the title *Finnegans Wake* – demonstrates Carroll's powerful influence in creating an American, fantastic form of surrealism.

Most of the writers and visual artists associated more or less closely with French surrealism and published in *transition* remain in posterity: Arp, Artaud, Baron, Bousquet, Brassaï, Breton, Crevel, Desnos, Eluard, Ernst, de Chirico, Gaillard, Goll, Leiris, Masson, Man Ray, Michaux, Nezval, Noll, Péret, Prévert, Queneau, Reverdy, Ribemont-Dessaignes, Soupault, Tanguy, Unik, Vitrac are names with which many people today are familiar. But who remembers Wayne Andrews, Whit Burnett, Robert Myron Coates, William Closson Emory, Murray Godwin, Leigh Hoffman, Charles Tracy, or George Whitsett? In all likelihood, only Harry Crosby still rings a bell for his work on the Black Sun Press. However, all of these American contributors to *transition* tried their hand at surrealist experiments, producing texts that together share some common traits. Some of them explicitly or implicitly associated their work with surrealism, while others reinterpreted surrealist themes and techniques, thus allowing the reader to establish connections with surrealism.

Charles Tracy republished his three contributions to *transition* in a book explicitly entitled *An American Sur-Realist*.[6] Wayne Andrews wrote in *The Surrealist Parade* that he submitted 'The Evocative Treason of 449 Golden Doorknobs' (his very first publication, which appeared in *transition*) to Breton in 'the summer of 1934', and that Breton's 'stamp of approval on [his] prose poem' won Andrews's 'eternal loyalty'.[7] William Closson Emory and Whit Burnett published 'scenarios' ('Love in the West' and 'Home Edition', two titles to which the word 'scenario' was added respectively), a genre which signals the influence of French surrealism.[8] In 'Dreams 1928–1929' (*transition* 18), Harry Crosby tried his hand at automatic writing while Leigh Hoffman in 'Anamnesis' (*transition* 11) and Robert Myron Coates in 'Conversations n°7' (*transition* 1) and 'In Memoriam' (*transition* 6) reworked the surrealist *topos* of the hunted woman.[9] As for Murray Godwin, it was Nathanael West, the author of the surrealist novel *The Dream Life of Balso Snell* (1931), who referred to Godwin's two extracts of 'Work on Sidetrack' in *transition* as representatives of 'an American superrealism'.[10] George Whitsett's case is slightly different: his two pieces in *transition* are probably less connected to surrealism than those of the other contributors under study, but are included because of the characteristics they share with the other experiments.[11]

While these texts are connected in one way or another to surrealism, they are strikingly different from the experiments of the French surrealists that were also published in the pages of *transition* and elsewhere. The main difference between *transition*'s American surrealist experiences and French surrealism lies in their propensity to create imaginary worlds,[12] in congruence with the second statement of *transition*'s 'Revolution of the Word' manifesto published in 1929: 'The imagination in search of a fabulous world is autonomous and unconfined.'[13] One could say that unlike these American surrealist texts, heavily based on the creation of a fantastic world, French surrealist experimentations tend to rely on the 'marvelous'. In 1962, Breton remarked that the spirit 'would like to distinguish with certainty the true marvelous from the fantastic, the strange, the illusive sparkling'.[14] Such a distinction was crucial to Breton, who established the superiority of the marvelous over the fantastic: 'The fantastic almost always derives from some unimportant fiction, whereas the marvelous glimmers at the extreme end of the vital movement and entirely engages affectivity'.[15] In other words, one could say that the 'marvelous' emerges from reality, whereas the 'fantastic' opposes reality. The marvelous comes primarily from language ('the earth is blue like an orange' for example), whereas the fantastic relies on visual shock: the American surrealist experiments in *transition* are based on phantasmagorias that, like in *Alice in Wonderland*, are usually safely contained within the limits of a parallel world, whether it is a dream or a scenario. Reality itself is not radically put into question. A good example of this partition is to be found in Hoffman's 'Catastrophe': 'How long we fought I do not know, but what seemed hours afterwards I regained consciousness lying in the bed of the room where the struggle had been, sore and badly bruised, with a nurse beside me who declared that I had fallen down a flight of stairs'.[16]

Based on impressive personifications of animals and animations of plants and objects, the rewriting of genres such as the fairy tale and the nursery rhyme, and a reassuring separation between a dream world and the real world, the American surrealist experiments in *transition* point to a connection with Lewis Carroll's Wonderland, where animals are humanized and where playing cards and flowers come to life. Let us look at the American surrealist texts in *transition* more closely in order to underline this link better. George Whitsett, for example, animates plants and objects while revisiting the genre of the nursery rhyme in 'Dancing Rope' and 'Hotel'. 'Hotel' starts: 'Mr Mango, you are nominated to the phone';[17] and this is the beginning of 'Dancing Rope', in which Carroll's and Joyce's influences – through puns reminiscent of both *Alice* and 'Work in Progress', and personifications that echo Carroll's world – as well as the principles of the 'Revolution of the Word' manifesto can be felt:

> Lice night
> And the nice before.
> Lambs and cuttlefish came to my door,
> The lambs wore plumes,
> The cuttlefish said,
> And a spray of almond over their head.[18]

Personifications and puns also characterize Whit Burnett's writings in *transition*. 'An Essay in Compostography or the Life in the Day of the Squidge', published in June 1930, stages a 'squidge' (defined as 'an old Wightword from Wedgeworms lying midway between the ichytherapeutical stream and the shelless crustaceans'[19]), who is the hero of the fairy tale on which the text relies: 'Fourteen years before the fall of Tyre there lived on the Isle of Wight a Squidge'.[20] Similarly, Charles Tracy's *An American Sur-Realist* also develops from the fantastic world of the fairy tale, with accents that are noticeably reminiscent of Joyce's experiments in 'Work in Progress' and, because of the cultural intertextuality with *Alice*, are also underlined by the critical essays published in *transition* on 'Work in Progress' and Carrollian influence. For example, this is the beginning of 'Seven Ages of Women' published in *transition* 24:

> In the kingdom of glad no
> quirk can creep to flay
> the nap of serene.
> She rides
> feather's fluff flitters in
> in the golden gleam of ERBS
> idle glitter.[21]

The same kind of fantastic, enchanted fairy-tale atmosphere can be found in 'Mother of a Clown', also by Charles Tracy, in *transition* 25:

> In everland silken grass pink-tipped
> [...] bending and swaying in endless
> curve-forms sings in the breath
> of windless breezes [...] [22]

Personifications are a recurrent feature of almost all the American surrealist experiments published in *transition*. Whit Burnett's 'Home Edition, A Scenario' starts:

> Enter, bowing, Page One, followed by Mr. Calvin Coolidge in high hat, the Average Citizen with abashed look, Crime, Coal Strikers, Chicago Riots, Missing Clue, Police in Hot Pursuit, Miss America, and other Atlantic City Beauty Contestants who play leap frog gracefully over a series of headline-hurdles up to the point of arriving gracefully, with legs crossed, on the shoulder of the Statue of Liberty.[23]

The burlesque nature of this personification is counterbalanced by a more poetic type of fantastic further down the text: 'Accidents join hands, dancing along a radio wave.'[24] Another experimental text by Whit Burnett, published in the following issue, also oscillates between the burlesque and the poetic. In 'Balls, Or Simple Error', 'A pair of ear muffs bow and do a polka' while 'Two pairs of black rimmed spectacles do a hesitation waltz'.[25] Later on, a more poetic atmosphere prevails: 'Mr. Wedgewood Homes. Vainly he strikes at the jolly animal. It laughs. It turns into a hoop, a ball, and rolls away.'[26] Harry Crosby's 'Dreams', published in November 1929, also display a poetic fantastic, as for example section 17: 'a giraffe is gorging himself on sunflowers a Parisian doll is washing herself in a blue fingerbowl while I insist on their electrocution on the grounds of indecency'.[27] The connection with Carroll is strengthened when the speaker 'do[es] not find it strange that a blue bird should fall in love with a playing card because the playing card in question happens to be the queen of hearts'.[28] 'The Evocative Treason of 449 Golden Doorknobs' – the surrealist text Wayne Andrews said he submitted to Breton – also relies on the animation of objects, most prominently with the doorknobs of its title:

> The entry, rather 'solemn', to be sure, of 449 golden doorknobs cautioned a dreamheavy evening, and I listened to the inaudible words of April which thrilled the golden doorknobs into magic letters, so contemporary that one could no longer say
> 'Evening has fallen'
> without a betraying blush.
> Meanwhile, the 449 golden doorknobs had arranged themselves before a worn but purple tapestry with appropriate years for the more human exclamation marks and other fragilities.
> Although April's lips, a cool adagio, were as slow as the more penetrating pendulums of timepieces on less tragic planets, the doorknobs beat a warm allegro.[29]

The connection between Andrews and Carroll appears even more clearly in Andrews's other *transition* piece, entitled 'Take a Number from One to Ten': here, roses talk, just before 'some capricious chapelier' is conjured up.[30]

Whereas Andrews's 'The Evocative Treason of 449 Golden Doorknobs' oscillates between the poetic and the burlesque, Godwin's surrealist experiment clearly embraces the grotesque. Godwin's 'Work on Sidetrack' (two extracts of which were published in *transition*) stages a 'Pford' car (referred to as 'she') soothed by a 'Pfordnurse' before giving birth to a smaller Pford. Here again, personifications and puns are reminiscent of both Carroll and Joyce. But it is probably William Closson Emory's scenario, 'Love in the West', which conjures up the most impressive series of burlesque personifications. In this text, whose heroine is a personified one-hundred-dollar bill, 'Large Idaho Potato stalks back and forth under canopy opening limousines and handing in and out turnips, oysters and carnations that are constantly arriving and departing.'[31] When Hundred Dollar Bill and her fiancé go on a trip, Easter eggs carry their luggage: 'They walk briskly down the platform followed by colored easter eggs carrying arm loads of luggage. Turnips and asparagus accompany them from train.'[32] Later on, 'A bologna sausage paces up and down in front of the night club yawning.'[33]

The wide – and wild – personifications these texts have in common are all the more striking since neither the French surrealists nor Joyce – undoubtedly another crucial influence on young American readers of *transition* and would-be writers – used this device. Further seeming references to Carroll punctuate the reading of two more texts. In 'Conversations n°7', Robert Myron Coates seems to push the Mad Hatter's riddle joke one step further by not even asking the riddle he mentions at the beginning of the text: '*Listen! I was lying in my bed dreaming.* but I will tell you a joke or rather ask you a riddle.'[34] In 'Anamnesis', Leigh

Hoffman's narrator sees a woman disappearing into a cavern and follows her. He is immediately caught by a powerful wind: 'The cavern, I found, was nothing more than a vacuous tube with a strong suction at either end. I was drawn powerlessly back and forth through the length of the tunnel, from first one end to the other.'[35] The scene seems to combine the French surrealists' *topos* of the hunt of the woman with Alice's fall down the Rabbit Hole.

Interestingly, the connections between the American surrealist experiments published in *transition* and Carroll's world do not derive only from references to famous scenes in *Alice*, or from similarities with the way Carroll creates wild and strange personifications. The connections are also induced by the magazine itself; in other words, it is not just about the texts themselves; the publishing and reading contexts matter. How? Firstly, although they are not presented as a group by the editors, these American experiments, which share a certain number of striking characteristics, tend to give the impression to the assiduous reader[36] of *transition* that they exist as a group. Within this context, the influence of Carroll, which might not be always obvious when reading each text individually, becomes much more unmistakable when considering all the texts together: indeed, the same connections with Carroll keep appearing (mostly through a specific type of personification, arguably owing much to Wonderland, and through references to famous scenes from the *Alice* books). Second, the connection with Carroll is suggested by the fact that *transition* published many references to Wonderland, in particular through Joyce's 'Work in Progress'. Large extracts of 'Work in Progress' were published for the first time in *transition* from the first issue of the magazine in April 1927 to the last in the spring of 1938, and the first references to *Alice's* world in 'Work in Progress' appeared early in the history of the magazine, in the first issue of *transition* in April 1927 – 'The great fall of the offwall entailed at such short notice the schute of Finnegan, erse solid man, that the humptyhillhead of humself prumptly sends an unquiring one well to the west in quest of his tumptytumptoes' – and in August 1927.[37] This gave rise to early references to Carroll in critical essays on Joyce's work that were published in *transition* as early as 1928, 1929, and 1930 (namely 'Mr Joyce's Treatment of Plot' by Elliot Paul in *transition* 9, 'The Dubliner and His Dowdili' by Michael Stuart in *transition* 18, and 'Astropolis' by Stuart Gilbert in *transition* 19–20), significantly predating other Carrollian connections to Joyce in the critical canon.[38]

Wonderland thus has an important influence on the shaping of these American surrealist experiments; but there is more: Carroll's world is also an important distinctive feature of this early expression of American literary surrealism. Indeed, the French surrealists, whose writings were much translated and published in *transition*, and who inspired these experiments, as we saw, were not influenced, or were not as obviously influenced by Carroll. Although Carroll is frequently mentioned as one of the precursors of French surrealism, critics such as Michel Remy and Isabelle Nières-Chevrel have shown that he did not become an object of interest for the French surrealists before Aragon, probably prompted by his lover Nancy Cunard, translated *The Hunting of the Snark* in 1929 and wrote an article on Carroll in *Le Surréalisme au service de la révolution* in December 1931.

As for Breton, he did not mention Carroll before 1934 in *What Is Surrealism?* In other words, *transition*'s American contributors' interest in *Alice* was not primarily mediated by French surrealism. So where did this influence come from? 'Work in Progress', and all the attention it attracted, is probably part of the answer, as we saw. Another part of the answer probably lies in the vivid presence of *Alice* in American culture. At the end of the 1920s, when *transition*'s first surrealist texts were published, *Alice* had long been a strong cultural reality across the various social layers of the United States, and its influence was on the rise.

In 1905, an advert for Peter's chocolate in *Life* magazine entitled 'Alice in Petersland' already relied on the *Alice* imagery.[39] In fact, as Carolyn Sigler showed in *Alternative Alices*, Carroll's writings gave birth to several American imitations and parodies as early as 1885. The 1920s saw a rekindled interest in Carroll's world. Fifty-six Alice comedies were produced by the Disney brothers between 1924 and 1927.[40] 'The 1920s', Sigler writes, 'is also the period when Carroll's work was discovered and appropriated by high literary artists, critics, and theorists, such as William Empson, Virginia Woolf, and Edmund Wilson'.[41] She further adds that Americans' interest in Carroll and *Alice* reached a new height when Alice Liddell Hargreaves had to sell the original manuscript in April 1928. This manuscript sold for a record price to an American rare-book dealer and was exhibited at the New York Public Library from November 1928 to January 1929. Sigler also indicates that both Carroll and *Alice* received even more popular and critical attention in 1932 when the hundred-year anniversary of Carroll's birth was celebrated.[42]

This provides interesting context for the understanding of *Alice*'s influence on our *transition* pieces, which were primarily published in the late 1920s (especially around 1928), with some of them published in the 1930s. As we saw, *transition* itself made many references to Wonderland, in particular in connection with Joyce's 'Work in Progress'. Stuart Gilbert, one of *transition*'s editors, wrote about the French surrealists in February 1933, stating that 'They turned away from realism towards romantic wonderlands',[43] thus using Carroll, a well-known reference to his English-speaking readers, to explain surrealism, which, to them, remained a rather obscure avant-garde movement. In fact, a study of the reception of *transition*, and, more broadly, a study of the reception of surrealism in the American local press of the time reveal that Carroll's world was a recurring comparison when reporting on *transition*'s editorial line or on the surrealists' programme. As Karen Leick has remarked:

> The first issue of *transition* was discussed by reviewers all over America and became the subject of numerous jokes about incomprehensible modern literature. A cover story appeared in the *Saturday Review of Literature*, 'Gyring and Gimbling (Or Lewis Carroll in Paris)', and focused on the contributions by 'the half mythical JJ and that lesser mistress of experimental prose, the prophetic Gertrude Stein'.[44]

The 30 April 1927 review of the *Saturday Review of Literature* mentioned by Leick was followed by more reviews linking *transition*'s puzzling editorial line with Carroll's wanderings in Wonderland. 'Lewis Carroll Redivivus', a *Literary Digest* review of the 'Revolution of the Word' issue of *transition* (published in June 1929), also insists on Carroll's legacy, and quotes a sarcastic extract from the New York *Sun* suggesting that 'the [Revolution of the Word] rebels ought certainly to acknowledge their debt and establish Humpty Dumpty as their prophet'.[45] A substantial extract from the same New York *Sun* review was reprinted in *transition* 18, in November 1929, as part of the magazine's self-promotion strategy consisting in implicitly turning into ridicule the sarcastic reviews written on *transition*. The first sentence of the excerpt reads: 'All unsuspecting in his mad whimsicality, Lewis Carroll discovered the new tenets of writing which were to be hailed in 1929 as the ne plus ultra of artistic creation, hailed upon the first page of the current issue of *transition* as the revolution of the word'.[46] Carroll was again mentioned in connection with the 'Revolution of the Word' in an extract from a London *Daily Express* review reprinted in *transition* 23: 'A new number of that enthrallingly esoteric periodical *Transition* has just reached us [...]. It also contains an installment of a *Revolution of the Word* dictionary with some portmanteau neologisms which would have pleased Lewis Carroll'.[47] That same year, in 1935, a Detroit *Free Press* paper stated: 'Actually, Jolas sounds post-Carroll of "The Jabberwock".'[48] And in 1937 in the *Chicago Daily Tribune*, an editorial entitled 'Gibberish' ran another comparison between *transition* and Carroll, which worked against *transition*: 'Dean Swift and Lewis Carroll were fascinated by the unborn possibilities of syllables, but they were vulgar enough to fasten meaning on most of the words they coined'.[49] From the early days of *transition* to its end, Carroll's Wonderland therefore appears as a recurrent – today one could even say viral – useful, common reference to try to explain the magazine's project, often perceived as elitist, to a rather large audience spanning from the readers of literary publications, such as the *Saturday Review of Literature*, to the readers of the local press, such as the Detroit *Free Press*.

However, Carroll was not just used to introduce *transition*'s eccentricities to an American public; surrealism at large was often explained by referring to Alice's spiritual father, and Joyce's 'Work in Progress' was also often connected to Wonderland's verbal creativity. In 1930, in the Louisville, Kentucky *Courier-Journal*, Carroll was considered as a forerunner to both Joyce and the surrealists, and all of them were rated according to 'whether the trick comes off or not. It certainly did with Carroll and I believe it does with Joyce – in spots. The revolutionary Surrealist, less original and without gayety in his makeup, will not come off, but he will go off instead, and soon'.[50] In 1935, the *Cumberland Evening Times* in Maryland had a hard time trying to define surrealism: 'The newest thing in art is known as "surrealism." This term seems to mean superrealism. A surrealistic picture must be more real than reality itself'.[51] A reinterpretation of 'that brilliant Alice in Wonderland idea' then became a way of trying to make sense of one of Dalí's paintings, whose meaning the author of the paper failed to understand: 'The second [painting] may be a new version of that brilliant Alice in Wonderland idea – the Cheshire cat vanishing and leaving her grin behind'.[52] The same rhetoric was used by the *Reno Gazette-Journal* in Nevada in 1936, about a modern art exhibition in San Francisco. In a paper entitled 'Abstract Art Is Puzzle to S. F. Patrons', and subtitled 'Lecturers Attempt to Tell Visitors What It Is All About', one of the paintings is described as follows: 'An indefinite painting, dark gray tones with splashes of color suggesting steel framework and the puppet oyster ballet in "Alice in Wonderland," carries the title "Progressive Lines Plus Dynamic Sequences".'[53] Other examples of this connection can be found in the late 1930s in newspapers such as the *Indianapolis Star* or the Zanesville, Ohio *Times Recorder*, with an article which well illustrates how references to Carroll in the local press often partook of a larger mission to make surrealism accessible to the widest possible audience. Indeed, after tracing the origins of surrealism to medieval art, Shakespeare and Lewis Carroll ('whose "Alice in Wonderland" still delights and charms people with its nonsensical words'), its author concludes by stating that 'surrealism is not the exclusive property of artists. The typical Zanesville joke about turning left in the middle of the bridge illustrates the illogical and confusing character to be found in the paintings.'[54]

But the reference to *Alice* was used far beyond the social sphere of the local press. Some art critics themselves established a link between surrealism and Wonderland. The title of the famous 1936 MoMA exhibit, 'Fantastic Art Dada Surrealism', is in itself quite telling, as it brings together the 'fantastic' and 'surrealist', suggesting a radically different vision of surrealism from the one the leader of the French movement, Breton, defined.[55] Moreover, Lewis Carroll was mentioned in the 'Fantastic Art' section of the catalogue and represented by one of the original illustrations from *Alice* ('Change Lobsters and Retire in Same Order').[56] More connections between the exhibit, surrealism, and Wonderland were established. When the MoMA touring exhibit opened at the Philadelphia Museum of Art in January 1937, *The Evening Times* wrote: 'According to Fiske Kimball, director of the museum, Surrealism is supposed to represent a sort of "Alice in Wonderland" in art.'[57] As for art critic James Johnson Sweeney, one of the MoMA's leading figures from 1930 on, and one of *transition*'s late editors, from 1936 to 1938, he described Saul Schary's illustrations of *Alice in Wonderland* as 'superrealist' (meaning, surrealist) in *The New Republic* in 1935.[58] This draws our attention to Schary's little-known surrealist illustrations of *Alice*, painted years before Dalí's and Ernst's famous pictorial homages to Carroll in the 1950s and 1960s. A rather obscure American painter and illustrator, Saul Schary, born in 1904, seems to have been a rather traditional artist, as his obituary in the *New York Times* stated in 1978, but he illustrated *Alice's Adventures in Wonderland* in a less traditional way between 1926 and 1935, producing a series of seven gouache and watercolour paintings. One of them, 'The Walrus and the Carpenter', was part of the 'Abstract Painting in America' exhibition held at the Whitney Museum in February–March 1935, while 'Down the Rabbit-Hole' was reproduced in the May 1937 issue of *Scribner's*.

Thus, Wonderland was a much-used reference to convey to a broader audience living in the United States and not necessarily concerned by the avant-gardes, a sense of the – confusing – artistic endeavours undertaken in Paris by *transition*, surrealism, and Joyce. As Heinz Ickstadt has suggested, considering 'the perspective from outside', the reception of the European avant-gardes in the United States tended to be marked by a blurring of their differences into 'a single gesture of rebellion' as they 'swept together in a simultaneous reception a temporal sequence of manifestos and events'.[59] *Alice* helped to make sense out of the abundant and disconcerting production of the numerous European avant-gardes at a time when it was tasteful – and standard, as study of the local press reveals – in the United States to dedicate a lot of attention to European artistic creations. The wide circulation of the Wonderland analogy probably builds on a conjunction of factors, such as the strong presence of *Alice* within the American culture and across social groups, or the striking scope of the didactic mission of the American local press, consisting in trying to report on and sometimes explain culturally, socially, and geographically distant artistic events to 'ordinary' readers. The fact that Joyce's 'Work in Progress' was influenced by Carroll, connected to *transition* and surrealism by the critics, *and* received a lot of attention, including in the local press, probably helped as well to circulate the Alice analogy. Drawing parallels with familiar cultural realities, such as Wonderland, is obviously likely to create a bias in the comprehension of cultural novelties such as the avant-gardes. Joyce was annoyed by the frequent analogies between *Finnegans Wake* and Wonderland, so much so that in May 1927 he wrote to Harriet Weaver to complain about how some of these critics had misconceived what he was doing.[60] As it influenced the American understanding of the European avant-gardes – in particular French surrealism and Joyce's modernism – this 'misconception', as Joyce put it, in other words this *Alice* bias, heavily affected the way these avant-gardes were reinterpreted by American writers and artists; it also helped to give birth to a rich, interesting, and still underestimated early form of American surrealism whose aesthetics owe much to Carroll and Wonderland.

Notes

1   For more information on French surrealism in *transition*, see Céline Mansanti, 'Présence du surréalisme français dans la revue américaine *transition* (Paris, 1927– 38): Eugène Jolas entre André Breton et Ivan Goll', *Mélusine* (Paris, L'Âge d'Homme), 'Métamorphoses' 26 (February 2006): 277–304.

2   A few other little magazines (such as *The Little Review* and *Broom*) also did so, albeit to a lesser extent. At the time, French surrealism was relatively new (Breton's first manifesto dates back to 1924), and there seemed to be little interest in the United States for French literary surrealism, as Eugene Jolas explains in his autobiography: 'In fact, a proposed anthology to be composed of translations of Surrealist prose and poetry, with illustrations of the painters and sculptors identified with the movement, was turned down by a number of New York publishers when they were approached by Maria [Jolas's wife] in 1928. "Nobody would be interested", was the invariable reply' (Eugene Jolas, *Man from Babel*, ed. Andreas Kramer and Rainer Rumold [New Haven and London: Yale University Press, 1998], 90.)

3   See, for example, Ron Sakolsky, *Surrealist Subversions: Rants, Writings and Images by the Surrealist Movement in the U.S.* (Brooklyn, NY: Autonomedia, 2002) and Franklin Rosemont, *The Forecast Is Hot!: Tracts and Other Collective Declarations of the Surrealist Movement in the U.S.: 1966–76* (Chicago: Black Swan Press, 1997).

4   The exhibit was organized by Julien Levy in Hartford, Connecticut, in December 1931, and was followed by the first New York exhibit, at the Julien Levy Gallery, the following year.

5   On *transition*'s American surrealist literary experiments as a counter-proposal to French surrealism, see Céline Mansanti, *La Revue transition (1927–1938), le modernisme historique en devenir* (Rennes: Presses Universitaires de Rennes, 2009), 215–49. For a journal issue that surveys early American surrealisms and their close connections to the 1920s and 1930s international, transatlantic culture, see Céline Mansanti and Anne Reynes-Delobel, eds., 'Early American Surrealisms, 1920–1940', Special Issue, *Miranda* 14 (2017) and the issue's introduction 'Americanizing Surrealism: Cultural Challenges in the Magnetic Fields', *Miranda* 14 (2017). DOI: 10.4000/miranda.9759.

6   'Seven Ages of Women', 'Mother of a Clown', and 'Ho to AA, A Stage Playlet in Two Scenes' were published in *transition* 24, 25, and 26, respectively.

7   Wayne Andrews, *The Surrealist Parade* (New York: New Directions, 1990), ix–x. Wayne Andrews's two contributions to *transition*, 'The Evocative Treason of 449 Golden Doorknobs' and 'Take a Number from One to Ten' were published in *transition* 23 and 24, respectively.

8   The scenario is a hybrid form between literature and cinema much used by the French surrealists and best exemplified by Artaud's 'The Shell and the Clergyman' and Buñuel's 'An Andalusian Dog'. On this question, see, for example, Richard Abel, 'Exploring the Discursive Field of the Surrealist Film Scenario Text', *Dada/ Surrealism* 15 (1986): 58–71. William Closson Emory's scenario 'Love in the West' was published in *transition* 13. Whit Burnett published 'Home Edition, A Scenario' in *transition* 13. He also published two other texts with a surrealist dimension, 'Balls, Or Simple Error' and 'An Essay in Compostography or the Life in the Day of the Squidge' respectively in *transition* 14 and *transition* 19–20.

9   Another experiment by Hoffman linked to surrealism is 'Catastrophe', published in *transition* 13.

10   In a letter written to William Carlos Williams in 1931, West suggested contributors' names for *Contact*, the new magazine they were about to launch, and wrote about Godwin: 'Do you remember his dream factory stories in *transition* – what I meant by an American superrealism (?)' (Nathanael West, *Novels and Other Writings*, ed. Sacvan Bercovitch [New York: The Library of America, 1997], 770). 'Superrealism' is an antiquated equivalent of surrealism, used until the beginning of the 1930s. See Jonathan Veitch, *American Superrealism, Nathanael West and the Politics of Representation in the 1930s* (Madison: University of Wisconsin Press, 1997), 15. Godwin's two extracts of 'Work on Sidetrack' were published in *transition* 4 and 15.

11   Whitsett's two experiments, 'Dancing Rope' and 'Hotel', were published in *transition* 24.

12   For a discussion of the fantastic, see, for example, Eric S. Rabkin, *The Fantastic in Literature* (Princeton: Princeton University Press, 1977).

13   'Revolution of the Word', *transition* 16–17 (June 1929): 13.

14   L'esprit, 'voudrait distinguer avec certitude le merveilleux véritable du fantastique, de l'étrange, des illusoires miroitements' (André Breton, 'Preface to Pierre Mabille', in *Le Miroir du merveilleux* (1962) [Paris: Éditions de Minuit, 1977], 21). My translation.

15   'le fantastique est presque toujours de l'ordre de la fiction sans conséquence, alors que le merveilleux luit à l'extrême pointe du mouvement vital et engage l'affectivité toute entière' (ibid., 16).

16 Leigh Hoffman, 'Catastrophe', *transition* 13 (summer 1928): 78.
17 George Whitsett, 'Hotel', *transition* 24 (June 1936): 38.
18 George Whitsett, 'Dancing Rope', *transition* 24 (June 1936): 38.
19 Whit Burnett, 'An Essay in Compostography or the Life in the Day of the Squidge', *transition* 19–20 (June 1930): 185.
20 Ibid.
21 Charles Tracy, 'Seven Ages of Women', *transition* 24 (June 1936): 29.
22 Charles Tracy, 'Mother of a Clown', *transition* 25 (fall 1936): 22.
23 Whit Burnett, 'Home Edition, A Scenario', *transition* 13 (summer 1928): 199.
24 Ibid.
25 Whit Burnett, 'Balls, or Simple Error', *transition* 14 (fall 1928): 121.
26 Ibid., 125.
27 Harry Crosby, 'Dreams 1928–1929', *transition* 18 (November 1929): 35.
28 Ibid., 34.
29 Wayne Andrews, 'The Evocative Treason of 449 Golden Doorknobs', *transition* 23 (July 1935): 8.
30 Wayne Andrews, 'Take a Number from One to Ten', *transition* 24 (June 1936): 43.
31 William Closson Emory, 'Love in the West', *transition* 13 (summer 1928): 35.
32 Ibid., 37.
33 Ibid.
34 Robert Myron Coates, 'Conversations n°7', *transition* 1 (April 1927): 83.
35 Leigh Hoffman, 'Anamnesis', *transition* 11 (February 1928): 66.
36 It would probably be wrong to think that this assiduous reader of *transition* never existed, and is just, in a way, the scholar who, years after the magazine folded, pays scrupulous attention to each text in order to try to defend a thesis. Many testimonies by contributors such as John Glassco, Josephine Herbst, Henry Miller, Harry Crosby, Kay Boyle, and others show that the magazine was considered as a vital source of inspiration, and that each issue of *transition* was much anticipated.
37 James Joyce, 'Opening pages of a "Work in Progress"', *transition* 1 (April 1927): 9; and 'To all's much relief one's half hypothesis of that jabberjaw ape amok the showering jestnuts of Bruisanose was hotly dropped and his room taken up by that odious and still today insufficiently malestimated notesnatcher, Shem the Penman' (James Joyce, 'Continuation of a "Work in Progress"', *transition* 5 [August 1927]: 31). Moreover, on page 22 of the same issue, the word 'alices' appears.
38 This is much earlier than what is usually considered to be early analogies between Joyce and Carroll. See, for example: 'Lewis Carroll seems an obvious precursor of James Joyce in the world of elaborate wordplay, and critics have long thought so. Harry Levin suggested in 1941 that Carroll's Humpty Dumpty was "the official guide" to the vocabulary of *Finnegans Wake*' (Michael Wood, 'Quashed Potatoes', *The London Review of Books* 32, no. 24 [16 December 2010]: 19).
39 'Alice in Petersland', Advertisement, *Life* 45, no. 1166 (2 March 1905): 268.
40 Robert Douglas-Fairhurst, *The Story of Alice: Lewis Carroll and the Secret History of Wonderland* (London: Harvill Secker, 2015), 392.
41 Carolyn Sigler, ed., *Alternative Alices: Visions and Revisions of Lewis Carroll's Alice Books* (Lexington: The University Press of Kentucky, 1997), xvi.
42 Carolyn Sigler, *Lewis Carroll's Alice's Adventures in Wonderland: A Documentary Volume, Dictionary of Literary Biography*, vol. 375 (Detroit: Gale Research, 2014), 264–5.
43 Stuart Gilbert, 'Five Years of *transition*', *transition* 22 (February 1933): 141.

44 Karen Leick, *Gertrude Stein and the Making of an American Celebrity* (New York: Routledge, 2009), 96.

45 'Lewis Carroll Redivivus', *The Literary Digest* (10 August 1929): 23.

46 '*transition* and Its Contemporaries: "Some Opinions"', *transition* 18 (November 1929): 290.

47 '*transition* and Its Contemporaries', *transition* 23 (July 1935): 204.

48 '*transition* 1934–1935', *Detroit Free Press* (4 August 1935): 36.

49 'Gibberish', *Chicago Daily Tribune* (2 January 1937): 8.

50 'Surrealism', *Courier-Journal*, Louisville, Kentucky (16 February 1930): 29.

51 'Surrealism', *Cumberland Evening Times*, Cumberland, Maryland (16 January 1935): 2.

52 Ibid.

53 'Abstract Art Is Puzzle to S. F. Patrons', *Reno Gazette-Journal*, Reno, Nevada (3 August 1936): 14.

54 *The Indianapolis Star*, Indianapolis, Indiana (5 March 1939): 50; Stewart Leonard, 'Stewart Leonard Adds More Notes Upon "Surrealism"', *The Times Recorder*, Zanesville, Ohio (28 February 1937): 10.

55 Recall the distinction, already quoted in this chapter, that Breton made between the fantastic and the marvelous, the marvelous being what, according to him, defined surrealism: the spirit 'would like to distinguish with certainty the true marvelous from the fantastic, the strange, the illusive sparkling' (Breton, 'Preface', 21).

56 *Fantastic Art Dada Surrealism*, ed. Alfred H., Barr Jr. (New York: The Museum of Modern Art, 1936), 253.

57 'Surrealist Art Is Shown by Museum', *The Evening Times* (15 March 1937): 5. Similarly, 'Surrealism', Julien Levy's 1932 surrealist exhibit – the first surrealist exhibit in New York – was considered by the *Brooklyn Daily Eagle* as 'merely a 20th-century manifestation of the age old spirit of fantasy', with a painting by Dalí recalling 'the absurdities of the croquet party in *Alice in Wonderland*' ('In the Galleries', *Brooklyn Daily Eagle* [24 January 1932]: 60).

58 James Johnson Sweeney, 'A Note on Abstract Painting', *The New Republic* (17 July 1935), https://newrepublic.com/article/90639/note-abstract-painting.

59 Heinz Ickstadt, 'Deconstructing/ Reconstructing Order: The Faces of Transatlantic Modernism', in *Transatlantic Modernism*, ed. Martin Klepper and J. C. Schöpp (Heidelberg: C. Winter, 2001), 19.

60 See 'On this day [...] 31 May', The James Joyce Centre, http://jamesjoyce.ie/on-this-day-31-may/.

Chapter 5

ALICE AND THE EXPANSION OF THE AMERICAN WEST: MODERNISM, THE NORTHERN PACIFIC RAILROAD'S WONDERLAND ROUTE, AND KATE CHOPIN'S *THE AWAKENING*

Michelle E. Moore

Lewis Carroll's *Alice in Wonderland* begins rather abruptly: Alice bored with reading a book runs after a rabbit and finds herself falling down, down, down a deep hole practically into 'the centre of the Earth'.[1] When she reaches the bottom with a 'thump' she finds herself in a 'long passage' and upon opening a tiny door at the end, sees another 'passage' that leads her into 'the loveliest garden you ever saw'.[2] She can't fit through the door and this begins the narrative of Alice eating and drinking strange concoctions, meeting new creatures, and changing size and shape. In the decades before the turn of the twentieth century, the word 'Wonderland' began to expand in meaning to include the American West. The Northern Pacific Rail Road (NPRR) coupled this linguistic change with a new reading of Alice as traveller and created an advertising campaign which used the figure of Alice as an adult traveller in order to promote railroad travel for women and with it Western Expansion in the United States.

This chapter will first show how the NPRR transformed the figure of Alice in Wonderland into an advertising image designed to woo turn-of-the-century Victorian women to the American West. It will then argue that the railroad advertising imagery used the Alice image and its narrative to revise the traditional Victorian gender codes ascribed to the Western frontier through nineteenth-century paintings and in women's journals. In doing so, the popular advertising campaign added an additional layer to Lewis Carroll's already-complex novels by redrawing Alice as a consuming tourist, poised between being a late Victorian lady and a progressively modern woman. The final section of this chapter will analyse Kate Chopin's *The Awakening* as an example of how turn-of-the-century feminist writers borrowed the images and metaphors of Wonderland from Carroll's novels and the NPRR campaign. The novel subtly suggests that adult women need to behave as an adult Alice as she appears in the NPRR advertising imagery and leave the domestic world behind through travel and education.

The Victorian Gendering of Train Travel

By the middle of the nineteenth century, US industrialists were expanding the railways at a feverish pace, which allowed them to capitalize on the West by selling the resources and potential land investments found there to the new upper and middle classes in the form of consumer goods and adventure travel. Amy G. Richter points out, 'In fiction and nonfiction, cities and railroads revealed themselves as chaotic sites characterized by unpredictable encounters with strangers.'[3] She argues, 'Only train travel demanded the constant and simultaneous negotiation of both urban social disorder and the systematic ordering associated with the rise of larger business enterprises and managerial capitalism.'[4] Travel, associated with the business of westward expansion and capitalism, was thus a decidedly masculine enterprise.

Popular Victorian lady's journals published numerous stories that warned of the dangers of train travel for unaccompanied ladies. Anna Despotopoulou has shown that 'the majority of stories appearing in journals present women who find themselves in difficult or even dangerous situations in trains and who need to adopt a domestic, docile attitude in order to survive.'[5] In the stories, a woman could find herself assaulted by improper sights or smells, verbal or physical abuse, and exposure to passengers of varying classes. She could be pestered and taken advantage of by seductive con artists or the train workers. The stories indicate strongly that by travelling alone and by train, women open themselves to abuse and even violence.

While the danger most often came from men in the stories in lady's journals, these narratives also indicate that other women in the train cars could pose a different but equally damaging threat to the unescorted lady traveller. Desptopoulou continues: 'Other stories aimed at discursively regulating the mobility of women targeted "fast" women, whose freedom of manners in public spaces threatened to extinguish the ideal of feminine innocence.'[6] The woman who was not targeted as a victim could be even more dangerous, as her lack of victimhood was a threat to the mystique of femininity in general. At the end of the stories, these women 'readily and even gladly acknowledge their inability to deal with the mental and physical challenges of travel', and this 'confirms their successful internalization of a femininity constructed as weak and vulnerable.'[7]

George Pullman's vision directly and deliberately contradicted the popular narratives about train travel that warn women riders to stay off the rails. In 1862, Pullman established his company on the edge of Chicago and built luxury sleeping cars, which featured carpeting, draperies, upholstered chairs, libraries, and card tables. Richter has pointed out that 'the opulent decoration of his Pullman Palace Car Company's sleeping cars, hotel cars, dining cars, and parlor cars was unprecedented and reflected his commitment to domesticity and its ability to imbue public life with morality.'[8] For Pullman, the opulence of the train would serve to domesticate its passengers, male and female. The luxury appointments and materials would metaphorically lift up the train car morally and socially and therefore its inhabitants would be inspired to lift up, too, and behave as if in a high-class drawing room. It would then be ensured that women be treated equally well on Pullman's cars as they would be in the privacy of their own homes by their own families.[9]

Richter writes that Pullman's vision was to 'establish a public home on rails as an agent of civilization'.[10] His vision translates the imagery of nineteenth-century paintings depicting masculine work and feminine inspiration, into a metaphor for train travel where the train itself is the feminine and muse-like agent of civilization. Pullman believed that the mere presence of virtuous women would bring civility to the train travel as well as to the West.[11] Pullman, while remaining firmly entrenched in a Victorian vision of women as possessing inherent domestic virtue and innocence, believed that their presence would overcome any stereotypically masculine tendencies towards coarseness, roughness, or abuse. Women would domesticate the West, in Pullman's vision, rather than be corrupted just getting there. His vision changed the possibilities for railroad travel for women and in doing so, opened up new possibilities for commercial tourism in the American West.

The Northern Pacific Rail Road (NPRR) and the Wonderland Route

In the decades after the invention of the Pullman car, the word 'Wonderland' began to expand in meaning to include the American West. The May 1871 issue of *Scribner's Monthly*'s cover article is simply titled: 'The Wonders of Yellowstone'.[12] In 1877, Henry N. Maguire published *The Black Hills and America's Wonderland* and in 1878, Edwin James Stanley wrote *Rambles in wonderland, or, Up the Yellowstone: and among the geysers and other curiosities of the national park.* Colgate Hoyt wrote of his September 1878 trip to Yellowstone: 'It contains in the same space probably a greater number of natural wonders & curiosities than any other region of the entire globe & thus is rightly named Wonderland.'[13] In 1882, William Wallace Wylie published *Yellowstone National Park, or, The great American wonderland: a complete description of all the wonders of the park, together with distances, altitudes, and such other information as the tourist or general reader desires: a complete hand, or guide book for tourists.* In 1883, the Chicago and North Western Railway Company published *The Early History and Rapid Progress of That Wonderland, Central Dakota.*

In 1883, the NPRR began rail service to Yellowstone and built lavish hotels for the new wilderness tourist. On 2 July 1864, the US Congress chartered the NPRR to build a line from Lake Superior to a port on the Pacific coast. The railroad used Congress' land grant of forty million acres as collateral to raise money in the East and Europe for construction. Even with the land, it proved quite difficult to find financial backing for its venture into a mostly unsettled wilderness. When Philadelphia banker Jay Cooke raised 100 million dollars for funding, construction could finally begin in 1870. In 1873, the railroad was approaching Bismarck, in the Dakota Territory, when Cooke's bank collapsed and the railroad had to go into receivership, stopping construction for six years. In 1878, Henry

Villard took over the railroad and continued its Westward expansion to Helena in the Montana Territory. Once in Helena, the railroad connected its tracks to the Oregon Railway to Seattle in the Washington Territory. In 1882, the NPRR reached Livingston, Montana, and soon they added a spur close to the north end of Yellowstone National Park at Gardiner. For the last decade, since the park had opened in 1872, there had been few visitors because of its remote location, difficult access, and primitive accommodations. In 1883, the NPRR began direct rail service to the 'Wonderland of Yellowstone'. The company saw the possibilities for the growth of the new wilderness tourism industry that was bringing middle- and high-class Americans across the West in train cars to see the Wonderland for themselves.[14]

In 1884 the NPRR began an annual publication to compete with other railroads and convince readers that their route to and through Wonderland was a must-see for any tourist. The first issue of the NPRR's series was titled *Alice's Adventures in the New Wonderland*, a direct reference to Lewis Carroll's popular 1865 book and a not-so-subtle marketing suggestion that a woman who takes their train route may find herself having adventures equally astonishing as Alice's. The title of the next issue was the same, but its subtitle was more explicit: *Alice's Adventures in the New Wonderland: The Yellowstone National Park*. The marketing campaign was so successful that multiple guides, pictures, and maps were published each year, including one to Alaska written by the journalist Elia Peattie, all dedicated to the Wonderland Route and to the image of an adult train-riding Alice, until the entire campaign ended in 1906.

The cover of the 1885 NPRR brochure entitled *Alice's Adventures in the New Wonderland: The Yellowstone National Park* shows a young woman on a rugged mountain path, filled with stones, sharp points, and no greenery. The font used to write *Alice's Adventures in the New Wonderland: The Yellowstone National Park* seems to mimic the mountain path by using jagged points, uneven kerning, and a neutral brown colour. The words frame the female figure, suggesting that she is a grown-up Alice who wears a Victorian blue dress, just like the younger Alice in Carroll's novels, with a bustle and brown gloves and belt. She cuts a decidedly feminine figure and her peaceful gaze indicates that she is quite at home, despite the contrast to the landscape offered by her fashionable dress, more suited for the parlour than for the rocky Western path.

Carroll's *Alice* can be read as providing the same warning to curious women as the lady's journals, and so the advertisement must also rely on the audience's memory of Tenniel's drawings to rewrite the Alice story slightly. In Carroll's version, from the moment young Alice drops down the Rabbit Hole, her body and entire psyche are threatened by violence. She may hurt herself from falling into Wonderland. She changes size and shape after disobeying directions left on food and drinks. She is even in danger of losing her head. Similarly, the inhabitants of Wonderland speak at times very rudely to young Alice and she soon forgets her own manners and taught behaviours and speaks rudely in return. She both encounters violence on her journey and loses her manners as a result of exposure to the coarseness of those she encounters.

Instead of replicating Carroll's warning messages for little girls, the advertising image replicates the messages of popular paintings of the American West, in which female figures inspire men to move westward and struggle with the land's hardships in order to make it submit. John Gast's *American Progress* (1872) is perhaps the best known of the type. In Gast's painting, the female figure, dressed as a Greek Goddess, holds a schoolbook and leads male settlers westward while Native Americans and animals flee from her influencing powers of progress and modernity. Janis P. Stout has shown how Gast's figures repeat traditional Victorian gender binaries.[15] The pious female muse floats above the landscape, untouched and unsullied by the inhospitable climate and conditions below. From her position above, she inspires the men below who actually create civilization by physically conquering the difficult climate, building, carving, and blasting their way westward. The brochure's Alice, then, in her bustle and blue dress, seems to call to men to join her on the frontier and speaks directly to male land speculators. She promises to be a civilizing force as the men march westward, buying up land and making homesteads, presumably from the Northern Pacific parcel and route, to aid in financing the often-struggling railroad.

Gast's muse and the brochure's Alice have remarkably similar dreamy and peaceful expressions on their faces. The same expression can also be found on Alice's face in John Tenniel's first illustration to *Through the Looking-Glass*. In Tenniel's first portrait of Alice, she sits in an armchair contentedly looking out the window. Nina Auerbach points out that 'two Victorian domestic myths' lie behind Tenniel's illustration: 'Wordsworth's "seer blessed", the child fresh from the Imperial Palace and still washed by his continuing contact with "that immortal sea," and the pure woman Alice will become, preserving an oasis for God and order in a dim tangled world.'[16] She argues that Victorians 'saw little girls as the purest members of a species of questionable origin, combining as they did the inherent spirituality of child and woman'.[17] Both Gast's muse and the brochure's Alice have this same look of contented seeing, which implies that both characters have a childish innocence and a pure womanly virtue, just like Tenniel's Alice. Because the Victorian female figures are believed to hold these qualities in tandem, they can inspire men to settle westward. The NPRR advertisement must promise to its late Victorian middle-class and morally correct readers that women can maintain the qualities of innocence and virtue, just as Gast's muse can, as its female passengers float across the western Wonderland. The NPRR advertisement uses the picture of a grown-up Alice to indicate visually that riding the Northern Pacific will allow ladies to see the American West without having to endure physical, psychic, or spiritual attacks on their innocence or virtue.

The NPRR's brochure also counters the lady's journal narratives with the full length and detailed image of the adult Alice. The reader can see from the drawing that she has not been physically or psychically stretched or reshaped as a result of her experiences while taking the train through Wonderland. She looks pious and serene rather than vulnerable and traumatized, and still wears her bustle, gloves, and fashionable dress, all indicators that she has kept her Victorian drawing room morality intact. Because the grown-up Alice in the advertisement is whole, just like the child Alice in Tenniel's illustration, she demonstrates visually that the Northern Pacific Railroad will deliver its female passengers to their destinations without any of the worrisome violence or trauma the lady's journal's stories about train travel predicted and warned against.

The Alice in Wonderland campaign, then, subtly implies through Alice's serene gaze and fashionable outfit, that the NPRR trains are comfortable, domestic spaces that will protect its female riders and their femininity from harm. Pullman's ideas extended culturally so far beyond his own brand of Pullman cars that even though the NPRR did not use Pullman cars on their route, their campaign relies heavily on implying his ideas about transforming train travel into something suitable for Victorian ladies. The NPRR's picture of Alice shows her with her Victorian femininity intact, just in the new landscape of the West. She presumably got there because of the well-appointed, highly civil, and genteel train cars provided by the NPRR and her curiosity about that new Wonderland, the American West.

The second issue of the NPRR brochure is supposed to be a letter written by the now grown-up Alice who is travelling on the Northern Pacific from Chicago. Alice describes to her friend, Edith, all of the things she sees and stops she makes as she travels on the railroad. She describes the lush landscape in beautiful and breathtaking detail.[18] The brochure even includes a picture of Alice at her writing desk, presumably on the train or in a hotel, and the pages of her letter falling down into the brochure's margin. The campaign plays with the idea of the letter as transmission that connects Alice in the New Wonderland with Edith's drawing room back home, reducing the space physically and psychically between the women. Jean Ratzinger has commented that with train travel, 'Conceptions of space and time become less stable. As travel is eased, distant places seem more accessible and thus closer.'[19] Even though Alice is still experiencing odd changes in time and space as a result of travelling through Wonderland, because of the wonders of train travel these changes become useful rather than strange and frightening. Through reading Alice's travel narrative, Edith may join in on the fun promised by the curiosities in Wonderland, while at the same time Alice feels as if she never strays too far from home.

The NPRR advertising campaign used the representation of Carroll's Alice, who is 'curiouser and curiouser',[20] as a direct appeal to the late-nineteenth-century belief in women's 'natural curiosity' about 'natural curiosities'.[21] The first few NPRR brochures consisted of a single sheet, folded so as to present fifteen pages of text and illustrations, opening out to show a map on the opposite side, the whole 'descriptive of the region tributary to the Northern Pacific Railway',[22] spotlighting one or more attractive tourist destinations, presumably visited by the grown-up Alice. Alice's 'letter' emphasizes the curious nature of Yellowstone National Park, too, by highlighting its 'curiosities': strange topography, a uniquely untouched American landscape preserved and protected due to its status as the only national park of the time, 'curious natural oddities', and 'wondrous and curious freaks of Nature'.[23] Both the park and Alice herself who has had new adventures become increasingly curious to the reader of the brochure.

Alice's curiosity is the feature that separates Carroll's Alice from Tenniel's passively gazing rendition of the little girl. Nina Auerbach explains:

> The pun on 'curious' defines Alice's fluctuating personality. Her eagerness to know and to be right, her compulsive reciting of her lessons ('I'm sure I can't be Mabel, for I know all sorts of things') turn inside out into the bizarre anarchy of her dream country, as the lessons themselves turn inside out into strange and savage tales of animals eating each other. In both senses of the word, Alice becomes 'curiouser and curiouser' as she moves more deeply into Wonderland; she is both the croquet game without rules and its violent arbiter, the Queen of Hearts.[24]

Alice, for Auerbach, 'speaks with two voices'.[25] She speaks as a curious little girl, keen to accumulate knowledge and eager to recite the rules and manners she's been taught in the drawing room. She also speaks as a result of her immersion in Wonderland, emotional and savage, a curiosity in her own right. This dual nature of Alice, the result of exposure to curiosities as a result of being curious, describes perfectly the result of travel on the individual traveller. She is both properly learning and adding to the civilized total of knowledge and at risk of becoming nativized as she may acclimate to what she finds in wonderland at the edges of the empire.

Because she speaks two languages and is poised between two worlds, Alice begins to seem like a bit of a tourist in Carroll's novels, far before the NPRR used the figure to advertise their new train line. Joseph Urgo applies Victor and Edith Turner's analysis of the Christian pilgrimage in order to define the process of tourism. Travellers must first separate from their familiar surroundings, leaving ordinary acquaintances and routines behind. They then enter a state of liminality, an 'anti structure'.[26] New bonds with fellow travellers emerge and new communities based on the shared bonds of travellers emerge. Upon returning home, travellers must reintegrate into their former social worlds, but often find that they are lifted up to a higher rung by the pilgrimage experience.[27] Alice's fall down the Rabbit Hole casts her into a world of anti-structure, one where she must learn to rely not just on herself but on the strange community of new creatures she finds there. Upon returning, the experience of Wonderland has helped her grow up, a major point of most critical studies on the novels. Because the novels already follow a pattern established by the nineteenth-century travel industry, the NPRR brochures draw doubly from already-established tourism narratives.

Anne Friedberg constructs the idea of the 'tourist gaze' further, by considering what she calls the 'mobilized virtual gaze'.[28] She compares the static film viewers' gaze to that of the moving gaze of the pedestrian, window shopper, or traveller. Ellen Strain considers the proliferation of this kind of gaze across American culture as happening because of a kind of continuity that existed through transmissions 'between the tourist and the armchair traveler', naming this transmission 'a "tutoring" of the armchair gaze'.[29] This is exactly the kind of transmission that seems to happen in the brochure when Alice writes home to her friend with great visual detail and excitement about what she sees as she moves from place to place on the train.

Strain explains that the 'blow' of loss must be 'parried', arguing: 'Visual fascination is part and parcel of this dodging effort, the rehearsal of which is actually sought in order to strengthen the illusion of impenetrability, autonomy, and coherence. Exoticization is this fetishization process at work during the confrontation with extreme cultural difference.'[30] The tourist gaze then emerges as the process becomes solidified and capitalized upon by the tourist industry. When Carroll's Alice reprimands the other characters for being ill-mannered and rude and recites her nursery manners, she separates herself from Wonderland. Instead of being fully consumed, as she is in other moments, she separates herself to save herself. In this case, her shock at bad manners actually saves her from being culture shocked and rendered fully lost. The letter written by the grown-up Alice in the NPRR brochure fetishizes and exoticizes all of the 'Wonders' that she sees in 'Wonderland'. In doing so, she shows that it is the process of being a tourist that has allowed her to stay psychologically safe, despite the distance she has travelled, the things that she has seen, and the people she has met.

The 'letter' teaches the brochure's female audience how to view the sites of Wonderland as a safe tourist, without the threat of losing themselves or their connections to home. At the same time, it teaches its female audience how to teach others by writing letters home about their experiences riding the Wonderland Railroad. The letter's opening sentence, 'When Mr. Carroll wrote that funny book about one of my childish dreams', mocks the little girl who loses herself completely in an adventure. Carina Garland argues that 'Lewis Carroll's *Alice* texts are all about "malice" (Cohen, *Interviews* 108): that is, the often spiteful attempts of the male author to suppress and control Alice's agency so that Carroll can desire and own her.'[31] The writers of the second edition of the brochure seem to agree with this reading of the child Alice and felt the need to counter such possible readings. By introducing Alice's own voice into the brochure and no longer co-opting it into a third-person narrative, the brochure shows her to be a thoroughly independent woman capable of travelling, writing, and dreaming without that 'Mr. Carroll'. The brochure updates the Alice story, itself the travel narrative of a little girl, by reimagining what had been presented as dangerous as adventurous instead.

The picture on the second brochure leads us to assume Alice's curiosity has led her to this rugged landscape, the new Wonderland. Her gloves and belt appear made out of a hearty fabric that can stand up to the rigors of the mountain path and tucked behind her is a functional hat to protect her from the harsher climate. All three items stand out in contrast to the blue dress because they replicate the colours of the rocks behind her. The image transforms from a passive muse into a woman who possesses a new rugged version of femininity and whose contours and colours replicate the Western landscape she surveys. James Kincaid has also noticed Alice's tendency to mimic the contours of and relax into Carroll's Wonderland. He points out, 'By the end of *Alice in Wonderland*, though, most of this ambivalence disappears and Alice establishes herself clearly as an adult, ironically pretty much at home at the grotesque trial and "quite pleased to find that she knew the name of nearly everything [in the courtroom]".[32] The NPRR advertising image of a new adult Alice suggested to a generation of young, modern women the possibilities provided by train travel for her and promised that she, too, can become figuratively part of America's West, as an explorer in her own right, not as a passive muse or shocking child.

Auerbach, too, suggests that Alice is more than just a depiction of an innocent and Romanticized child. She points out, 'Other little girls traveling through fantastic countries, such as George Macdonald's Princess Irene and L. Frank Baum's Dorothy Gale, ask repeatedly "where am I?" rather than "who am I?" Only Alice turns her eyes inward from the beginning, sensing that the mystery of her surroundings is the mystery of her identity.'[33] The NPRR image suggests that Alice, completely at ease in her surroundings, can explore the mystery of herself. In doing so, the NPRR created a brochure that will capture the attention of a young late-nineteenth-century girl who fancies herself to be changing into a new, modern woman, just like grown-up Alice.

The campaign proved so popular that by 1890, the NPRR expanded the series from brochures and pamphlets to guidebooks and that year put out the 108-page book, *A Journey through Wonderland: The Pacific Northwest and Alaska with a description of the country traversed by the Northern Pacific Railroad*. This was the first signed guidebook and Elia Peattie's name as the author features prominently on the cover beneath the title.

Peattie was very well known from her journalism and publications in lady's magazines. Her family moved to Chicago from Michigan in 1876, when she was fourteen, and she became the *Tribune*'s first 'girl reporter' in 1885. She married in 1883 and when they moved to Omaha, her writing took a profound turn towards fictional and realistic renderings of the frontier with a particular emphasis on those issues pertinent to women: suffrage, domestic troubles, and the plight of children. She also wrote long, uplifting pieces on the beauty of the United States. She wrote the 700-page *The Story of America* the same year, 1889, as her pamphlet for the Northern Pacific Wonderland series touting the amazing splendour of Alaska for women travellers. She published regularly in popular magazines like *Lippincott's* and *Cosmopolitan*. Her writing began to win her prizes and she took advantage of her popularity by earning extra money on the side lecturing on literary topics that would elevate the listener.[34]

Peattie's well-known adventures as a journalist and a proponent of travel for women made her a perfect choice to continue the campaign that continues the story of a grown-up Alice exploring the American West. However, unlike the previous iterations, Peattie's version of the campaign makes no direct references to the *Alice* novels or Tenniel's illustrations. Instead, it subtly references the beginning of *Through the Looking-Glass*, where Alice takes a railway journey and chronicles all of the interesting sights she sees and people she meets. Peattie had just returned from a trip to Alaska, and the narrative continues her interest in promoting to her female readers the freedom and excitement that comes from seeing America's splendours. The Wonderland campaign was already in full swing and it could now simply employ a writer whose work was already synonymous with promoting freedom, education, and curiosity through travel for women. What was implied visually and through narrative in the first Wonderland brochures and pamphlets is now made explicit simply by employing Elia Peattie.

The field guide is a kind of imaginative literature, particularly if a child stumbles across it. Peattie's guide follows Alice's instructions for a good story, with lots of pictures and interesting conversations, much as Carroll does. The travel narrative is illustrated with twenty-three pictures, several of which show the interiors of lushly appointed hotels to stay at along the route including: 'Detroit Lake and Hotel Minnesota, Detroit, Michigan'; 'Mammoth Hot Springs Hotel, Yellowstone National Park'; and 'Hotel Broadwater, Helena, on N.P.R.R.'[35] The second and third pictures reveal the lushness of the 'Dining Car Interior on the Wonderland Route' and the 'Sleeping Car Interior on the Wonderland Route'.[36]

The dining car picture shows a well-dressed woman sitting opposite of a well-dressed man and woman being served tea by an African American porter. The picture continues to represent the safety and comfort for women travellers and is juxtaposed by Peattie's story, written in the first person, about the first two days of travel. The narrator meets a man, 'a good-natured young man – indeed he was too good natured, for he never looked at me without smiling', who remarks, "'I should like to see you [...] after you caught the fever"'.[37] The fever here is 'the western fever'.[38] The 'lumberman' gets off at Deluth, and she meets a great many other men in her travels, with whom she has engaging and factual conversations about the territory they cross, and these conversations continue in later letters. The effect is exactly that promised by the earlier pamphlets: travel is safe, despite the stories of strange men approaching women. Even further, the narrator of Peattie's guidebook asks multiple straightforward questions and displays the desire for education and curiosity that the earlier pamphlets gesture to through the allusion to a grown-up Alice.

Peattie then inaugurates a thoroughly grown-up Alice, who through travelling educates herself and becomes increasingly curious. Her journey, unlike Carroll's original Alice, is a safe one, and provides a clear route forward for turn-of-the-century curious and literary feminist women.

Kate Chopin's The Awakening: *An Example of One Feminist Writer's Uses of the* Alice *Novels*

The NPRR Wonderland campaign was enormously popular and succeeded in countering the lady's magazines warning about train travel for unaccompanied young ladies. They added a new layer to Carroll's Victorian novels by transcribing Alice into a modern and grown-up curious woman who learned by travelling the United States safely and alone. Popular and literary references to *Alice's Adventures in Wonderland* would now carry the additional meanings of Alice as curious, female traveller that would be legible to readers well-familiarized with the NPRR campaign. Turn-of-the-century feminist writers, inspired by all of Peattie's life and work, would refer to the trappings of Wonderland in a way now informed by the NPRR advertising campaign. They did so to critique the Victorian culture that still dictated women remain at home to be good, unquestioning wives and mothers. The remainder of this chapter will consider how Kate Chopin's novel *The Awakening* alludes to the *Alice* novels and assumes knowledge of the NPRR campaign in order to create new narratives about a female heroine looking to escape the expectations of Victorian womanhood. The novel stands as a strong warning to women who remain trapped in their homes and small communities, afraid to be curious, travel, and explore.

The Awakening begins with a warning from a 'green and yellow parrot', who hangs 'in a cage outside the door' and cautions any visitors, as well as the reader, to go away: "'Allez vous-en! Allez vous-en! Sapristi! That's all right!'"[39] Edna Pontellier, the novel's protagonist, listens to the parrot all day and though his words don't repeat ever again in the novel, the warning underpins Edna's subsequent attempts at transforming herself. She will try to move away from the domestic life inside the house with the parrot in the doorway and remains within the French Quarter among the French Creoles with whom she has made her life. She never just 'goes away'. The novel, informed by Carroll's novels and the NPRR Wonderland campaign, strongly asserts that Edna needs to just 'go away', not by drowning, but perhaps by train or another mode of transportation that will take her far away from the childish Wonderland in which the French Creole mother-women must live out their lives. She is not curious about life outside of the French Quarter, despite being a transplant there from Kentucky, and remains stuck, unable to imagine a way that gives her a new kind of life while remaining where she is.

The Awakening gives a single literal clue that Edna's story should be seen as a new version of the *Alice* novels that draws from the Wonderland campaign. A third of the way through the narrative 'Edna began to feel like one who awakens gradually out of a dream, a delicious, grotesque, impossible dream'.[40] In the first chapter of *Alice's Adventures in Wonderland*, the narrator observes: 'So many out-of-the-way things had happened that Alice had begun to think that very few things were indeed impossible.'[41] When Alice meets the White Queen in the sequel, *Through the Looking-Glass*, she reveals that she has shifted from believing in the impossible to not even trying to believe in 'impossible things': Alice says, 'There's no use trying [...] one *ca'n't* believe impossible things.'[42]

Alice's abrupt reversal demonstrates that her experiences in Wonderland have caused her beliefs about impossible things to shift, shutting off future possibilities for the little girl. The White Queen chides Alice in response to her new disbelief in the impossible: "'I daresay you haven't had much practice, [...] When I was your age, I always did it for half-an-hour a day. Why, sometimes I've believed as many as six impossible things before breakfast.'"[43] The queen's words indicate that one can believe in impossible things as a child, and Alice, as a result of her Wonderland experiences, is growing up. Alice's change of heart about impossible things reveals that staying too long in Wonderland will cause the adventurer to lose their beliefs and dreams.

Edna's awakening from an 'impossible dream' highlights the interweaving of the novel's sleep metaphors with the Wonderland novels and complicates traditional readings of Edna's awakening as being indicative of her becoming increasingly aware of the cultural patterns that circumscribe her life as a woman. Robert Levine has noted: 'It is one of the curiosities of Kate Chopin's *The Awakening* that the "awakening" heroine does so much sleeping.'[44] He argues that previous critics wrongly ascribe her sleepiness to being duped by illusions and instead shows 'A close study of this rhythmic pattern demonstrates the logical though tragic connection between Edna's sleep habits and her suicide and reveals the radical rebellious tendencies of her character.'[45] Her disrupted sleep patterns are a sign of rebellion against the rhythms around her, especially those of her husband and expected of women. Levine notices: 'Resisting sleep, Edna becomes open and receptive to the call of the "sea": passional, nonrational sources. The act of resistance paradoxically creates a passivity of consciousness that nurtures these internal stirrings.'[46] Her sleeplessness renders her vulnerable and her mind becomes dis-eased and dis-ordered as a result of her rebellious insomnia. This pattern becomes even clearer through her connection to Alice, who oscillates between madness and rebellion throughout her journey in Wonderland.

Alice experiences odd changes in time and space as a result of travelling through Wonderland and the Wonderland campaign constructs these changes as useful, even educational, rather than strange and frightening. Edna's abrupt changes as she is 'awakening' cannot always be characterized as good, healthy, or useful, and yet these are the signals of her rebellion. She wakes up from her dream-like state in Wonderland, a childish place and at the same time, her sleepiness from not-sleeping aligns her with Alice who dreams she is awake in Wonderland. Edna's awakening from an 'impossible dream' reveals that she is simultaneously rebelling against being a white queen trapped in the stultifying New Orleans Creole culture and trapped in that same culture, she will not leave.

Edna casts Madame Ratignolle as The White Queen, a key figure in Wonderland who believes in the 'impossible dreams' that Edna rebels against:

> [Edna] stood watching the fair woman walk down the long line of galleries with the grace and majesty which queens are sometimes supposed to possess. Her little ones ran to meet her. Two of them clung about her white skirts, the third she took from its nurse and with a thousand endearments bore it along in her own fond, encircling arms. Though, as everybody well knew, the doctor had forbidden her to lift so much as a pin![47]

This White Queen is dowdy and childish. Madame Ratignolle is repeatedly ill throughout the novel from her pregnancy and enjoys the fuss made about her and her condition. The queen imagery that Chopin borrows from Carroll allows her to write against the Victorian standard for ideal femininity. The White Queen lives backwards and so is a version of a Victorian women's novel heroine who also lives backwards, because she spends the plot projecting forward to her wedding day. Chopin creates Edna as the opposite of these heroines who seek a life of queen-like domesticity. The reader is told: 'Mrs. Pontellier was not a mother-woman.'[48] If she becomes a perfect Creole wife, she would be stuck in societal dreams of impossible things for an adult woman and would wither and die. Edna, just as when Alice matures in Wonderland, wakes up, speaks against the White Queen and puts away her beliefs in 'impossible things'.

She falls easily for Robert. He adores the metaphorical White Queen, and so adores 'impossible things', including wooing married women who would never leave their husbands. When Edna and Robert tell each other of their feelings towards the end of the novel, he declares: 'Oh! I was demented, dreaming of wild, impossible things, recalling men who had set their wives free, we have heard of such things.'[49] Robert dreams of impossible things, aligning himself fully with the White Queen, and her love of doing impossible, childish things.

Edna replies as Alice does to the White Queen further aligning Robert with his love of White Queens: 'You have been a very, very foolish boy, wasting your time dreaming of impossible things when you speak of Mr. Pontellier setting me free! I am no longer one of Mr. Pontellier's possessions to dispose of or not. I give myself where I choose. If he were to say, "Here, Robert, take her and be"'.[50] She speaks to him as a grown-up Alice, who no longer dreams of what is impossible. But she also credits Robert with her awakening and wants to run away with him: an impossible dream within Creole culture and Robert's history with other women.

Yet, Edna wears white throughout the novel and sleeps in Madame Antoine's 'white bed',[51] just like the one she slept in while vacationing on the island at the novel's beginning. She commits suicide naked, and her body and feet are emphatically 'white'.[52] Her rebellion against the White Queen doesn't take her away from the childish dream of Wonderland, and instead pushes her deeper into the dream-like state of Wonderland. The longer she stays awake, the dreamier she becomes; like Alice, her rebellion is marked by taking on and understanding the characteristics of Wonderland. Edna is stuck in the paradox of Wonderland like Alice. Both become smarter about Wonderland while simultaneously being unable to free themselves from its grip through waking up.

Christine Roth has argued that Wonderland holds both of these ideas in tension for an adult reader:

> By imagining both the space's native Others and child Others as negations (bodies that lack a story of their own), Carroll, Barrie and their adult readers perform a kind of erasure, clearing a space for the expansion of an adult imagination and for the pursuit of adult desires within such a fantasy space; however, the adult presence comes through the child's perspective and experience, passively commenting on what they could see and feel.[53]

Because Edna will not leave the French Quarter outside of the prescribed trips to the beach resort and home to Kentucky, she remains trapped in a fantasy space, superimposing her adult desires over what must be seen as a space still occupied by childish Queens. What appears as movement forward for a new woman becomes the movements of someone trapped within a fantasy, whether that fantasy is freedom from marriage, being a mother, having a passionate love affair with Robert, or being a female artist.

Edna is horrified and hurt when she hears that Robert 'is leaving for Mexico that evening' exclaiming, 'Impossible!' She then asks, 'How can a person start off from Grand Isle to Mexico at a moment's notice, as if he were going over to Klein's or to the wharf or down to the beach?'[54] For Edna, travel away seems childish, even ridiculous, and it is here that she becomes stuck in a double bind. On the one hand, she grows up and away from the 'impossible things' of being a kept and childish Queen in the Wonderland of Creole New Orleans. On the other, she refuses to embrace the wonders of train travel, which the NPRR promotes as the ideal for a grown-up Alice. Only once is a train mentioned and rather ominously: 'There was the whistle of a railway train somewhere in the distance and the midnight bells were ringing.'[55] The train signals that there are other opportunities for Edna elsewhere, as promised by the Wonderland campaign, if she would just leave the Quarter.

Edna and the reader hear the train whistle when she brings Alcee, her new lover to 'the pigeon house' she just acquired while her husband does business in New York. Just like the parrot yelling, 'Go Away' at the beginning of the novel, the train whistle is both an instruction to Edna and a warning. Edna tells him: "'Ellen is afraid to mount the ladder. Joe is working over at the 'pigeon house' – that's the name Ellen gives it, because it's so small and looks like a pigeon house – and some one has to do this." Arobin pulled off his coat, and expressed himself ready and willing to tempt fate in her place.'[56] The name of Edna's new abode alludes to another of Alice's encounters in Wonderland. Alice shrinks and finds a large Pigeon who sits on a nest of eggs. In *Alice*, the pigeon's house is her nest full of eggs, making her a clear caretaker of both house and children, a figure of ideal Victorian womanhood. The pigeon is convinced that Alice is a serpent and trying to steal her eggs, which she is not, and squawks loudly at her to go away, much like the parrot at beginning of *The Awakening*. She is afraid Alice is a homewrecker, who like Eve in the Garden of Eden aligns herself with snakes and will cause the Fall of Mankind. The allusion suggests that Edna's desires, like Alice's and Eve's, will cause sure destruction, wrecking homes and children's lives by having an affair with this 'ready and willing man' who wants to 'tempt fate' in the pigeon house.

The allusion also reasserts that Edna remains in Wonderland the more she wakes up to passion. The 'pigeon house', her place of escape and rebellion, is just another house in the French Quarter, and she remains just as trapped there as she always was. Edna tries to make her movements mean something new and fails each time she becomes ensnared yet again into her life. Alice tries to claim to the pigeon that she is not a serpent, but rather, 'a little girl', but she says it 'rather doubtfully, as she remembered the number of changes she had gone through that day'.[57]

James Kincaid points out, 'Indeed, throughout the stories, Alice's awkward position as a child possessed by an adult consciousness is continually exaggerated by barely governable growth spurts, and, given Alice's shape-shifting in so many scenes, we begin to see her as both a prelapsarian child and a postlapsarian (or "fallen") adult.'[58] Edna, too, is trying to negotiate between wanting the childish things of Wonderland and being seen as a 'fallen' adult. However, Edna is not a child, and so has the option of leaving Wonderland, which Alice does not. Because she does not exercise this option, she appears trapped and fated as she marches forward, giving a 'mad' dinner party and then drowning herself, the final judgement for this woman who cannot escape from Wonderland on the train heard in the distance.

Alice in Wonderland mentions the train only once, in chapter 2, 'The Pool of Tears':

> As she said these words her foot slipped, and in another moment, splash! she was up to her chin in salt-water. Her first idea was that she had somehow fallen into the sea, 'and in that case I can go back by railway,' she said to herself. (Alice had been to the seaside once in her life, and had come to the general conclusion, that wherever you go to on the English coast, you find a number of bathing-machines in the sea, some children digging in the sand with wooden spades, then a row of lodging-houses, and behind them a railway-station.) However, she soon made out that she was in the pool of tears which she had wept when she was nine feet high.[59]

Even Alice recognizes the possibilities of being saved by the proximity of train routes to seaside towns. This passage may have inspired the Wonderland campaign, and Alice's new courage and strength appears precisely because she understands that there's always a way out. In fact, she excels at leadership in the water, leading the other creatures in the water as they swim back to shore.

It turns out that Alice's 'sea' is actually a puddle of her own tears made when she had grown large. When she shrinks, she finds herself in the puddle, which now appears as large and vast as the sea. The story then is about a girl who is strong enough to overcome her own sadness and get herself out of a worrisome situation through her own strength and understanding of the possibilities of travel. Edna is not a strong swimmer, a fact pointed out throughout the novel by Edna herself and Mme. Reisz, the artist who dislikes water and doesn't swim herself. Edna is not strong enough to remove herself from her sadness, and she doesn't even recognize that there is a way out, a 'railway station' behind every row of beach houses. Instead, she drowns in her tears, trapped inside of a childish Wonderland that made her small, just as she believed she was growing larger.

Kate Chopin relies on her reader's knowledge of the NPRR Wonderland campaign in order to make sense of Edna's disturbing story and fate. In doing so, it operates as a warning for women against being trapped in the idea of a childish, Victorian Wonderland. The novel subtly suggests Edna needed to behave as an adult Alice as she appears in the NPRR advertising imagery and leave the domestic world behind through travel and education. The novel provides one strong example of how turn-of-the-century literary feminists employed the enormously successful NPRR advertising imagery in their fiction to signal the way forward for modern women.

Notes

1   Lewis Carroll, *Alice's Adventures in Wonderland* and *Through the Looking-Glass*, ed.
    Hugh Haughton (London: Penguin, 1998), 11.
2   Ibid., 11–12.
3   Amy G. Richter, *Home on the Rails: Women, the Railroad, and the Rise of Public
    Domesticity* (Chapel Hill and London: University of North Carolina Press, 2005), 14.
4   Ibid.
5   Anna Despotopoulou, '"Running on Lines": Women and the Railway in Victorian and
    Early Modernist Culture', in *Women in Transit Through Literary Liminal Spaces*, ed.
    Teresa Gomez Reus and Terry Gifford (Houndmills: Palgrave Macmillan, 2013), 49.
6   Ibid.
7   Ibid., 50.
8   Richter, *Home on the Rails,* 73.
9   Ibid., 73–4.
10 Ibid., 73.
11 Ibid., 74.
12 Chris Bruce, curator, *Myth of the West*, The Henry Art Gallery, University of
    Washington, Seattle (Seattle: Henry Art Gallery Association, 1990), 70.
13 James S. Brust and Lee H. Whittlesey, '"Roughing It Up the Yellowstone to
    Wonderland": The Nelson Miles/Colgate Hoyt Party in Yellowstone National Park,
    September 1878', *Montana: The Magazine of Western History* 46 (spring 1996): 59.
14 Henry Jacob Winder and William C. Riley, *The Official Northern Pacific Railway
    Guide: For the Use of Tourists and Travelers Over the Lines of the Northern Pacific
    Railroad and Its Branches* (St. Paul: W. C. Riley Publisher, 1897), 13–18.
15 Janis P. Stout, *Picturing a Different West: Vision, Illustration, and the Tradition of
    Austin and Cather* (Lubbock: Texas Tech University Press, 2007), 117–19.
16 Nina Auerbach, 'Alice and Wonderland: A Curious Child', *Victorian Studies* 17, no. 1
    (September 1973): 31–2.
17 Ibid., 32.
18 'Alice's Adventures in the New Wonderland [brochure]', *National Park Service Website*,
    National Park Service (18 January 2012), https://www.nps.gov/yell/blogs/Alices-
    Adventures-in-the-New-Wonderland-brochure.htm.
19 Jean P. Ratzinger, 'Framing the tourist Gaze: Railway Journeys Across Nebraska,
    1866–1906', *Great Plains Quarterly* 18, no. 3 (1998): 214.
20 Carroll, *Alice*, 16.
21 'Alice's Adventures in the New Wonderland [brochure]'.
22 Ibid.
23 Ibid.
24 Auerbach, 'Alice and Wonderland', 33–4.
25 Ibid., 33.
26 John Urry, *The Tourist Gaze* (London: SAGE Publications, 1990), 10.
27 Ibid.
28 Anne Friedberg, *Window Shopping: Cinema and the Postmodern* (Berkeley and Los
    Angeles: University of California Press, 1993), 15.
29 Ellen Strain, *Public Places: Private Journeys: Ethnography, Entertainment and Tourist
    Gaze* (New Brunswick: Rutgers University Press, 2003), 15.
30 Ibid., 18.

31 Carina Garland, 'Curious Appetites: Food, Desire, Gender, and Subjectivity in Lewis Carroll's *Alice Texts*', *The Lion and Unicorn* 32, no. 1 (2008): 22.

32 James R. Kincaid, 'Alice's Inversion of Wonderland', *PMLA* 88, no. 1 (1973): 94.

33 Auerbach, 'Alice and Wonderland', 33.

34 Susanne George Bloomfield, *Elia Peattie: An Uncommon Writer, An Uncommon Woman*, University of Nebraska's Center for Digital Research in the Humanities, plainshumanities.unl.edu/peattie/about.html.

35 Elia Peattie, *A Journey Through Wonderland: A Journey Through the Pacific Northwest and Alaska* (Chicago: Rand McNally, 1890), 5.

36 Ibid.

37 Ibid., 7.

38 Ibid., 8.

39 Kate Chopin, *The Awakening*, ed. Margaret Culley (New York: Norton, 1976), 3.

40 Ibid., 32.

41 Carroll, *Alice*, 13.

42 Ibid., 174.

43 Ibid., 174.

44 Robert S. Levine, 'Circadian Rhythms and Rebellion in Kate Chopin's *The Awakening*', *Studies in American Fiction* 10, no. 1 (spring 1982): 71.

45 Ibid.

46 Ibid., 72.

47 Chopin, *The Awakening*, 14.

48 Ibid., 10.

49 Ibid., 106.

50 Ibid., 106–7.

51 Ibid., 37.

52 Ibid., 113.

53 Christine Roth, 'Looking Through the Spyglass: Lewis Carroll, James Barrie, and the Empire of Childhood', in *Alice Beyond Wonderland: Essays for the Twenty-first Century*, ed. Cristopher Hollingsworth (Iowa City: University of Iowa Press, 2009), 24.

54 Chopin, *The Awakening*, 42.

55 Ibid., 91.

56 Ibid., 84.

57 Carroll, *Alice*, 48.

58 Roth, 'Looking Through the Spyglass', 28.

59 Carroll, *Alice*, 20.

Chapter 6

'OPEN ALICE'S DOOR': LEWIS CARROLL'S INFLUENCE ON ELIZABETH BISHOP AND SYLVIA PLATH

Jessica R. McCort

In a 1958 journal entry, after outlining the plot of a story she wanted to write for the children's magazine *Jack and Jill* and musing about her intended first novel, Sylvia Plath, then twenty-six, directed herself to 'Open Alice's door': 'Begin there: 10 years of childhood before the slick adolescent years & then my diaries to work on: to reconstruct. [...] Recreate life lived: that is renewed life. [...] Open Alice's door, work & sweat to pry open the gates & speak out in words and worlds.'[1] Faced with the locked doors of writer's 'paralysis', Plath locates in *Alice's Adventures in Wonderland* a childhood favourite that remains a seminal text throughout her life, a key she believed would unlock her imagination: writing about her experiences of coming of age in an attempt to transform personal experience into art. In a similar vein, Elizabeth Bishop also drew upon the *Alice* books in her more autobiographical work to expose the problems of articulating identity, especially her narrators' ambivalent responses to the ideals of girlhood and womanhood they were expected to adopt. Both writers' appropriations of Carroll remark most upon the disorienting dislocation of the self in the world and the power of patriarchal authority; they primarily use allusions to Carroll to demonstrate their narrators'/ speakers' feelings of distress when trying to articulate their own identity and creativity or their place in the world in relationship to others. In this chapter, I will explore specific examples of such appropriations to demonstrate the ways in which Plath and Bishop used Carroll's Alice to speak out in their own 'words and worlds'.

A 'rigmarole of props': Bidding Farewell to 'Seem'

When it comes to the appropriation of source texts, Sylvia Plath was a prolific dabbler in children's literature, especially Grimm's fairy tales, nursery rhymes, and Lewis Carroll's *Alice* stories.[2] In the Plath home, as in many English and American households, the fantasy worlds in such children's books provided a regular source of entertainment. As Plath's mother describes in her introduction to *Letters Home*, her children loved being read to, and she obliged. Concentrating on the poetry to which she introduced Sylvia and her younger brother, Aurelia recounts the various texts with which she regularly amused them, including 'the children's favourite anthology *Sung Under the Silver Umbrella*' (a book explicitly targeted towards young children, containing poems by such authors as Edward Lear, Walter de la Mare, Christina Rossetti, and Sara Teasdale), 'Dr. Seuss's hilarious *Horton Hatches an Egg*', and Tolkien's *The Hobbit*.[3] This reading incited Plath's girlish creativity and lingered in her adult imagination. In a November 1962 review of children's books for *The New Statesman*, Plath, then twenty-nine, turned back to the books she loved as a child to recommend *Horton Hatches the Egg*, remarking on the continued presence of Seuss's poetic rhythms in her mind: 'Horton was hatching it in America when I was eight, and 22 years later, I still have by heart the trump couplet.'[4] The 'trump couplet' to which Plath refers reads in the original: 'Horton trumpets throughout the book the following lines: "I meant what I said and I said what I meant [...] / An elephant's faithful, one hundred per cent!"'[5]

Though Plath's mother does not include Carroll's *Alice* stories in the list of books she remembers having read to her children, Plath's allusions to them throughout her letters, journals, poetry, and prose demonstrate that they had also been foundational to her imaginative world as a child. Plath often described her childhood past as one characterized by the magic of the 'fairy-tale world' and the wonder of Carroll's topsy-turvy dreamscapes, with these stories residing in her memories alongside her oft-acknowledged muse, the sea.[6] 'If I tried to describe my personality', she explained in a youthful letter to her long-distance confidante Eddie Cohen, 'I'd start to gush about living by the ocean half my life and being brought up on Alice in Wonderland and believing in magic for years and years.'[7] As Plath wrote in her journal during the winter of 1950, however, she found herself disillusioned: 'Not to be sentimental, as I sound, but why the hell are we conditioned into the smooth strawberry-and-cream Mother-Goose-world, Alice-in-Wonderland fable, only to be broken on the wheel as we grow older and become aware of ourselves as individuals with a dull responsibility in life?'[8]

Plath's early appropriations of children's literature demonstrate her attempts to relinquish the key that had opened her literary imagination while simultaneously using that key to unlock her creativity.[9] The majority of Plath's work from the late 1940s/early 1950s that appropriates children's literature contemplates the models of girlhood that this literature offers, particularly as she begins to realize how deeply it is intertwined with her conception of her artistic identity and her attempts to claim authority as a female writer.[10] The 1950s poem 'A Sorcerer Bids Farewell to Seem', for instance, explicitly contemplates this dilemma. Positioning herself in the poem's title as a 'Sorcerer' – a masculine role drawn from the realm of fairy and fantasy tales – Plath playfully considers the legacy of both children's literature and poetic tradition for the female artist by blatantly usurping a 'rigmarole of props' provided by both of Carroll's *Alice* books.[11] The poem begins as Plath's 'Daddy' ends, with the speaker's declaration of being 'through' with the past: 'I'm through with this grand looking-glass hotel / where adjectives play croquet with flamingo nouns; / methinks I shall absent me for a while / from rhetoric of these rococo queens.'[12] The use of the 'looking-glass hotel' here suggests that the place in which the speaker finds herself is transient, self-absorbed, derivative, and disorienting. Plath's references to Alice's attempts to play croquet with flamingos as mallets also call attention to the absurdity of her efforts to put words to use, the words coming alive and becoming unwieldy, just as inanimate objects often do in Carroll or, for that matter, in Plath's later poems, like 'Words'. Despite the speaker's declaration, however, the poem makes clear, as the closure of 'Daddy' also insinuates, that she is not at all through; she is instead inextricably bound to the texts on which she has modelled her work, since the 'props' she has borrowed formulate much of the content of the poem. As the poem continues, characters and symbolic emblems from both *Alice in Wonderland* and *Through the Looking-Glass* proliferate: the White Rabbit, the Gryphon, the Caterpillar's mushroom, the Mad Hatter, the Jabberwock, the Cheshire Cat, the Walrus and the Carpenter, and, above all, Alice herself, whom the poet singles out as 'my muse', albeit a muse she wants to 'send [...] packing'.[13]

Through these allusions, Plath dramatizes the impossible imperative of escaping the overwhelming influence of past texts as she attempts to simultaneously break out of and into 'the grand looking-glass hotel' of literary tradition, represented in the poem as inward-looking, self-repeating, and fickle.[14] These moves, coincidentally, echo many of Carroll's in his parodies of well-known poems that would have been easily recognizable to his readers.[15] Plath's poem links her narrator's troubles to the two central dilemmas that plague the young Alice in Carroll's books: the mutability of her identity and the inscrutability of language in the two nightmarish dream-worlds that she enters. The characters Plath references, for instance, regularly destabilize Alice's sense of who she is and her claim to language: the White Rabbit mistakes Alice for a common servant; the Mad Hatter repeatedly attacks Alice's statements, maddeningly using word play.[16] As Carroll's books progress, the real question obsessively becomes for Alice, as for Plath throughout her career, "'Who in the world am I?" Ah, *that's* the great puzzle!'[17]

The answer to this question can only be puzzled out in words, but, to Alice's dismay, her experiences in both Wonderland and the Looking-Glass world leave her feeling 'dreadfully puzzled' and at a linguistic loss – that is until she decides to rouse herself from her nightmares.[18] In 'A Sorcerer Bids Farewell to Seem', language and identity likewise become dreadfully intermingled, but Plath's narrator shows that there is no easy way to snap herself, like Alice, out of her nightmare. The poem in turn displays the speaker's anxiety of influence. The speaker's dismay is rooted in her struggle against both the 'rhetoric' of 'rococo queens', presumably represented in Plath's eyes by such aged 'poetic godmothers' as Edith Sitwell and Marianne Moore, and the masculine giants of modernist poetics, whom Plath links to the gigantic, monstrous 'jabberwock [who] will not translate his songs',[19] and the ridiculously erudite Humpty Dumpty, who demonstrates his authority over Alice by translating the nonsense poem 'Jabberwocky'.[20] The poem dramatizes, in turn, the younger poet's struggle for voice, recognition, and understanding.

For Plath's speaker, the only viable option in her battle for artistic originality, on the surface, seems to be a turn away from the tired props of childhood fantasy and back to her own reality. In other words, her only option is to tell things as she

sees them (not as they 'seem') by looking back through Alice's keyhole: 'it's time
to vanish like the Cheshire Cat / alone to that authentic island where / cabbages
are cabbages; kings: kings.'[21] And yet, even as she tries to escape Alice's world, she
returns. Imagining herself as the Cheshire Cat, a master of disguise and display
(and nebulous 'advice'), the speaker's final injunction to herself to be realistically
blunt is, in fact, an allusion to the poem 'The Walrus and the Carpenter' in the
'Tweedledee and Tweedledum' chapter of *Through the Looking-Glass*. This rhyme,
another parodic spin on poetry popular in Carroll's time, concentrates on death
and trickery. The Walrus's call to 'talk of many things: / Of shoes – and ships
and sealing-wax – / Of cabbages – and kings – And why the sea is boiling hot –
And whether pigs have wings' serves merely as a diversionary tactic to keep the
oysters he wants to eat unaware of their impending doom.[22] By the end of the
Walrus and the Carpenter's digressive speech, all of the oysters are dead, their
shells the only remnant of their existence. Through this allusion, 'A Sorcerer
Bids Farewell to Seem' likewise ends with an ironic twist, one concentrated on
surface and substance. Here, the speaker notes her plan to 'vanish' to an 'authentic
island' where words mean what they say – a cabbage is a cabbage and a king a
king, not a manipulative lie. However, Plath declares her allegiance to her own
vision through the very language she is trying to discard, wielding the language
of childhood fictions to imagine the artistic dilemma she faces at present.
Carroll's influence in the poem is finally ambivalent: it represents the early stages
of the poet's apprenticeship, but it also tries to offer a viable alternative to the
threatening Jabberwocky of poetic tradition as the poet seeks to articulate her
vision. The word 'vanish' always gives me pause, however. In seeking her own
place, she disappears and is left 'alone' on a deserted island. If the speaker has
gained her own voice, who is going to actually hear it?

As Plath's career progressed, she continued to manipulate children's literature as
a foundation on which to build her narratives of female experience. Increasingly
influenced by Freud's theories, Plath recurrently strove to re-enter childhood as a
way of developing her voice, melding children's literature to her progressively more
confessional and feminist poetics and provoking her readers' consideration of both
the enabling and disabling powers of children's fictions in girls' and women's lives.
Beginning in the mid-1950s, Plath explicitly aligned her own or her characters'
autobiography with elements of children's literature and began to splinter the
children's book, inserting its shards into her personae's imaginations.[23] In her
later poems, Plath continued to enter into a dialogue with the children's book that
made the language of children's literature part of the speaker's vocabulary as she
expresses the frustration, anger, and confusion that evolved out of her childhood
and adolescent experiences.[24] Plath's most famous poem, 'Daddy', for example, has
been viewed as an exercise in this sort of rebellion, replacing her earlier use of the
Alice books with nursery rhymes.[25]

The poem 'The Babysitters' is a good example of Plath's later appropriations
of Carrollian symbolism in her work. Written in 1961 near the end of October,
her always-productive birthday month, 'The Babysitters' enters an adult woman's
consciousness to consider how her girlhood self has been locked away in the past.

Rather than directly addressing Alice, here Plath plays upon the Carrollian motif of drifting along in water on a dreamy afternoon, the poem beginning with two girls rowing a boat out to 'Children's Island'.[26] This space alludes to both the past habitus of the girls' world and the destination of maternity, as suggested by the poem's reference to babysitting. The poem moves forward to consider the girls' early resistance to their future roles and their subsequent process of going into hiding. When the pair get to Children's Island, which has come in the adult woman's mind to symbolize both girls' lost pasts, they find it 'deserted – / A gallery of creaking porches and still interiors, / Stopped and awful as a photograph of somebody laughing, / But ten years dead'.[27] The woman narrator, now ten years removed from her adolescent past (and presumably one of the ten years dead), laments the loss of her girlish self by alluding subtly to the story of Alice in Wonderland. 'What keyhole have we slipped through?' the speaker wonders. 'What door has shut?'[28] This 'keyhole' and 'door' recall the 'little golden key' and 'the little door' Alice confronts after she falls down the Rabbit Hole into Wonderland.[29] Unlike Alice, who eventually bobs about in a pool of her own tears and escapes the flood she has created by floating into Wonderland, these two cannot escape; they remain forever floating in the locked-off space of the island. In the speaker's mind, they become 'two cork dolls', a phrase which suggests, given the doll symbolism in Plath's work, that the girls have been corked inside their Stepford Wife–like adult selves, their past selves forever encapsulated and deadened behind Alice's locked door.[30]

In Plath's work, sources like Carroll and the nursery rhyme are productive, if ambivalent. Her poetry and prose both celebrate and abhor the powerful influence of children's texts: they are a site in which the imagination can thrive, but at the same time, they are missives that mislead and distort girls' expectations, ultimately resulting in their disillusionment and disgust. At the core of her late style lies the particularization of her culture's tales, in this case an individualization of the texts that employs their most recognizable themes, forms, and plots to come to terms with her past, present, and future. The content and language of children's books like Carroll's equipped Plath with a vocabulary for articulating her experience. This vocabulary draws her readers into the world of her text and asks them to recognize the powerful shaping influence of children's books in their own earliest experiences of culture.

'Who are you?': Elizabeth Bishop's Alice Figures

For Elizabeth Bishop, Carroll's *Alice* books likewise became emblematic of displacement, loss, and the child's confusion when confronted with social rules, gender roles, and the contradictory rigidity and fluidity of both identity and language. In her work, Bishop often uses symbolism from Carroll to frame her speakers' explorations of identity, especially in the confrontation between adolescence and adult femininity. As Judith Little notes in her essay on Alice as a 'female hero', 'Alice [...] responds to the Victorian ideal of womanhood with obvious ambiguity'.[31] 'When a figure resembling Alice does reappear', Little argues, 'her story always includes an energetic critique of the social clichés which tend to pedestal female domesticity. It usually includes as well the female hero's assertion of autonomy, of freedom from patriarchal condescension and control.'[32] Bishop's adaptations of Carroll often centre on narrators who contemplate and critique the controls placed on individuals. The 1951 poem 'Insomnia', for example, begins with the narrator contemplating the moon's reflection in the mirror, then 'drop[ping]', like Alice through the vehicle of the dream, 'down the well / into [a …] world inverted'.[33] The poem eventually imagines a place where the moon can 'tell [the Universe] to go to hell'.[34] Feeling 'deserted' by the world around her, 'she' creates a place 'where left is always right, where the shadows are really the body',[35] and where the person the speaker desires requites her love. Though Carroll's influence on this poem is certainly subtler, Bishop uses the inverted world of Wonderland much as Plath's speaker does in 'A Sorcerer Bids Farewell to Seem': the speaker creates a universe that operates by a different set of rules that better suit the needs of the writer.

Carroll's influence on Bishop is perhaps most readily apparent during the 1950s and 1960s. During this time, she returned to her own experiences of childhood, producing multiple pieces of short fiction and memoir that explored the roots of her life. Bishop's use of Carrollian motifs, images, characters, and language in these texts mark the importance of his books to the aesthetics of childhood and, especially, of girlhood that she sought, at that time, to develop. Her attention came to focus more and more on two aspects of Carroll's texts that consistently resonated for other modern and postmodern women writers. First, as Murray Knowles and Kristen Malmkjaer explain in their study of language and control in children's literature, Carroll's work reflects 'the essential instability and uncertainty of the language through which material "facts" are reprinted', which makes it difficult to 'maintain a clear distinction between fiction and reality'.[36] Secondly, this difficulty becomes linked to the essential instability and uncertainty of identity; Alice loses 'linguistic control' as she loses the ability and the confidence to 'name herself'.[37] As Gilles Deleuze explains in *The Logic of Sense*, Alice's transformations throughout her adventures 'have one consequence: the contesting to Alice's personal identity and the loss of her proper name'.[38] As I previously noted, the great question that Alice has to answer in both Wonderland and the Looking-Glass world is 'Who am I?' – a question that she is less and less able to answer as the books go on. 'I wonder if I've been changed in the night?' Alice wonders at one point: '"I'm sure I can't be Mabel, for I know all sorts of things and she, oh, she knows such a very little! Besides, *she's* she, and *I'm* I, and – oh dear, how puzzling it all is!"'[39] Catherine Driscoll further extends Deleuze's reading to focus on girls' identities, arguing that the 'special relevance to girlhood' in Alice's dilemma is that it is rooted in 'Alice's transitions in body, power, and identity'.[40] As her body begins to change and she confronts adult after adult trying to tell her who and what she should be, her confidence in her identity begins to slip away.

Drawing on Carroll's preoccupation with both language and identity, Bishop subtly frames some of the representations of girlhood she produces during this period on Alice's disorienting journeys. Her prose piece 'The Country Mouse', for example, intersects mainly with Carroll's second book *Through the Looking-Glass*, and depicts an orphaned girl being whisked away from the stable, much-loved home of her maternal grandparents to a new life in America with her deceased father's family. The piece opens on a train, the disorienting journey echoing Alice's hallucinatory train ride in the Looking-Glass world. In *Through the Looking-Glass*, the train-ride symbolizes another leg in Alice's journey towards becoming a queen, her queenship, or womanhood, the endpoint of the surreal chess-game she has been invited to play. Like the frightening train which 'scream[s]' 'shrill[y]' in Carroll,[41] the 'gritting, grinding, occasionally shrieking' train in Bishop's story is bearing the girl – as the train conductor in *Through the Looking-Glass* tells Alice, '"You're travelling the wrong way"'[42] – further and further away from home and, like Alice, deeper and deeper into a new and increasingly strange world.[43] Bishop's dominant subject in 'The Country Mouse' is the girl's disturbing discovery of what it means to be a proper 'little girl'. As the narrator moves deeper into the strange new world of her American home, she progressively loses the sense of whom she had been in her previous one, and becomes increasingly conscious of the feminine, American-girl role she is expected to perform. 'There seemed to be much, much more to being a "little girl" than I had realized,' the narrator muses, '[and] the prospect was beginning to depress me.'[44] The voice through which Bishop renders the child's confusion is akin to Carroll's questioning Alice, who is utterly bewildered by the peculiar use of language in Wonderland and the Looking-Glass world. Alice's interactions with the Mad Hatter, for example, reflect this confusion: 'Alice felt dreadfully puzzled. The Hatter's remark seemed to her to have no sort of meaning in it, and yet it was certainly English. "I don't quite understand you," she said, as politely as she could.'[45] As Bishop's narrator comes into contact with gender codes in particular, she asks similar questions, her confused response mirroring Alice's confrontations with a world that is, as W. H. Auden wrote of the Looking-Glass world, 'governed by laws to which she is unaccustomed'.[46]

In 'The Country Mouse,' Bishop roots the child's confusion in response to language in her grandmother's way of speaking, echoing Alice's disorienting conversations with the Red and White Queens in *Through the Looking-Glass*. On the train journey, for example, the narrator remarks, 'I was beginning to enjoy myself a little, if only Grandma hadn't had such a confusing way of talking. It was almost as if we were playing house. She would speak of "grandma" and "little girls" and "fathers" and "being good" – things I had never before considered in the abstract, or rarely in third person.'[47] Here, the girl recognizes and wonders at the multiple meanings of single words (one of the dominant forms of wordplay in Carroll's books, as in the Mad Hatter's riddles of 'ravens' and 'writing-desks'), meanings that she had never contemplated before (despite her certain prior awareness of her position as daughter, granddaughter, and girl). As Juliet Dusinberre describes in her examination of how Carroll influenced writers like Virginia Woolf, Carroll 'identif[ies] the linguistic centre of a child's subjection to the adult world'.[48] As the passage above indicates, the girl's subjection to the adult world is rooted in learning new definitions of 'father', 'little girls', and 'being good' – in other words, the definition of proper feminine behaviour in the eyes of the

American patriarchy. The girl's ultra-femme, 'doll-like' grandmother, like the aged Red and White Queens, is responsible for teaching the little girl how to behave.[49]

The conversations between Alice and the Queens in the 'Queen Alice' chapter of *Through the Looking-Glass* are similarly focused on manners and lessons, and the older women don't often give Alice the chance to speak, much like the grandmother in 'The Country Mouse':

> 'I daresay you've not had many lessons in manners yet?'
> 'Manners are not taught in lessons,' said Alice. 'Lessons teach you to do sums, and things of that sort.' […]
> 'She ca'n't do Substraction,' said the White Queen. 'Can you do Division? Divide a loaf by a knife – what's the answer to *that*?'
> 'I suppose——' Alice was beginning, but the Red Queen answered for her. 'Bread and butter, of course.'[50]

By the end of this conversation, Alice 'couldn't help thinking to herself "What dreadful nonsense we *are* talking!"'[51] While these lessons seem dreadful nonsense to Alice, they are painfully real to the narrator in Bishop's story. In this new world, she struggles to decipher language that 'baffle[s]' and ultimately silences her, much of which is related to American domesticity and femininity, such as her young, ultra-femme playmate's use of the phrase 'apple-pie order'.[52] In Bishop's memoir, the girl's ultimate response to the 'Who am I?' question is 'You are you'.[53] This answer, however, is anything but satisfying for the child. 'You are you' seems threatening, nonsensical, and complicates the reading of the self as being situated in external particulars: others looking upon the 'I' read the child as a 'you', thereby cancelling out the girl's ability to define herself. Coming tellingly from a voice that seems disembodied from the child, this assertion reads like a prison sentence handed down from above: '"You are you," something said. "How strange you are, inside looking out. You are not Beppo, or the chestnut tree, or Emma, you are *you*, and you are going to be *you* forever."'[54] Instead of Alice's emphatic declarative '*I'm I*', here we get a more damning, deploring 'you are *you*', with the emphasis placed on 'you' instead of on 'I am'. Whereas Alice is able to draw a line between herself and other girls on her own, in the first person, stating what she *is*, Bishop's child mainly defines herself by what she is *not*, finally settling on the 'you' that she is to other people. This suggests a sense of identity not classified by self-definition but by outside particulars.

In 'The Country Mouse', Bishop makes good use of the internal monologue, a motif Carroll uses frequently in the *Alice* books. By the end of Bishop's memoir, however, the child's internal monologue is usurped by 'something', which suggests her realization that she will be defined by the new culture in which she is being forced to live – the Looking-Glass world of American femininity.[55] This point is brought home when the narrator gazes into the mirror in her grandfather's bedroom. While Carroll's Alice greets her reflection in the mirror with surprise and wonder, Bishop's girl is afraid of the reformulated image of an American 'little girl' that meets her eyes: 'my ugly serge dress, my too long hair, my gloomy and frightened expression'.[56] The shame, disgrace, and dissolution of the self that the girl experiences when she sees herself in the mirror, akin to Virginia Woolf's childhood memory of seeing a terrifying animal face appear over her shoulder in 'A Sketch of the Past', depicts the girl's sudden recognition of her fall into gender as a loss of power and self-definition.

Bishop's use of Carrollian motifs to capture the mutability of language when it comes to identity was a thread that carried through into her later work, especially in her memoir writing. Bishop's pieces 'Efforts of Affection' and 'North Haven', written for Marianne Moore and Robert Lowell respectively, further examine the intersection of linguistic ambiguity and identity that Carroll's books seemed to represent for Bishop. 'Efforts of Affection', for example, ends with an allusion to Carroll's *Alice* that calls attention to the difficulty of using language to make 'sense' of someone's identity. She writes:

> I find it impossible to draw conclusions or even to summarize. When I try to, I become foolishly bemused: I have a sort of subliminal glimpse of the capital letter *M* multiplying. I am turning the pages of an illuminated manuscript and seeing the initial letter again and again: Marianne's monogram; mother; manners; morals; and I catch myself murmuring, 'Manners and morals; manners *as* morals? Or is it morals *as* manners?' Since, like Alice, 'in a dreamy sort of way,' I can't answer either question, it doesn't much matter which way I put it; it *seems* to be making sense.[57]

This passage echoes language from *Alice's Adventures in Wonderland*, in the chapter 'Down the Rabbit-Hole', where Alice falls into a new world through a dream and discovers identity's disorienting lack of fixity. '[H]ere Alice began to get rather sleepy,' Carroll writes, 'and went on saying to herself, in a dreamy sort of way, "Do cats eat bats? Do cats eat bats?" and sometimes "Do bats eat cats?" for, you see, as she couldn't answer either question, it didn't much matter which way she put it.'[58] Alice's puzzlement over cats versus bats echoes Bishop's puzzlement when it came to Moore's manners and their connection to morality, especially what it was and was not proper to write about (Moore, for example, notoriously called 'Insomnia' a 'trite love poem').

The language Bishop includes from Carroll suggests the prismatic description of Moore that Bishop offers in the essay; she is, at once, a contradiction of various selves – impractical and dogmatic, decorous and indecorous, fragile and formidable, child-like and aged.[59] Bishop's positioning of herself as Alice in the fantastic world that Moore inhabited demonstrates the world of new rules that she had entered, the inverted 'otherworldl[iness]' of Moore's life (which the younger Bishop had the sensation of sinking into via 'diving bell').[60] However, Bishop's use of this specific passage alludes particularly to the mutability and inaccuracy of language, the spontaneous production of linguistic associations that occur when a person tries to pin down the meaning of someone or something – language itself refuses to remain stable at the end of the memoir, similar to the functionality of language in both Wonderland and the Looking-Glass world that Alice enters.

Bishop again used language from this same passage in her 1978 memorial poem for Robert Lowell in an effort to capture the divagation necessary in recording identity and addressing the meaning of it in the face of death: 'The islands haven't shifted since last summer, / even if I like to pretend they have / – drifting in a dreamy sort of way, / a little north, a little south or sidewise, / and that they're free within the blue frontiers of bay.'[61] 'Drifting in a dreamy sort of way' represents in both Carroll's books and Bishop's allusions to them a fall into consciousness, death, loss, and abrupt change prompting a new way of looking at the old world and the recognition of both the power and unwieldiness of language. Here, however, Bishop concentrates more on spatial constructs, the islands moving around in her imagination, even though they remain fixed in reality, and they seem to find freedom in their wandering. The theme of wandering is important in both Bishop's oeuvre and Carroll's books, as it is in their wandering that the characters learn more of the world and of themselves. However, by the end of the poem, with Lowell's death, the wandering of her imagination in relation to his identity seems to be at an end; her attempts to pinpoint Lowell's resonance in her life seem as stopped as a ship in a bottle: 'You can't derange, or re-arrange, / your poems again. [...] The words won't change again. Sad friend, you cannot change.' Words seem to fail the speaker here again, as in the Moore memoir; however, this time they fail because, instead of words multiplying like echoes, they have ceased movement, become statue-like. In 'North Haven', the wordplay and drifting come abruptly to stasis.

In most of Bishop's applications of Carroll, the central motif seems to be struggle – struggle with language, identity, people in positions of power and authority, cultural difference, grief. Carroll's work, for her, seems also to have been emblematic of confusion, particularly in relation to a person's attempts to navigate a world that seems nonsensical and strange or to describe other people. In this regard, Bishop's allusions to Carroll operate much as Plath's do; both Plath and Bishop seem to dredge Alice up from memory when trying to articulate their own or their speakers' confrontations with things that don't make sense, whether they are the rules their society has constructed for their behaviour or the loss of a beloved mentor or friend.

Breaking the Glass

Viewed together, the work of these two authors showcases the strategies that several other twentieth-century women writers also used during this period to write themselves out of the wonderlands of their pasts, their mentorships, and the Looking-Glass world of 'proper' femininity. Both authors critically engaged and appropriated Carroll's work in an effort to claim artistic authority and to demonstrate the influence of girls' imaginative lives on adult women's creativity. Plath's and Bishop's inclusions of Carroll specifically tend to serve two underlying purposes: to focus the reader's attention on the narrator's/speaker's/author's anxiety of influence and/or to call attention to the unwieldiness of language when it comes to articulating identity. Furthermore, both authors converge around similar Carrollian tropes: the authoritative adult who speaks gibberish or nonsense, wandering, floating in water, mirrored surfaces, the locked door and its key, interior monologues. Through these allusions, Plath and Bishop contend with and sometimes reject literary history, their mentors' influence on their work, their families' attempts to change their behaviour, their desire to break out of the moulds that had been set in place for them by others. They also attempt to assert their own creative identity by wielding the shards of Carroll's tales in new and interesting ways.

Notes

1   Sylvia Plath, *The Unabridged Journals of Sylvia Plath*, ed. Karen V. Kukil (New York: Anchor, 2000), 305. Sarah Kate Stephenson, in her unpublished dissertation 'The Disquieting Muse: Childhood and the Work of Sylvia Plath' (University of Virginia, 2001), notes that 'Plath's work in the production of children's literature surfaces at precisely the time she began to think of herself as a serious poet, suggesting that her poetry intersects with a prolonged meditation on childhood' (i). Stephenson incorrectly asserts, however, that Plath's first reference to writing for children is on 23 April 1959 in *The Bed Book* (24). However, Plath first refers to writing for children as early as January of 1958. The years 1958 and 1959, during which Plath wrote for children, also mark Plath's regular attempts to enter the adult prose market, writing story after story that resonated with her interest in children's literature.

2   For a full discussion of Bishop's and Plath's use of children's literature as structuring framework and source of allusion, see 'The "interrupted story": Children's Literature and Elizabeth Bishop's Exploratory Aesthetics' and 'Sylvia Plath through the Looking-Glass' in Jessica McCort, 'Getting Out of Wonderland: Elizabeth Bishop, Sylvia Plath, Adrienne Rich, and Anne Sexton' (PhD Diss., Washington University in St. Louis, 2009), 36–212, http://openscholarship.wustl.edu/etd/234.

3   Sylvia Plath, *Letters Home: Correspondence 1950–1963*, ed. Aurelia Plath (New York: Harper & Row, 1975), 19.

4   Plath, 'Oregonian Original', *The New Statesman* (9 November 1962), 660.

5   Seuss, *Horton Hatches the Egg* (New York: HarperCollins, 2011), 16.

6   Plath, *Unabridged Journals*, 34.

7   Quoted in Kathleen Connors, 'Living Color: The Interactive Arts of Sylvia Plath', in *Eye Rhymes: Sylvia Plath's Art of the Visual*, ed., Kathleen Connors and Sally Bayley (Oxford: Oxford University Press, 2007), 17.

8   Plath, *Unabridged Journals*, 5.

9   See Plath's poem 'Bluebeard', which riffs on the fairy tale about a gentleman and his closet full of dead wives. Plath uses the source text here to investigate the male gaze and its dangerous invasion of female sexual desire.

10 In this, Plath echoes Joyce Carol Oates's assessment of the early influences of sources like the *Alice* books. In her article on the importance of Lewis Carroll to her aesthetics, Oates explains that there are two primary influences in a writer's life: (1) 'those that came so early in childhood, they seem to soak into the very marrow of our bones and to condition our interpretation of the universe thereafter' and (2) those that come later when the writer is more aware of the strategies and emotions of art

(Joyce Carol Oates, 'First Loves: From "Jabberwocky" to "After Apple-Picking"', in *The Faith of a Writer: Life, Craft, Art* [New York: Plume, 2003], 13).

11 Sylvia Plath, *The Collected Poems*, ed. Ted Hughes (New York: Harper Perennial, 1992), 324.

12 Ibid.

13 Ibid.

14 Ibid. In his brief discussion of this poem in his overview of Plath's 'juvenilia' (a contested term, based on Ted Hughes's delineation of the stages of her work in his version of the *Collected Poems*), Steven Gould Axelrod also calls attention to the inescapability of textuality that this poem recounts: 'In ostensibly seeking to escape textuality[, Plath] alludes to a host of prior texts, including Shakespeare's *Hamlet*, Lewis Carroll's *Alice in Wonderland*, and Wallace Stevens's "The Emperor of Ice-Cream" (with its resonant, if impossible imperative to "Let be be finale of seem")' ('The Poetry of Sylvia Plath', in *The Cambridge Companion to Sylvia Plath*, ed. Jo Gill [Cambridge: Cambridge University Press, 2006], 75).

15 See, for example, 'How Doth the Little Crocodile' or 'Twinkle, Twinkle, Little Bat' (Lewis Carroll, *Alice's Adventures in Wonderland* and *Through the Looking-Glass*, ed. Hugh Haughton [London: Penguin, 1998], 19, 63).

16 Carroll, *Alice*, 31–3, 62–8.

17 Ibid., 18.

18 Ibid., 62.

19 Plath, *Collected Poems*, 324.

20 Plath, *Unabridged Journals*, 360. Plath has called attention to the relationship between Sitwell's and Carroll's worlds elsewhere. In a college essay on Sitwell in 1953, as Kathleen Connors notes, Plath 'likened Sitwell's "acute and vivid observations" to that of "a terribly clever and technically adroit child" who awakens "in a very personal and intimate wonderland" – a child that sounds very much like the young Sylvia Plath. She went on to describe the other side of this "bucolic world" where the "storybook animals turn harsh and grunting and all is mired" in what Sitwell called "heavy brutish greedy darkness"' (Connors, *Eye Rhymes*, 74). Through allusions to Carroll's characters and landscapes, Plath considers the unsettling quality that she found in Sitwell's work, which led to a greater consideration of how consciousness develops.

21 Plath, *Collected Poems*, 324. The poem 'Two Lovers and a Beachcomber by the Real Sea' can be read as a similar attempt to excise the influence of childhood fantasy. In this poem, Plath contemplates the imagination, especially the failure of the imagination. The adult mind cannot play as the child's had; it cannot create, for example, fantastic imaginings of 'mermaid hair' in the sea, an allusion to Andersen's 'The Little Mermaid'. The poem ends with the speaker's realization that childhood gullibility cannot persist through an allusion to Mother Goose's 'The Man in the Moon': 'No little man lives in the exacting moon / And that is that, is that, is that' (327). Plath's turn from fantasy toward the 'Real Sea', with 'The imagination / Shut[ting] down its fabled summer house', is akin to Plath's injunction to turn towards an island where the real is the coldly observable visual, with no fabled adornments added (237).

22 Carroll, *Alice*, 161.

23 See, for example, my previous work on Plath's appropriations of Carroll in her piece 'Stone Boy with Dolphin', in Jessica McCort, 'Alice in Cambridge: Sylvia Plath, Little Girls Lost, and "Stone Boy with Dolphin"', *Plath Profiles* 1 (summer 2008): 175–86.

24 As Sandra Gilbert and Susan Gubar argue in *No Man's Land*, Plath's late style relies on creating a double-layered quality in her poetry that calls attention to her artistic defiance and originality. 'Behind the apparently ragged, defiantly irregular lines of the "real" text', they assert, 'we sense the rhythm of a kind of ghost text' (Sandra Gilbert and Susan Gubar, *No Man's Land: The Place of the Woman Writer in the Twentieth Century*, vo!. 3, *Letters from the Front* [New Haven: Yale University Press, 1988], 291). While the ghost text represents a mastery of poetic form, the printed text represents a wilful breaking or 'shredding' of that prosody. As Gilbert and Gubar also briefly suggest, the shredding of children's literature is often readily apparent in Plath's late style.

25 For more information on how Plath uses children's nursery rhymes in 'Daddy', see 'Sylvia Plath through the Looking-Glass', in Jessica McCort, 'Getting Out of Wonderland: Elizabeth Bishop, Sylvia Plath, Adrienne Rich, and Anne Sexton', 107–212.

26 Plath, *Collected Poems*, 174.

27 Ibid., 175.

28 Ibid.

29 Carroll, *Alice*, 12.

30 Plath, *Collected Poems*, 175. Plath originally planned to title the poem, 'Madonna of the Refrigerators', an allusion to Amy Lowell's poem 'Madonna of the Evening Flowers', in which Lowell describes looking for and being unable to find anything but traces of a woman until she enters the garden (Amy Lowell, 'Madonna of the Evening Flowers', in *The Norton Anthology of Literature by Women: The Tradition in English*, ed. Sandra M. Gilbert and Susan Gubar [New York: Norton, 1985], 1298).

31 Judith Little, 'Liberated Alice: Dodgson's Female Hero as Domestic Rebel', *Women's Studies* 3 (1976): 195.

32 Ibid.

33 Elizabeth Bishop, *The Complete Poems: 1927–1979* (New York: Farrar, Straus and Giroux, 1983), 70.

34 Ibid.

35 Ibid.

36 Murray Knowles and Kirsten Malmkjaer, *Language and Control in Children's Literature* (London: Routledge, 1996), 225.

37 Ibid., 233.

38 Gilles Deleuze, *The Logic of Sense*, trans. Mark Lester and Charles Stivale, ed. Constantin V. Boundas (New York: Columbia University Press, 1990), 3.

39 Carroll, *Alice*, 18.

40 Catherine Driscoll, *Girls: Feminine Adolescence in Popular Culture and Cultural Theory* (New York: Columbia University Press, 2002), 197.

41 Carroll, *Alice*, 148.

42 Ibid., 146.

43 Elizabeth Bishop, *The Collected Prose*, ed. Robert Giroux (New York: Noonday, 1984), 13.

44 Ibid., 16.

45 Carroll, *Alice*, 62.

46 W. H. Auden, 'Today's "Wonder-World" Needs Alice', in *Aspects of Alice: Lewis Carroll's Dreamchild as Seen through the Critics' Looking Glasses, 1865–1971*, ed. Robert Phillips (New York: Vanguard, 1971), 9.

47 Bishop, *Collected Prose*, 16.

48 Juliet Dusinberre, *Alice to the Lighthouse: Children's Books and Radical Experiments in Art* (New York: St Martin's, 1999), 166.
49 Bishop, *Collected Prose*, 16.
50 Carroll, *Alice*, 221–2.
51 Ibid., 223.
52 Bishop, *Collected Prose*, 22. In her essay on Bishop's appropriation of Carroll in 'The Country Mouse', one of the few essays which consider Bishop's work and children's literature, Gail Dayton argues that, in 'The Country Mouse', 'Bishop produces an aesthetic rendering of her autobiography, and she finds her unified self in the exploration of past memories' (Gail H. Dayton, 'Elizabeth Bishop: Child of Past, Child of Present in "The Country Mouse"', in *'In Worcester, Massachusetts': Essays on Elizabeth Bishop from the 1997 Elizabeth Bishop Conference at WPI*, ed. Laura Jehn Menides and Angela G. Dorenkamp [New York: Peter Lang, 1999], 35).
53 Bishop, *Collected Prose*, 41.
54 Ibid., 33.
55 Ibid.
56 Ibid., 29.
57 Ibid., 156.
58 Carroll, *Alice,* 11.
59 Kathryn R. Kent roots this reference in *Through the Looking-Glass*, 'where the mirror, instead of mirroring and reflecting back Alice's image, leads her into other fantastical spaces' (*Making Girls into Women: American Women's Writing and the Rise of Lesbian Identity* [Durham: Duke University Press, 2003], 175). Kent rightly notes that 'the *M* multiplying [...] signif[ies] abundance, the many identificatory possibilities that Moore offers Bishop' (178), calling up the multiplication of images that occur in the space of the mirror.
60 Bishop, *Collected Prose*, 137.
61 Bishop, *Complete Poems*, 188.

Chapter 7

BECOMING A CHILD: LEWIS CARROLL AND VIRGINIA WOOLF'S POETICS OF FLUIDITY AND PERMANENCE

Teresa Prudente

Published in December 1939, Woolf's review of *The Complete Works of Lewis Carroll* both recapitulates Woolf's extensive (and multifaceted) work on childhood perception and singles out the essence of Carroll's work, by offering insight into the peculiarities of the fellow writer while also displaying Woolf's reflection on her own poetics. Woolf's view of Carroll as a 'conglomerate object',[1] escaping fixed definition, is strongly connected to her emphasis on the 'confuse, diffuse, tumultuous' nature of the human soul,[2] and, as I will show, also anticipates Deleuze's analysis of Alice's adventures as performing the 'paradox [...] which destroys common sense as the assignation of fixed identities'.[3] In this chapter, I intend to use Woolf's remarks on Carroll as a point of departure in order to retrace the pattern connecting the two authors, particularly following their shared interest in recreating the complex relationship between perception and language in childhood. As we shall see, this pattern entails elements of convergence and divergence, as well as of fluidity and permanence, especially in relation to what Deleuze has defined as 'the paradox of pure becoming', wherein 'it is language which fixes [...] the limits, but it is language as well which transcends the limits and restores them to the infinite equivalence of an unlimited becoming'.[4] Many of the elements constituting the 'common ground' between Woolf and Carroll, as well as the differences between them, seem indeed to rotate around the double-faceted quality that renders language simultaneously as a fixed/fixing element and as an ever-moving phenomenon – an aspect which, interestingly, Deleuze observes in both Woolf's and Carroll's writing.[5]

Woolf's review of the edition of Carroll's *Complete Works* published by Nonesuch Press in 1939 coincided with her work on two very different forms of life writing: her biographical *Roger Fry* (1940) and her autobiographical 'A Sketch of the Past' (1939). In both cases Woolf was confronted with the task of rendering the unfolding of the events of a life, an idea which challenged the very nucleus of her experimentation, pointed at crystallizing life perceived not as 'a series of gig lamps symmetrically arranged', but rather as 'a luminous halo, a semi-transparent envelope surrounding us from the beginning of consciousness to the end'.[6] With

'A Sketch of the Past', Woolf was free to recreate the past – through glimpses of her childhood – by displaying the interdependence of *moments of being* and *moments of non-being* and the fragmented nature of one's progression in time. For *Roger Fry*, the writer instead strongly felt the conventions imposed by the genre of biography,[7] especially its very assumption of providing an exhaustive account of a life. The point interestingly coincides with her remarks on the impossibility of getting the 'complete' Lewis Carroll, either through his work or through his life:

> So there is no excuse – Lewis Carroll ought once and for all to be complete. We ought to be able to grasp him whole and entire. But we fail – once more we fail. We think we have caught Lewis Carroll; we look again and see an Oxford clergyman. We think we have caught the Rev. C. L. Dodgson – we look again and see a fairy elf. The book breaks in two in our hands. In order to cement it, we turn to the Life. But the Rev. C. L. Dodgson had no life.[8]

In this sense, Woolf's review meaningfully intersects with her coeval work on forms of life-writing, while also touching upon central points of her poetics: the permanence of the past into the present, and the way childhood shapes one's identity. Along the same lines, reviewing Carroll's work also offered Woolf the opportunity to reconsider a predecessor who had an influence in shaping the imagination of her generation[9] and make him obliquely converge with her development as a writer.

In 'A Sketch of the Past', Woolf was free to go back to her most typical treatment of memory, which had fully emerged in *To the Lighthouse*: the interplay between linear unfolding and re-presencing of the past through flashes. As opposed to the 1927 novel, narration in the first person as well as the idea itself of drawing a 'sketch' produced, in this case, an original mixture of diary and fiction, where the expanded moment recollected from the past co-exists with the narrative extension provided by the unfolding of the history of the family. This idea of development – or, as I will show, of constant transformation in time – indeed proves to be a key concept in Woolf's writing, and is one of the issues that I intend to tackle in relating her work to Carroll's oeuvre. In order to do so, I will place Woolf's ideas on Carroll in the context not only of the aforementioned 'Sketch of the Past', but also the slightly earlier *The Waves* (1931). Woolf's interest for the modalities of recollection of childhood memory and perception is prominent throughout her work, and famously central to *To the Lighthouse* (1927), for which she meant to have 'all characters boiled down; & childhood; & then this impersonal thing […] the flight of time, & the consequent break of unity in my design'.[10] With *The Waves* Woolf appears to expand on the impersonal element ('this shall be Childhood; but it must not be my childhood […] unreality; things oddly proportioned'),[11] and the novel provides a poignant example of the dynamics of permanence and fluidity, especially in the way language is employed and reflected upon. In this sense, I will retrace convergences between Woolf's and Carroll's poetics both in her review and in *The Waves*, a work that the writer expected 'to form in me could I let my mind lie asleep',[12] and that displays similarities to Carroll's 'wildly inconsequent, yet perfectly logical world [...] the world of sleep [...] the world of dreams'.[13] At the same time, the analysis of *The Waves* will allow me to show how her emphasis on processes – of language acquisition, of experience re-elaboration – taking place in time unveils divergence from Carroll's 'pure and entire' recreation of the dimension of childhood.[14]

The Crystal of Childhood

In her review, Woolf's portrayal of Carroll employs a set of dichotomies that touch upon the foundation of her work on childhood, perception, and language. The focus is especially on the dynamic interaction between hard and soft – or more accurately, malleable – matter. Carroll's life is seen by Woolf as an 'untinted jelly': he 'passed through life [...] melted passively', and 'slipped through the grown up world like a shadow, solidifying only on the beach of Eastbourne'.[15] In contrast to the blurred nature of his life, his 'solidif[ication]' of personality occurs in his preservation of childlike perception within himself: the 'hard block of pure childhood' which 'lodges in him pure and entire'.[16] Significantly, Woolf sees the childhood that Carroll 'could not disperse' as 'a perfectly hard crystal',[17] thus mobilizing a central image of her own work on the dynamics between permanence and fluidity. The metaphor of the crystal traverses Woolf's oeuvre in multiple directions, from the process of fixing the fleeting 'moment of being' ('any turn in the wheel of sensation has the power to crystallise and transfix the moment upon which its gloom or radiance rests'[18]) to 'the crystal, the globe of life',[19] described by Bernard in *The Waves*. The multiform nature that the image of the crystal acquires in Woolf may explain why Carroll's 'hard block of pure childhood' is also portrayed as an 'impediment' which 'starved the mature man of nourishment'.[20] This, I argue, unveils a difference of focus in the two writers' portrayal of childhood, as Carroll's ability of returning to that phase ('he could recreate it, so that we too become children again')[21] is something that 'no one else has ever been able to do',[22] but also implies renouncing the chance of looking at it from a distance, a feature that Woolf stresses as fundamental for retrieving meaning from past experience. In providing her famous definition of 'moments of being', Woolf underlined how such moments of intensity could only be mastered and understood in time: 'I was conscious – if only at a distance – that I should in time explain it [....] This suggests that as one gets older one has a greater power through reason to provide an explanation.'[23]

Similar to the multi-directionality characterizing the solid bodies of crystals, Woolf's employment of the crystalline metaphor is charged with several opposing implications. In the early short story 'The Evening Party' (1920), the image is already related to childhood perception:

Don't you remember in early childhood, when, in play or talk, as one stepped across the puddle or reached the window on the landing, some imperceptible shock froze the universe to a solid ball of crystal which one held for a moment—I have some mystical belief that all time past and future too, the tears and powdered ashes of generations clotted to a ball; then we were absolute and entire; nothing then was excluded; that was certainty – happiness.[24]

The images and vocabulary featuring here will appear again in 'A Sketch of the Past', where the author changes the above 'shock [that] froze the universe into a solid ball of crystal' into the famous 'shock-receiving capacity' that the author identifies as 'what makes me a writer'.[25] Nonetheless, the 'solid ball of crystal' also connects with the images of solid, circular figures pervading *The Waves*, but the crystal appears there to have undergone a meaningful transformation: 'the crystal, the globe of life as one calls it, far from being hard and cold to the touch, has walls of thinnest air. If I press them all will burst'.[26]

The crystal serves then as a transforming metaphor across Woolf's works, embodying both a stable, 'absolute and entire' nucleus ('some absolute good, some crystal of intensity'[27]), and a malleable element which loses its hard quality to become porous and expanding to the bursting point. As previously mentioned, emphasis on fluidity and on the capacity of questioning conventions and fixed identity is a shared trait in Woolf's and Deleuze's views of Carroll's work. It is thus meaningful that Deleuze's characterization of Carroll's writing resorts to the same image of the crystal seen, not as a fixed element, but rather as ever-expanding material. For Deleuze, Carroll takes up the operation 'inaugurated by the Stoics' and 'examines the difference between events, things and states of affairs'.[28] The conception of events in Carroll entails an inversion between surface and depth,[29] as:

> events are like crystals, they become and grow only out of the edges, or on the edge. This is first secret of the stammerer or the left-handed person: no longer to sink, but to slide the whole length in such a way that the old depth no longer exists at all, having been reduced to the opposite side of the surface.[30]

The crystal is a topical image in Deleuze's thinking, and especially in his work on cinema, where it comes to represent the mutual interchange of actual and virtual images taking place in the cinematic medium. As such, the crystal-image, a coalescence of actual and virtual ('distinct but indiscernible'), is both solid ('the solidity of finished crystal') and internally subdivided ('ultimately a peak or point, but a physical point which has distinct elements [a bit like the epicurean atom]'), 'visible and limpid' as well as 'invisible, opaque and shadowy'.[31] This double nature is closely tied to the relationship the Deleuzean crystal-image entertains with time:

> What constitutes the crystal-image is the most fundamental operation of time: since the past is constituted not after the present that it was but at the same time, time has to split itself in two at each moment as present and past, which differ from each other in nature, or, what amounts to the same thing, it has to split the present in two heterogeneous directions, one of which is launched towards the future while the other falls into the past. [...] Time consists of this split, and it is this, it is time, that we *see in the crystal*. The crystal-image was not time, but we see time in the crystal.[32]

According to Deleuze, the paradoxical nature of the crystal-events portrayed by Carroll establishes a bi-directionality, showing 'the capacity to elude the present [...] the infinite identity of both directions or senses at the same time – of future and past, of the day before and the day after'.[33] This indubitably connects with Woolf's focus on the fleeting moment as a convergence of past, present, and future. Nevertheless, Woolf's insistence that childhood seemed to have remained in Carroll in its 'absolute and entire' quality also appears to point to the two authors' different perspectives. The process of gradual fading and the presence of the past in the present in the form of fragments – key features of Woolf's poetics – are in fact the forms of experience that Carroll seems to have evaded, according to Woolf: 'for childhood normally fades slowly. Wisps of childhood persist when the boy or girl is a grown man or woman. Childhood returns sometimes by day, more often by night. But it was not so with Lewis Carroll'.[34] The two authors appear thus to look at childhood from different perspectives: whereas Carroll recreates infancy from within, as an intact dimension, Woolf rather focuses on its retrospective and fragmented re-appropriation. For Woolf this entails recreating in writing those processes, unfolding in time, which transform the subject's relationship with perception and language: a transformation that, as I will show, requires negotiation with limits and conventions, but also provides the hermeneutic tools to bestow meaning on one's experience.

'I can't explain myself': Language and the Challenge of I-less Perception

According to Woolf, Carroll's ability to make us 'become children' lies in his portrayal of the world of childhood as a land akin to dreams, where 'time races, then stands still; where space stretches, then contracts' with the characters 'turning and changing one into the other [...] skipping and leaping across the mind'.[35] Perception out of proportion is also what Woolf underlines in her own recollection of childhood in 'A Sketch of the Past': 'many bright colours; many distinct sounds; some human beings, caricatures; comic; several violent moments of being; always including a circle of the scene which they cut out: and all surrounded by a vast space'.[36] In this sense, the experience of childhood is portrayed as navigating a space that exceeds normal proportion but also displays a complex structure ('that great Cathedral space which was childhood').[37] This is rendered by the paratactic prose employed by Woolf in the passage and, in particular, by her use of semi-colons, which help recreate the simultaneous sense of disjunction ('distinct') and inter-connectedness among the elements composing the scene.[38] Moreover, both in her review of Carroll's works and in 'A Sketch of the Past', Woolf's stress is on movement, the perpetual transformation which is the essence of the kaleidoscopic world of childhood:

> But somehow into that picture must be brought, too, the sense of movement and change. Nothing remained stable long. One must get the feeling of everything approaching and then disappearing, getting large, getting small, passing at

different rates and speed past the little creature; one must get the feeling that made her press on, the little creature driven on as she was by growth of her legs and arms, driven without her being able to stop it, or to change it, driven as a plant is driven up out of the earth, up until the stalk grows, the leaf grows, buds swell. That is what is indescribable, that is what makes all images too static, for no sooner has one said this was so, then it was past and altered.[39]

The above-quoted passage contains remarkable similarities to Carroll's depiction of Alice's perception, not only with respect to her confrontation with an ever-changing world, but also to her passivity as she is 'driven', to use Woolf's word, to a series of experiences she can hardly grasp. The disjunct between Alice and the surrounding Wonderland characters obviously amplifies the child's passivity and becomes especially visible in the various instances when interaction is precluded: when Alice first goes trough the looking-glass ('I feel somehow as I was getting invisible),[40] and when she asserts her presence with a question, 'the King took no notice of the question: it was quite clear that he could neither hear her nor see her'.[41] Language becomes thus the opposite of a tool of communication and rather magnifies the untellability of the child's experience. For Woolf, the key to this ineffability ('what is indescribable') lies in movement, as the 'static' quality of language seems unable to catch the dynamism of childhood perception. This is clearly a paramount issue of Carroll's portrayal of Alice's adventures, from the relentless moving of time ('"the rest next time – " "It *is* next time!"'[42]) to the perennial transformation affecting both the character and the world surrounding her. Nonetheless, with both writers, this extends beyond the portrayal of a specific perceptual stage, and instead addresses the very relationship between language, subject, and experience.

As Robin Lakoff has singled out, Alice's 'subversive' adventures destabilize many of our certainties about the pragmatic function of language, starting with the idea of reference, which 'depends crucially upon object and personal constancy':

If language is to refer reliably to reality, so that speakers can be confident of its ability to transmit meaning, those objects and persons referred to must remain, in some sense, the same. Constancy is implicit in and basic to the social contract that enables us to live as social beings, devising and using linguistic conventions and making sense to ourselves and one another. But in W/LG constancy cannot be counted upon.[43]

If in both *Alice* books the dynamism pertains especially to the fantastic external reality that the character is experiencing, it is nonetheless clear that the portrayed instability symbolically mirrors how the *in fieri* nature of the child makes them a highly unsteady deictic centre of experience. This is overtly alluded to in the way Alice's identity is questioned throughout her fantastic journeys: the Caterpillar asks '"Who are you?"' and Alice responds '"I – I hardly know, sir, just at present – at least I know who I *was* when I got up this morning, but I think I must have been changed several times since then."'[44] Moreover, the relentless changes Alice is subjected to ('I must have been changed') result in what Deleuze terms 'the loss of the proper name',[45] an event which first affects her linguistic abilities, since, as Alice discovers, utterances are grammatically and pragmatically bound to the identification of the speaker:

> 'What do you mean by that?' said the Caterpillar sternly, 'Explain yourself!'
> 'I ca'n't explain *myself*, I'm afraid, Sir,' said Alice, 'because I'm not myself, you see [....] I'm afraid I ca'n't put it more clearly [...] for I ca'n't understand it myself, to begin with; and being so many different sizes in a day is very confusing [....] Well, perhaps *your* feelings may be different [...] all I know is, it would feel very queer to *me*.'
> 'You!' said the Caterpillar contemptuously. 'Who are *you*?'
> Which brought them back again to the beginning of the conversation.[46]

The circularity in which – here as well as in many other instances in both books – dialogic interaction is trapped depends heavily on the *literal* sense bestowed by the characters on utterances, an issue to which I will return. What is relevant, however, in this specific example, is how the questioning of identity deconstructs the conventions on which the speech act rests: the fact that the deprivation of a solid meaning bestowed on the 'I' also determines the questioning of the employment of the same pronoun as one of the deictic coordinates for the speech act.[47]

It is on this point, specifically, that I would like to look at potential convergences between Carroll's linguistic deconstruction in *Alice's Adventures in Wonderland* and *Through the Looking-Glass* and Woolf's challenge at recreating 'eyeless' (and I-less) perception in *The Waves*.[48] Among the most striking features of the 1931 novel is the fact that the 'series of dramatic soliloquies' structuring the work[49] – a form to which Woolf had come after many revisions[50] – point to I-centred narration, while, in fact, they orchestrate a perspectival deconstruction aimed at making 'one thing, not enduring – for what endures? – but seen by many eyes simultaneously'.[51] The first chapter of the novel, in particular, which portrays the six characters in childhood, opens precisely on a series of short statements positioning each character as the isolated centre of perception:

> 'I see a ring,' said Bernard, 'hanging above me. It quivers and hangs in a loop of light.'
> 'I see a slab of pale yellow,' said Susan, 'spreading away until it meets a purple stripe.'
> 'I hear a sound,' said Rhoda, 'cheep, chirp; cheep chirp; going up and down.'
> 'I see a globe,' said Neville, 'hanging down in a drop against the enormous flanks of some hill.'
> 'I see a crimson tassel,' said Jinny, 'twisted with gold threads.'
> 'I hear something stamping,' said Louis. 'A great beast's foot is chained. It stamps, and stamps, and stamps.'[52]

These initial utterances recreate the child's experience in purely sensorial terms, similar to how – as we have seen – Woolf will later describe it in 'A Sketch of the Past', and they also set a frame of confrontation between language and the senses. The overtly fictive linguistic competence bestowed here on the characters seems to align their complex sensorial experience to language, filling that gap between perception and expression, which dominates childhood and which is also one major element of Alice's wondering through lands exceeding her interpretative and communicative skills.[53] At the same time, the unrealistic hyper-competence of the characters and the anti-mimetic form of their exchange come to compose a minute account of the stages involved in the processes of perception and expression, both synchronically – via the de-construction of the perceptual act into its single components – and diachronically, tracing the entire parabola of language acquisition (and ultimately, as I will show, dis-acquisition).

Already in these initial pages, the problem of 'subject and object and the nature of reality' disarticulates the utterances in stages,[54] where firstly objects are seen from the perspective of the self, and, secondly, they are given in a more objective form: '"The leaves are gathered round the window like pointed ears," said Susan.'[55] Time is initially erased from the suspended dimension from which the children speak, which is tied to the present tense of description. Subsequently, motion enters time in the form of a series of successive nows,[56] and then in that of the present perfect tense ('Biddy has smacked down the bucket on the kitchen flags'[57]), providing the scene with the temporal depth it had until that moment lacked. In the passage from I-centred ('I see') to object-centred expression ('The leaves') another meaningful expressive shift takes place, as Bernard's act of pointing ('Look at the spider's web'[58]) opens a space of shared deixis among the characters, whom the readers had first encountered as isolated perceptual subjects deprived of a clear spatio-temporal location. This inaugurates the constant atomistic movement of distancing and re-assembling of the characters that dominates the novel, making them, at the same time, six individual entities as well as – at times – one single undifferentiated organism: '"But when we sit together, close," said Bernard, "we melt into each other with phrases. We are edged with mist. We make an unsubstantial territory."'[59] Interestingly, the dynamism between indistinguishability and differentiation, which marks the pattern of development of the characters of *The Waves*, shares several similarities with the fluidity of identity and language in the *Alice* books.

As we have seen, Alice's bewilderment when she enters Wonderland ('"How queer everything is to-day! And yesterday things went on just as usual."'[60]) is expressed by her wondering about her identity, which appears to have changed along with the metamorphosis of the surrounding world. For Alice, searching for her identity means, in the first place, trying to retrieve what distinguishes her from other subjects:

> 'I'm sure I'm not Ada,' she said, 'for her hair goes in such long ringlets, and mine doesn't go in ringlets at all; and I'm sure I ca'n't be Mabel, for I know all sorts of things, and oh, she! She knows such a very little! Besides, *she's* she, and *I'm* I, and – oh dear, how puzzling it all is!'[61]

A similar pattern emerges in *The Waves* when the characters progress from the osmotic perception of early childhood to acknowledging their individual identities. Bernard defines himself at the end of the novel, like Alice, by differentiating himself from others: "'Therefore,' I said, 'I am myself, not Neville,' a wonderful discovery."[62] At the same time, the pattern traced by *The Waves* does not entail a univocal movement of progression, but rather it draws an elastic temporal arch constituted by intermittent phases: "'We changed, we became unrecognizable,' said Louis. "Exposed to all these different lights, what we had in us (for we are all so different) came intermittently, in violent patches, spaced by blank voids, to the surface as if some acid had dropped unequally on the plate. I was this, Neville that, Rhoda different again, and Bernard too."'[63] Thus, the emergence of individual identities ('some crack in the structure – one's identity'[64]) co-exists with moments when the characters re-experience the blurring of the boundaries between their minds. This happens, in particular, when they re-assemble in their youth, and their communication again takes the form of the complementary soliloquies featured at the beginning of the novel.[65] Nonetheless, the passing of time has changed their perspective on that initial osmosis, inserting that sense of loss which is one of the key elements of Woolf's retrieval of childhood. As Bernard recalls from yet another temporal perspective:

> We saw for a moment laid out among us the body of the complete human being whom we have failed to be, but at the same time, cannot forget. All that we might have been we saw; all that we had missed, and we grudged for a moment the other's claim, as children when the cake is cut, the one cake, the only cake, watch their slice diminishing.[66]

The sense of collectivity, of being able to go in and out each other's minds is now felt, from the perspective of adult life, as an impossible dream, something that becomes even unthinkable, as it happens with the voices *thinking* in chorus in *Through the Looking-Glass*:

> Alice thought to herself 'Then there's no use in speaking.' The voices didn't join in *this* time, as she hadn't spoken, but to her great surprise, they all *thought* in chorus (I hope you understand what *thinking in chorus* means – for I must confess that *I* don't), 'Better say nothing at all. Language is worth a thousand pounds a word!'[67]

In *The Waves*, the sense of melting with other subjects ('I am not one person; I am many people; I do not altogether know who I am – Jinny, Susan, Neville, Rhoda, or Louis; or how to distinguish my life from theirs'[68]) or, better, the memory of that lost osmosis, keeps shaking the sense of identity of the characters. In this sense, the novel's dissolution of the 'I' originates both from a self-emptying process ('I have been traversing the sunless territory of non-identity'[69]), and from the act of merging with others. Similarly, Alice's identity is questioned by Humpty Dumpty's remarks on her indistinguishability from others: "'I shouldn't know you again if we *did* meet [...] you're so exactly like other people.'"[70]

As mentioned, it is this undermining of identity which, in the first place, challenges the limits of language by depriving the linguistic medium of one of its main deictic referents. In *The Waves*, this ignites a process of linguistic deconstruction that, as we shall see, will ultimately bring the subject back to the 'inarticulate' expression capable of conveying the perpetually mobile nature of both the world and the self:

> But how describe the world seen without a self? There are no words. Blue, red
> – even they distract, even they hide with thickness instead of letting the light
> through. How describe or say anything in articulate words again? – save that
> it fades, save that it undergoes a gradual transformation, becomes, even in the
> course of one short walk, habitual – this scene also.[71]

'To be very literal': Learning and Un-Learning Language

In both the *Alice* books and *The Waves*, the definition of individual identity, and how flexible this will then prove to be, goes hand in hand with the acquisition of knowledge. As we have seen, Alice quickly shifts from comparing herself to the other children in physical terms to contrasting their mental abilities, or more appropriately, the possession of notions acquired through education. This, however, proves now, in the new dimension she has entered, entirely useless:

> 'I'll try if I know all the things I used to know. Let me see: four times five is twelve,
> and four times six is thirteen, and four times seven is—oh dear! I shall never get
> to twenty at that rate! However, the Multiplication-Table doesn't signify: let's try
> Geography. London is the capital of Paris, and Paris is the capital of Rome, and
> Rome—no, that's all wrong, I'm certain! I must have been changed for Mabel!'[72]

Symbolically, this appears to question knowledge acquired through accumulation, linear proceeding, and definitions, a form of learning whose inflexibility becomes readily useless when the subject is displaced in a dimension where reference points have shifted. The role of education is similarly depicted in *The Waves*, when the characters transition from the purely sensorial experience of early childhood to the 'orderly progress' of school.[73] Education is seen as providing the comfort of order and safe belonging: "'Now we march, two by two," said Louis, "orderly, processional, into chapel. I like the dimness that falls as we enter the sacred building [....] We file in; we seat ourselves. We put off distinctions as we enter"'.[74]

At the same time, education is also what deprives the subject of their individual identity: "'the purple light," said Rhoda, "in Miss Lambert's ring passes to and fro across the black stain on the white page of the Prayer Book. [...] We shall write our exercises in ink here. But here I am nobody. I have no face. This great company, all dressed in brown serge, has robbed me of my identity"'.[75] Rhoda's inability to adapt to the order and categories imposed by education is part of her incapability of translating into language 'the arrows of sensation',[76] 'the rushing stream of broken dreams'[77] of perception:

> 'Louis writes; Susan writes; Neville writes; Jinny writes; even Bernard has now begun to write. But I cannot write. I see only figures. The others are handing in their answers, one by one. Now it is my turn. But I have no answer. […] The figures mean nothing now. Meaning has gone.'
>
> 'There Rhoda sits staring at the blackboard,' said Louis, '[…] her mind lodges in those white circles, it steps through those white loops into emptiness, alone. They have no meaning for her. She has no answer for them. She has no body as the others have[.]'[78]

In the novel, words first enter the children's perception as external elements belonging to the same living world they are exploring: '"They flick their tails right and left as I speak them," said Bernard. "They wag their tails; they flick their tails; they move through the air in flocks, now this way, now that way, moving all together, now dividing, now coming together."'[79] Woolf provides a similar description of words in her essay 'On Craftmanship': 'They hate anything that stamps them with one meaning or confines them to one attitude, for it is their nature to change. Perhaps that is their most striking peculiarity – their need of change. It is because the truth they try to catch is many-sided, and they convey it by being themselves many sided, flashing this way, then that.'[80] This living quality does not prevent words, however, from providing the subject with the sense of order and the categories that will allow them to begin mastering experience: '"Each tense," said Neville, "means differently. There is an order in this world; there are distinctions, there are differences in this world, upon whose verge I step. For this is only a beginning."'[81] In this sense, language is portrayed both as a limited/limiting tool and as an element essential to tie the subject to the 'real world', as it allows them to circumscribe their perception and single out their identity. Interestingly, in *Through the Looking-Glass*, Humpty Dumpty's famous questioning of reference[82] – '"When I use a word," Humpty Dumpty said in rather scornful tone, "it means just what I choose it to mean – neither more nor less"'[83] – also relies on the example of verbs as the most imposing of grammatical categories: '"They've a temper some of them – particularly verbs: they're the proudest – adjectives you can do anything with, but not verbs – however, I can manage the whole lot of them! Impenetrability! That's what *I* say!"'[84] Words are seen here, like in *The Waves*, as living organisms:

> 'When I make a word do a lot of work like that,' said Humpty Dumpty, 'I always pay it extra.'
> 'Oh!' said Alice. She was too much puzzled to make any other remark.
> 'Ah, you should see 'em come round me of a Saturday night,' Humpty Dumpty went on, wagging his head gravely from side to side, 'for to get their wages, you know.'[85]

Woolf's and Carroll's shared emphasis on how language operates both as a living organism and as an imposing convention also finds a theoretical meeting point in Bertrand Russell's work, to which both authors have been connected.[86] In *The Waves*, the stages of language acquisition undergone by the children show several overlaps with the philosopher's distinction between 'knowledge by acquaintance' and 'knowledge by description'.[87] Acquaintance with objects comes to be exemplified when at the end of the novel Bertrand recollects the path that has led the children to adult life: 'But meanwhile, while we eat, let us turn over these scenes as children turn over the pages of a picture-book and the nurse says, pointing: "That's a cow. That's a boat."'[88] The act of learning by establishing a one-noun/one-meaning relationship strongly re-echoes Russell's language of 'givenness' of 'presentation' which takes form in the act of naming, or 'simply pointing': 'The only true "logically proper name" is the demonstrative "this" [....] A term like "this" refers to an object of acquaintance, particular or universal. It gives no information beyond indicating its presence.'[89] Nonetheless, knowledge through acquaintance fails to account for 'things not present, not apprehensible', that require instead 'knowledge by description, which includes knowledge of non-apprehensible entities, either absent or non-existent',[90] a problem famously alluded to in *To the Lighthouse* ('think of a kitchen table [...] when you're not there'[91]).

In Russell's theory of descriptions, 'the language which refers to absent objects can [...] fail to denote any object at all without being nonsensical',[92] and this has been linked to Carroll's famous treatment of 'nobody' as a quantifier in *Through the Looking-Glass*: '"I see nobody on the road", said Alice. "I only wish *I* had such eyes", the King remarked in a fretful tone. "To be able to see Nobody! And at that distance too! Why, it's as much as *I* can do to see real people, by this light!"'[93] Such questioning of the referentiality of language leads us back to one of the aspects underlined by Woolf in her review: the fact that becoming children, for Carroll, also means 'to be very literal'.[94] Many of the aforementioned misunderstandings present in the *Alice* books appear to result from a *literal* employment of language that unveils the conventions underlying the linguistic medium:

> Edwin and Morcar, the earls of Mercia and Northumbria, declared for him; and even Stigand, the patriotic archbishop of Canterbury, found it advisable –
> 'Found *what*?' said the Duck.
> 'Found *it*', the Mouse replied rather crossly: 'of course you know what "it" means.'
> 'I know what "it" means well enough, when *I* find a thing', said the Duck: 'it's generally a frog, or a worm. The question is, what did the archbishop find?'[95]

Carroll's works come to shake the idea of univocal reference in two opposing directions ultimately nullifying the concept: on the one hand, the infinite proliferation of meanings of Humpty Dumpty's portmanteaus and, on the other, the reduction of language to pure designation – in Russell's terms – in the episode of the wood 'where things have no name'.[96] The fact that both episodes belong to *Through the Looking-Glass* reinforces the idea of a shift between the first and the second book, as 'in LG [Alice] is older and somewhat wiser: having discovered that there are rules, like all new converts (and early language learners) she expects everything to work by those rules: she overgeneralizes'.[97] Thus, the misunderstanding in the quoted passage from *Alice's Adventures in Wonderland* – when the preparatory object 'it' is revealed in its redundant nature, as the sentence is stopped before the actual object is introduced – evolves into the more radical unveiling of the void of reference behind grammatical particles in the passage about 'nobody' in *Through the Looking-Glass*. In this sense, the literal employment of language that Woolf underlines in Carroll seems to point to the ability of the nineteenth-century author to recreate an 'innocent' language that unveils the semantic gaps of linguistic conventions; it is also an 'irresponsible' language ('only Lewis Carroll [...] has made us laugh as children laugh, irresponsibly'[98]) that lays bare the illusion of referentiality.

This last point, however, seems also to disclose how Carroll and Woolf display different focuses in their portrayals of childhood. As mentioned, the process depicted by Woolf in *The Waves* provides a double-faceted view of the relationship between subject and language. Russell's idea of language as a scaffolding, a logical form, indubitably requires the subject to accept the symbolic nature of the relationship linking experience and expression. A sign of this is shown early in the novel: when the characters shift from I-centred to object-centred description, they also immediately resort to figurative language ('"The leaves are gathered round the window like pointed ears," said Susan'[99]), thus showing how the analogic language of simile is needed to fill the gap of referentiality between perception and expression. Nonetheless, in the novel, language is also portrayed as allowing the subject to filter their experience ('I must make phrases and phrases and so interpose something hard between myself and the stare of housemaids.'[100]) and come to order it in a sequence: 'Let him describe what we have all seen to that it becomes a sequence. Bernard says there is always a story. I am a story. Louis is a story.'[101]

Yet, with a further reversal, in the last chapter of the novel the character of the writer, Bernard, expresses his need to revert to 'inarticulate' forms of expression. He starts: 'Also, how I distrust neat designs of life that are drawn upon half-sheets of note-paper. I begin to long for some little language such as lovers use, broken words, inarticulate words, like the shuffling of feet on the pavement. [...] Of story, of design, I do not see a trace then'.[102] Then later: 'Out rush a bristle of horned suspicions, horror, horror, horror – but what is the use of painfully elaborating these consecutive sentences when what one needs is nothing consecutive but a bark, a groan?'[103] In search of an impossible 'exactitude' ('There is about both Neville and Louis a precision, an exactitude, that I admire and shall never possess.'),[104] Bernard has been 'eternally engaged' in the process 'of finding some perfect phrase that fits this very moment exactly'.[105] The 'perfect phrase', however, has always escaped him, and he is in fact 'breasting the world with half-finished sentences',[106] or, as described in the last chapter, 'unfinishing phrase[s]'.[107] What intervenes in the last section of the novel seems to be a new awareness of the imperfect relation entertained by the subject with language, one that entails accepting the degree of mystification involved in linguistic expression: 'Let us again pretend that life is a solid substance, shaped like a globe, which we turn about in our fingers. Let us pretend that we can make out a plain and logical story, so that when one matter is despatched – love for instance – we go on, in an orderly manner, to the next.'[108]

This seems to reposition the subject into the frame of the overlapping of fiction and reality characterizing childhood (as per Alice's phrase: "let's pretend"[109]), while at the same time pointing to the subject's awareness of the illusion of coherence and significance provided by linguistic and narrative conventions. These conventions seem essential to making communication possible, as they allow the mastering of the 'cauldron' from which Bernard 'retrieve[s experience] from formlessness with words'.[110] In *The Waves*, refusing them leaves the subject on the dangerous verge of the impossible: 'I said life had been imperfect, an unfinishing phrase. It had been impossible for me, taking snuff as I do from any bagman met in a train, to keep coherency.'[111] The same happens to Alice as the character plunges into a dimension which 'precedes all good sense and all common sense'[112]: 'For, you see, so many out-of-the-way things had happened lately, that Alice had begun to think that very few things indeed were really impossible.'[113] In the paradoxical dimension of Wonderland, as Deleuze notices, language itself 'seems impossible, having no subject which expresses or manifests itself in it, no object to denote, no classes and no properties to signify according to a fixed order'.[114] In *The Waves*, the conscious turn from the infinite possibilities – bordering with the impossible itself – of childhood to adult life entails instead the acceptance of language, in both its fertile possibilities and the imperfect way it mediates communication:

> But unfortunately, what I see (this globe, full of figures) you do not see. You see me, sitting at a table opposite you, a rather heavy, elderly man, grey at the temples. You see me take my napkin and unfold it. You see me pour myself out a glass of wine. And you see behind me the door opening, and people passing. But in order to make you understand, to give you my life, I must tell you a story – and there are so many, and so many – stories of childhood, stories of school, love, marriage, death, and so on; and none of them are true.[115]

Woolf's insistence on Carroll's recreation of the 'perfectly hard crystal of childhood' seems indeed to unveil how the *Alice* books represent for her the portrayal of a self-enclosed world – 'the world upside down as a child sees it,'[116] as Woolf puts it – whose rules include the impossibility of the subject distancing themselves and looking at it from a temporally distant perspective. This is instead what happens in the last chapter of *The Waves*, when Bernard looks back at the sensorial experience of childhood:

> And by some flick of a scent or a sound on a nerve, the old image – the gardeners sweeping, the lady writing – returned. I saw the figures beneath the beech trees at Elvedon. The gardeners swept; the lady at the table sat writing. But I now made the contribution of maturity to childhood's intuitions – satiety and doom; the sense of what is unescapable in our lot; death; the knowledge of limitations;

how life is more obdurate than one had thought it. Then, when I was a child, the presence of an enemy had asserted itself; the need for opposition had stung me. I had jumped up and cried, 'Let's explore.' The horror of the situation was ended.[117]

Meaningfully, the passage shows many similarities with how Woolf describes the interdependence between moments of being and the process of writing in 'A Sketch of the Past'. Here she also reflects on the role of writing in her passage from childhood innocence to adult experience:

> I hazard the explanation that a shock is at once in my case followed by the desire to explain it. I feel that I have had a blow; but it is not, as I thought as a child, simply a blow from an enemy hidden behind the cotton wool of daily life; it is or will become the revelation of some order; it is token of some real thing behind appearances; and I make it real by putting it into words. It is only by putting it into words that I make it whole; this wholeness means that it has lost its power to hurt me; it gives me perhaps because by doing it I take away the pain, a great delight to put the severed parts together.[118]

As we have seen, the capacity of language of offering the subject the tools to master and express their experience is in fact treated problematically in *The Waves*. Instead, language appears, no less than in Carroll's works, to translate the subject's perception in an imperfect way, one that only provides an illusion of order, sequence, and – ultimately – meaning. Bernard's awareness of language as the medium providing the subject with the possibility of conveying and sharing their experience goes hand in hand with his realization that such an attempt at expression will always be arbitrary and partial: 'Whatever sentence I extract whole and entire from this cauldron is only a string of six little fish that let themselves be caught while a million others leap and sizzle, making the cauldron bubble like boiling silver, and slip through my fingers.'[119] The ever-moving quality of experience, its unlimited borders and ever-evolving nature, determine a permanent failure in the way the 'static' components of language try to adhere to the 'pure becoming' of experience: 'for no sooner has one said this was so, then it was past and altered'.[120] At the same time, in both Carroll's and Woolf's work, language is challenged in a way capable of making the limits and the infinite potentialities of the medium emerge simultaneously, by encapsulating the awareness of the potential void of reference inherent in language via a 'litterature'[121] made of 'a litter of fragments'.[122] In this sense, the work of the two authors appears to intersect in that both question the fixity of conventions – of language and identity – via the recreation of the fluid, porous and ever-moving state of childhood; at the same time their modalities of writing take different directions in terms of temporal reconfiguration. Woolf's perspective on Carroll proves revealing to understand such divergent paths, as her stress on how Carroll allows the reader to plunge again into the 'intact' dimension of childhood unveils her different focus, more pointed at recreating how our relationship with childhood and language transforms in time. The two authors' complementary, yet divergent perspectives allow the elements structuring the experience of childhood – and the adult retrieval of it – to emerge in that same multifaceted form of the crystal which has served as a central metaphor for this chapter: perfect and entire yet fluid, ever-present yet distant, and characterized by an uncompromising, unconventional relationship with language that remains, in adult life, under the form of an awareness of that lost original first meeting between experience and expression.

Notes

1   Virginia Woolf, 'Lewis Carroll' (1939), in *Collected Essays*, vol. 1 (London: The Hogarth Press, 1966), 255.
2   Virginia Woolf, 'The Russian Point of View' (1925), in *Collected Essays*, vol. 1 (London: The Hogarth Press, 1966), 242.
3   Gilles Deleuze, *The Logic of Sense*, trans. Mark Lester and Charles Stivale, ed. Constantin V. Boundas (London: The Athlone Press, 1990), 3.
4   Ibid., 2–3.
5   The observation on Woolf can be found in Felix Guattari, *Capitalism and Schizophrenia: A Thousand Plateaus*, trans. Brian Massumi (London: Continuum Books, 2004), 309. Deleuze's *The Logic of Sense* explores this with reference to Carroll.
6   Virginia Woolf, 'Modern Fiction' (1919), in *The Crowded Dance of Modern Life: Selected Essays*, vol. 2 (London: Penguin, 1993), 8.
7   See Woolf's essay 'The Art of Biography' (1939), in *The Crowded Dance of Modern Life: Selected Essays*, vol. 2 (London: Palgrave, 1999), 144–51. On Woolf's relationship with the *genre* of biography see Elena Gualtieri, 'The Impossible Art: Virginia Woolf and Modern Biography', *Cambridge Quarterly* 29, no. 4 (2000): 349–61; Federico Sabatini, 'Archiving the Unarchivable: The Role of Archives in the Biographical Writing of Virginia Woolf and Lytton Strachey', *Textus, English Studies in Italy* 27, no. 3 (2015): 119–38.
8   Woolf, 'Lewis Carroll', 254.
9   Juliet Dusinberre, *Alice to the Lighthouse* (London: Palgrave Macmillan, 1999), 2. On the topic see also: Lois Gilmore, 'Where Childhood's Dreams Are Twined": Virginia Woolf and the Literary Heritage of Lewis Carroll', in *Virginia Woolf and Heritage*, ed. Jane deGay, Tom Breckin, and Anne Reus (Clemson: Clemson University Press, 2018), 121–6.
10   Virginia Woolf, *The Diary of Virginia Woolf*, vol. 3, ed. Anne Olivier Bell and Andrew McNeillie (London: Penguin, 1982), 36.
11   Woolf, *Diary*, 236.
12   Ibid., 249.
13   Woolf, 'Lewis Carroll', 255.
14   Ibid., 254.
15   Ibid.
16   Ibid.
17   Ibid.
18   Virginia Woolf, *To the Lighthouse* (London: Penguin, 1996), 9.
19   Virginia Woolf, *The Waves* (Oxford: Oxford University Press, 1992), 214.

20 Woolf, 'Lewis Carroll', 254.

21 Ibid.

22 Ibid.

23 Virginia Woolf, 'A Sketch of the Past', in *Moments of Being: Unpublished Autobiographical Writings* (London: The Hogarth Press, 1978), 72.

24 Virginia Woolf, 'The Evening Party', in *A Haunted House. The Complete Shorter Fiction*, ed. Susan Dick (London: Vintage, 2003), 92.

25 Woolf, 'Sketch', 78.

26 Woolf, *Waves*, 214.

27 Woolf, *Lighthouse*, 197.

28 Deleuze, *Logic of Sense*, 9.

29 The concept of 'event' would need an extensive treatment for its philosophical and linguistic implications. I will have to omit discussing the point here for reasons of space, but I would like to point out at least one significant occurrence of the term in *The Waves*: 'While one straightens the fork so precisely on the table-cloth, a thousand faces mop and mow. There is nothing one can fish up in a spoon; nothing one can call an event. Yet it is alive too and deep, this stream' (Woolf, *Waves*, 213).

30 Deleuze, *Logic of Sense*, 9.

31 Gilles Deleuze, *Cinema 2: The Time Image*, trans. Hugh Tomlinson and Robert Galeta (London: The Athlone Press, 1989), 70.

32 Ibid., 81.

33 Deleuze, *Logic of Sense*, 2.

34 Woolf, 'Lewis Carroll', 254.

35 Ibid., 255.

36 Woolf, 'Sketch', 79.

37 Ibid., 81. For the representation of space in Carroll's work, also with reference to the coeval debate on Euclidean and non-Euclidian geometry, see Gillian Beer, *Alice in Space: The Sideways Victorian World of Lewis Carroll* (Chicago: Chicago University Press, 2016).

38 On Woolf's use of semi-colons see Maria DiBattista, 'Virginia Woolf and the Language of Authorship', in *The Cambridge Companion to Virginia Woolf*, ed. Sue Roe and Susan Sellers (Cambridge: Cambridge University Press, 2000), 127–45; Elena Minelli, 'Punctuation Strategies in the Textualization of Femininity: Virginia Woolf Translated into Italian', *New Voices in Translation Studies* 1 (2005): 56–69; Teresa Prudente, *A Specially Tender Piece of Eternity. Virginia Woolf and the Experience of Time* (Lanham: Lexington Books, 2009); Teresa Prudente, '"The Daily Bread of Experience": The Transfiguration of Materiality in Woolf and Joyce', *English* 60, no. 229 (2011): 142–58.

39 Woolf, 'Sketch', 79.

40 Lewis Carroll, *Alice's Adventures in Wonderland* and *Through the Looking-Glass*, ed. Hugh Haughton (London: Penguin, 1998), 128.

41 Ibid., 129.

42 Ibid., 6.

43 Robin T. Lakoff, 'Lewis Carroll Subversive Pragmaticist', *Pragmatics* 3, no. 4 (1993): 372.

44 Carroll, *Alice*, 40–1.

45 Deleuze, *Logic of Sense*, 3.

46 Carroll, *Alice*, 41.

47 As per Lyons's classical definition of deixis: 'By deixis is meant the location and
    identification of persons, objects, events, processes and activities being talked about,
    or referred to, in relation to the spatiotemporal context created and sustained by the
    act of utterance and the participation in it, typically, of a single speaker and at least
    one addressee' (John Lyons, *Semantics* [Cambridge: Cambridge University Press,
    1977], 637). See also Judith F. Duchan, Gail A. Bruder, and Lynne E. Hewitt, eds.,
    Deixis in Narrative. A Cognitive Science Perspective (Hillsdale: Lawrence Erlbaum
    Associates, 1995).

48 'That was to be an abstract mystical eyeless book: a playpoem' (Woolf, *Diary*, 203).
    On how 'eyeless' may be interpreted also as 'I-less' see Julia Briggs, 'The Novels of
    the 1930s and the Impact of History', in *The Cambridge Companion to Virginia Woolf*
    (Cambridge: Cambridge University Press, 2000), 72–90.

49 Woolf, *Diary*, 312.

50 On Woolf's compositional process of *The Waves* see Julia Briggs, *Virginia Woolf:
    An Inner Life* (London: Penguin, 2005); Finn Fordham, *I Do, I Undo, I Redo: The
    Textual Genesis of Modernist Selves in Hopkins, Yeats, Conrad, Forster, Joyce, and
    Woolf* (Oxford: Oxford University Press, 2010); Teresa Prudente, 'From "The Aloe"
    to "Prelude" and from The Moths to The Waves: Drafts, Revisions and the Process
    of "Becoming-Imperceptible" in Virginia Woolf and Katherine Mansfield', *Textus,
    English Studies in Italy* 27, no. 3 (2015): 95–118.

51 Woolf, *Waves*, 104.

52 Ibid., 5.

53 On this point see especially Nina Auerbach, 'Alice and Wonderland: A Curious Child',
    Victorian Studies 17 (1973): 31–47, and Jan B. Gordon, 'The Alice Books and the
    Metaphors of Victorian Childhood', in *Aspects of Alice: Lewis Carroll's Dream-Child as
    Seen through the Critics' Looking-glasses*, ed. Robert Phillips (New York: The Vanguard
    Press, 1971), 93–113.

54 Woolf, *Lighthouse*, 38.

55 Woolf, *Waves*, 5.

56 Ibid., 6.

57 Ibid., 7.

58 Ibid., 5.

59 Ibid., 11.

60 Carroll, *Alice*, 17.

61 Ibid., 18.

62 Woolf, *Waves*, 201.

63 Ibid., 103.

64 Ibid., 94.

65 Ibid., 91–120.

66 Ibid., 231.

67 Carroll, *Alice*, 146.

68 Woolf, *Waves*, 230.

69 Ibid., 95.

70 Carroll, *Alice*, 192.

71 Woolf, *Waves*, 239.

72 Carroll, *Alice*, 18–19.

73 Woolf, *Waves*, 25.

74 Ibid., 25–6.

75 Ibid., 25.

76 Ibid., 200.

77 Ibid., 213.

78 Woolf, *Waves*, 15–16.

79 Ibid., 14.

80 Virginia Woolf, 'On Craftsmanship' (1937), in *The Crowded Dance of Modern Life: Selected Essays*, vol. 2 (London: Penguin, 1993), 143.

81 Woolf, *Waves*, 15.

82 In the philosophy of language, the issue is referred to as the 'Humpty Dumpty Problem'. See Eliot Michaelson and Marga Reimer, 'Reference', *The Stanford Encyclopedia of Philosophy*, ed. Edward N. Zalta (spring 2019), https://plato.stanford.edu/archives/spr2019/entries/reference/. See also *Semiotics and Linguistics in Alice's Worlds*, ed. Rachel Fordyce and Carla Marello (Berlin: de Gruyter, 1994).

83 Carroll, *Alice*, 186.

84 Ibid.

85 Ibid., 187.

86 Russell also famously offered a solution for Carroll's 1895 re-proposal of the Zeno paradox. For more elements of connection between Russell and Carroll, among which the strange resemblance of Tenniel's Mad Hatter to Russell, see S. P. Rosenbaum, *Aspects of Bloomsbury* (London: Palgrave, 1998), 41–2.

87 Ann Banfield, *The Phantom Table: Woolf, Fry, Russell, and the Epistemology of Modernism* (Cambridge: Cambridge University Press, 2000), 85–8.

88 Woolf, *Waves*, 200.

89 Banfield, *Phantom Table*, 86. See also Deleuze on this point: 'There are many relations inside a proposition. […] The first is called denotation or indication. It is the relation of the proposition to an external state of affairs (*datum*). […] certain words in the preposition, or certain linguistic particles, function in all cases as empty forms for the selection of images, and hence for the denotation of each state of affairs. It would be wrong to treat them as a universal concept, for they are formal particulars (*singuliers*) which function as pure "designators" or, as Benveniste says, as indexical (*indicateurs*). These formal indexicals are: this, that, it, here, there, yesterday, now, etc.' (Deleuze, *Logic of Sense*, 13).

90 Banfield, *Phantom Table*, 86.

91 Woolf, *Lighthouse*, 38.

92 Banfield, *The Phantom Table*, 87.

93 Carroll, *Alice*, 194.

94 Woolf, 'Lewis Carroll', 255.

95 Carroll, *Alice*, 25.

96 Ibid., 152.

97 Lakoff, 'Pragmaticist', 371.

98 Woolf, 'Lewis Carroll', 255.

99 Woolf, *Waves*, 5.

100 Ibid., 22.

101 Ibid., 28.

102 Ibid., 199.

103 Ibid., 210.

104 Ibid., 54. On the idea of exactitude see also the interesting portmanteau 'exactually' in *Through the Looking-Glass*: '"I'm seven and a half, exactly." "You needn't say 'exactually'", the Queen remarked' (Carroll, *Alice*, 174).

105 Woolf, *The Waves*, 54.

106 Ibid., 55.
107 Ibid., 236.
108 Ibid., 210.
109 Carroll, *Alice,* 14, 124.
110 Woolf, *Waves*, 214, 225.
111 Ibid., 236.
112 Deleuze, *Logic of Sense*, 79.
113 Carroll, *Alice*, 13.
114 Deleuze, *Logic of Sense*, 79.
115 Woolf, *Waves*, 199.
116 Woolf, 'Lewis Carroll', 255.
117 Woolf, *Waves*, 224.
118 Woolf, 'Sketch', 72.
119 Ibid., 214.
120 Ibid., 79.
121 In his 'Preface' to *Sylvie and Bruno*, Carroll uses the term 'litterature': 'I found myself at last in possession of a huge unwieldy mass of litterature – if the reader will kindly excuse the spelling – which only needed stringing together, upon the thread of a consecutive story, to constitute the book I hoped to write'(Lewis Carroll, 'Preface to *Sylvie and Bruno*', in *The Complete Work by Lewis Carroll* [London: Nonesuch Press, 1939], 256).
122 Woolf, *Diary,* 287; see also: 'what a litter – what a confusion' (Woolf, *Waves*, 237).

Chapter 8

'REELING AND WRITHING' IN BENJAMIN'S *ARCADES*: THE CURIOUS CASE OF THE GIRL WHO WASN'T THERE

Lisa Mullen

In his *Passagenwerk* (*The Arcades Project*), Walter Benjamin is emphatic. 'Task of childhood: to bring the new world into symbolic space', he writes. 'The child, in fact, can do what the grown up absolutely cannot: recognize the new once again.'[1] The figure of the child as a conduit of the new is explicitly linked to the dreamer in Benjamin's political imagination. The dreaming child is not innocent or passive: she is a revolutionary, a powerful agent of change, infused with radical insight. Yet Benjamin's reference to her – embedded here in the file marked 'Dream City and Dream House, Dreams of the Future, Anthropological Nihilism, Jung'[2] – is harder to unpack than it might first appear. What might it mean to carry a hermeneutically unencumbered new world into a realm of symbols pre-populated by existing archetypes? What meanings might fuse or rupture? And how, except in paradox, can the new, which has never been seen before, be recognized *again*?

This chapter suggests that we may find a key to such questions in the 'Dream City and Dream House' of Lewis Carroll's two *Alice* books. For is not the curious Alice precisely the kind of fearless 'child-critic' who was Benjamin's ideal interpreter of the capitalist world?[3] As he writes elsewhere, quoting Baudelaire: 'The child sees everything in a state of newness; [s]he is always drunk. [...] It is by this deep and joyful curiosity that we may explain the fixed and animally ecstatic gaze of a child confronted with something new.'[4] As the nineteenth-century prototype of the acquisitive modern consumer, entranced by novelty, the insatiably curious Alice personifies consumption: she is always on the look-out for invitations to 'EAT ME' or 'DRINK ME',[5] though she discovers that Wonderland's tempting products transform her in ways she did not expect or want. Falling asleep on the Oxford riverbank in the first book, or by the crackling fireside in the second, she dreams of the nineteenth century in all its self-contradictions, strictures, and reified symbols of the old order. When she awakens, she enters into a new kind of empowered consciousness, just as any good Benjaminian critic ought to do. Moreover, her two adventures seem to map a distinctly Benjaminian terrain of troubling thresholds: in Wonderland, she free-falls vertically into the 'dream-city' hierarchy of the

Queen of Heart's chaotic *polis*, and emerges by overturning the illusionary house of cards; in the Looking-Glass world, she crosses sideways through the domestic 'Dream House' mirror and discovers the dizzying possibilities revealed when the social rules of a homely *oikos* are confronted by a restless imagination. In both, she approaches the meaning-void of nineteenth-century social structures with an unflinching gaze, and awakens to a modernity in which things can no longer be expected to conform to a bourgeois idea of rationality and linear progress. 'As a matter of fact', as Benjamin records, 'if the rule of the bourgeoisie were one day to be stabilized [...] then the vicissitudes of history would in actuality have no more claim on the attention of thinkers than a child's kaleidoscope, which with every turn of the hand dissolves the established order into a new array.'[6]

From different directions, Benjamin and Carroll arrive at a similar intimation: that the apparent stability of the norms and expectations of industrial society is an illusion. Carroll the logician was aware that any claim of truth was built on lines of carefully calibrated contradiction and tension; Benjamin the Marxist saw capitalism, not as an iron-clad economic construct, but as a rickety contraption which functioned only by the smoke-and-mirror workings of fetishization and reification. He also understood that this collective hallucination found its most meaningful manifestation far away from the factories and smoke-stacks of industrialized labour; rather, it was revealed in the immersive phantasmagorias of popular amusement: in the glassed-in wonderlands of shopping arcades and the cock-eyed pavilions of world exhibitions; in the immersive illusions of cheap dioramas and waxwork displays; in domestic interiors clogged with plush fabrics whose nap recorded every scuff and fingerprint; in the grubby backstreets where smoky coffee-rooms and gambling dens sprouted. Carroll sent Alice down such strange passageways in order to refresh the adult world with her curious gaze. The modernist subjects who followed in her wake could move through these same conceptual spaces in twentieth-century Paris. They were enwreathed by the faded glamour of the nineteenth-century flâneur, but they also inhabited a realm of dreams. Like Alice, they were out of their element: clue-hunters, engaged in an interpretative experiment, where signs become more meaningful the more their instability is acknowledged, and the solution is contained in the confusion. This chapter, then, will twist the Carrollian/Benjaminian kaleidoscope back and forth: moving in one direction, it will suggest a Benjaminian reading of the *Alice* books which discloses an emergent critique of the established order of the nineteenth-century bourgeois thing-world; rotating the other way, it will look for clues and traces left by Alice in the ruins of Benjamin's *Arcades*. The first of these tasks is sanctioned by Benjamin's own approach to literary interpretation; the second, by his professed interest in the *Alice* books.

As a reader, Benjamin rejected mere commentary as the fruitless labour of a drudge: like Carroll's Gryphon, he favoured intellectual 'adventures first' because 'explanations take such a dreadful time'.[7] The critic's job – according to Benjamin's essay on 'Goethe's Elective Affinities' – is to abjure paraphrase and exegesis in favour of a radical unveiling of the text's immanent but occluded salience.[8] In the *Arcades Project*, he compares his type of critical history with the Eiffel Tower, which offers a 'slender but sturdy scaffolding' that 'hangs suspended in the air' and through which 'things stream' and 'lose their distinctive shape, swirl[ing] into one another'.[9] This could just as well be a description of the *Alice* books themselves as it is of the 'immanent critique' which Benjamin favoured, and which this chapter also attempts. Inevitably, such a reading is implicitly ideological, and if Carroll's books shrug off simplistic political allegory, we nevertheless find within them a sharp unease about his era's obsession with empty status (as represented by the despotic idiocy of royalty) and value (where a hatter might be doomed to wear a perpetual price tag on his own self-made hat). There is evidence in Carroll's pamphlets and letters to newspapers that he had a pragmatic sense of politics as a means of achieving ethics and justice.[10] More importantly, his literary interest in paradox and nonsense, which clearly lampoons the contradictions and aporias of rigid rationalism, goes some way to sanctioning a reading of Alice's dream-world as a place of dialectical images and revolutionary stirrings.

Benjamin clearly found it so. In a letter to Gretel Karplus, wife of Theodor Adorno, from January 1936, he writes, rather testily: 'Naturally I am familiar with *Alice in Wonderland*. It is in fact the only book of which I know a few pages in English. For it is those pages that I chose as the basis for my useless attempts to teach myself that language.'[11] He was responding to a letter Karplus had written in which she declared she was 'utterly captivated by the famous children's book' and found it a pity he could not read enough English to enjoy it himself.[12] Benjamin's reply suggests that he considered it an essential text which any intellectual might be expected to know: he went on to explain that he had not only read it in translation, but had seen the 1933 film version by Norman Z. McLeod: 'It is an extraordinary affair', he writes, 'and is naturally also held in high esteem by the Surrealists.'[13]

It is easy to imagine why an attempt to learn English by reading *Wonderland* might have faltered in the text's thicket of unexplained allusions, untranslatable puns, and unresolved ambiguities. For Benjamin, though, translation was never a matter of mere transfer from one language to another; rather, it exemplified a necessary and dialectical deferral of semantic closure. In 'The Task of the Translator' (1923), he examines the relative translatability of different texts, arguing that attempting to find blurry equivalences, or render basic information intelligible by brute force, was 'the hallmark of bad translations': 'No translation would be possible if in its ultimate essence it strove for likeness to the original',[14] he writes. Good translations, on the other hand, arise from works of a richly poetic and symbolic nature, and should reveal fundamental truths about language itself; the mismatch between one language and another is a 'representation of hidden significance', suggesting meaning through 'analogies and symbols'.[15]

Alice is just the kind of text that would make this kind of rich translation so complicated. Like the Mad Hatter's insoluble riddle – 'Why is a raven like a writing desk?'[16] – Carroll's phantasmagorias both promote and collapse analogy whenever possible, overtly challenging any notion of an algebraic equivalence between the symbolic and the real ('Alice felt dreadfully puzzled. The Hatter's remark seemed to her to have no sort of meaning in it, and yet it was certainly English'[17]). Metaphor comes to literal – and recalcitrant – life in Alice's encounters with communal English folk images, such as the mad March hare (first print appearance in 1528); hackneyed similes like the grinning Cheshire cat (a commonplace since 1788); or the mad hatter (a more recent addition to the cliché lexicon, dating to 1829). Though these comparisons have since become vividly and permanently associated with Carroll, when he was writing they were the kind of worn-out images so embedded in their habitual meaning that they cease to mean anything at all. In his text they spring back defiantly into the realm of the creaturely. The Cat, the Hare, and the Hatter are in revolt against their own symbolic burden, shaking off the shackles of their algorithmic equivalences in order to stand up and speak for themselves. And what they speak of is the upsetting of rules. The Cat and his grin, rather than signifying smug satisfaction, become instead a sinister harbinger of the disintegration of normality: 'We're all mad here. I'm mad. You're mad'.[18] These animated tropes partake of the particular kind of fluid signification which Benjamin found in key works across centuries of textual history, from the Kabbalah to surrealism; as he wrote in his thesis on German baroque tragedy: 'The many obscurities in the connection between meaning and sign [...] did not deter, they rather encouraged the exploitation of ever remoter characteristics of the representative objects as symbols [...] so that one and the same object can just as easily signify a virtue as a vice, and therefore more or less anything.'[19] Nor is this semiotic waywardness relevant only to Benjamin's literary criticism; it is the key to his political understanding of the mythologies of commodification as well: 'Any person, any object, any relationship can mean absolutely anything else. With this possibility a destructive but just verdict is passed on the profane world: it is characterized as a world in which the detail is of no great importance.'[20]

In Carroll's universe, this collapse of meaning is presented as playful, but it is predicated on a deeply unsettling premise. Alice's encounter with Humpty Dumpty, during her excursion through the looking-glass, highlights her struggle with an eruption of semantic waywardness:

> 'When *I* use a word,' Humpty Dumpty said, in a rather scornful tone, 'it means just what I choose it to mean – neither more nor less.'
> 'The question is,' said Alice, 'whether you *can* make words mean so many different things.'
> 'The question is,' said Humpty Dumpty, 'which is to be master – that's all.'[21]

Yet Humpty Dumpty's oppressive 'mastery' of meaning leads to semantic sterility. Cut off from ambiguity and nuance, he is unable to function either personally or poetically. He produces a piece of plodding doggerel in place of an amusing poem, and admits that he cannot distinguish one individual from the next: 'I shouldn't know you again if we *did* meet [...] you're so exactly like other people.'[22] In this, he is precisely the opposite of the child-critic as a super-recognizer of novelty; his fall will shatter him, and though Alice sees the king's horses and men arrive, she is not interested enough to find out whether or not his fragments can be put back together. In this, he contrasts sharply with the childlike White Knight, whose facility with wild, nonsensical invention is revealed in his chaotically assembled get-up – which survives repeated tumbles from his horse – and in his rambling, variously titled poem 'Haddocks' Eyes', which Alice listens to 'in a half-dream'. Crucially, this liminal state adds clarity rather than vagueness. Alice's experience of this 'whole scene' is drenched in the vividness of a snapshot: the dazzling gleam of the sun, the shadows of the forest, 'all this she took in like a picture' so that it remained sharp 'for years afterwards [...] as if it had been only yesterday'. The special quality of the Knight's performance is emphatically underlined; 'Of all the strange things that Alice saw in her journey', we are told, it was this that she 'always remembered most clearly'.[23]

For Benjamin, too, a story's value could be measured by its ability to access the listener at a semi-conscious level, and this was key to the power of the oral epic as well as the folktale, which delivered important knowledge through images received in an almost trance-like state. As he writes in 'The Storyteller' (1936): 'The first true storyteller is, and will continue to be, the teller of fairy tales. Whenever good counsel was at a premium, the fairy tale had it, and where the need was greatest, its aid was nearest.'[24] For Carroll a successful teller of tales, like the White Knight, was likewise a teller of deep truth: a magician with the power to entrance the listener, but also to map the exploratory potential of the imagination itself. One of Alice's repeated tasks is to request and listen to stories, and to tell her own. Crucially, though, as we see in her conversation with the Mock Turtle in *Wonderland*, second-hand tales emerge transformed into something new in her recounting. At the same time, her own autobiography is similarly unstable, overtaken by the eternal present of the new: 'It's no use going back to yesterday', she tells the Mock Turtle, 'because I was a different person then.'[25]

When he first began work on the *Passagenwerk* in 1927–8, Benjamin was already describing it as a kind of radically transformative bedtime story, a 'dialectical fairy tale' [*dialektische Feerie*] which would 'liberate the enormous energies of history that are slumbering within the "once upon a time" of classic historical narrative'.[26] It seems likely that this interest in dream-narratives was what drew him to Carroll's books. According to his letter to Karplus, Benjamin read the translation of *Alice* in 1934, at a time when his project was entering a particularly urgent phase of reconfiguration.[27] He had decided that his embryonic history of nineteenth-century materialism was not sufficiently political, and in 1934 he returned to his notes with a new sense of purpose, embarking on a fresh round of conceptual shaping, and recalibrating the work as a more explicitly revolutionary project: in his words, 'less a galvanisation of the past than anticipatory of a more humane future'.[28] That this coincided with his exposure to Carroll adds an intriguing insight into this process. The new tranche of work culminated in a 1935 exposé of the project, written for Horkheimer's Institute for Social Research. In this outline, Paris's arcades become emblematic of the double history Benjamin wanted to write, because they speak both of the congealed material culture of the last century and the energizing ruptures which rippled out from the past through the present and into the future. These semi-derelict spaces 'are residues of a dream world', wherein '[t]he realization of dream elements, in the course of waking up, is the paradigm of dialectical thinking. [...] Every epoch, in fact, not only dreams the one to follow but, in dreaming, precipitates its awakening.'[29] If Alice is the ultimate nineteenth-century dreamer, perhaps what she dreams is the future collapse of her epoch's nonsensical fantasies: codes embedded in the text, and in the dusty rubbish of the Arcades, for Benjamin to decipher, decades later.

The historian's 'task of dream-interpretation',[30] as Benjamin describes it, involves reading and writing the past as a story which produces, in the telling, a collective of readers and listeners: co-dreamers capable of restructuring social relations from scratch. This insight arguably also functions as a political reading of the endings of Alice's two adventures. In the first, she awakens from Wonderland only when she defies the court of the King and Queen of Hearts to tell a revolutionary truth: that those who wield such total but petulant power are 'nothing but a pack of cards'.[31] This breaks the dream and brings her back to the reality of the Oxford riverbank, but it is not the end of the book: she then immediately recounts what she has dreamed, piecing it together in an act of interpretation which in turn triggers the reactivation of the same dream in another dreamer. In fact, fulfilling the role of the storyteller, the effect of Alice's tale is that her sister dozes into a reverie of her own, and 'the whole place around her bec[omes] alive with the strange creatures of her little sister's dream'.[32] For Benjamin, in 'The Storyteller', this kind of cognitive contagion was the mark of a tale which could bypass subjective narration and operate at a haptic, or even neurological, level: 'The more natural the process by which the storyteller foregoes psychological shading', he writes, 'the greater becomes the story's claim to a place in the memory of the listener, the more completely is it integrated into his own experience, the greater will be his inclination to repeat it to someone else someday, sooner or later.'[33]

The idea that dreams might not be personal, but may pass from individual to individual or are nested one within another, precisely describes the basis of political utopianism. It also informs the ending of the *Looking-Glass* dream: when Alice awakens to her wintry fireside, she does so in response to another uproar, this time at a feast where out-of-control domestic objects are in active revolt against their masters, and have started to get up out of their places and move around autonomously. Alice breaks this dream by accelerating the revolution, pulling the tablecloth out from under the objects piled upon it, so that they crash to the floor. She then shakes the Red Queen 'into a kitten',[34] before demanding that Kitty – who had 'been along with [her] all through the Looking-Glass World'[35] – help her to work out 'who it was that dreamed it all': '"it *must* have been either me or the Red King. He was part of my dream, of course – but then I was part of his dream, too!"' she muses.[36] This interpenetration of imaginative worlds extends even further, to the reader, in Carroll's closing question: 'Which do *you* think it was [that dreamed it all]?'[37] At this moment, the collective consciousness bursts through the covers of the physical book itself, to make contact with the reality of the reader, just as the materiality of the book-as-object is co-opted by Tenniel's two famous illustrations of Alice going through the Looking-Glass, which were printed on either side of the same page, and use the reader's physical act of turning it back and forth to flip Alice over from reality into dream-world.[38] The book itself is thus one of many uncanny objects the reader encounters, and takes its place among the animated and unruly objects in Carroll's dream-world.

Carroll's books are not, then, mere reveries suspended in a pillowy dreamtime: they contain sharp edges and rude awakenings of their own. Moreover, they prefigure exactly the type of modernist aesthetic work which most interested Benjamin, tapping into the mythology of their age and exposing it *as* myth, a seductive narrative riven by flaws and contradictions. For him, 'capitalism was a natural phenomenon with which a new, dream-filled sleep came over Europe and, through it, a reactivation of mythic forces'.[39] The temporal relationship between dream and history is a key part of Benjamin's political aim of interrogating the difference between the individualistic time of lived experience in the now, and the long-view, Marxian time of dialectical materialism. He felt that the best way of doing this was by examining the currents of art and literature for the 'dialectical images',[40] which emerge with a whizz and a bang from the conjunction – correctly perceived by the right kind of curious intellect – of the apparently banal objects and detritus which have washed up after the storm of industrialization and commodity culture. The meaning of such temporal flotsam is no longer fixed, but open to interpretation. 'Preserved in the arcades are types of collar studs for which we no longer know the corresponding collars or shirts', he writes, and the very fact that such out-of-date things have survived their own use-value shows that time and history do not progress smoothly by days and hours, but stutter and fold back around inanimate objects which have persisted from one era to the next.[41] While other modernist thinkers in Europe, influenced by Henri Bergson or Albert Einstein, were susceptible to the idea that time might intersect with human subjectivity in slippery ways, Benjamin specifically links this fluidity with the churn of value to which the most abject, mass-produced objects succumb: objects capable of revealing a whole philosophy of modernism in a flash of dialectical insight. 'We can speak of two directions in this work', he writes in an early sketch: 'in one which goes from the past into the present and shows the arcades, and all the rest, as precursors, and one which goes from the present into the past so as to have the revolutionary potential of these "precursors" explode in the present'.[42] Thus, the objects which wash up in the Arcades long after their heyday have something to tell modernism about the imminent, inevitable collapse of the monolithic certainties of the now.

Alice is the prototype of the curious, questioning modernist who can perceive this imminent precarity, and her thing-world is stuffed with objects out of time. From the moment the White Rabbit lures her down into Wonderland with his cry of 'Oh dear! Oh dear! I shall be too late!', it is the doubleness of time – the co-existence of the synchronic with the diachronic – that she is forced to confront.[43] The Mad Hatter, condemned for 'murdering the time' during a performance of 'Twinkle Twinkle Little Bat', helps her to understand history's troublesome dialectic with his eternal teatime ruled over by a watch that has stopped at six o'clock. And his plight is not just a logician's thought experiment. Like everything else in Wonderland, Time is concretized and given form and personality. 'Now if only you kept on good terms with [Time]', the Hatter explains to Alice, 'he'd do almost anything you liked with the clock'.[44] Like Benjamin's collector, whose job it is to notice and preserve history and truth in the residues of consumption, Alice must engage in a creative process of reading and writing – or, as Carroll would have it, 'Reeling and Writhing'[45] – as she passes through Wonderland, coaxing her own meanings out of the nonsense she finds at every turn, and tussling with language in her attempt to read a nineteenth-century cultural milieu which is attempting, in its turn, to wriggle off the hook.

In *The Arcades Project*, this process of reeling and writhing takes place through the mechanism of quotation, which constitutes so much of the material of the project itself. Quotation has an affinity with the dialectical image, because cut-up texts remind us that all meaning is contingent and friable. Benjamin's quotations readily come unstuck from their original context, as soon as he claims them as his own and sets them turning within new constellations of radical ideas. In this sense, too, Alice is a Benjaminian reader/writer. Once she discovers that she can no longer fit the bourgeois manners and rules of her upbringing onto the slithery framework of Wonderland logic, her very identity is assailed by ontological doubt ('Who are you?', the Caterpillar asks insistently, to which Alice replies 'I – I hardly know, Sir, just at present'[46]). And when she tries to remember herself through quotation – by 'repeat[ing] her lessons'[47] – she finds that the didactic moral texts she learned at home have been mangled by their new Wonderland context. Thus, 'Twinkle Twinkle Little Star' becomes a vivid but ridiculous image of a bat that is 'like' a tea tray; and Isaac Watts's moralistic poem 'How Doth the Little Busy Bee' is reconfigured as a self-sabotaging warning against the virtues of work, with the industrious bee transformed into a grinning crocodile who 'welcomes little fishes in, / With gently smiling jaws!'[48] In her baffling conversations with the creatures she meets, Alice comes to realize that the rules by which she has hitherto been defined cannot survive any sustained interrogation. It is not that Wonderland has subsided into nonsense, but that it exposes the flaw at the heart of her culture's ontological and epistemological suppositions, which purport to be common sense until they are put under the pressure of their own internal logic. Alice must reverse these discursive norms in order to see truly, and to do that she must undergo a series of translations and transformations.

The threshold between the dream-world and the waking world is always heralded, for Alice, by the uncanny presence of something that has passed between two states: the White Rabbit is the first example, while the black kitten which accompanies her back from her Looking-Glass dream is the rabbit's reverse analogue. Benjamin understood the importance of such transitional figures. In *The Arcades*, he notes that thresholds are properly presided over by modern, technological household gods: 'Threshold magic. At the entrance to the skating rink, to the pub, to the tennis court, to resort locations: *penates*. The hen that lays the golden praline-eggs, the machine that stamps our names on nameplates, slot machines, fortune-telling devices, and above all weighing devices [...] – these guard the threshold.'[49] Thresholds attract such instances of the uncanny because they are ambiguous spaces, 'neither on the inside nor truly in the open'.[50] In a passage reminiscent of Alice's looking-glass room, where 'the pictures on the wall next the fire seemed to be all alive, and the very clock on the chimney-piece [....] had got the face of a little old man',[51] Benjamin notes that 'the same magic prevails more covertly in the interior of the bourgeois dwelling. Chairs beside an entrance, photographs flanking a doorway, are fallen household deities, and the violence they must appease grips our hearts even today at each ringing of the doorbell.'[52]

In Benjamin's Paris, the arcades are themselves thresholds, signalling the importance of the city's interstitial spaces, hidden in plain sight. 'A new precinct begins like a step into the void,' he writes, so that the curious explorer finds themselves tumbling down rabbit holes at every turn.[53] Such observations lead Benjamin to ponder the deeper porosity of Paris: the catacomb-riddled ground it stands on providing a secret subterranean topography like the suppressed pre-industrial history of the city itself, where the 'lightning-scored, whistle-resounding darkness' of the Métro is presided over by 'sewer gods, catacomb fairies': 'Our waking existence [...] is a land which, at certain hidden points, leads down into the underworld – a land full of inconspicuous places from which dreams arise. All day long, suspecting nothing, we pass them by, but no sooner has sleep come than we are eagerly groping our way back to lose ourselves in the dark corridors.'[54] Again, Alice haunts this passage as a dweller in the rabbit warren who is ever alert to secret entrances, though many doors are locked and there are substances which Alice must eat and drink in order to gain entry into different parts of Wonderland. For Benjamin, Paris's glassed-in arcade passageways – themselves 'neither on the inside nor truly in the open' – operate as thresholds in the same way, presenting a moment of difficulty by which the dialectical dreamer will be alerted to the suspension of normal rules, and must be ready to adjust. Alice's transit through the Looking-Glass is likewise complicated by the magical powers that guard the threshold: she must negotiate a series of paths which seem to lead the right way, but twist confusingly back on themselves until she realizes she has to walk in the opposite direction.

For Benjamin, such looking-glass difficulties are to be expected. For him, mirrors are an essential component of the mythologizing glamour of capitalist illusion; their profusion in the arcades, he wrote, fills the space with 'the whispering of gazes'.[55] One of his notes reads:

A look at the ambiguity of the arcades: their abundance of mirrors, which fabulously amplifies the spaces and makes orientation more difficult. For although this mirror world may have many aspects, indeed infinitely many, it remains ambiguous, double-edged. It links: it is always this one – and never nothing – out of which another immediately arises. The space that transforms itself does so in the bosom of nothingness.[56]

Mirrors complicate the very notion of thresholds: 'Where doors and walls are made of mirrors', he writes, 'there is no telling outside from in.'[57] They are also at the heart of the optical novelties which Benjamin found so fascinating, and which, like a telescope-resembling kaleidoscope, seem to offer a view of the distance, but on examination only reveal their own tightly sealed, shifting interior, filled with the glass shards of history. The opening of Benjamin's 'Theses on the Philosophy of History' describes a famous mirror-based illusion, The Mechanical Turk, which dates back to the late eighteenth century and evokes Alice's encounter with both the hookah-smoking Caterpillar, and the Looking-Glass chess game:

> The story is told of an automaton constructed in such a way that it could play a winning game of chess, answering each move of an opponent with a countermove. A puppet in Turkish attire and with a hookah in its mouth sat before a chessboard placed on a large table. A system of mirrors created the illusion that this table was transparent from all sides. Actually a little hunchback who was an expert chess player sat inside and guided the puppet's hand by means of strings.[58]

As we have seen, the conceptual architecture of Wonderland – dreams and awakenings, tunnels and mirrors, fairy tales and childhood – repeatedly resonate with Benjamin's political imagination. *The Arcades Project* unearths the nineteenth-century thing-world which was Alice's playground, and which was archived both in Carroll's books and in the piles of old junk that mouldered in Paris's neglected shopping arcades. As Benjamin saw it, this archive not only produced but defined modernity. The Industrial Revolution had promised an abundance of mass-produced possessions accessible to all, but the result was the destruction of stable relationships between objects and the people who owned and used them; in place of this long-lost stability there came a constant, discomforting churn of value and devaluation which locked consumers into a Wonderland-style 'caucus race' for acquisition, with each individual running around in a frenzy with no sense of who was winning but a clear conviction that 'all must have prizes'.[59] 'In the nineteenth century', Benjamin wrote in 1935, 'the number of "hollowed out" things increases' because 'technical progress is continually withdrawing newly introduced objects from circulation'.[60] Commodities then become receptacles of fear and desire, just like the hollowed out but entrancing things Alice found, but could never quite grasp, on her own shopping trip: 'The shop seemed to be full of all manner of curious things – but the oddest part of it all was that, whenever she looked hard at any shelf, to make out exactly what it had on it, that particular shelf was always quite empty, though the others round it were crowded as full as they could hold.'[61]

Of course, Carroll himself was no enemy of commerce. In 1889 he invented his own piece of novelty merchandise, the Wonderland Postage-Stamp Case, to promote his books.[62] It performed a simple magic trick: on the front of the outer slip-cover was printed a picture of the Cheshire Cat in his tree, and the case inside bore the same picture, but with the Cat gone and just his grin in place; slipping the case in and out of its cover, you could make the Cat appear and disappear at will. This chapter has attempted something similar, using *The Arcades Project* and the *Alice* books as the two parts of a Wonderland Postage-Stamp Case: when we slide Carroll's fairy tale over Benjamin's sprawling, unfinished critique of capitalist history, each summons and reveals the other, disclosing their shared, playful attention to the kaleidoscopic fragment, the palimpsest, and the puzzle. And this accounts for another shared quality: the infinite interpretability of these entangled texts. Each reader appropriates *Alice* for themselves as Benjamin did, awakening new meanings from it according to their critical perspective. Likewise, Benjamin's magic mirror both invites and deflects the reader who seeks definitive positions and insights: look into it, and Alice is just one of many images which may shimmer into view.

Notes

1   Walter Benjamin, *The Arcades Project*, trans. Howard Eiland and Kevin McLaughlin (Cambridge, MA: Harvard University Press, 1999), 390. This collection of files containing notes, quotations, and theoretical positions was curated and assembled by Benjamin between 1927 and 1940, and published posthumously, first in German in 1982, and then in English translation in 1999.
2   Benjamin, *Arcades*, 388–404.
3   See Esther Leslie, *Walter Benjamin: Overpowering Conformism* (London: Pluto Press, 2000), 76.
4   Benjamin, *Arcades*, 239.
5   Lewis Carroll, *Alice's Adventures in Wonderland* and *Through the Looking-Glass*, ed. Hugh Haughton (London: Penguin, 1998), 13–14.
6   Benjamin, *Arcades*, 339.
7   Carroll, *Alice*, 91.
8   Benjamin, 'Goethe's Elective Affinities', in *Selected Writings*, vol. 1 of 4, trans. Marcus Bullock et al. (Cambridge, MA: Harvard University Press, 1996–2003), 297.
9   Benjamin, *Arcades*, 459. Benjamin is quoting Siegfried Giedion.
10 See, C. L. Dodgson, *The Political Pamphlets and Letters of Charles Lutwidge Dodgson and Related Pieces: A Mathematical Approach*, ed. Francine F. Abeles (Charlottesville: Virginia University Press, 2001).
11 Gretel Adorno and Walter Benjamin, *Correspondence 1930–1040*, trans. Wieland Hoban, ed. Henri Lonitz and Christoph Gödde (Cambridge: Polity, 2008), 176.
12 Ibid., 175.
13 Ibid., 175–6. In his 1934 lecture, 'Qu'est-ce que le surréalisme?' André Breton included Carroll in a list of surrealists; he included a French translation of 'The Lobster Quadrille' in his *Anthologie de l'humour noir*. Adrienne Monnier had also written about the film in the January 1935 issue of the *Nouvelle Revue Français*: ('Alice au pays des merveilles', *Nouvelle Revue Français* 256 [January 1935]: 172–4). For an account of the influence of Lewis Carroll on French surrealist art, see Catriona McAra, 'Surrealism's Curiosity: Lewis Carroll and the *Femme-Enfant*', *Papers of Surrealism* 9 (summer 2011): 1–25.
14 Walter Benjamin, 'The Task of the Translator', in *Illuminations*, trans. Harry Zorn (London: Pimlico, 1999), 70–82; 73.
15 Ibid., 73.
16 Carroll, *Alice*, 60.
17 Ibid., 62.
18 Ibid., 57.
19 Benjamin, *The Origin of German Tragic Drama*, trans. John Osbourne (London: Verso, 1998), 174. Benjamin is quoting Carl Giehlow.

20 Benjamin, *Origin*, 175.
21 Carroll, *Alice*, 186.
22 Ibid., 192.
23 Ibid., 214.
24 Benjamin, 'The Storyteller', in *Illuminations*, trans. Harry Zorn (London: Pimlico, 1999), 102.
25 Carroll, *Alice*, 91.
26 Benjamin, *Arcades*, 863.
27 Adorno/Benjamin, *Correspondence*, 176. For a full chronology of Benjamin's composition of his notes, see Susan Buck-Morss, *The Dialectics of Seeing: Walter Benjamin and the Arcades Project* (Cambridge, MA: MIT Press, 1991), 48–52.
28 Letter from Benjamin to Adorno dated 18 March 1934 (Walter Benjamin, *Gesammelte Schriften*, vol. 5, ed. Rolf Tiedemann and Hermann Schweppenhauser [Frankfurt am Main: Surkamp, 1972], 1102). Translation taken from Buck-Morss, *Dialectics*, 49.
29 Benjamin, *Arcades*, 13.
30 Ibid., 464.
31 Carroll, *Alice*, 108.
32 Ibid., 109.
33 Benjamin, 'The Storyteller', 91.
34 Carroll, *Alice*, 234.
35 Ibid., 238.
36 Ibid., 239–40.
37 Ibid., 240.
38 Ibid., 215–26.
39 Benjamin, *Arcades*, 391. Benjamin's reading of the Paris finds mythology everywhere, from shop signage and building sites to the labyrinthine subway tunnels and ceremonial archways. He explores this mythological topography of the city most fully in Convolute C, 'Ancient Paris, Catacombs, Demolitions, Decline of Paris', 82–100.
40 Ibid., 11.
41 Ibid., 922.
42 Ibid., 862.
43 Carroll, *Alice*, 10.
44 Ibid., 63.
45 Ibid., 85.
46 Ibid., 41.
47 Ibid., 19.
48 Ibid., 63, 19.
49 Benjamin, *Arcades*, 214. See also similar notes on 86 and 88.
50 Ibid., 88.
51 Carroll, *Alice*, 127.
52 Benjamin, *Arcades*, 214.
53 Ibid., 88.
54 Ibid., 84.
55 Ibid., 878.
56 Ibid., 542.
57 Ibid., 537.
58 Walter Benjamin, 'Theses on the Philosophy of History', in *Illuminations*, trans. Harry Zorn (London: Pimlico, 1999), 245.
59 Carroll, *Alice*, 26.

60 Benjamin, *Arcades*, 466.
61 Carroll, *Alice*, 176.
62 See Lewis Carroll, *The Annotated Alice: The Definitive Edition*, ed. Martin Gardner (New York: Forum Books, 2000), 67, n5.

Chapter 9

'THESE TAUTOMERIC CHANGES': THE FIGURES OF ALICE AND HUMPTY DUMPTY IN THE WORK OF W. H. AUDEN

Allan Pero

Auden's 1962 essay titled 'Today's "Wonder-World" Needs Alice' reveals not only his long appreciation of Lewis Carroll's works, but also the way in which they offer useful lessons about the relationship of language to desire. If the contemporary world is, as Auden suggests, as arbitrary and chaotic as Wonderland, then Alice's level-headedness – her flexible-but-disciplined, imaginative-but-controlled notions of social and linguistic propriety – is surely meant to function as a tonic. Moreover, she, like an archetypal hero, is already what she will become.[1] In his 1954 review of Isaiah Berlin's study of Tolstoy, *The Hedgehog and the Fox*, Auden goes so far as to come up with his own classifications of men – not into steady, system-oriented hedgehogs or the glittering, magpie pursuits of foxes (a classification that Berlin derives from Archilochus), but instead into Alices and Mabels.[2] Mabel, of course, is Alice's dull, foolish schoolmate, against whom Alice compares herself at a moment of ontological crisis. Auden's Alice, we are told, possesses 'strong nerves' and 'a morality that was aesthetic' in character, while a Mabel embodies 'the intellectual with weak nerves and a timid heart', who thinks in utter binaries.[3] Yet Auden's point is more complex, more trifocal; as the experiences of Wonderland repeatedly show us, one's relationship to language is both personal and individual, both unconscious and conscious. Indeed, in Auden's introduction to his own edition of the *Oxford Book of Light Verse*, he singles out Carroll and Edward Lear as 'masters' of the kind of nonsense verse that 'appeals to the Unconscious and of poetry for children who live in a world before self-consciousness'.[4] One could say, then, that nonsense verse and Carroll's creation of 'a world where the divisions of class, sex, occupation did not operate'[5] lay bare not only the arbitrariness of these divisions, but also how we unconsciously and self-consciously repair to these discourses to contend with the nonsense that informs these divisions. In effect, Carroll's work is absurd and disturbing precisely because it applies pressure to the 'I', to the subject who is negotiating the failure of language to make seamless sense of Wonderland, to the 'I' who occupies the space between the Unconscious and self-consciousness. The 'I' who speaks thus occupies a third space, the gap between the individual and the personal, between what Jacques Lacan calls conscious speech and its unconscious enunciation. That is to say, as Auden repeatedly contends, *pace* Martin Heidegger – whom he read eagerly, but with ideological suspicion, in the 1940s and early 1950s – we are not the masters of language: language masters us. The subject's frustrated attempts to become the master of language, of meaning, that make up much of the Wonderland books, take on a special cast in Alice's encounters with Humpty Dumpty. Their clashes are linguistic, but they are also unconscious. They occupy the space between unconscious desire and the conscious desire to be the master of language, of meaning. This gap or disjunction is perhaps why Auden was so fascinated by Humpty Dumpty, as he included his 'song' in the *Oxford Book of Light Verse*, and wrote a long poem about the character early in his career.

In *Secondary Worlds*, his series of 1967 Memorial Lectures to T. S. Eliot, Auden links the desire to speak to other people to a need to find the words necessary to articulate what one has in mind. They are not 'ready-to-hand' in the way that purely informational and impersonal requests are.[6] In this respect, our individual use of language is actually a speaking of ourselves into consciousness and a self-consciousness that begins with our being named. Language shapes perception and consciousness by naming, by calling things into being; it does not merely designate or give names to objects. That said, our linguistic power is not nearly as Adamic as we might like to think. For Heidegger, poetry is offered as a privileged site precisely because it is less concerned with expression/communication than with creation through imagination; language speaks 'purely' in the sense that it can 'deny the poet's person and name' in its creation of worlds.[7] Auden attributes his appreciation of Alice in part to the fact that she knows that she is attempting to make sense, imaginative sense, out of Wonderland's anarchy, but also that that requires a fidelity to a particular phenomenal sense. As he puts it in the fourth and final lecture, 'Words and the Word': 'Now, however, there is no reason why any one [*sic*] should be either a doctrinaire naturalist or a doctrinaire aesthete, for the scientists have discovered that objective knowledge of things-in-themselves is not attainable.'[8] Auden concludes:

> We seem to have reached a point where, if the word *real* can be used at all, then the only world which is 'real' for us, as the world in which all of us, including scientists, are born, work, love, hate and die, is the primary phenomenal world as it is, as it always has been, presented to us through our senses.[9]

In this way, the secondary worlds of art and poetry are meant to be put in conversation with the primary one, rather than to be put in competition with it. This is perhaps why Auden invokes Alice in 'The Door', the first poem in his 1940 sonnet sequence, *The Quest*. We encounter the door as a liminal space opening onto 'Enigmas, executioners, and rules', a waiting Wonderland in 'sunshine' to which 'Enormous Alice' is drawn, and that 'Simply by being tiny, made her cry'.[10] If the quest is figured here as a site of existential becoming, then for Auden, Alice is herself an archetype of the kind of ideal hero, one who longs to step into the dream that is Wonderland, even as the anxieties of consciousness, naming, and decision are marked by the 'enraged phenomena' that attack and undermine the desire informing language, the very basis of consciousness and community.[11] As an aesthetic problem, it is for Auden also an existential one, one that he decides to investigate by coming at the question from another angle: by subjecting one of the *Looking-Glass* characters to the poetic and ontological rigours of dreamwork.

By way of example, I shall turn to a very early poem of Auden's, composed in summer 1926, titled 'Humpty Dumpty'. As Katherine Bucknell has noted, it carries echoes of T. S. Eliot and Edith Sitwell in its modernist fascination with the darker implications of nursery rhyme.[12] Since the poem is not one of Auden's better-known works, I shall begin with a long quotation:

> Dawn rose for hunting, trampling on the hills,
> Pushing the shadows down from lower ridges,
> Till one stood up and bared itself for glory,
> A clear horizon, and a single tree
> With dancing ring of children who would carry
> May to the village underneath them soon.[13]

As we see, the poem begins with the break of day, 'Pushing the shadows down from lower ridges', revealing not the sun, but a figure who 'stood up and bared itself for glory'. In the context of the poem's title, Auden's use of the term 'glory' immediately reminds us of Alice's encounter with Humpty Dumpty in *Through the Looking-Glass*. As Humpty Dumpty extols the quantitative virtues of un-birthday presents over birthday ones, he exclaims 'There's glory for you!'[14] Alice is puzzled, since he clearly does not mean glory in the sense of renown or magnificence, but sees it instead as the pledge and seal of his 'nice knock-down argument'.[15] A word like 'glory', he reminds Alice, 'means just what I choose it to mean – neither more nor less'.[16] As Lacan contends, what matters to Humpty Dumpty is thus not the meaning per se, but the enjoyment of exercising control over the troublesome parts of speech, of being the master of the signifier, but not of the signified.[17] He avoids the difficulties of the puzzle that is signification by claiming that whatever he proposes as logical is perforce logical.

Perhaps more crucially, Lewis Carroll contends that logic is not the means of mastering language (i.e., arbitrarily assigning meaning), but that it can be used to 'see *your way* through the puzzle',[18] linguistic or otherwise. Symbolic logic, once mastered, provides a clarity of thought, and the ability, 'more powerful than all, to detect *fallacies*' and thus avoids the deluding snares bedevilling those 'who have never taken the trouble to master this fascinating Art'.[19] We can counter Humpty Dumpty's private speech with a tautology, one upon which Heidegger asks us to meditate: 'Language is language.'[20] What is the difference between the subject and its predicate here? The visible difference is the capital 'L'. A tautology is a statement that apparently offers no new information. It is something that is logically the case, but it is not an example of empirical truth; one of the odd things about a tautology is that 'it is actually an analytical truth that depends logically on nothing in experience for its truth value'.[21] A lack of symbolic sense in tautology points, in a negative way, towards the limits of our ability to master signification; more specifically, it limits our capacity to master the signified. As George Pitcher, in his reading of Carroll and Wittgenstein, tells us, there is an important difference between a notion in the mind and its articulation in language, and it is wrong to assume that the clarity of the notion will necessarily make its translation into language a simple affair.[22] It frustrates the absolute determinism we might prefer language to have. Why? Because it opens up the abyss to which Heidegger refers; the apparent 'sameness' of subject and predicate places us in the position of looking at the abyss of tautology. What do we discover? Language, our master, represents language for and through us; it speaks. This is the truth of language; it speaks, not we.

Auden comes at the problem in another way, but arrives at a similar conclusion. We are individuals and persons, he reminds us, not one or the other: 'If we were only individuals, we should all be the same, and art could tell us nothing. If we were only persons, everyone's experience would be unique, and communication would be impossible.'[23] By implication, Alice's frustration with Humpty Dumpty is that he thinks exclusively like a person who imagines himself utterly sui generis, as the master of language, while everyone else, including Alice, is meant to behave and respond only like a mass of individuals, utterly the same, and thus unable to tell Humpty Dumpty anything he does not already know.

We, each of us, live with the illusion that the phrase 'I speak' is an ontological condition of being; Heidegger suggests that language produces a space for being, for us to exist. In this respect, we must draw a distinction between 'speech' and 'enunciation' (something that Lacan does in his reading of the subject's relation to language).[24] Language, for Lacan, is the unconscious operating at the level of enunciation. Speech is the conscious articulation of/by the ego to the world; enunciation is the unconscious articulation of the subject in language. Here again, we strike the limit of the subject's ability to master language. There is thus a gap or space between speech and enunciation; this gap is what we as subjects inhabit. In this space, which Auden calls the secondary imagination, we call forth a world. Poetry invents a world – that is, 'finds out' (from the Latin *inventus* – 'discover, find out') or 'invites in' the thing in its active (or, more specifically, actual) sense.[25] Language is, however idiosyncratically, granted a kind of power of invocation against which Humpty Dumpty arrogantly struggles. In this respect, even Humpty Dumpty does acknowledge that he is not an absolute master of language – verbs, especially, are deeply and perhaps unconsciously slippery, and remain resistant to his riddling 'impenetrability'.[26] It thus raises the question: If Alice is dreaming, or in the realm of the unconscious, is Humpty Dumpty an other who struggles with the difference between speech and enunciation, or is he a manifestation of Alice's own struggle with conscious and unconscious language? Is he an enigma, or does he operate in a space between speech as conscious citation and enigma as unconscious enunciation? In short, who is the dreamer and who is the dream? These questions emerge in the form of a riddle; just as Carroll's own 'Humpty Dumpty's Song' is a riddle, so, too, is Auden's poem 'Humpty Dumpty'. The answer may be as much about the intersection of the worlds of symbol and metaphor, of primary and secondary imagination, as it is about the works of Lewis Carroll.

If we turn back to Auden's poem, let us consider the following passage:

> Above them were the fells, the unused day,
> Cloaked shepherds motionless among their sheep
> Like Monoliths amid a ring of boulders,
> Below a world about to stretch itself ....
> Noon followed in the valley presently,
> Where trees were darkly cool as under water,
> And Lovers in the shadow of stone idols
> Stirred not till evening touched them, and they saw
> Flushed necks of waterfalls far-off, that spouted
> From hanging valleys; Death seemed no more than
> The echo of an axe, and life so lovely
> Time's snarl sank in his throat to leave him staring,
> And Change froze with his mattock in the air.[27]

Here we notice that Humpty Dumpty is granted sacred features in this secondary world. He is figured as a Druidic amulet, while the 'dancing ring of children', mentioned earlier, mirrors Stonehenge, invoking the summer with the bringing in of May and the banishing of Death. In this case, Humpty Dumpty is being compared to the adder stone or serpent's egg of Druidic tradition. But, for Auden, there is more to Humpty Dumpty than that. He is also an enigma, here returned to his original function; at one time, we were meant to guess the nature of Humpty Dumpty's being (that he is, in this incarnation, an egg) from the nursery rhyme. Again, Heidegger provides some clarification. In bringing together the monoliths, the ring of dancing children, and the riddle, Auden offers a particular insight into the way in which poetry makes, and makes sense, of a world, of earth and sky, of divinities and mortals. As Heidegger puts it:

> The mirror-play of world is the round dance of appropriating. Therefore, the round dance does not encompass the four like a hoop. The round dance is the ring that joins while it plays as mirroring. Appropriating, it lightens the four into the radiance of their simple oneness. Radiantly, the ring joins the four, everywhere open to the riddle of their presence. The gathered presence of the mirror-play of the world, joining in this way, is the ringing. In the ringing of the mirror-playing ring, the four nestle into their unifying presence, in which each one retains its own nature. So nestling, they join together, worlding, the world.[28]

Language speaks us into existence as consciousness; speech is figured as a space (abode or dwelling) for the being of mortals in what Heidegger calls 'the fourfold' (earth, sky, divinities, mortals). Our sense of being-in-the-world is predicated upon a being-with. In gathering together, in the mirroring act of forming a ring, each 'I' comes to constitute, in its joining with others, the riddle of the 'we'. The ring can be thought of in terms of its constitution, its unity in language, but can also be thought of as the 'O' or nothingness at its centre, symbolized by the shape of an egg. This nothingness at the centre of being is another index of the fact that we are not masters of language; language, Heidegger insists, is our master. This is why he resists the fantasy of reducing it to a mere concept or faculty of being human; in Auden's poem, Humpty Dumpty becomes a sign that is equally resistant to this fantasy.

When Heidegger speaks of language as a dwelling, he is referring more specifically to the way in which we have been gathered 'into the appropriation' or *Ereignis*, the event;[29] but the question arises: The appropriation of what? Here, appropriation for Heidegger means to take or make as one's own, as our ways of making sense of the world are transformed over time; the invocation of bringing in May is one such appropriation. But we must be attendant to the subtlety; language has gathered us into *its* space. We live with the necessary illusion that we 'made' language. Rather, language has made *us*. Although Auden may have restored Humpty Dumpty to his status as enigma, he remains suspicious of whether the ways in which mirroring and ringing can leave us, as Heidegger suggests, in the fourfold, 'open to the riddle of their presence'.[30] As Auden shows us in *The Sea and the Mirror*, his meditation on Shakespeare's *The Tempest*, the sea is the source of a world, a reality that can itself reflect surfaces even more puzzling than the cresting waves above 'full fathom five', even as the dazzling mirror can reveal enigmatic depths that the sea obscures or withholds.

In returning to Auden's poem, we see that the change of season does not bring fecundity and growth but a kind of loneliness or isolation in which Humpty Dumpty, in his idiolectic determinism, his indifference to linguistic difference, causes Change itself to 'freeze with his mattock in the air'.[31] The Druidic warning that, to prevent its hatching, the serpent's egg must not touch the earth is given its absurd echo in Humpty Dumpty's famed appearance on a wall.

It is at this point that the poem breaks, and then proceeds to invoke Job's lament, '"Let the day perish wherein I was born"',[32] in effect cursing his birthday as Humpty Dumpty does in *Through the Looking-Glass* (though for very different reasons). Meanwhile, another figure, the Watcher, reads the quotation as a graffito on the very wall on which we would expect to find Humpty Dumpty. But in a gesture that anticipates turning 'away/ Quite leisurely from the disaster' in Auden's 'Musée des Beaux-Arts', the grim wit of the tag prompts the Watcher to turn to 'Wonderland the backside of indifference'[33] and focus instead on the primary world of lived experience, or, perhaps more precisely, prior poetic meditations on lived experience – an Eliotic one, evoking 'The Love Song of J. Alfred Prufrock' in its 'Streets that follow like a tedious argument / Of insidious intent',[34] or a Sitwellian one, as in 'Clowns' Houses': 'Tall houses; like a hopeless prayer / They cleave the sly dumb air'.[35] By way of comparison, here is Auden's 'Humpty Dumpty': 'Squat tenements in streets that imitate / Infinity but never get so far. / Houses were dumb till wind blew doors away / Displaying fragments fitted into frames'.[36] In short, this is 'a world of slag-tips, chimneys / More eloquent of Death than cypresses'.[37] As Richard Bozorth argues, the logic informing the appearances and attitudes of the Montmere figure of the Watcher is one of borders between states of being, 'straddling the "razor-edge" of psychic schism'.[38] As Carroll puts it in *The Game of Logic*, we can understand the space the Watcher occupies in propositional terms as a contradictory one; one side may have a positive quality shared by the other side, but they are otherwise in opposition. Which world to choose? The primary one or its secondary counterpart? Carroll uses a red counter as a place holder in this particular game of proposition; one cannot definitely choose one side or the other. Borrowing an American phrase, Carroll tells us that the placing of the red counter in this particular contradiction is analogous to sitting 'on [...] the fence'.[39] As a result, in a phrase that even more pointedly suggests both the problem of the Watcher and the logical contradictions espoused by Humpty Dumpty, 'he sits astride, poor fellow, dangling his legs, one on each side of the fence!'[40]

What is striking about this shift is that the Watcher is paradoxically spurred on to an engagement with the primary world, and away from the secondary one, by indifference; indifference becomes the means of making a choice when puzzled by contradiction. As Andrew Hass explains in his reading of Auden's complex relationship to 'O', to nothingness, 'The O is always and forever present, negating both the positive and negative that leaves neither side the same as before'.[41] As we have already seen, Change itself is negated, frozen. Further, 'the unused day'[42] ultimately lies fallow, and Death appears no more final 'than / The echo of an axe'.[43] The Watcher is an ambivalent figure, one of mockery and respect, who first appeared as the 'Watcher in Spanish' (i.e. vigilante) in a few of the (largely unfinished) Montmere fantasy stories, co-written by Christopher Isherwood and Edward Upward when they were undergraduates and commemorated in Isherwood's *Lions and Shadows*:

> He appeared to us, we said, at moments when our behaviour was particularly insincere [...]. He made no gesture, never spoke. His mere presence was sufficient reminder and warning. Mutely, he reminded us that the 'two sides' continued to exist, that our enemies remained implacable, beneath all their charming, expensive, scholarly disguises; he warned us never to give ourselves away by word or deed. He was our familiar, our imaginary mascot, our guardian spirit. We appealed to him, made fun of him, tried to deceive him.[44]

The Watcher's presence in Auden's poem takes on a similarly critical quality, observing the plosive alliteration of 'A poet prattling prettily of love',[45] the Watcher gazing upon him 'Indulging his plush insincerity / His gulping courage, and his sexual day-dreams, / And all his facile armament of tears'.[46] The effect is that of a check or curb on the extravagance and insincerity that can mar the work of the secondary imagination.

One could say that Auden has, in the figure of the Watcher, produced an auditor of the dream poem even as it is being constructed. Auden claimed that he wrote only one poem – 'O What Is that Sound' – in which one is expected to 'read as if the reader were dreaming it'.[47] But it is clear that 'Humpty Dumpty', composed some six years earlier, follows a similar pattern: a dream is broken or interrupted by the appearance of a secondary figure.

But why the break? Perhaps one answer is that if engaging the secondary imagination is a game, as Auden insists, then it has laws and rules. Indeed, one of the reasons Auden finds Alice praiseworthy is her capacity for flexibility in the games she must play, however chaotic or anarchic the worlds of Wonderland and the Looking-Glass might be.[48] In other words, fantasy is circumscribed by a kind of logic in the same way reality is. The logics may differ, one may be empirical and the other symbolic, and their effects may diverge, but each world must possess some consistency, imposed or otherwise.[49] If, in 'Humpty Dumpty', the world of change has frozen, it has done so in the name of critique, of parody – as Auden's text devolves ironically into a bathetic version of Keats. (We should keep in mind that Auden is not criticizing Keats, whom he admired for possessing 'a rare combination of witty and original intelligence with common sense'.[50]) The 'Watcher in Spanish' becomes an uncanny emblem of one of the presumed sites of Keats's writing: Spaniards Inn. Here the charged products of Keats's famed 'negative capability' meditate upon the intimations of louche sexual experience, rather than a Keatsian meditation on mortality and imagination.

In Auden's version, it is not the song of a nightingale, but of 'a chorister's sweet treble', that captures the attention of a curate, bringing lustful moisture to his 'nether lip'.[51] Just as the Watcher comes upon college intellectuals who, in a now-direct invocation of 'Ode to a Nightingale', 'Oped magic casements', we discover that these casements do not open out to the foam of perilous seas, but instead onto other texts: the 'Columbus tales' of such singular, roving figures as Lord Alfred Douglas and the then-Prince of Wales.[52] In other words, the Watcher offers another tempering perspective on the problem of dreaming and waking that marks the conclusion not only of Keats's poem, but also of the space of Carroll's *Alice* texts.

The poem then breaks again, turning back to Humpty Dumpty's fate in the phrase "'All the king's horses and all the king's men/ Could not – '",[53] halting before Alice's misremembered phrase '*put Humpty Dumpty in his place again*'.[54] Of course, Humpty Dumpty tells Alice that this is precisely what the king's men will do, but she, the critical reader and thinker, remains understandably sceptical – both critiquing his confidence and expressing her disapproval of the excessive number of syllables in the final line of the nursery rhyme. Importantly, Alice voices her scepticism 'almost out loud, forgetting that Humpty Dumpty would hear her'.[55] This moment of suspension redounds upon my earlier discussion of Change being frozen, whereas it is now stilled by the world of the dream. Through this particular looking-glass, the Watcher provides an unconscious mirror of Humpty Dumpty toppling into unconsciousness, into an anxiety dream: 'and he dreamed / Of equilibrium and a noiseless fall / Which shattered and said nothing till the grass / Had spelled forgetfulness on the spot'.[56] In this passage, we confront what Humpty Dumpty cannot quite accept. Just as he attempts to escape the bonds of language and meaning, blindly hoping to avoid a fate that Alice knows is, in effect, preordained by the nursery rhyme, Humpty Dumpty dreams of the very equilibrium and the presumably harmless fall that he bargains for himself.

Remarkably, the fall shatters the fantasy of equilibrium and inconsequence, but not the dream itself.

As we have seen, the wall on which Humpty Dumpty sat is marked by text, but so, too, is the grass upon which the dream would seem to shatter. But rather than waking, he continues to dream, the grass having been literally marked by the word 'forgetfulness'.[57] In his essay 'Psychology and Art Today', Auden warns against the notion that fantasy is necessarily an important dimension of being an artist, but also warns that no artist is utterly 'disinterested' and that the dissatisfaction inherent in being human is essential to the artist. The artist is not an Olympian, passive observer; rather all artists are active, engaged. As he puts it, 'To retire into a life of phantasy' is the choice of 'the schizophrene', and that 'perfect satisfaction would be complete unconsciousness'.[58] Unlike Humpty Dumpty, who retreats utterly into the dream of perfect mastery, of perfect satisfaction, the role of the artist is 'To understand the mechanism' of such traps.[59] Of course, Freud claims that a particular form of forgetfulness can be 'motivated by repression'.[60] Auden, like Freud, believed that people live their lives controlled by forces unknown or unconscious to them.[61] The dream is thus sustained in part by unconscious forgetting; the trauma of shattering produces repression instead of the 'death' of the subject or the end of the dream. In psychological terms, Auden described repression as 'eristic' precisely because it attempts to avoid truth by focusing on contradiction and argument.[62]

Antagonism and forgetfulness cannot be explained away by purely materialistic means; as Auden himself said of Freud, 'his love of truth was great enough to give him the courage to transcend the materialist, even mechanistic philosophy which went almost unchallenged when he was growing up'.[63] It is thus not insignificant that one etymology of the ancient Greek word for truth, *aletheia*, is 'unforgetting'; by implication, forgetfulness can be a way of denying truth. When we consider the implications of this assertion in the context of Wonderland, we encounter the means by which the narrative frame – that is, Alice's dream – like Humpty Dumpty's in the poem, is able to prolong itself, despite its nightmarish quality.

In psychoanalytic terms, the very debates and fractious, anarchic arguments and linguistic contests that pepper the *Alice* texts are paradoxically, in addition to Wonderland's tendency to 'forget' logic, the eristic means by which the dream is sustained. As Lacan contends, the logic of a dream is that of the unconscious, a logic that cannot represent or capture desire directly; since the purpose of the dream is to lengthen the subject's brief escape from reality, the decentredness of the subject is perforce mirrored in the distortions of desire that manifest themselves in the dream.[64]

Just as Humpty Dumpty is 'taken' in his role as chess piece, thus mirroring his fall, the king and his tripping soldiers appear in Carroll's text. As Auden's poem proceeds, the kings (Red and White?) appear, but their impotence, their defeat in the face of the fall is staged in various allegorical ways; the 'hairpin kings forsook/ Their palaces'[65] and 'went crawling on their hands and knees',[66] their horses transformed into 'tethered motors rusting under trees'.[67] The phrase 'hairpin kings' hearkens back to the repeated episodes involving untidy hair in *Through the Looking-Glass*, and of Alice's attempts to put hirsute chaos to rights. The irony deepens as the kings fail to acknowledge their defeat, and as Humpty Dumpty overhears them calling upon the victor (in this case, Alice) to 'Sing us one of the songs of Sion',[68] evoking Psalm 137:3, in which the Babylonians mockingly call upon the exiled, tormented Israelites to entertain their captors with a sacred song. The poem then plucks a literally half-remembered line from Carroll's text, '"What's one and one and one and one and one and one and one and one and one and one?"',[69] in which the Red Queen turns a question of manners into a lesson of addition: the 'ones' who form the ring of community (bound by rules like etiquette) are here separated and unable to come together. In Carroll's text, the Red Queen is asking what adds up to ten. In Auden's, the number is halved, perhaps because Humpty Dumpty is split in two. Of course, the ambiguity of having 'Queen' Alice, the ultimate victor in the chess match with the Red King, assume the role of the grieving Israelite, mirrors her anxiety that her very existence may be nothing more than as a fragment populating the Red King's dream. In the case of Auden's intertextual poem, she may very well be nothing but a character in Humpty Dumpty's dream. But as is often the case, Wonderland is more complicated than that:

> 'So I wasn't dreaming, after all,' she said to herself, 'unless – unless we're all part of the same dream. Only I do hope it's *my* dream, and not the Red King's! I don't like belonging to another person's dream,' she went on in a rather complaining tone: 'I've a great mind to go and wake him, and see what happens!'[70]

Alice has hit upon one of the keys to her predicament; in this secondary world, fantasy functions like a dream, held together by a conflict that is not simply external, or between persons, but is structured by a conflict that is also internal, unconscious, in the gap between the individual and the person.

When one is able to determine who is dreaming, one can confront the implications of that determination for one's own being. Alice faces precisely the same problem of how the primary and secondary worlds relate to each other, but in reverse; she must work to name the secondary world of Wonderland into a site of conversation – a personal one, fraught with implications for individual responsibility – with her experience of the primary world on this side of the looking-glass. In terms of the dream problem, Alice's dilemma has similarities to Lacan's reading of Choang-tsu (Zhuangzi), who dreamt of being a butterfly. Choang-tsu wonders if, upon waking, he is in fact a butterfly who dreams he is Choang-tsu. On the surface, the question is an absurd one, but it points to the very gap between the individual and the person, to the insight that he is not self-identical.[71]

This is precisely the insight that Alice is groping towards; on one level, she knows this is a dream. But unlike Humpty Dumpty, because she knows there is a gap or difference between the person and the individual, between speech and enunciation, she cannot know for sure whether she is dreaming of being through the looking-glass or is simply a 'butterfly', as it were, in the Red King's dream. In being tempted to find out the answer by waking him, she recognizes that she is confronting an ontological question. The 'strong nerves' and aesthetic morality that Auden identifies in her allow the possibility for her to discover that she may be nothing – a figment, however formidable, of the Red King's dream realm – but that, more importantly, her ability to contend with the various linguistic and ontological crises of the Looking-Glass world is the fantasy-being that structures both her relationship to the dream and the reality that lies outside it. (This is one of the several reasons why Alice is an Alice, and not a Mabel.) In the case of the poem, Alice plays a crucial role in keeping Humpty Dumpty's dream alive; her role in his fall (i.e., being taken in the chess game) paradoxically sustains the illusion that there can be a master of the game, of the signifier, 'even if', as Lacan reminds us, 'he is not the master of the signified from which his being derived its shape'.[72] Another way of putting it is to say that Humpty Dumpty takes such enjoyment from words, from being their master, that he can forget that he is not truly the master of their meanings, even after he falls, no matter how 'handsome' his shape might be.[73]

In repressing or forgetting his fall, Humpty Dumpty occupies an uncanny, phenomenological space between life and death, where dreaming makes it possible to come to 'the edge of Things',[74] to the Abyss that makes even Tom o' Bedlam turn away in horror. In effect, the kings and their men arrive at the signified from which Humpty Dumpty's being takes its shape: the 'O', or nothingness. The wall upon which Humpty Dumpty sits is transformed, becoming the wall or barrier separating signifier from signified; it is the gap or abyss of contradiction that informs Humpty Dumpty's being. The wall is dangerous, strewn 'with bottle glass along the top' as the men grope, lost in the coming darkness.[75] As they approach death or nothingness, the men find themselves 'nearer their Antipodes'.[76] The line evokes Alice's own fall, in the inverted space of Wonderland: 'I wonder if I shall fall right *through* the earth! How funny it'll seem to come out among the people that walk with their heads downwards! The Antipathies, I think [...]'.[77] But her misuse of the word 'Antipathies' instead of 'Antipodes' is significant in that she has indeed entered a world of antipathies, and is not literally falling to the other side of the earth. So why does Auden use the word Antipodes instead? He uses the word metaphorically, to refer to the other side of life, of death and the abyss, rather than to the 'underside' of the earth. The abyss in the poem is a kind of necropolis, filled with fragments of memory, traces of those who had made a mark, however humble, 'in the silent valleys of broken chimneys',[78] with no egress 'But crazy tramlines and a choked canal'.[79] Thus entrapped, there is no escape from the abyss. Only another 'O', the moon, 'fraily sad', bears witness to 'a world that guttered and went out'.[80] And with that, the world of this particular dream ends.

Upon waking, Humpty Dumpty, the enigma himself, puzzles over the 'Persistent questions doors and chimneys ask',[81] evoking the moment in *Through the Looking-Glass* when Alice finishes his sentence about the king's promise to him, should he ever fall:

'The King has promised me—with his very own mouth—to—to——'
'To send all his horses and all his men,' Alice interrupted, rather unwisely.

'Now I declare that's too bad!' Humpty Dumpty cried, breaking into a sudden passion. 'You've been listening at doors—and behind trees—and down chimneys—or you couldn't have known it!'[82]

In his accusation, Humpty Dumpty suggests that doors, trees, and chimneys are sites of knowledge, where one's secrets may be overheard. But in meditating on his dream, these sites are transformed. They are not places where secrets may be discovered, but are instead hectoring objects whose questions are themselves enigmatic. In his dream, the enigma is thus confronted with the enigma of his own being, but in a specific way: in plumbing the nothingness at the centre of his tautological thinking, he experiences what Auden calls 'tautomeric changes of the mind'.[83] But the question arises: What is the difference between tautology and tautomerism? Tautomerism is a term from chemistry referring to an interconversion of isomers that are composed of the same molecular formulae, but that have different, although interchangeable, structures. That is to say, the surface or skeleton of the compound remains the same, even if the position of a particular particle (a proton or electron) changes. It is, in psychological terms, a shift in perspective.

If tautology constructs itself over the abyss between subject and predicate, then the confrontation with the abyss in the dream creates a world in which Humpty Dumpty witnesses the ontological, 'tautomeric' shift between a tautological subject and its predicate. His dream-fall produces an atomic shift in consciousness. In this case, the king's promise to arrive with his men should Humpty Dumpty fall, is rendered tautologically equivalent to his being saved; this assumption has hitherto been the foundation of his fantasy of self-identity. As Angelika Zirker ably demonstrates, 'Egg-shaped Humpty Dumpty himself is an appropriate symbol of the recursive and endlessly regressive process of understanding.'[84] Recursion and regression are demands that having an unconscious entails, since, like any riddle, the process of understanding the unconscious is elusive and fragmentary. Humpty Dumpty's dream opens up and occupies the temporal abyss – in short, the disavowed consequence of his fall – between these presumed equivalencies. In the conclusion to Auden's poem, Humpty Dumpty experiences not a conversion, but an interconversion. The secondary worlds he constructs are 'palimpsests upon reality', upon the primary world, mere traces to be blotted out until there is 'an end of worlds'[85] – an end that is, like desire, deferred, at least for now: 'while crocuses/ And waltzes still have something to recall / Of Adam's brow, and of the wounded heel'.[86] The tides of the world, like the revolutions, the recursions, and the regressions of a waltz – these phenomenological realities continue – hold within them another reminder: the 'O' of nothingness, of death, that marks Adam's fall into mortality and the fateful vulnerability of Achilles. But why the reference to crocuses? Humpty Dumpty's being provides an answer: 'crocus' is a Semitic loanword in ancient Greek, from the Hebrew *karkom*, meaning 'egg yolk'. He has come full circle; his dream having invented a world in which nothingness is made to happen – to him. He is still Humpty Dumpty, but upon waking, he comes to confront not a literal cracking, but rather the crack in being, and the shifting yolk around which the truth of nothingness nurtures itself.

Notes

1   W. H. Auden, 'Today's "Wonder-World" Needs Alice', in *The Complete Works of W. H. Auden,* vol. IV, ed. Edward Mendelson (Princeton: Princeton University Press, 1996), 422.

2   W. H. Auden, 'Chester Kallman, a Voice of Importance', in *The Complete Works of W. H. Auden,* vol. III, ed. Edward Mendelson (Princeton: Princeton University Press, 2008), 487.

3   Ibid., 487–8.

4   W. H. Auden, 'Introduction', in *Oxford Book of Light Verse*, ed. W. H. Auden (Oxford: Oxford University Press, 1973), xviii.

5   Ibid.

6   W. H. Auden, *Secondary Worlds: T. S. Eliot Memorial Lectures* (London: Faber and Faber, 1967), 121–2.

7   Martin Heidegger, *Poetry, Language, Thought*, trans. Albert Hofstadter (New York: Harper Perennial, 1971), 193.

8   Auden, *Secondary Worlds*, 143.

9   Ibid., 143–4.

10 W. H. Auden, 'The Door', in *Selected Poems: New Edition*, ed. Edward Mendelson (New York: Vintage, 1979), 99.

11 Ibid., 109.

12 W. H. Auden, *Juvenilia: Poems, 1922–1928*, ed. Katherine Bucknell (Princeton: Princeton University Press, 1994), 152.

13 W. H. Auden, 'Humpty Dumpty', in *Juvenilia: Poems, 1922–1928*, ed. Katherine Bucknell (Princeton: Princeton University Press, 1994), 149.

14 Lewis Carroll, *Alice's Adventures in Wonderland* and *Through the Looking-Glass*, ed. Hugh Haughton (London: Penguin, 1998), 186.

15 Ibid.

16 Ibid.

17 Jacques Lacan, *Écrits: The First Complete Edition in English*, trans. Bruce Fink, Héloïse Fink, and Russell Grigg (New York: Norton, 2006), 242.

18 Lewis Carroll, *Symbolic Logic* and *The Game of Logic* (New York: Dover Publications, 1958), xvii.

19 Ibid.

20 Heidegger, *Poetry*, 189.

21 Allen Thiher, *The Power of Tautology: The Roots of Literary Theory* (Vancouver: Fairleigh Dickinson University Press, 2000), 20.

22 George Pitcher, 'Wittgenstein, Nonsense, and Lewis Carroll', *The Massachusetts Review* 6, no. 3 (1965): 604.

23 W. H. Auden, 'Phantasy and Reality in Poetry', in *'In Solitude, for Company': W. H. Auden after 1940*, ed. Katherine Bucknell and Nicholas Jenkins (Oxford: Clarendon, 1995), 178.

24 Jacques Lacan, *The Four Fundamental Concepts of Psychoanalysis*, trans. Alan Sheridan (New York: Norton, 1981), 139–40.

25　Heidegger, *Poetry*, 79.

26　Carroll, *Alice*, 186.

27　Auden, 'Humpty Dumpty', 149.

28　Heidegger, *Poetry*, 178.

29　Ibid., 188.

30　Ibid., 178.

31　Auden, 'Humpty Dumpty', 149.

32　Ibid., 149, Line 20; *The Bible*, Authorized King James Version (Oxford: Oxford University Press, 1998), Job 3:3.

33　W. H. Auden, 'Musée des Beaux-Arts', in *Selected Poems: New Edition*, ed. Edward Mendelson (New York: Vintage, 1979), 80. Auden, 'Humpty Dumpty', 150.

34　T. S. Eliot, 'The Love Song of J. Alfred Prufrock', in T. S. *The Poems of T. S. Eliot*, vol. 1, ed. Christopher Ricks and Jim McCue (London: Faber and Faber, 2015), 5.

35　Edith Sitwell, 'Clowns' Houses', in *Collected Poems* (London: Macmillan, 1957), 114.

36　Auden 'Humpty Dumpty', 150.

37　Ibid.

38　Richard R. Bozorth, *Auden's Games of Knowledge* (New York: Columbia University Press, 2001), 75.

39　Carroll, *Game of Logic*, 9.

40　Ibid.

41　Andrew W. Hass, *Auden's O: The Loss of Sovereignty in the Making of Nothing* (Albany: State University of New York Press, 2013), 151.

42　Auden, 'Humpty Dumpty', 149.

43　Ibid.

44　Christopher Isherwood, *Lions and Shadows: An Education in the Twenties* (Norfolk: New Directions, 1947), 53–4.

45　Auden, 'Humpty Dumpty', 150, Line 36.

46　Ibid.

47　Auden, 'Phantasy', 193.

48　W. H. Auden, *Forewords and Afterwords*, ed. Edward Mendelson (New York: Random House, 1973), 289.

49　Auden, 'Phantasy', 188–9.

50　W. H. Auden, 'Keats in His Letters', in *The Complete Works of W. H. Auden*, vol. III, ed. Edward Mendelson (Princeton: Princeton University Press, 2008), 263.

51　Auden, 'Humpty Dumpty', 150.

52　Ibid.

53　Ibid.

54　Carroll, *Alice*, 182.

55　Ibid.

56　'Humpty Dumpty', 150.

57　Ibid.

58　W. H. Auden, 'Psychology and Art Today', in *The English Auden: Poems, Essays and Dramatic Writings, 1927–1939*, ed. Edward Mendelson (New York: Random House, 1977), 334–5.

59　Ibid., 335.

60　Sigmund Freud, *The Psychopathology of Everyday Life*, trans. A. A. Brill (New York: Macmillan, 1914), 13.

61　Edward Mendelson, *Later Auden* (New York: Farrar, Strauss, and Giroux, 1999), 28.

62   W. H. Auden, 'As Hateful Ares Bids', in *The Complete Works of W. H. Auden,* vol. II, ed. Edward Mendelson (Princeton: Princeton University Press, 2002), 289.

63   Auden, 'Phantasy', 179.

64   Lacan, *Écrits*, 521.

65   Auden, 'Humpty Dumpty', 150.

66   Ibid.

67   Ibid.

68   Ibid.

69   Carroll, *Alice,* 221.

70   Ibid., 205.

71   Jacques Lacan, *The Seminar of Jacques Lacan Book XI: The Four Fundamental Concepts of Psychoanalysis*, trans. Alan Sheridan, ed. Jacques-Alain Miller (Sheridan, NY: Norton, 1998), 76.

72   Lacan, *Écrits*, 242.

73   Carroll, *Alice*, 182.

74   Auden, 'Humpty Dumpty', 51.

75   Ibid.

76   Ibid.

77   Carroll, *Alice*, 11.

78   Auden, 'Humpty Dumpty', 150.

79   Ibid.

80   Ibid.

81   Ibid.

82   Carroll, *Alice,* 182–3.

83   Auden, 'Humpty Dumpty', 150.

84   Angelika Zirker, '"All about Fishes?" The Riddle of Humpty Dumpty's Song and Recursive Understanding in Lewis Carroll's *Through the Looking-Glass and What Alice Found There*', *Victorian Poetry* 56, no. 1 (spring 2018): 97.

85   Auden, 'Humpty Dumpty', 150.

86   Ibid.

Chapter 10

Nightmares of History: Modernism and Colonialism in Lewis Carroll and Jorge Luis Borges

David Conlon

Introduction: Fantasy and Modernism in Latin America

Gabriel García Márquez began his 1982 Nobel Prize acceptance speech by recalling the Florentine navigator Antonio Pigafetta's description of his passage through South America in the early 1500s, 'a strictly accurate account that nonetheless resembles a venture into fantasy'.[1] Throughout Latin America's history, the blurring of boundaries between what registers as real and fantastical has been a recurring cultural phenomenon,[2] which, as García Márquez suggests, did not abate with the advent of modernity. On the contrary, it has become almost a commonplace to read fantastical elements from texts such as Lewis Carroll's *Alice's Adventures in Wonderland* (1865) and *Through the Looking-Glass, and What Alice Found There* (1871) as prefiguring what García Márquez called the 'outsized reality' of the all-too-real problems that have faced Latin America over the past century, ranging from the baroque excesses that often characterize bureaucracy in the region, to the human rights abuses perpetrated by a succession of tragicomically grandiose military dictators. Over the years, the Alice novels have been variously adapted, cited, or mobilized by Latin American artists as a way of diagnosing a variety of public ills. For instance, Argentine film director Eduardo Plá's 1976 adaptation of *Alice's Adventures in Wonderland* served as a critique of the 1976–83 military junta (in spite of barely straying from the source text); the film's theme song, 'Canción de Alicia en el país' ('Song of Alice in the Country') by the rock group Serú Girán, subsequently became an unofficial anthem of resistance during the twilight years of the regime. A decade later, Cuban director Daniel Díaz Torres's 1991 openly satirical adaptation *Alicia en el pueblo de Maravillas* (*Alice in Wondertown*) was denounced as an attack on the Castro regime – and even on socialism itself – and was subject to censorship upon release.[3] More recently, Mexican writer Juan Pablo Villalobos's 2010 fantastical novella *Fiesta en la madriguera* (translated by Rosalind Harvey as the more explicitly Carrollian *Down the Rabbit Hole*) adapted Wonderland imagery as a way of representing the excesses of Mexico's drug war.[4] More recently again, the Mexican-American writer Ilan Stavans re-wrote the novel in Spanglish as *Alicia's Adventuras en Wonderlandia* (2021), and subsequently lauded Carroll's work as 'an extraordinarily compelling metaphor for Latin Americans entering an entirely different world in the United States and the pressure they face through assimilation.'[5]

Given this tendency for the fictional to fold into the factual in both implicit and overt homages to Alice's legacy, the question of how a primarily cultural trend such as literary modernism might aid in the recuperation and assessment of Carroll's influence in Latin America becomes difficult to separate from the socio-political. Indeed, even the term 'modernism' itself has been the subject of continued controversy in Latin American studies, in spite of it being arguably a more persistently mainstream literary trend in Latin America than in either Europe or North America.[6] This is partly owing to the fact that the term is freighted with the baggage of an equivalent Spanish term, *modernismo*, which predates Anglo-American modernism and generally describes a thematically and formally distinct literary phenomenon. Although Latin America's *modernismo* anticipated and influenced Continental European modernism in certain respects, its influence was thereafter subject to a gradual process of erasure from the literary-historical archive.[7] Later movements contemporary with Anglo-American high modernism, such as the formally analogous *vanguardismo* or the more locally inspired *regionalismo* and *indigenismo*, are diminished in stature by literary histories that interpret their innovations in terms of a reaction to a supposed European centre.[8] Even Latin American writers who seem to satisfy the outward requirements of a rigged, Eurocentric definition of modernism are generally disregarded for the purpose of general studies or anthologies.[9] As an alternative, some scholars have located a Latin American modernism in the formally innovative 1960s 'boom' narratives by Mario Vargas Llosa, Julio Cortázar, Carlos Fuentes, and García Márquez, among others,[10] a movement which seemed to herald 'modernization' in a broader sense, too, in tandem with the widely felt optimism generated by the triumph of the Cuban Revolution in 1959.[11] However, an irony arises from the unavoidable fact that the boom derived its meaning at least partly through its success as a marketing phenomenon; its singular achievement is therefore inseparable from its reception in mainstream European and North American literary cultures, in which virtually all of these authors have been (usually inaccurately) pigeon-holed as 'magical realist'.[12] In sum, and in spite of the fact that it has in recent years become more common to speak of many modernisms rather than one Anglo-American modernism,[13] the conversation on modernism in Latin America remains difficult to engage for very long without invoking the core/peripheral questions that are more commonly associated with postcolonial studies and that urge us to attend to the international division of intellectual labour and the legitimizing function of cultural power operations that determine the location of Latin America in the global imagination.

The Argentine writer (and Lewis Carroll aficionado) Jorge Luis Borges (1899–1986) is a case in point, in that his relationships to both modernism and colonialism could be said to mutually complicate each another. On the one hand, Borges is often subtracted from his Latin American context, and his well-known appropriations of the Victorian-era Englishman Carroll might easily be subsumed within the reductive yet still entrenched idea that his Anglophilia is evidence of his disembodied status as (at best) mild-mannered freeman of the world republic of letters or (at worst) a reactionary escapist.[14] The origin of these canards is often Borges himself, who notoriously praised the 1976 military junta as 'the only gentlemen capable of serving the country'.[15] Among his compatriots, Borges sometimes stands accused of purveying an inverted neo-colonial gaze targeted at Argentina itself,[16] a view that is in some respects abetted by knowledge of his fascination with his own family's illustrious military history, which Borges could trace back to River Plate conquistadores; to veterans of the Independence wars; and to the fabled 'Colonel Borges', a leader in the 1880s military campaigns aimed at subduing the country's remaining indigenous peoples.[17] On the other, Borges was dismissive of precisely those forms of Latin American modernism that overtly set out to redress colonialism and its legacies. In his famous 1955 essay 'The Argentine Writer and Tradition', for instance, he dismissed the then-voguish 'local colour' of *regionalismo* as an inferior literary mode founded on a conceptual fallacy.[18]

In the same essay, however, Borges goes on to herald the 'Argentine writer' as a harbinger of a kind of global citizen-to-come, and draws analogies with the 'Irish writer', anticipating the now-widely accepted idea that the supposed geographical and cultural peripheries of former colonies are productive sites from which to engage with tradition and modernity. But this relationship also works in the opposite direction. For Gina Apostol, for instance (whose assessment occurs in the context of a polemical rebuke to a *New Yorker* article that she perceived as a rehash of the 'apolitical Borges' trope), it is precisely the modernist, modernizing, and post-modernist involutions of Borges's oeuvre that generate the 'profound echoes for the postcolonial citizen' that she identifies throughout his work.[19] Consequently, the postcolonial Borges emerges in part as a function of the negotiation of the problematic relationship between Anglophone and Latin American modernisms, and which must be brokered in terms of the core-periphery postcolonial paradigm. Borges's Pascalian solution was arguably to 'undermine [the] centre by stretching it out to infinity',[20] thereby cashing in on modernism's emancipatory promise of a universal locus that was constituted out of its own peripheries.[21]

Although Gabriel Josipovici includes Borges among his five writers who most clearly embody 'the essential spirit of modernism',[22] the work for which he is best known was written after high modernism's watershed moment had passed, and he tends not to be included in the movement's histories or anthologies. He is instead sometimes considered as a transitional figure positioned on the 'borderland' between modernism and postmodernism,[23] on account of a perceived playful reflexivity and suspicion of meta-narratives. Nor has Borges traditionally been credited as a postcolonial writer. Since the appearance of Apostol's 2013 article, however, Edna Aizenberg's idea of a Borges as 'postcolonial precursor' has gained increased visibility, most notably with the 2017 publication of Robin Fiddian's landmark book *Postcolonial Borges*.[24] Less in question is the influence Lewis Carroll exerted on the writer, evinced by the plentiful references to Carroll throughout Borges's oeuvre, and occasionally subject to scholarly analysis, most notably in John Irwin's 1996 book *The Mystery to a Solution*. What I want to suggest here is that the points at which these various affiliations intersect can serve as a useful way of framing the place of Alice in the work of Borges, insofar as the meeting point of modernist and postcolonial strategies in the stories of Borges can be understood as bearing a roughly analogical relationship with the collusion of these elements in Carroll's famous novels. I will argue that this analogical similarity hinges on a shared tendency to (a) lampoon the temporal and spatial coordinates of imperialism, (b) reject the implicitly 'realist' subjectivities inherent to both nineteenth-century Victorian travel writing and twentieth-century Latin American ethnographical narrative, and (c), through recourse to one of modernism's recurring tropes, the dream space, to articulate the connection between imperial language and colonial violence. Borges's implicit allusions to and explicit deployments of Alice, taken collectively, can be understood to capitalize on a latent postcolonial complication of the Carrollian legacy and can be capitalized on, in turn, in the ongoing project to read and decipher Borges. My contention is that this way of framing both authors can help us to identify how and why they can be considered in relation to twentieth-century literary modernism.

Modernism and Imperial Time and Space

For Peter Childs, modernism's relation to postcolonialism can be mapped along the trajectory that goes from a default colonial perspective to 'a distinctive discourse characterized by ambivalence'.[25] According to Fredric Jameson's influential account, modernism 'is at one with the contradiction between the contingency of physical objects and the demand for an impossible meaning'.[26] This contradiction in turn arises out of an epistemological fault-line that is a product of 'the representational dilemmas of the new imperial world system' and the attendant 'spatial disjunction [which] has as its immediate consequence the inability to grasp the way the system functions as a whole'.[27] Modernism, suggests Simon Gikandi, is 'generated by a crisis of belief in the efficacy of colonialism, its culture, and its dominant terms – a progressive temporality, a linear cartography, and a unified European subject'.[28] According to schemas such as these, and as is signalled by Borges in 'The Argentine Writer and Tradition', it would be precisely the 'peripheral artist' who has privileged access to both centre and periphery that would be therefore best placed to grasp the radical spatial disjunction diagnosed by Jameson.[29] Borges's apparently harmless classification of Carroll as 'un inglés excéntrico' might here be open to a literal and radical meaning (i.e. ex-centric)[30]: both Carroll, at the heart of empire, and Borges, at one of its outer edges, were adept at mimicking the tropes and rhetorical formulae of imperialism and of logically extending its implications to absurd effect.[31]

Carroll began writing *Alice's Adventures in Wonderland* in Victorian England in the 1860s, when the world's largest empire was entering into its most ambitiously expansionist phase, and this context inevitably shaped the text itself. In chapter 4 alone (the iconic scene in which an outsized Alice is trapped inside the White Rabbit's house) at least two unmistakable signifiers of colonial discourse appear: the obsequious stage-Irishisms of 'Pat', evidently a servant in the employ of the White Rabbit, and the languid Orientalism of the hookah-smoking Caterpillar. However, *Alice* has generated some uncertainty regarding whether it abets or upends the governing narratives of the imperial project. Laura E. Ciolkowski forwards the idea of Alice as embodying the role of the emergent European bourgeois subjectivity whose adventures are 'a curious and unsettling rite-of-passage';[32] the story would then serve as a moral lesson on the triumph of Western rationality over the culturally Other, with Wonderland itself figuring as a kind of vanishing mediator in the process of the ideological education of impressionable children. But other scholars argue that Alice's encounters with the Wonderland inhabitants satirize and critique the Victorian-era travel narratives that lent legitimacy to the imperial project;[33] backed up by the veiled and overt references to violence that can be discerned throughout, and which make it clear that it is Alice herself rather than the natives that might constitute the real threat, these readings serve to reconfigure *Alice* as a text that both unveils and undermines the ideological operations at the root of the epistemological wing of the imperial project. In either case, the ambiguity that is generated by this aspect of Carroll's work is prescient, particularly if we take modernism to constitute 'the art of a world from which many of the traditional certainties had departed, and a certain sort of Victorian confidence [...] in the very solidity and visibility of reality itself [had] evaporated'.[34]

References to Carroll, and particularly to the *Alice* novels, occur frequently throughout Borges's fiction and nonfiction.[35] The novels formed an undoubted part of the Argentine author's childhood treasury and continued to operate as an important touchstone throughout his intellectual development. Some tropes have become mutually synonymous with both authors (to name just a few: the ontology of the dreamed dreamer explored in the *Alice* novels and 'The Circular Ruins'; the alternative societies and rituals depicted in Wonderland and 'The Babylon Lottery'; the eerie mirrors and symmetries that characterize Looking-Glass house and the villa of Triste-le-Roy in 'Death and the Compass'), and Borges hints at this affinity in his prologue to an Argentine edition of Carroll's collected works, published by Corregidor in 1976. The duality of the austere Oxford don who constructed 'logico-mathematical paradoxes' that were observant of the 'secret exactitudes of chess' while at the same time enthralling children with 'adventures of the imagination' no doubt appealed to Borges, and in some ways parallels his own dual fascination with profound philosophical problems and free-wheeling adventure yarns.[36] Intentionally or not, when Borges describes Carroll as '[the] celibate who wove the unforgettable fantasy',[37] he foreshadows a guiding narrative thread that will inform many of his own posthumous biographies (that by Edwin Williamson, for instance). In the same text, Borges attributes one of modernism's key distinctions to Carroll: he reminds us that whereas William Faulkner is usually given credit for teaching Borges and his contemporaries how to 'play with time',[38]

Carroll had already set this precedent with, for example, the Mad Hatter for whom it is perpetually six o'clock; the Unicorn who reveals to Alice that the correct way to divide a cake is to share it out before cutting it; and the White Queen who not only cries out in pain before her finger is cut, but explains to Alice that the King's Messenger is in jail prior to judgement for a crime that has not yet been committed. The subversion of linear time is of course a motif which was embraced by Borges in major fictions such as 'The Garden of Forking Paths', which posits the simultaneous existence of infinite parallel worlds, and 'The Secret Miracle', in which an instant of time is stretched out into a near-infinite realm.

But as Borges knew, historical memories of conquest and colonization had already presented Latin American societies with the kinds of epistemological and juridical absurdities that have come to be associated with Carroll's texts. Even as Carroll supplies Borges with the conceptual and literary coordinates for reckoning with the temporal innovations of modernism, the possibilities opened up by a fictive 'playing with time' had been a pan-regional concern for upwards of four centuries. From the perspective of both colonizer and colonized, the world-historical event of the 1492 Colombian encounter with Amerindian civilization threw various orthodoxies off their axes, temporal and spatial as well as ethical and doctrinal. Indeed, Walter Mignolo argues that it was this event that gave rise to a conception of people and cultures as primarily located in time, as opposed to space, and to enduring notions of the 'present' of history as located in Western Europe, and of the inherent 'belatedness' of everybody else.[39] But the day-to-day specifics of the business of colonial expansion also created absurd scenarios that would not be out of place in the Wonderland court, given the Queen of Hearts's 'Sentence first – verdict afterwards' decree,[40] or 'Rule Forty-Two',[41] which Alice claims to have been arbitrarily 'invented' by the King. It was often the case, for example, that ad hoc legislative decisions in the Americas resulted in atrocities that would be subject to *a posteriori* debate in Spain years or even decades later. Particularly notorious was the *requerimiento*, a legal text that was to be read out to indigenous peoples about to be conquered by Spaniards in the 1500s; unless they immediately affirmed their subordination to the Crown, the Spanish military was legally permitted to apply untrammelled force.[42] According to the temporal logic of this requirement, indigenous peoples were called upon to understand and assent to a complex legal formulation before having had the opportunity to learn the language in which it was formulated.

Throughout the period of conquest, which in Argentina's case continued until at least the 1880s desert campaigns carried out by the independent republic, linear temporality was also subverted in the sense that legislative and cartographic documents described normative, projected relations with the territory and its inhabitants rather than existing circumstances. As García Márquez noted in the aforementioned Nobel speech, the keenly sought yet ultimately non-existent space of El Dorado 'appeared on numerous maps for many a long year, shifting its place and form to suit the fantasy of cartographers'.[43] Just as these projections attempted to codify space before it had been physically traversed, key works by both Borges and Carroll trouble the boundary between the map and the territory, and in various ways dramatize the moment in which imperial subjectivity must negotiate the terms of a confluence between the terrain as fantasy object and the terrain itself. The archetypal figure for this, and the one to which Borges will repeatedly return, is the chessboard in *Through the Looking-Glass*; what in essence begins as an overhead perspective of the board as a finite set of deontological, rule-governed propositions, segues into Alice's traversal of the board as a series of muddy ambiguities and epistemologically unsettling encounters. Indeed, it could be argued that chess is an obvious metaphor for the colonial project, particularly when Alice observes that 'It's a great huge game of chess that's being played – all over the world – if this is the world at all, you know.'[44] Clear parallels emerge between this and at least two of Borges's three detective stories, 'The Garden of Forking Paths', a geopolitical-turned-metaphysical puzzle which posits 'a riddle whose answer is chess'[45] (and which, as Daniel Balderston observes, plays with 'a series of fractured colonial histories'[46]), and 'Death and the Compass', in which the protagonist sleuth Erik Lönnrot wrongheadedly and fatally attempts to investigate a real murder through the use of rarefied religious doctrine and dizzying geometrical abstractions.

An even more clear-cut appropriation from Carroll is found in Borges's 'On Exactitude in Science', which relates the mania of an empire that seeks to attain exact correspondence between word and world through the fabrication of a map that bears a 1:1 relationship to the territory represented. This idea was first formulated in Carroll's final novel, *Sylvie and Bruno Concluded* (1893), wherein Mein Herr describes how the proclivity for extreme map-making where he comes from has resulted in 'a map of the country, on the scale of a mile to the mile!', though it 'has never been spread out' on account of complaints from farmers that it would block the sunlight.[47] As Benoît Faucher avers, the full implementation of radical mimesis would here literally 'kill off' the object represented.[48] In the Borges story, the discordance between imperial representation and its object is similarly associated with destitution: the map is found to be of little use and is left to decay into pieces – 'the Tattered Ruins of that Map'[49] – which eventually come to be inhabited by beggars and itinerant animals. These tendencies towards ruin are enacted in both texts by a territorialization of the map; the radical materialization of the sign amounts to a decoding of the map's hidden signature, the secret violence harboured by the words as much as by the weapons of empire.

Towards Ethnographic Modernism

Literary modernism, according to perhaps its most basic working definition, entailed a rejection of nineteenth-century realism, and an undermining of the 'interpretive stability' that had characterized this mode through a variety of narrative strategies.[50] If we approach Carroll and Borges in purely chronological terms with respect to the literary historiographical timeline, it seems untenable or (in the case of Borges) unremarkable that either can be taken as having 'rejected' realism. However, both authors represent a significant troubling of the orthodoxies of realist subjectivity, insofar as this subjectivity is implicated in scientific discourse and, especially, the interrelated disciplines of anthropology and ethnography. Alice, for example, is often interpreted as performing the role of a child-ethnographer; Emma D. Graner argues that by satirizing the Victorian-era travel narratives, Carroll is effectively undermining the 'raw data of Victorian ethnography' which was 'directly implicated in the formation of scientific theories about the nature of primitive societies.'[51] Carroll's reading and writing against the grain of nineteenth-century travel narratives offers a useful template for considering Borges's own significant engagement with ethnography and ethnographers, a figure to which he turns with some regularity, overtly so in 'The Ethnographer' and 'Doctor Brodie's Report' but also through the use of ethnographer avatars in 'The South' and 'The Gospel According to Mark'. It is a mark of Borges's fictions that these protagonists will be systematically divested of their claims on scientific objectivity.

Borges's reaction was perhaps not to nineteenth-century realism per se, but to a specific realist vein of narrative that had come to prominence in Latin America in the 1920s and 1930s, namely the *novela de la tierra*, or telluric novel, whose practitioners sought to depict local customs, character, landscape, and society as mutually constitutive. According to Roberto González Echevarría's influential hypothesis, the telluric novel was ideologically of a piece with a wider predominance enjoyed by anthropology in Latin America, to the extent that it had acquired the status of what González Echevarría terms a 'hegemonic' or 'totalising' discourse;[52] in effect, it had become an over-riding paradigm through which Latin America attempted to explain itself and the basis for a new Latin American master-story. Like the ethnographic writing of the time, the telluric novel was characterized by adherence to belated nineteenth-century realist literary conventions, even as both attempted to promote belief in a quasi-mystical relationship between inhabitants and environment. While partaking of a superficial realism in their descriptive modus operandi, these texts were nonetheless products of artifice, a technique which Borges simply amplified and exposed. González Echevarría argues that the prime example is 'Tlön, Uqbar, Orbis Tertius' which, with its pseudo-anthropological account of a completely invented realm, radically critiques the ideological operation that underlay the telluric form. By mimicking the illusion of precision, but applying it to the obviously fictional Tlön, Borges unveils the mode's fantastic dimension.[53] Without using the more overt trappings that have come to be associated with the split modernist subject, Borges nonetheless undermines the telluric's belatedly realist idiom by comprehensively deconstructing it from within; with a performative sleight-of-hand resonant of Carroll, the author's mastery of prevailing codes allows him to stretch them beyond breaking point. In the case of both authors, therefore, modernism occurs neither in accordance with a centrally mandated timeframe, nor as the manifestation of a set of inherent textual characteristics, but instead as a function of the text's interaction with and undermining of existing realist practices.

Both also evidently shared a fondness for rogue taxonomies, whose ultimate target was not only the objects of ethnographical fieldwork, but ordered systems of knowledge in a more general sense. Perhaps the most famous example in

Borges's case is the 1942 essay 'The Analytical Language of John Wilkins', in which the narrator outlines an animal classification system, which he claims is drawn from an ancient Chinese encyclopaedia called the *Celestial Emporium of Benevolent Knowledge*. The system divides all animals into fourteen categories, among which are 'Fabulous Ones', 'Stray Dogs', and 'Those that are included in this classification'.[54] This disorienting classification scheme was later deployed with verve in the opening paragraph of Michel Foucault's *The Order of Things*,[55] which Foucault claimed to have been partially inspired by Borges, but the same spirit of epistemological estrangement is present at several junctures throughout the *Alice* novels: in the 'Advice from a Caterpillar' chapter, Alice is confronted with one of the strange classification systems evidently operative in Wonderland, in this case put forward by a pigeon, who infers that Alice must be 'a kind of serpent' because she eats eggs;[56] in 'The Mock Turtle's Story', confusion is sown over whether mustard should be considered animal, vegetable, or mineral;[57] later in the same chapter, the Turtle lists 'Ambition, Distraction, Uglification, and Derision' as the branches of Arithmetic.[58] In his prologue to Carroll's collected works, Borges returns to the theme of taxonomy, but on this occasion via a reading of chapter 2 of Carroll's *Symbolic Logic* (1896). Here, Borges notes, Carroll 'wrote that the universe consists of things that can be ordered into categories and that one of these categories is the category of impossible things'.[59] Although the animal taxonomy devised by Borges was interpreted by Louis Sass as exhibiting schizophrenic logic on account of the absurdity of its sheer arbitrariness,[60] it has since been argued and even convincingly demonstrated that the gulf between it and the operating logic of conventional Western epistemology is not necessarily greater than that encountered between extant non-Western cosmologies.[61]

In effect, Carroll and Borges both shatter the surface illusion of objective realism through foregrounding the artifice of what in Latin American postcolonial discourse has come to be called the 'locus of enunciation', a term coined by Walter Mignolo to designate the fallacy of the universal vantage-point or 'nonplace',[62] 'the epistemic location from where the world was classified and ranked'.[63] Mignolo argues that this mode of knowledge production entails a pageant of 'imaginary constructions', and draws particular attention to the obverse, namely 'to the fact that if reality is constructed, it is always constructed by someone who is located somewhere specific, with some particular purpose in mind'.[64] The dubiously constructed non-place of scientific subjectivity is lampooned by Borges in 'The Aleph', with its near-literal descent 'down the rabbit-hole' of a basement at Garay Street in Buenos Aires, and wherein the titular conceit allows one to observe the entirety of the cosmos, but only from an absurdly specific location, namely the mediocre poet Carlos Argentino Daneri's underground stairwell. Conversely, Borges's questing protagonists can often be found in the process of ascending to elevated vantage points from which to observe the world: the tower in 'The Approach to Al-Mu'tasim'; the villa at Triste-le-Roy ('almost as tall as the black eucalypti which surrounded it'[65]) in 'Death and the Compass'; and the plain overlooking the marshland where the 'Yahoos' dwell in 'Doctor Brodie's Report'. Similarly, among Alice's first acts in both novels is the establishment of an elevated purview, whether unwittingly in Wonderland through rapid growth, or consciously upon exiting the Looking-Glass house, when she reasons that she 'should see the garden far better' if she were to get to the top of a nearby hill.[66] In Wonderland, however, Alice's growth 'like the largest telescope that ever was',[67] far from enhancing her observational capacities, actually diminishes her ability to see even her own feet, and the apparent route to the hill, 'more like a corkscrew than a path',[68] leads back to the house she has just exited. In each of the Borges stories, the protagonist's ultimate quest is unsuccessful, ending in proliferating mystery in 'The Approach to Al-Mu'tasim', death in 'Death and the Compass', and the committing of murder in 'Dr. Brodie's Report'.

One of the most persistent ways in which Carroll destabilizes the objective 'realism' of Victorian-era ethnography is found in the figure of Alice herself, who evinces a slippery subjectivity that has the effect of troubling the detached perspective with which she is identified. Alice grows, but also shrinks, alternating between implication and detachment, between the colonizer who commits violence simply by being present, and the disembodied gaze that withdraws from the scene of the crime. Her assumption of universal 'non-situatedness' can be inferred from the persistence with which she attempts to subtract herself: when berated for interrupting the Mock Turtle's story, she desires 'to sink into the earth';[69] in chapter 8, she responds to the Queen's murderous enquiries about the identity of the gardeners by stating that 'It's no business of *mine*'[70] (and her desire to self-efface is here perhaps sublimated into the figure of the Cheshire Cat, seemingly able to disappear from view at will); she is invisible to the inhabitants of the Looking-Glass house, and floats down the stairs without her feet touching the ground. But in spite of Alice's ethnographical impulse towards self-effacement, the text is littered with examples of how she is reminded of her own situatedness, notably by the hookah-smoking Caterpillar, and what Nabokov called his 'elenctic'[71] insistence that it behoves Alice to explain who *she* is, a reversal of the standard colonial assignment of subject-object roles; by the insistence of the Mouse and the Dodo that Alice herself receive a prize from her own pocket following the caucus race in chapter 3; by the flowers' insistence that Alice be classified alongside them as a category of flower; by the inopportune growth spurt during the court hearing in chapter 11, following which she is called upon to give evidence; by her materialization upon exiting the Looking-Glass house, following which she is enlisted to substitute for one of the chess pieces; and (in a further reversal of colonial roles) by the Lion's query concerning whether Alice herself is animal, vegetable, or mineral, before the Unicorn proclaims her to be 'a fabulous monster'.[72]

As in both *Alice's Adventures in Wonderland* and *Through the Looking-Glass*, the planting of perspectival confusion and meticulously plotted border panic within deceptively straightforward tales will be key to Borges's modernist turn in respect of ethnography. A good example of this is 'The South', since it precisely mimics the telluric tradition to which González Echevarría refers. Juan Dahlman is cast as the city-dwelling descendant of a dual lineage who, like Borges himself, typifies one of the multiple historical schisms that cleave Argentine national identity, expressed in the case of Dahlman's forebears as a split between the colonizer as evangelizing vehicle of European values and Argentine creole as member of the rural aristocracy. Though he has lost all practical knowledge of the Argentine countryside, Dahlman retains an idealized notion of the pampa and gaucho culture. He travels to the country's heavily mythologized 'South' as part of a process of recuperation following a mysterious illness, and plans to take up residence in the inherited family ranch.[73] En route, Dahlman filters the natural surroundings through what he has read; his reading material for the duration of the journey consists of a copy of the *Thousand and One Nights*, an indicator, perhaps, of the Orientalist gaze (or, to use a more specifically Latin American term coined by Walter Mignolo, the 'Occidentalist' gaze) that Dahlman brings to bear upon his process of reconnaissance of the national terrain. Shortly after arrival, he is inexplicably harassed in a tavern and then faced with almost certain death at the hands of the locals, becoming engulfed by a semiotic economy of gestures and knives that contains the (in this context) haplessly illiterate Dahlman himself as just one sign among many. Ultimately, the encounter adumbrates the existence of realities 'in the field' that exceed and overwhelm any discursive savoir faire that Dahlman can bring to the situation. This structure occurs again in 'The Gospel According to Mark', in which the story of the Crucifixion imparted by the 'cultured' protagonist Espinosa is appropriated by the 'barbaric' Gutre family, who will subsequently enlist Espinosa himself as an unwitting player within their local re-working of Christian eschatology.

Time and again, Borges's works will perform this same critique of the delusion of ethnographical impartiality. Fred Murdock, protagonist of 'The Ethnographer', is almost entirely effaced by the narrator, who claims that '[t]here was nothing singular about him',[74] a rhetorical staging of science's claim to dispassionate objectivity while pulling off what Donna Haraway calls 'the god-trick of seeing everything from nowhere'.[75] Murdock is a PhD student at a North American university who goes to live among members of an Amerindian tribe, with the aim of acquiring knowledge about the tribe's esoteric rites. After a prolonged period, and with the requisite knowledge obtained, Murdock returns to his university, but does not complete his dissertation, and ends up working in the university library. No clear explanation is given for this decision; although Murdock affirms the 'beauty' of the secret, and the 'frivolity' of the scientific discipline,[76] the reader is denied the cliché that what he has discovered is inexpressible in Western language or thought. As per Idelber Avelar's analysis, although in tone, length, and structure the story projects the sense of being a parable, it crucially withholds the disclosure of any decipherable moral instruction. Instead, it instantiates what Avelar identifies as a 'split between *producers of thought* and *producers of objects for thought*'.[77] Thus duplicating the problems of theorizing modernism in Latin America, Borges's ethnographic texts articulate the core-peripheral imbalance concerning the production and legitimation of systems of knowledge. Echoing the paradigms that Alice brings, and eventually applies to Wonderland (imperial conceptions of time, space, taxonomy, logic, mathematics, law, and causality), these stories by Borges are structured around a hypothetical total knowledge, which proves to be the product of a conspiracy ('Tlön, Uqbar, Orbis Tertius'), or an irrecoverably lost object ('The South'; 'The Ethnographer'). They generate anxieties around the status of epistemologies, not only by prying open or revealing gaps in discourse, but by having the unwitting hitherto producers of knowledge walk into the open jaws of an alternative epistemic system.

Murder and the Dream of the Other

While Gabriel Josipovici did not explain why he considered Borges as embodying 'the essential spirit of modernism' when he originally made the claim, he does provide a clue in a later piece, arguing that the idealist world of Tlön described in Borges's 'Tlön, Uqbar, Orbis Tertius' 'helps to bring out something that is often overlooked in studies of literary modernism: that to write about politics without recognising the complicity of the forms of writing with the formation of political consciousness is to betray the cause one thinks one is serving.'[78] The history of colonialism is of course steeped in the dehumanizing effects of form and rhetoric. In nineteenth-century Argentina, the ostensibly scientific, fact-finding excursions of naturalists such as Charles Darwin and early ethnographers such as Lucio Mansilla were tinged by association with the violence of the campaigns of extermination of the indigenous peoples, in which both men were tacitly complicit.[79] For Darwin, the 'lower races' on board the HMS Beagle (who had spent some years in England), precisely because of their ability to speak some English and adopt the thought processes of the civilized, embodied a 'living link' between different stages of 'the evolutionary ladder';[80] indigeneity was thereby construed as an intermediary between human and animal. The act of classifying, though not outwardly violent in and of itself, nonetheless lays the groundwork for violence to take place, and this process is demonstrated in one of Borges's most well-known later tales, 'Doctor Brodie's Report', which consists of a 'found' first person account of a lengthy field trip undertaken in Africa by a Victorian-era Scottish ethnographer. Alarmingly, Dr Brodie decides to refer to the people among whom he lives as 'Yahoos',[81] claiming that 'the total absence of vowels in their harsh language' means that 'an exact transliteration is virtually impossible'.[82] However, a more consequential act of erasure occurs when Brodie describes the 'Ape-men' who live nearby, and whom he later refers to as 'animals' at the same time as he makes the startling revelation that he once killed two of them with his rifle.[83] A similar manoeuvre occurs in Wonderland when, following the Mouse's tale (whose clear message concerns the mortal danger posed to mice by household pets), Alice offhandedly mentions her cat Dinah, 'a capital one for catching mice' who would 'eat a little bird as soon as look at it!'[84] This pronouncement is followed by her Wonderland companions hastily departing her company, though its underlying ideology is implied by virtue of the metonymic chain connecting the 'creatures',[85] as Alice initially calls them, to unspoken categories of undesirable vermin or prey. Violence is never far from the surface in the *Alice* novels, mostly at the hand of Alice herself: her initial arrival among the inhabitants of Wonderland begins with Alice almost drowning several of them in the pool of tears that she weeps while nine feet high, and her propensity to visit harm on the residents of the Looking-Glass house and its environs is underlined by her unsolicited handling of the chess pieces, and shortly afterwards in the garden of live flowers, to whom Alice (who 'didn't like being criticized') issues the ultimate threat: 'If you don't hold your tongues, I'll pick you!'[86]

Epistemic panic finally resolves into physical harm at the conclusion of Alice's course across the board in *Through the Looking-Glass*. Seated in the large hall between the Red and White Queen, Alice becomes increasingly disoriented by the 'dreadful confusion',[87] before finally seizing and pulling the tablecloth, leading to the reduction of 'plates, dishes, guests, and candles' into 'a heap on the floor';[88] she blames the Red Queen as 'the cause of all the mischief',[89] and shakes her 'backwards and forwards with all her might',[90] precipitating the complete destruction of Looking-Glass world. This move reveals the ultimate connection between ideology (or what Bivona calls Alice's 'missionary zealotry'[91]) and colonial violence, which in this case amounts to the power to destroy a society 'simply by declaring it null'.[92] While this is quickly sublimated into Alice's waking reality and the poetic digression that closes the novel ('Lingering in the golden gleam – / Life, what is it but a dream?'[93]), these latter events cannot fully occlude the violent endpoint of the dream, nor indeed of the chess-game, which ends in the checkmating and hence 'death' of the Red King. As John Irwin shows, this specific event is one that Borges worked and re-worked into his narratives, perhaps most notably in 'Death and the Compass', a story defined by its resistance to epistemic closure.[94] In this metaphysical detective story, the murder of a Jewish scholar in a hotel room is misinterpreted by investigator Erik Lönnrot as the first part of a series of coordinated crimes based on the Tetragrammaton, or the Hebrew name of God. The culprit turns out to be a professional criminal named Red Scharlach, whose ancient grudge against Lönnrot has led him to capitalize on the latter's misapprehension by carrying out a series of murders, in fulfilment of Lönnrot's own reader-generated expectations. Scharlach ultimately ensnares Lönnrot at the remote villa of Triste-le-Roy, and kills him in accordance with the requirements of the sequence that Lönnrot himself has devised in his foolishly abstract and doctrinaire attempts to apprehend the killer. As Irwin demonstrates through an identification of the German, Swedish, and Old Norse components that make up the name of 'Erik Lönnrot', the victim can be interpreted as signifying 'hidden red king'.[95] The story therefore can be linked to Carroll via an example of what Borges himself famously referred to as the myriad 'inlaid' details that he had deliberately planted in 'Death and the Compass'.[96]

As Ana María Barrenechea explains, the conclusion to the story demonstrates how, for Borges, 'language is an interpretation and organisation of the universe'.[97] But 'Death and the Compass' supplies a violent codicil to this proposition; what becomes increasingly clear throughout the story is the capacity of murder not just to generate readings in the form of investigations, but to itself be generated as the collateral damage caused by over-adherence to textual constructs. It is perhaps on the basis of this fatality ascribed to semiotic systems that Borges would later (in 'The Argentine Writer and Tradition') describe 'Death and the Compass' as 'a kind of nightmare, a nightmare in which there are elements of Buenos Aires, deformed by the horror of the nightmare'.[98] 'Nightmare' (or *pesadilla*) is also the precise term that Borges most consistently used to describe the *Alice* novels. In a 1967 interview, recounting his first childhood encounter with *Alice's Adventures in Wonderland*, he suggests that he probably wasn't 'conscious of its being a nightmare book'.[99] Nevertheless, he claims that he did intuit 'something eerie, something uncanny about it' and that, as a grown-up, he can't but encounter the text's 'nightmare touches'.[100] In a text published a couple of years earlier, he had suggested that it was impossible to know whether Carroll 'felt that in that unstable world of figures that dissolve into one another there is nightmare's beginning'.[101] And in the aforementioned prologue (published a decade later), Borges contends that both of Alice's dreams border on nightmares.[102] Given that Alice's moment of greatest consternation occurs when the proposition is put to her that she is a component of the Red King's dream, and therefore may not be real, we can perhaps infer that, for Borges as reader of Carroll, the nightmare derives from the state of finding oneself ensconced inside the Other's dream (or, in 'Death and the Compass', as a cipher inside the Other's abstraction), and therefore in a position not only of epistemological but ultimately of ontological precariousness: the threat of being snuffed out by virtue of existing only as a function of an external authorial design. Indeed, Daniel Bivona locates the segue from dream into nightmare as occurring at the juncture where Alice fails to successfully interpret, organize, and assimilate events in the large hall, and like Lönnrot, therefore fails to obtain mastery over what she has encountered.[103]

As Borges reminds us in his prologue to Carroll's collected works, dreaming and the illusory are made by Carroll to approximate fatality, with Alice warned that if the Red King awakens she will 'go out [...] just like a candle!'[104] This points towards what is perhaps Borges's most well-known and most direct appropriation from the *Alice* novels, the incomplete conditional clause 'And if he left off dreaming about you ...' that appears as the epigraph to 'The Circular Ruins',[105] and which might then be taken as a synecdoche for what is ultimately at play in the relationship between Carroll and Borges. The full line is uttered by Tweedledee, as he warns Alice that she may be merely a character from the dream of the sleeping Red King: 'And if he left off dreaming about you, where do you suppose you'd be?'[106] 'The Circular Ruins' concerns a sorcerer tasked with dreaming an apprentice into being, only to discover '[w]ith relief, with humiliation, with terror [...] that he too was a mere appearance, dreamt by another',[107] i.e. that he himself is the dreamed figure of a prior sorcerer. A variation on the theme occurs in the anti-Orientalist story 'Averroës's Search', which begins as an account of the titular philosopher's failure to translate the Aristotelian concepts of 'tragedy' and 'comedy' into Arabic, but which turns out to be a story about Borges's own failure to successfully imagine the life of Averroës, who vanishes into thin air before the story concludes, a Carrollian snuffing out that is vaguely anticipated by the imperfectly dreamed-up protagonist himself mid-way through the story, when he is momentarily assailed by the realization 'that he was old, useless, unreal'.[108]

These anxieties cannot but formally reproduce the postcolonial condition of modern Latin American subjectivity as mandated from afar (and, by extension, of Latin American modernism), which García Márquez described in his Nobel speech as the state of being akin to 'a pawn without a will' subject to '[t]he interpretation of our reality through patterns not our own',[109] a situation that has a perhaps even more accurate analogy in a curious incident from chapter 1 of *Through the Looking-Glass*. Alice first picks up the White King chess piece against his will, then inexplicably decides to take control of his pencil and thereby dictate his attempts to write in his own memorandum.[110] In other words, having decided to write down 'the horror' of being picked up, the White King now has to suffer the ignominy of having his trauma related for him, on his behalf, by his tormentor. For Gina Apostol, the postcolonial condition of existential precariousness derives from 'the sense that who you are is a fiction, the result of texts constructed by others'.[111] The modernist moment common to both Carroll and Borges can be seen to be operative in these figures of authorial and epistemological inversion, whereby the interpretive gaze that was imagined to constitute and comprehend the territory from without is instead made into the subject of a flash of interpellation, and thereafter unveiled as no more than an expression of what Borges calls the 'arbitrary and speculative' nature of all claims to hierarchically ordered knowledge.[112] While Borges's deployment of Alice throughout his oeuvre may appear superficially light of touch and even conservative in the metonymic chain of associations it sets into play, closer inspection reveals an Alice that serves as cipher for this flash of epistemological complication, occurring at the junctures where imperial monologue is supplanted by alterity, agents are revealed to be subjects, and where the hidden violence of colonial wordings becomes de-sublimated. We can conclude that both authors were engaged, often in strikingly similar fashion, with a thoroughly modernizing process of undermining and taking apart the systems, hierarchies, and abstractions that make up the fever-dream of colonialism, or, to paraphrase the terms set forth by Stephen Dedalus in Joyce's postcolonial modernist novel *Portrait of the Artist as a Young Man* (1916), of trying to finally wake up from, and reckon with one of history's longest and most persistent nightmares.

Notes

1   Gabriel García Márquez, 'The Solitude of Latin America', in *Gabriel García Márquez and the Powers of Fiction*, ed. Julio Ortega (Austin: Texas University Press, 1988), 87.

2   Amelia S. Simpson, *Detective Fiction from Latin America* (London: Associated University Press, 1990), 119.

3   Laura-Zoë Humphreys, *Fidel between the Lines: Paranoia and Ambivalence in Late Socialist Cuban Cinema* (Durham: Duke University Press, 2019), 90.

4   Juan Pablo Villalobos, *Fiesta en la madriguera* (Barcelona: Anagrama, 2013).

5   Arturo Conde, 'Alicia en Wonderlandia? The Case for Spanglish on World Book Day', *NBC News*, 23 April 2021, https://www.nbcnews.com/news/latino/alicia-en-wonderlandia-case-spanglish-world-book-day-rcna741.

6   Gerald Martin, 'Narrative Since c. 1920', in *A Cultural History of Latin America: Literature, Music and the Visual Arts in the 19th and 20th Centuries*', ed. Leslie Bethell (Cambridge: Cambridge University Press, 1998), 157.

7   As a transatlantic phenomenon, *modernismo* (and the poetry of Rubén Darío in particular) marked the first time the former colonies succeeded in influencing literary culture in Spain. See Anthony L. Geist and José B. Monleón, 'Modernism and Its Margins: Rescripting Hispanic Modernism', in *Modernism and Its Margins: Reinscribing Cultural Modernity from Spain and Latin America*, ed. Anthony L. Geist and José B. Monleón (New York: Garland Publishing, 1999), xxi. Alejandro Mejías-López gives an indication of what later became of the legacy of *modernismo* by tracking how the term registers in successive editions of the *Princeton Encyclopedia of Poetry and Poetics*. In the 1965 edition, the entry on 'modernism' describes a late-nineteenth-century Hispanic literary movement, which, in the words of the *Encyclopedia*, offered 'a cosmopolitan perspective, a new concinnity of language, and a new poetic direction' as its 'main contributions […] to Western literature' (Princeton: Princeton University Press, 1965, 527). In the second edition (1974), the entry remains unchanged, but now appears under the Spanish, *modernismo*. In the 1993 *New Princeton Encyclopedia of Poetry and Poetics*, there once again appears an entry on 'modernism', but with no reference to the Hispanic literary movement or any Hispanic poets, which continue to appear under *modernismo*; the latter entry has been amended, however, and the reference to *modernismo*'s contributions to Western literature has disappeared. See Alejandro Mejías-López, *The Inverted Conquest: The Myth of Modernity and the Transatlantic Onset of Modernism* (Nashville: Vanderbilt University Press, 2009), 1–2.

8   George Yúdice, 'Rethinking the Theory of the Avant-Garde from the Periphery', in *Modernism and Its Margins: Reinscribing Cultural Modernity from Spain and Latin America*, ed. Anthony L. Geist and José B. Monleón (New York: Garland Publishing, 1999), 53.

9   Geist and Monleón, 'Modernism', xix.

10 Neil Larsen, *Reading North by South: One Latin American Literature, Culture, and Politics* (Minneapolis: Minnesota University Press, 1995), 68; Gerald Martin, 'Spanish American Narrative since 1970', in *The Cambridge Companion to Modern Latin American Culture*, ed. John King (Cambridge: Cambridge University Press, 2004), 105.

11 Santiago Colás, *Postmodernity in Latin America: The Argentine Paradigm* (Durham: Duke University Press, 1994), 24.

12 As Liam Connell convincingly argues: 'The formal characteristics of a literature described as Magic Realist are hard to distinguish from the formal characteristics of early-twentieth-century Modernism; to that end, attempts to keep these movements distinct through the categorization of one sort of literature as modern and another as magical, as well the various attempts to define the genre through a series of extra-literary criteria, merely serve to codify a set of prejudices about Western European and non-Western societies and their respective modes of thinking' (Liam Connell, 'Discarding Magical Realism: Modernism, Anthropology, and Critical Practice', *Ariel: A Review of International English Literature* 19, no. 2 [April 1998]: 95).

13 Rajeev S. Patke, *Modernist Literature and Postcolonial Studies* (Edinburgh: Edinburgh University Press, 2013), xxv.

14 George Steiner, 'Tigers in the Mirror', in *Critical Essays on Jorge Luis Borges*, ed. Jaime Alazraki (Boston: G. K. Hall & Co., 1987), 119; Bernard McGuirk, *Latin American Literature: Symptoms, Risks, and Strategies of Post-Structuralist Criticism* (London: Routledge, 1997), 122.

15 José Eduardo González, *Borges and the Politics of Form* (New York: Garland, 1998), 169.

16 Juan José Hernández Arregui, 'La imagen colonizada de la Argentina: Borges y el Martín Fierro', in *AntiBorges*, ed. Martín Lafforgue (Buenos Aires: Javier Vergara, 1999), 158–62.

17 Edwin Williamson, *Borges: A Life* (London: Penguin, 2004); Ricardo Piglia, 'Ideología y ficción en Borges', *Punto de Vista* 2, no. 5 (March 1979): 3–4.

18 Jorge Luis Borges, 'The Argentine Writer and Tradition', in *Labyrinths* (London: Penguin, 2000), 211–20. The title of the essay is widely regarded as containing an allusion to T. S. Eliot's 'Tradition and the Individual Talent'.

19 Gina Apostol, 'Borges, Politics, and the Postcolonial', *Los Angeles Review of Books*, 18 August 2013, https://lareviewofbooks.org/article/borges-politics-and-the-postcolonial/.

20 Yúdice, 'Rethinking', 53.

21 Geist and Monleón, 'Modernism', xxi.

22 Gabriel Josipovici, *The Lessons of Modernism and Other Essays* (London: Macmillan, 1977), 26.

23 Graciela Keiser, 'Modernism/Postmodernism in "The Library of Babel": Jorge Luis Borges's Fiction as Borderland', *Hispanófila* 115 (September 1995): 45.

24 Edna Aizenberg, 'Borges, Postcolonial Precursor', *World Literature Today* 66, no. 1 (winter 1992): 21–6. See also Robin W. Fiddian, *Postcolonial Borges: Argument and Artistry* (Oxford: Oxford University Press, 2017).

25 Peter Childs, *Modernism and the Post-Colonial: Literature and Empire 1885–1930* (London: Continuum, 2007), 1.

26 Fredric Jameson, 'Modernism and Imperialism', in *Nationalism, Colonialism, and Literature*, ed. Terry Eagleton, Fredric Jameson, and Edward Said (Minneapolis: Minnesota University Press, 1990), 55.

27 Ibid., 49; 50–1.

28 Simon Gikandi, *Maps of Englishness: Writing Identity in the Culture of Colonialism* (New York: Columbia University Press, 1996), 161.

29 Geist and Monleón, 'Modernism', xxiii.

30 Jorge Luis Borges, *Introducción a la literatura inglesa* (Madrid: Alianza, 1999), 35.

31 Colonialism in Argentina has historically been complex and ambiguous: although nominally a concern of the Spanish empire up until independence in 1810, it was additionally mediated through the 'informal empire' established by British economic interests in the region for the hundred years leading up to the outbreak of the First World War, and, to a lesser extent, the hemispheric control mandated by the Monroe Doctrine to the north. The republic's colonization of its own rural interior continued up to the 1880s, culminating in the bloody and euphemistically titled 'Conquest of the Desert', and matters were complicated further by a series of mid-century civil wars pitting the 'enlightened' and 'civilised' Unitarianism of Buenos Aires with the 'barbarian' Federalism of the *provincias*, perceived as a regressive culture of warlords

and gauchos. See the collection of essays *Informal Empire in Latin America: Culture, Commerce, and Capital*, ed. Matthew Brown (Oxford: Blackwell, 2008).

32   Laura E. Ciolkowski, 'Visions of Life on the Border: Wonderland Women, Imperial Travelers, and Bourgeois Womanhood in the Nineteenth Century', *Genders* 27 (1998), https://www.colorado.edu/gendersarchive1998-2013/1998/02/01/visions-life-border-wonderland-women-imperial-travelers-and-bourgeois-womanhood.

33   See, for example, Emma D. Graner, 'Dangerous Alice: Travel Narrative, Empire, and *Alice's Adventures in Wonderland*', *CEA Critic* 76, no. 3 (November 2014): 252–8 and Daniel Bivona, 'Alice the Child-Imperialist and the Games of Wonderland', *Nineteenth-Century Literature* 41, no. 2 (September 1986): 143–71.

34   Malcolm Bradbury and James McFarlane, *Modernism: 1890–1930* (Harmondsworth: Penguin, 1976), 57.

35   References to Carroll throughout Borges's work are helpfully enumerated in Daniel Balderston, *The Literary Universe of Jorge Luis Borges: An Index to References and Allusions to Persons, Titles, and Places in His Writings* (New York: Greenwood Press, 1986).

36   Jorge Luis Borges, *Prólogos, con un prólogo de Prólogos* (Buenos Aires: Editorial Torres Agüero, 1975), 109.

37   Ibid.

38   Ibid.

39   Walter Mignolo, 'The Enduring Enchantment: (Or the Epistemic Privilege of Modernity and Where to Go from Here)', *The South Atlantic Quarterly* 101, no. 4 (fall 2002): 933.

40   Lewis Carroll, *Alice's Adventures in Wonderland* and *Through the Looking-Glass*, ed. Hugh Haughton (London: Penguin, 1998), 107.

41   Ibid., 104.

42   Roberto González Echevarría, *Myth and Archive* (Cambridge: Cambridge University Press, 1990), 56.

43   García Márquez, 'Solitude', 87.

44   Carroll, *Alice*, 141.

45   Borges, 'The Garden of Forking Paths', *Labyrinths*, 53.

46   Daniel Balderston, 'Ficciones', in *The Cambridge Companion to Jorge Luis Borges*, ed. Edwin Williamson (Cambridge: Cambridge University Press, 2013), 117.

47   Lewis Carroll, *The Complete Illustrated Lewis Carroll* (Hertfordshire: Wordsworth Editions, 1996), 556–7.

48   Benoît Faucher, 'By Indirections Find Directions Out: Thinkable Worlds in Abbott and Vonnegut' (PhD diss., Université de Montréal, 2013), 4.

49   Jorge Luis Borges, 'On Exactitude in Science', in *The Aleph*, trans. Andrew Hurley (London: Penguin, 1999), 181.

50   Stephen Kern, *The Modernist Novel: A Critical Introduction* (Cambridge: Cambridge University Press, 2011), 179.

51   Graner, 'Dangerous Alice', 252–3.

52   González Echevarría, *Myth*, 150.

53   Ibid., 162–3.

54   Jorge Luis Borges, 'The Analytical Language of John Wilkins', in *Selected Non-Fictions* (London: Penguin, 1999), 231.

55   'This book first arose out of a passage in [Jorge Luis] Borges, out of the laughter that shattered, as I read the passage, all the familiar landmarks of my thought – our thought that bears the stamp of our age and our geography – breaking up all the

ordered surfaces and all the planes with which we are accustomed to tame the wild profusion of existing things, and continuing long afterwards to disturb and threaten with collapse our age-old distinction between the Same and the Other. This passage quotes a "certain Chinese encyclopaedia" in which it is written that "animals are divided into: (a) belonging to the Emperor, (b) embalmed, (c) tame, (d) suckling pigs, (e) sirens, (f) fabulous, (g) stray dogs, (h) included in the present classification, (i) frenzied, (j) innumerable, (k) drawn with a very fine camelhair brush, (l) et cetera, (m) having just broken the water pitcher, (n) that from a long way off look like flies". In the wonderment of this taxonomy, the thing we apprehend in one great leap, the thing that, by means of the fable, is demonstrated as the exotic charm of another system of thought, is the limitation of our own, the stark impossibility of thinking that' (Michel Foucault, *The Order of Things* [New York: Pantheon, 1970], xv).

56 Carroll, *Alice*, 48.
57 Ibid., 79–80.
58 Ibid., 85.
59 Borges, *Prólogos*, 109.
60 Louis A. Sass, *Madness and Modernism: Insanity in the Light of Modern Art, Literature, and Thought* (New York: Basic Books, 1992), 119–22.
61 George Lakoff, *Women, Fire, and Dangerous Things: What Categories Reveal about the Mind* (Chicago: Chicago University Press, 1987), 92; Eduardo Viveiros de Castro, 'Cannibal Metaphysics. Amerindian Perspectivism', *Radical Philosophy* 182 (November/December 2013): 21.
62 Mignolo, 'The Enduring Enchantment', 938.
63 Walter D. Mignolo, *The Idea of Latin America* (Oxford: Blackwell, 2005), 42.
64 Walter D. Mignolo, 'Editor's Introduction', *Poetics Today* 15, no. 4 (winter 1994): 505.
65 Borges, 'Death and the Compass', *Labyrinths*, 113.
66 Carroll, *Alice*, 135.
67 Ibid., 16.
68 Ibid., 135.
69 Ibid., 83.
70 Ibid., 72.
71 Vladimir Nabokov, *The Real Life of Sebastian Knight* (London: Penguin, 2001), 101.
72 Carroll, *Alice*, 201.
73 As Eva-Lynn Alicia Jagoe explains, the term transcends geographical referentiality and functions as a placeholder for a complex idea of the rural intertwined with national identity. Jagoe elaborates: 'The South in Argentina is protean. In geographical terms, it incorporates Patagonia and Tierra del Fuego [....] Yet, in Argentine conceptions of their country, the South also includes the pampas, which extend south and west, even stretching somewhat to the north of Buenos Aires. A striking example of this disregard for the compass can be found in the capital's Retiro bus terminal where Mendoza, a city situated west by northwest of the capital, is included in the timetables' southern itineraries. The South in Argentina, then, holds little cartographic allegiance. Instead, it functions as a signifier of a time and space that is incorporated into different cultural and political projects and ideologies from post-independence to the present day. It is present in the evocative mythologies of the gaucho, the Indian, the horse, and the vast expanse of land; in Borges's image of a street with city on one side and desert on the other, and in the discourse of underdevelopment and crisis that threatened the foundations of Argentine identity in 2001' (Eva-Lynn Alicia Jagoe, *The End of the World as They Knew It: Writing*

Experiences of the Argentine South [Lewisberg: Bucknell University Press, 2008], 12–13).

74 Jorge Luis Borges, 'The Ethnographer', in *Collected Fictions* (London: Penguin, 1999), 334.

75 Donna Haraway, 'Situated Knowledges: The Science Question in Feminism and the Privilege of Partial Perspective', in *Women, Science and Technology. A Reader in Feminist Science Studies*, ed. Mary Wyer, Mary Barbercheck, Donna Cookmeyer, Hatice Orun Ozturk, and Marta L. Wayne (New York: Routledge, 2014), 459.

76 Borges, 'The Ethnographer', 335.

77 Idelber Avelar, *The Letter of Violence: Essays on Narrative, Ethics, and Politics* (New York: Palgrave, 2004), 59.

78 Gabriel Josipovici, 'Borges and the Plain Sense of Things', in *Borges and Europe Revisited*, ed. Evelyn Fishburn (London: University of London. Institute of Latin American Studies, 1998), 62.

79 González Echevarría, *Myth*, 149.

80 Virginia Richter, *Literature after Darwin: Human Beasts in Western Fiction 1859–1939* (London: Palgrave, 2011), 86.

81 The obvious allusion to Swift is mentioned in Borges's preface, in which he claims that 'Apart from the text that gives this book its title and that obviously derives from Lemuel Gulliver's last voyage, my stories are – to use the term in vogue today – realistic' (Jorge Luis Borges, 'Preface to the First Edition', in *Doctor Brodie's Report*, trans. Norman Thomas di Giovanni [London: Bantam Books, 1972], ix).

82 Borges, 'Doctor Brodie's Report', in *Doctor Brodie*, 134.

83 Ibid., 134.

84 Carroll, *Alice*, 29.

85 Ibid., 23.

86 Ibid., 137.

87 Ibid., 232.

88 Ibid., 234.

89 Ibid.

90 Ibid., 235.

91 Bivona, 'Alice the Child-Imperialist', 148.

92 Graner, 'Dangerous Alice', 254.

93 Carroll, *Alice*, 241.

94 McGuirk, *Latin American Literature*, 122.

95 John T. Irwin, *The Mystery to a Solution: Poe, Borges, and the Analytic Detective Story* (Baltimore: Johns Hopkins University Press, 1996), 74.

96 Donald L. Shaw, *Borges' Narrative Strategy* (Leeds: Francis Cairns, 1992), 119.

97 Ana María Barrenechea, *Borges the Labyrinth Maker*, trans. Robert Lima (New York: New York University Press, 1965), 82.

98 Borges, 'The Argentine Writer and Tradition', in *Labyrinths*, 215–16.

99 Jorge Luis Borges, *Conversations* (Jackson: Mississippi University Press, 1998), 34.

100 Ibid.

101 Borges, *Introducción*, 35.

102 Borges, *Prólogos*, 109.

103 Bivona, 'Alice the Child-Imperialist', 170.

104 Carroll, *Alice*, 165.

105 Borges, 'The Circular Ruins', in *Labyrinths*, 72.

106 Carroll, *Alice*, 165.

107 Borges, 'The Circular Ruins', in *Labyrinths*, 77.
108 Borges, 'Averroës's Search', in *The Aleph*, 73.
109 García Márquez, 'Solitude', 89–90.
110 Carroll, *Alice*, 130.
111 Apostol, 'Borges, Politics, Postcolonial', n.p.
112 Borges, 'The Analytical Language of John Wilkins', in *Selected Non-Fictions*, 231.

Chapter 11

'SENTENCE FIRST VERDICT AFTERWARDS': CARROLL, NABOKOV, AND THE FRAGMENTED BODY

Yaeli Greenblatt

Lewis Carroll's importance to Vladimir Nabokov's writing is well established, evident first and foremost in Nabokov's celebrated 1923 Russian translation of *Alice in Wonderland*.[1] As Julian Connolly remarks, Nabokov's *Ania v strane chudes* is 'one of the most ingenious and delightful' versions of Carroll's work and should be seen as an 'adaptation or transposition' due to its own creative force.[2] Connolly points to the translation as marking Nabokov's early 'predilection for verbal play, punning, and sound repetition'.[3] Beyond this tendency for Carrollian wordplay, Wonderland and its inhabitants remain a significant point of reference in nearly all of Nabokov's works, with a particular critical focus on the novels *Lolita* and *Pale Fire*. For example, Elizabeth Prioleau reads *Lolita* as a world of mirrors, and comments that '*The Real Life of Sebastian Knight* and *Ada*' are 'studded with Carrollian echoes and allusions'.[4] Julian Moynahan similarly argues for Carroll as a constant presence in Nabokov's entire body of work 'with its mirror images, dissolving perspectives and identities, and astonishing metamorphoses of scene and style' which 'shows affinity with the writings of that eccentric English mathematician and story teller from first to last'.[5]

In comparison, Nabokov's *Invitation to a Beheading*, the subject of this essay, has received less scrutiny as a work in dialogue with *Alice in Wonderland* and *Through the Looking-Glass*. The 1935 Russian novel, translated into English in 1959, depicts the last weeks in the life of Cincinnatus C., a prisoner who is condemned to death by a grotesque totalitarian regime. The novel's surreal setting follows Cincinnatus as he is put through a farcical theatre crafted by the prison jailers. By analysing Carroll's and Nabokov's treatment of decapitation, I argue that Carroll's texts are a crucial key to unlocking a thematic connection between language and body fragmentation. Likewise, their word-games are a catalyst for the body's undoing, the product of a modernist aesthetic in which the creative potential of language is made to coincide with its violent, destructive power – death and play bound up together within the narrative. In Carroll, the theme of the severed head is prominent throughout both of Alice's journeys. From her own expanding limbs to the Cheshire Cat's detached body, Alice's road to the decapitating court of the Queen of Hearts is filled with images of fragmented bodies. The constant threat of decapitation is presented through the unstable nature of language, as words unravel, reverse their meaning, and betray the speaker. In his account of Cincinnatus C.'s anxious wait for execution, Nabokov reimagines Carroll's depiction of wordplay and beheading in a dark phantasmagoria. The novel's anticipation of beheading further explores the role of language as a dynamic force, taking part in both the protagonist's imprisonment and unshackling. Through the use of puns, acronyms, synecdoche, and syllogisms, Nabokov emphasizes the inescapable presence of death in the narrative as wordplay unmasks Cincinnatus C.'s impending execution. The novel concludes in a retelling of the ending to *Alice's Adventures in Wonderland*.

What I will be reading as fragmented, broken, or detached bodies in the Wonderland narratives have been analysed through a variety of different paradigms, including the ethical, political, and psychoanalytical. Donald Rackin argues that bodies in Wonderland mark Carroll's de-sexualizing of the narrative, reading disembodiment as emblematic of a mind-body separation. The Cheshire Cat's smile, for example, becomes Carroll's own 'detached intelligence'.[6] In historicised readings of beheading the queen's 'off with their head' is presented as taking part in the debate on execution, contemporaneous with Carroll's time, as evident in Michelle Ann Abate's work on Carroll and the Anti-gallows movement.[7] The satirical portrayal of nonsensical decision-making in the ruling class is also a significant point of contact between Carroll's and Nabokov's narratives. Like the Queen of Hearts's capricious behaviour, Cincinnatus's world is plagued with arbitrary laws and illogical mechanisms. In the hands of these regimes, wordplay is a powerful and dangerous tool, used to frighten and torment.

The very first nonsensical statement Alice makes, as she falls down the Rabbit Hole, concerns her reaching the other side of the earth where she expects to meet 'people that walk with their heads downward! The antipathies'.[8] Though her misattributed word marks a reversal of the head's position, and not its detachment, this image sets the stage for Carroll's fascination with unnatural, or fragmented, bodies in Wonderland. Alice's own body is soon subjected to a series of transformations, growing and shrinking to abnormal sizes. Here we may observe one of Carroll's recurring techniques: taking bodies apart through animation of discrete parts. As Alice grows, 'opening out like the largest telescope',[9] the growing scale dissolves the unity of her body. No longer viewing her feet as connected to her, Alice considers the new relationship she must now have with them. Through an extended use of personification, Alice details a fantasy of fragmented physicality. The experience of alienation from her body is made clear as Alice asks her feet, 'who will put on your shoes and stockings for you now, dears?'[10] The feet as disembodied body parts are taken to the extreme through the detached head of the Cheshire Cat. To allow for his emblematic fluidity in appearing and disappearing, his body is fragmented, famously leaving 'a grin without a cat'.[11] The journey through Wonderland culminates in Alice's visit to the royal court of the King and Queen of Hearts, where execution by beheading is brought to the fore. There, the Cheshire Cat appears again not as a grin, but as a detached head, the authorities facing a dilemma as to how to carry out his sentence: 'The executioner's argument

Figure 11.1 *'You couldn't cut off a head unless there was a body to cut it off from'* (from John Tenniel, Illustration from *Alice's Adventures in Wonderland* [*Floating Head of the Cheshire Cat*], 1869).

was, that you couldn't cut off a head unless there was a body to cut it off from [....] The King's argument was, that anything that had a head could be beheaded.'[12] The threat of beheading constantly looms on the horizon, and is, I will show, frequently the result of words betraying their speaker.

Carroll repeats the mechanism in which a double meaning of a word is manipulated into a threat of decapitation. In this way, language becomes a dangerous tool to operate, its fluid, unpredictable nature a constant threat. As she leaves the Cheshire Cat behind, Alice encounters the Duchess. Trying to impress with her knowledge, Alice proclaims 'the earth takes twenty-four hours to turn round on its axis'.[13] The Duchess in response takes advantage of the available auditory pun: 'talking of axes [...] chop off her head!'[14] Alice is later threatened again by the queen herself: 'either you or your head must be off, and that in about half no time!'[15] Here again, wordplay seems to endanger Alice: the double meaning of 'off' is played on through a zeugma connecting the two different scenarios. Whether Alice chooses to leave, or is forcibly executed, the verb remains constant. In addition, Alice's head is personified by its implied ability to independently leave the scene. Granted autonomous agency, the head is once again detached from the body in a figurative doubling of the threat of decapitation. Complementing this highly condensed sentence is an additional word-game: the paradox of the expression 'half no time'. Dividing nothing by two is yet another act of fracturing, as time is shown to be simultaneously present and absent. In these two statements by the Duchess and Queen the inherent malleability of language, and its capacity to produce multiple meanings, is used to reveal the unexpected presence of death. A parallel case of the dangers inherent in language can be seen in the sentencing of the Mad Hatter. His crime, of badly reciting a poem in front of the queen, is proclaimed as 'murdering the time'.[16] Taken literally, the offense escalates in seriousness from being a bore to murder, and therefore merits execution. By reviving the dead metaphor in the expression (i.e. bored to death or killing time) and personifying the figure of Time, death is introduced both in the crime and in the customary threat of beheading that follows. Here again, it is not only the queen that poses a danger, but language itself.

A reversal of the pattern of body fragmentation can be found in the detachment not of a head, but of a tail. As with the Duchess's threat, here, too, a pun is the direct cause for undoing the Mouse's body. As he describes his 'long and sad tale',[17] the reader is presented with the typographical image of a tail translated by Alice into the shape of a winding line on the page of the book. Alongside John Tenniel's illustrations, the unique typography provides a material presence for the theme of severed bodies in Wonderland. Within this playful graphic synecdoche, the threatening aspect of the dismemberment is echoed in the content of the Mouse's story. Foreshadowing the farcical tart-stealing trial at the end of Alice's journey, the poem tells of a trial that must take place because that 'morning [Fury has] nothing to do'.[18] The Mouse attempts to negate the trial, saying it 'would be wasting our breath', but the cur promises: "'I'll be judge and I'll be jury," said cunning old Fury: "I'll try the whole cause and condemn you to death.'"[19] This gruesome sentence is not only the consequence of boredom, but necessitates from the poem's rhyme scheme, where the Mouse's interjection of wasted 'breath' anticipates his own doom when the poem ends with the expected rhyming word, 'death'.

Though the Queen of Hearts is absent from the sequel to *Wonderland*, Alice's return in *Through the Looking-Glass* is no less haunted by images of headlessness, and here, too, language is at the root. Signalling our entry into the sphere of decapitation is the image of the Knight chess piece. The severed horse's head is first drawn on the page adjacent to the 'Dramatis Personae' – before Alice's story begins – providing an index of moves and opening positions on the looking-glass chessboard, and then again in an enlarged form in Tenniel's illustrations of the first chapter, where the Knight is given a body with a grotesquely large head or helmet.[20] The fragmented bodies of these chess figures become even more tangible with the Red Knight who later dons the decapitated head of a horse '[taking] up his helmet (which hung from the saddle, and was something the shape of a horse's head)'.[21] It is when the chess game is won, and Alice becomes a queen, however, that the most striking of Tenniel's images of decapitation appears in the illustration of a headless leg of mutton, bowing his phantom head with a frilly napkin tied as a ruffle neck collar.

White Pawn (Alice) to play, and win in eleven moves

Figure 11.2 *The Head of the Chess Knight* (from John Tenniel, Illustrations from *Alice's Adventures in Wonderland* [*Chess Board*], 1897 and [*Knight*], 1871).

Upon stepping through the mirror and into the drawing room beyond, Alice is presented with a 'looking-glass book' in which she reads the ballad of the Jabberwocky.[22] The poem contains two of Carroll's most noted inventive poetic devices. The first is mirror writing, displaying the letters of the poem backwards: '*sevot yhtils eht dna, gillirb sawT*';[23] the second is the portmanteau: a creation of a new word out of the fragments of two others. In keeping with the tradition of the ballad, the poem concludes with the slaying of the foe. In this case, the beast is not only killed but is, more specifically, decapitated: the hero 'left it dead, and with its head / He went galumphing back'.[24] Where language is pulled apart, reversed, and fragmented, bodies follow suit.

The word 'portmanteau',[25] which explains the writing technique of 'Jabberwocky', is suggested to Alice by Humpty Dumpty later in the narrative. In this crucial scene, exploring the boundaries of language, images of fragmented bodies are also highly emphasized, not only through beheading but in their most creative forms. Acting as poetic interpreter, Humpty Dumpty presents Alice with a radical approach to language, proclaiming: 'When *I* use a word [...] it means just what I choose it to mean – neither more nor less'.[26] As Michael Hancher demonstrates, this segment is 'often cited as defining an extreme limit in semantic theory'.[27] Offering a defence of Humpty Dumpty's linguistic approach, Hancher suggests that it is a case of speech as 'stipulative definition', a term inspired by Carroll's assertion in his book *Symbolic Logic* that an author may change the meaning of a word if the new meaning is presented to the reader in advance.[28] Within his argument, Humpty Dumpty proposes the only relevant question is 'which is to be master';[29] can the speaker determine the meaning of a word, and maintain control over that meaning? Considering the danger and violence introduced by language manipulation throughout the *Alice* books, this question becomes of increasing importance, and can be reformulated as not only a question of communication, but also of agency.

The fragmentation of the portmanteau words, and of Humpty Dumpty's language, distancing words from their meaning, is dramatized through the fragmented bodies in the scene. Alice remarks that if Humpty Dumpty 'smiled much more the ends of his mouth might meet behind, [...] and then I don't know *what* would happen to his head! I'm afraid it would come off!'[30] This image of a severed head is elaborated in the full undoing of Humpty Dumpty's body as his fall fractures him into countless pieces. In Carroll's version of the rhyme '*All the King's Horses and all the King's men*' are unable to '*put Humpty Dumpty in his place again*'.[31] However, earlier variations of the nursery rhyme, including that in the Mother Goose collection, make the subtext of Humpty's fall much more explicit by ending with 'cannot put Humpty Dumpty together again'.[32] The nursery rhyme was originally presented as a riddle, the answer to which was that Humpty Dumpty is an egg.[33] As Tenniel's illustrations make this fact clear, the consequence of the fall can be deduced by the reader despite the gentler formulation of the rhyme. As she parts from Humpty Dumpty, another fracturing of Alice's body occurs. The

Figure 11.3 *The Headless Mutton* (from John Tenniel, Illustrations from *Alice's Adventures in Wonderland* [*Leg of Mutton*], 1871).

egg declares that he would not recognize Alice if the two were to meet again, as her face is so (un)remarkably 'the same as everybody has'.[34] Instead, he imagines a more memorable version of Alice's appearance: 'now if you had the two eyes on the same side of the nose, for instance – or the mouth at the top – that would be *some* help'.[35] This image of Alice's face, which is both grotesque and comical, repeats the disassembly of Humpty Dumpty's own body, a fragmentation that begins in his radical treatment of language.

Alice in Wonderland and *Through the Looking-Glass* abound in images of broken and beheaded characters. As the Queen of Hearts makes clear in her proclamation, 'sentence first – verdict afterwards',[36] words and sentences always precede threats of decapitation. It is no coincidence that Alice's education on the precariousness of the body in Wonderland's legal system is at the same time a lesson in grammar and syntax. Scenes in which bodily fragmentation is particularly significant mirror the treatment of language as fluid and erratic. Words are shown to master the characters, pulling the narrative towards a constant threat of corporeal fragmentation. The image of Humpty Dumpty's excessive smile severing his head perfectly captures Carroll's treatment of beheading as a singular combination of laughter and violence.

In Nabokov's Russian translation of 'sentence first – verdict afterwards', the Queen's pun is preserved, but the violent repercussion of such an arbitrary trial is intensified. As Victor Fet argues, Nabokov's version, which translates to 'execution first – sentence afterwards', is an intentional modification to adjust the story to twentieth-century Russian readers, who would have been all too familiar with such judiciary proceedings.[37] A similar sense of escalation can be noted in Nabokov's treatment of beheading. Against Carroll's abstracted visions of disassembled bodies, and the Queen of Hearts' constant (but nevertheless empty) threats of decapitation, Nabokov depicts the concrete physical reality of execution. By contrast, in the *Alice* books, headlessness is a temporary condition. With the exception of the Jabberwocky, bodies revert to their original state, or else the threat of their undoing never comes to fruition. However, in the dark Wonderland of *Invitation to a Beheading*, the anticipation of Cincinnatus C.'s execution looms concretely and oppressively over Nabokov's narrative. When he is instructed to prepare 'for those involuntary bodily movements that directly follow severance of the head',[38] the physical repercussions of such a sentence become shockingly vivid. At the same time, the surreal tendencies of the narrative allow for other varieties of disassembly and transformation, complicating the theme of beheading. Within this exploration, the connection between fragmented bodies and manipulations of language is preserved, as wordplay continually foreshadows the protagonist's death. The very crime for which Cincinnatus is incarcerated is connected to his perception, misuse, and perversion of words. As noted by Julian Connolly, 'from the perspective of his society, Cincinnatus reveals himself to be a subversive criminal as he manipulates words and images to "deconstruct" not only his body but ultimately the entire world which has imprisoned him'.[39] Attempting to regain control over words and letters is also Cincinnatus's bid for sanctuary and solace. While framing the final moment of Cincinnatus's sentence, the novel does not suppress the broken body. Images of dematerialized physicality abound, beheading extended beyond the arena of the final execution.

Paralleling the Duchess's subversion of Alice's innocent proclamation, making it into a threat, Cincinnatus's jailers taunt him with doubly inflected words. Always leaving the prisoner in a state of anticipation, the prison director refuses to name a specific time at which the execution will take place. When the moment arrives, and Cincinnatus is hurried into a carriage, the director's instructions maintain the uncertainty: 'you know where. Off to do chop-chop'.[40] The phrase 'chop-chop' as a colloquial expression for 'hurry up' provides a callous yet non-committal depiction of the destination and events that will follow. The same case is evident in reverse earlier in the narrative: "'Mercy," exclaimed the director, unmindful of the tactlessness of that word.'[41] The double meanings of words sign and un-sign Cincinnatus's sentence. The question arises as to who is tormenting Cincinnatus with language games: his jailers, the narrator, or as in Carroll, is language itself revealed as a dangerous, even deadly agency.

The meta-textual threat to Cincinnatus's life is encoded in the very structure of *Invitation* as a novel. This idea is explored by Gennady Barabtarlo in relation to a pun that operates on an external diegetic level, separate from the protagonist's awareness:

> Perhaps nowhere in the world's vast literature on decapitation does the obvious and jejune pun on the Latin for 'chapter' (caput) present itself so naturally and in such meaningful fashion as in *Invitation to a Beheading*. Cincinnatus's last days are literally numbered by the chapters' increments, a day per capita, and his confinement in the novel ends when, in the final chapter, he climbs the block to be beheaded. The hero and the book are 'decapitated' simultaneously (the original Russian, of course, preserves the pun in 'obezglavit').[42]

Nabokov stresses this analogy between the duration of Cincinnatus's life and that of the text through Cincinnatus's own thoughts on his approaching execution: 'we are nearing the end. The right-hand, still untasted part of the novel'.[43] In this multilayered metafictional reference, Cincinnatus imagines his last days alive as the remaining unread pages of a book that suddenly 'become quite meager'.[44] Three written narratives are counting down to the end of Cincinnatus's life. The first is envisioned by Cincinnatus, an image for his own sense of foreboding and the physical sensation of awaiting death. The second is the text Cincinnatus begins writing in his cell, scripted with a 'beautifully sharpened pencil, as long as the life of any man except Cincinnatus'.[45] He rushes to compose it, fearing he will be taken away before it is complete, but it is in the precise moment of its completion, when 'everything had in fact been written already', that he is escorted to the gallows.[46] The third narrative is the novel *Invitation to a Beheading*, where each chapter represents one of the last twenty days of Cincinnatus's life. On his way to the execution, a message is presented to Cincinnatus through a looking-glass. In this moment of foreshadowing, the letters on 'a glass door with the inscription "ffice"'[47] appear not only in 'mirrorlike inversion',[48] as in the first time he views them, but are themselves decapitated. The material erosion of the word's head, the letter 'O', voids the sign of meaning. A new nonsense word is then created, an apparition of death marking Cincinnatus's own nearing loss.

The fracturing of Cincinnatus's body ends in his beheading but begins with his crime. His incarceration is due to what is described as an inability to fully 'feign translucence'.[49] Unlike the other citizens of his world who possess 'transparent souls', he is 'opaque'.[50] This condition is described elsewhere as 'fleshy incompleteness',[51] suggesting that the integrity of his body is questioned. From the perspective of his peers, he is not a whole man. The translucence required of Cincinnatus is then enacted in the novel, through an unmaking of the body that begins with disassembly and reaches full transparency. Sitting in his cell, contemplating when his sentence will be carried out, Cincinnatus comes apart. He begins undressing his clothes, and continues to peel away his entire body: 'He took off his head like a toupee, took off his collarbones like shoulder straps, took off his rib cage like a hauberk. He took off his hips and his legs, he took off his arms like gauntlets and threw them in a corner.'[52] Calmly disassembling his own body, Cincinnatus finally becomes a Cheshire Cat figure as 'what was left of him gradually dissolved, hardly coloring the air'.[53]

Cincinnatus yearns for another form of existence to which he can escape. His depiction of this dream world, which he calls his 'native realm',[54] is described in a paragraph studded with bodily synecdoche until he becomes, once again, the Cheshire Cat. His 'howling heart', closed 'eyes', and 'eyelids' first appear detached from one another, as scattered pieces of a fragmented body.[55] The utopian world then comes into being with what 'slowly becomes first a languorous smile, then a warm feeling of contentment'.[56] In an echo of Carroll's cat '[vanishing] quite slowly, beginning with the end of the tail, and ending with the grin',[57] the rest of the body never materializes, remaining a detached smile.

The vision of this other hidden realm is inseparable from Cincinnatus's desire for expression. It is a place where language operates freely. Imagining that place, Cincinnatus exclaims: 'I shall really express myself, shall bring the words to bay.'[58] He intuits 'how words are combined, what one must do for a commonplace word to come alive', but is 'unable to achieve it'.[59] Cincinnatus's difficulty in operating within the linguistic restraints of his world can be seen earlier in the novel as he struggles to speak words in a form coherent to others. In order to communicate semantic content to the director, an inordinate degree of effort is needed to rearrange the initial formation of the words 'Kind. You. Very'.[60] Leona Toker interprets this phrase as Cincinnatus's struggle with the 'noncreative conventional behavior' of his world, which produces in language 'ready-made formulas'.[61] Making a similar claim, Connolly extends the perversion of language to scenes of writing in the novel. In the world of *Invitation*, writing 'has been sufficiently weakened or debased so as to pose no real threat to its members'.[62] Here again is the suggestion that language itself is a powerful agent. The prisoner 'awaits death in the prison fortress of the totalitarian state and, more important thematically, in the prison-house of language' as he attempts to 'express the inexpressible'.[63] In writing, as in speech, Cincinnatus is unable to fully express himself, experiencing a conflict with the language of his world. Like the decapitated o/ffice door, the materiality of letters on the page functions as a threat or warning. The novel *Quercus,* one of the few books allowed in the cell, contains 'a paragraph a page and a half long in which all the words [begin] with "p",[64] the initial letter of Pierre, a fellow prisoner and Cincinnatus's eventual executioner, whose controlling presence penetrates the pages of Cincinnatus's book. His own writing appears to him as 'only vestiges being the corpses of strangled words, like hanged men [...] evening silhouettes of gammas and gerunds, gallow crows'.[65] As Johnson argues 'the Greek gamma (Γ) [...] [conveys] the silhouettes of the gallows'.[66] We may recall Carroll's mouse tail and the way the visual form of the letters, and not their semantics, is used to break apart the body.

At the climax of Cincinnatus's vision of another world, language is animated, depicted as a compelling living force: 'Yes, that is the line beyond which I lose control [...]. Brought up into the air, the word bursts, as burst those spherical fishes that breathe and blaze.'[67] This is not a vision of mastery over language, but a surrender to its radical power. Cincinnatus's wish to find escape in language, to submit to words powerful enough to glow and move, is frustrated. In the hands of his oppressive regime, language is either suppressed, or incorporated to inflict pain. And yet, the novel itself, through Nabokov's writing, suggests a competing truth. Nabokov refers to *Invitation* as his 'most poetical novel',[68] and attests to writing its first draft in 'one fortnight of wonderful excitement and sustained inspiration'.[69] While Cincinnatus is barred from his fantasy of unfettered compelling language, Nabokov's readers are not.

The only condition in which Cincinnatus can reach his idyllic world becomes apparent in the ending of *Invitation,* and with it, the different variations of the fragmented body are unified. The final act of violence on Cincinnatus's body is his beheading. At the same time, he is fragmented in another way, split into two selves. Like Alice achieving her '[fondness] of pretending to be two people',[70] in doubling her world within the mirror, Cincinnatus experiences two separate realities: one in which the axe lands, another where reality disintegrates and he makes his way to join 'beings akin to him'.[71] Between these two separate experiences, Cincinnatus's fate is suspended, the ending maintaining its ambiguity. Noted by several scholars, the final scene of the novel can be read as a rewriting of the ending to the *Alice* books.[72] Like the Queen of Hearts's court turning back into a pack of cards that descend upon Alice, returning her to the bank with her sister, the execution gallery around Cincinnatus turns 'two-dimensional',[73] with the colours red and black dominating the scene. Roman, Cincinnatus's lawyer, becomes suddenly 'many times smaller',[74] shrinking like the Red Queen at the end of *Through the Looking-Glass.* This doubling is a culmination of a larger theme in *Invitation* and, as Connolly remarks, the narrative's tendency for duplication both of bodies and of language.[75] Hiding his opaque nature, Cincinnatus '[clutches] his own self to his breast, [removing] that self to a safe place'.[76] In both his life and his death Cincinnatus's body is duplicated, divided, dematerialized, and taken apart.

Reading the world of *Invitation* through gnostic philosophy, Moynahan returns once again to Carroll: Cincinnatus's 'pathos is that he is constantly encountering cryptic signs and hints which, if properly understood, would lead him through the blank wall as though through a curtain suddenly pulled back or behind a mirror and into Wonderland'.[77] However, as 'the signs mockingly refuse to yield their essential secret', it is 'death' that provides 'release'.[78] Revealing death through these obscured signs not only leads Cincinnatus to his own Wonderland but maintains Carroll's association of language and beheading.

Nabokov's notion of language as an access point to death is further explored in his later work *Pale Fire*. This highly complex novel is a parody of the act of commentary, containing the poem 'Pale Fire' by author John Shade, together with notes and interpretations by Charles Kinbote, both fictional characters invented by Nabokov. *Pale Fire* is one of Nabokov's works that is most clearly in dialogue with Carroll's Wonderland. Like *Lolita,* it has been described as a 'book of mirrors',[79] containing all of the elements of a Carrollian landscape – twins and doubles, red kings and queens and a 'mirror-realm, the Looking Glass of Alice' in the land of Zembla.[80] Following in Alice's footsteps, the characters of *Pale Fire* move through the time and space of the narrative like pieces on a chessboard. Nabokov acknowledges Carroll in his use of chess in a 1950 letter to Katharine White, in which he remarks that if Carroll's young readers are able to understand his 'very subtle and difficult chess problems' his own readers could not 'be more bewildered'.[81]

In Shade's poem and Kinbote's commentary, Nabokov continues to establish poetic devices as keys to unmaking the body and in doing so reaching the otherworldly. Games of words and letters are presented as the form in which we receive communication from the afterlife, as ghosts deliver messages and warnings. The poet John Shade's daughter, Hazel, attempts to communicate with a spirit manifesting as a 'roundlet of pale light' in a local haunted barn.[82] To begin with, Hazel shows a propensity for Carrollian word games with her fondness for 'twist[ing] words: pot, top// Spider, redips'.[83] A playful approach to language which, as Alice learns, also holds the potential for violent repercussions. In the barn séance, this talent is brought to use as the ghost communicates with Hazel by reacting to her recitation of the alphabet, eventually spelling a cryptic phrase: 'pada ata lane pad not ogo old wart alan ther tale feur far rant lant tal told'.[84] As Brian Boyd demonstrates, alluding to Nabokov's own explanation of this section in a letter to Andrew Field, the message is in fact coded. It is not, as Kinbote remarks, a 'jumble of broken words and meaningless syllables',[85] but a warning to Hazel about the tragic end to her father's life.[86] Much like Alice's encounter with the reversed writing of the 'Jabberwocky' or Humpty Dumpty's radical linguistic theory, the extreme manipulation of language works to conceal (and then reveal) danger, death, and the precarity of the body. In Nabokov's short story 'The Vane Sisters', a similar case of a ghostly scripted code can be seen, as the last paragraph of the story contains an acrostic message from one of the dead characters.[87] These allusions to ghost-writing have sparked an ongoing debate, and many imaginative theories regarding the true author of the poem and commentary of 'Pale Fire'. As Helen Sword argues, 'Nabokov's cryptopoetic gloss smacks of self-parody, exposing the slipperiness of the interpretive process itself'.[88] Sword criticizes the critical efforts to establish ghosts as a 'single, unifying' solution for the 'interpretive problems' of the novel.[89] Without attempting to conclusively determine the identity of the *Pale Fire* ghosts, or attribute parts of the narrative to one of these spirits, it is clear that their main form of action is language manipulation. In this way, we maintain the thematic exploration which, through *Invitation*, returns to Carroll in the question of mastery over language. In attributing a narrative or message to a ghost, a bodiless subject, what becomes embodied are the written words. In the absence of a corporeal body, the material letters receive the force of agency.

Like his daughter, John Shade receives a message from the afterlife. During a near-death experience following a heart attack, Shade has a vision of a white fountain. His belief in its validity is sanctioned when he reads a newspaper article of another woman who saw the same image in 'the land beyond the veil'.[90] The message, as it turns out, points not to the existence of heaven but to the subversive power of written language, as the article contained a mistake, printing the word 'fountain' instead of the original 'mountain'. As with the eroded office door sign in *Invitation*, language rewrites itself through material transformation. As a result, Shade does not experience a loss of faith, but shifts to seeing 'topsy-turvical coincidence' as life affirming.[91]

Through Kinbote's commentary on these lines, we receive, as James Ramey describes, another convoluted web of misprints, reminiscent of the threatening typographical play Nabokov employs in *Invitation*.[92] In Kinbote's extraneous aside, the material erasure of letters unmakes the subject and his body:

> A newspaper account of a Russian tsar's coronation had, instead of *korona* (crown), the misprint *vorona* (crow), and when next day this was apologetically 'corrected,' it got misprinted a second time as *korova* (cow). The artistic correlation between the crown-crow-cow series and the Russian *korona-vorona-korova* series is something that would have, I am sure, enraptured my poet.[93]

Through the supposedly innocent but systematic guillotining of letters in the English version, and the reshuffling of letters in the Russian, the tsar is transformed. Wordplay reifies the king, stripping away first his crown and then his humanity. As Ramey demonstrates, Kinbote's section on the Russian newspaper's misprint is significant as a steppingstone to the more prominent misprint of Shade's 'anagogic epiphany' of the white fountain. In both cases, forces even more abstract than Hazel's ghosts are manipulating the bodies of the narrative through wordplay.[94]

Shade's use of a syllogism in his poem is another case of language games overturning the intention of the speaker. Nabokov would have been familiar with Carroll's own fascination with syllogisms evident in his books *Symbolic Logic* and *Game of Logic*.[95] In Shade's formulation 'other men die; but I am not another; therefore I'll not die',[96] he attempts to produce the illusion of immortality. Instead, the logical failure and consequent resistance to the argument serves to emphasize the reverse. Shade's syllogism on death's certitude is later echoed in another of Nabokov's works. A similar set-up can be noted in the grammar textbook

Nabokov quotes in the epigraph to *The Gift*: 'An oak is a tree. A rose is a flower. A deer is an animal. A sparrow is a bird. Russia is our fatherland. Death is inevitable.'[97] In this case, the logical failure of the syllogism is much subtler. The concluding statement grammatically deviates from the series of simple categorizations. While the first five claims refer to facts that are true in the present, inevitability suggests an event that is still to come. By adhering to the pattern, death is implied to be immediate rather than eventual. Inevitability is then further dramatized in the movement of the sentence providing force to the last claim through inertia. Its truth is not only a result of the other claims, but of rhetorical manipulation. Toker suggests that 'each of the sentences of the epigraph [...] seems to be a fragment of a shadow syllogism'.[98] This pastiche of fractured sentences returns us to the hybridity of Carroll's portmanteau and its melding of disparate word fragments. A new formation in language that is both partial and whole.

Visiting his cell, Cincinnatus's mother recalls her childhood game of Nonnons in which 'shapeless, mottled' objects are placed in front of a distorted mirror and become wondrous images of 'flowers, a ship, a person, a landscape'.[99] The Nonnons represent Cincinnatus's secret world that is still out of reach; they are Nabokov's art of creating fiction; and they are also Carroll's Wonderland beyond the looking-glass. Nabokov's evocation of the *Alice* books in the last scene of *Invitation* is telling, not only as part of Carroll's vast influence on Nabokov's writing, but in pointing to a mutual exploration in both works. Manipulations of language through puns, rhymes, logical contradictions, and physically altered writing are systematically connected to unnatural conditions of the body, to images of disappearance, fragmentation, and beheading. Both Carroll and Nabokov portray language as mediating the otherworldly, as a destructive agent that reshapes, disassembles, and pulls bodies apart. Viewed through the terms of Humpty Dumpty's linguistic theory, the characters of Wonderland and of Nabokov's *Invitation* enact a conflict of mastery over language. These works explore the inherent tendency of words to subvert one meaning and replace it with another. Language is an unstable field on which to operate, and 'one of the most serious things that can possibly happen to one in a battle' as Tweedledee explains is 'to get one's head cut off'.[100] Once again, the elasticity of words extends into the bodies of the narrative, brutally de-materializing corporeal reality. The uncanny combination of death and humour is echoed in a scene depicting Cincinnatus reading *Quercus:* 'It was somehow funny that eventually the author must needs die – and it was funny because the only real, genuinely unquestionable thing here was only death itself, the inevitability of the author's physical death.'[101] Beyond the horror of his own execution, Cincinnatus finds in the certitude of death not only comfort, but a sense of elation.

Invitation and the *Alice* books chart corresponding trajectories to beheading. In Carroll's whimsical world the underlying oppression is always unexpected, whereas in Nabokov it is the use of humour and word-games within Cincinnatus's violent world that strikes a jarring note. By infusing brutality into one narrative and play into the other, both authors invest in an aesthetic that pivots on the crux of violence and joy.

Notes

1   In his 1967 interview with Nabokov, Alfred Appel, Jr. suggests an affinity between
     Carrollian nonsense and Nabokov's writing techniques in *Bend Sinister* and *Pale
     Fire.* On this occasion, Nabokov admits to being very 'fond of Carroll' but insists on
     separating his own 'invented [languages]' from those of Wonderland. Since this early
     establishment of a connection between the two authors, there have been countless
     studies of Carrollian allusions in Nabokov's works. Among the early critics who
     delve into the intertextual relationship, it is worth singling out Elizabeth Prioleau
     who, focusing on *Lolita,* speaks of Carroll as a 'powerful influence' on Nabokov
     (Elizabeth Prioleau, 'Humbert Humbert Through the Looking Glass', *Twentieth
     Century Literature* 21, no. 4 [1975]: 428–37). Excellent commentary on Nabokov's
     Russian translation of Carroll can be found in Julian W. Connolly, 'Ania V Strane
     Chudes', in *The Garland Companion to Vladimir Nabokov*, ed. Vladimir E. Alexandrov
     (London: Routledge, 2014), 18–25, and in Nina Demurova, 'Vladimir Nabokov,
     Translator of Lewis Carroll's *Alice in Wonderland*', in *Nabokov at Cornell*, ed. Gavriel
     Shapiro (Ithaca: Cornell University Press, 2003), 182–91. For a more recent study
     of Nabokov's place within the history of Russian translations of the *Alice* books,
     and the reverberation of Carroll's work within his early novels, see Julia Trubikhina,
     'Nabokov's Beginnings: "Ania" in Wonderland or "Does Asparagus Grow in a Pile of
     Manure?"', in *The Translator's Doubts* (Boston: Academic Studies Press, 2017), 38–85.
     Trubikhina also details correspondences between Alice and 'the many underage
     heroines of Nabokov's fiction' (ibid., 74). In addition to these focused investigations,
     Carroll is often alluded to in Nabokov studies in relation to their shared themes
     such as mirror worlds, doubles, chess, and card games. See, for example, D. Barton
     Johnson, 'Text and Pre-Text in Nabokov's "The Defense" or "Play It Again, Sasha"',
     Modern Fiction Studies 30, no. 2 (1984): 278, and Priscilla Meyer, 'British Subtexts:
     Lewis Carroll', in *Nabokov and Indeterminacy: The Case of The Real Life of Sebastian
     Knight* (Evanston: Northwestern University Press, 2018), 48–56. Carrollian themes
     can also be found in less frequently discussed texts such as the posthumously
     published "La Veneziana" ('The Venetian'): a short story set in an English castle
     in which a character travels in and out of a painting as if stepping through
     Alice's looking-glass. The story also includes a lamentation on life's overbearing
     consistencies: 'Our laws, though–our pulse, our digestion are firmly linked to
     the harmonious motion of the stars, and any attempt to disturb this regularity
     is punished, at worst by beheading, at best by a headache.' Of the '[splendid]'
     '[interruptions]' to 'the world's monotony' alluded to here by Nabokov, this paper
     will focus on disruptions to the laws of language which result in beheading and other
     acts of fracturing of the body. (Vladimir Nabokov, 'La Veneziana', in *The Stories of
     Vladimir Nabokov* [New York: Vintage, 2011], 105).

2   Connolly, 'Ania', 19.

3   Ibid., 24.

4   Prioleau, 'Humbert', 428.

5   Julian Moynahan, 'A Russian Preface for Nabokov's "Beheading"', *NOVEL: A Forum
     on Fiction* 1, no. 1 (1967): 16.

6   Donald Rackin, 'Mind over Matter: Sexuality and Where the "Body Happens to Be"
     in the Alice Books', in *Textual Bodies: Changing Boundaries of Literary Representation*,
     ed. Lori Hope Lefkovitz (Buffalo: SUNY Press, 1997), 169.

7   Michelle Ann Abate, '"The Queen Had Only One Way of Settling All Difficulties […]"
     "Off with His Head!": *Alice's Adventures in Wonderland* and the Anti-Gallows
     Movement', *Papers: Explorations into Children's Literature* 21, no. 1 (2011): 33–56.

8   Lewis Carroll and Hugh Haughton, *Alice's Adventures in Wonderland* and *Through the
     Looking-Glass and What Alice Found There* (London: Penguin Classics, 2009), 11.

9   Ibid., 16.

10   Ibid.

11   Ibid., 59.

12   Ibid., 76.

13   Ibid., 54.

14   Ibid.

15   Ibid., 81.

16   Ibid., 64.

17   Ibid., 27.

18   Ibid., 28.

19   Ibid.

20   Ibid., 113, 131.

21   Ibid., 206.

22   Ibid., 131.

23   Ibid.

24   Ibid., 132.

25   Ibid., 187.

26   Ibid., 186.

27   Michael Hancher, 'Humpty Dumpty and Verbal Meaning', *The Journal of Aesthetics
     and Art Criticism* 40, no. 1 (1981): 49.

28   Continuing this argument Hancher explains that the lack of a pre-definition is
     justified due to the reversal of all temporal sequences in the looking-glass world. For
     this reason, Humpty Dumpty explains his meaning only after uttering the word (ibid.,
     49–50).

29   Carroll, *Alice*, 186.

30   Ibid., 183.

31   Ibid., 182.

32   Blanche Fisher Wright, *The Real Mother Goose* (New York: Scholastic, 1994), 40.

33   Lucy Rollin, 'Dreaming in Public: The Psychology of Nursery Rhyme Illustration',
     Children's Literature Association Quarterly 19, no. 3 (1994): 105.

34   Carroll, *Alice*, 192.

35   Ibid.

36   Ibid., 107.

37   Victor Fet, 'Beheading First: On Nabokov's Translation of Lewis Carroll', *The
     Nabokovian* 63 (2009): 56.

38   Vladimir Nabokov, *Invitation to a Beheading*, trans. Dmitri Nabokov (London:
     Penguin, 2010), 6.

39   Julian W. Connolly, 'Cincinnatus and *Différance*: Subversive Discourse in *Invitation to
     a Beheading*', *Cyncos* 12, no. 2 (1995): 74.

40   Nabokov, *Invitation*, 166.

41   Ibid., 4.

42   Gennady Barabtarlo, 'Within and without Cincinnatus's Cell: Reference Gauges in
     Nabokov's *Invitation to a Beheading*', *Slavic Review* 49, no. 3 (1990): 391.

43   Nabokov, *Invitation*, 1.

44 Ibid.
45 Ibid., 2.
46 Ibid., 168.
47 Ibid., 171.
48 Ibid., 7.
49 Ibid., 11.
50 Ibid., 12.
51 Ibid., 92.
52 Ibid., 19.
53 Ibid.
54 Ibid., 70.
55 Ibid.
56 Ibid.
57 Carroll, *Alice*, 59.
58 Nabokov, *Invitation*, 69.
59 Ibid.
60 Ibid., 4.
61 Leona Toker, *Nabokov: The Mystery of Literary Structures* (Ithaca: Cornell University Press, 1989), 129.
62 Connolly, 'Cincinnatus and *Différance*', 74.
63 Barton D. Johnson, 'The Alpha and Omega of Nabokov's *Invitation to a Beheading*', in *Nabokov's Invitation to a Beheading: A Critical Companion*, ed. Julian W. Connolly (Evanston: Northwestern University Press, 1997), 123–4.
64 Nabokov, *Invitation*, 95.
65 Ibid., 67.
66 Johnson, 'Alpha', 126. In addition to Johnson's excellent analysis of this passage, a recent study has expanded on the material aspects of Nabokov's typography by focusing on 'synesthetic perception of typographic letters as images' (Zsuzsa Hetényi, 'The Texture of Type: Nabokov's Sensory Perception of Alphabetical Letters: The Semanticized Graphic Form', *Scando-Slavica* 66, no. 2 [2 July 2020]: 217–31.)
67 Nabokov, *Invitation*, 70.
68 Alfred Appel and Vladimir Nabokov, 'An Interview with Vladimir Nabokov', *Wisconsin Studies in Contemporary Literature* 8, no. 2 (1967): 138.
69 Ibid., 132.
70 Carroll, *Alice*, 14.
71 Nabokov, *Invitation*, 180.
72 See, for instance, Fet, 'Beheading First', 60, and Gleb Struve, 'Notes on Nabokov as a Russian Writer', *Wisconsin Studies in Contemporary Literature* 8, no. 2 (1967): 156.
73 Nabokov, *Invitation*, 180.
74 Ibid.
75 Connolly, 'Cincinnatus and *Différance*', 73.
76 Nabokov, *Invitation*, 12.
77 Moynahan, 'Russian Preface', 14.
78 Ibid.
79 McCarthy, 'A Bolt', viii.
80 Ibid., ix.
81 Vladimir Vladimirovich Nabokov, *Vladimir Nabokov: Selected Letters, 1940–1977*, ed. Dmitri Nabokov and Matthew J. Bruccoli (San Diego: Harcourt Brace Jovanovich, 1989), 99.

82 Vladimir Nabokov, *Pale Fire* (London: Penguin, 2000), 150.

83 Ibid., 39.

84 Ibid., 151.

85 Ibid.

86 Brian Boyd, *Vladimir Nabokov: The American Years* (Princeton: Princeton University Press, 1991), 454.

87 Vladimir Nabokov, 'The Vane Sisters', in *The Stories of Vladimir Nabokov* (New York: Vintage, 2011), 631.

88 Helen Sword, *Ghostwriting Modernism* (Ithaca: Cornell University Press, 2002), 150.

89 Ibid.

90 Nabokov, *Pale Fire*, 51.

91 Ibid., 53.

92 James Ramey, 'Parasitism and *Pale Fire*'s Camouflage: The King-Bot, the Crown Jewels and the Man in the Brown Macintosh', *Comparative Literature Studies* 41, no. 2 (2004): 194–5.

93 Nabokov, *Pale Fire*, 205.

94 Ramey, 'Parasitism', 195.

95 Lewis Carroll, *Symbolic Logic* and *The Game of Logic* (New York: Dover Publications, 1958).

96 Nabokov, *Pale Fire*, 35.

97 Vladimir Nabokov, *The Gift* (London: Weidenfeld and Nicolson, 1963), 11.

98 Toker, *Nabokov*, 176.

99 Nabokov, *Invitation*, 105.

100 Carroll, *Alice*, 167.

101 Nabokov, *Invitation*, 95.

Chapter 12

'YOU'RE NOTHING BUT A PACK OF CARDS!': CARROLLIAN INTERTEXTUALITY AND THE DETECTIVE FICTION OF DOROTHY L. SAYERS

Ann Martin

As a form of middlebrow modernism, Dorothy L. Sayers's detective fiction mediates modernity and its cultural productions for a wide readership. Intertextuality is integral to her exploration of the individual's place in interwar Britain, particularly in the Lord Peter Wimsey novels and short stories of the 1920s and 1930s. Her literary allusions form a narrative strategy through which Sayers and her characters engage with shifting perceptions of social identity and with authoritative uses of language. Sayers's references are often playful, emphasizing the game that is the mystery novel and offering – in the vein of Lewis Carroll – a tongue-in-cheek treatment of precursors and generic conventions. My focus is how this interactive literary dynamic works also to complicate the perceived limitations of her popular fiction and its associations with political conservatism and an unreflective nostalgia for the landed gentry. What emerges from a reading of Sayers's intertextuality as it intersects with the influence of Lewis Carroll within the context of modernity is a social vision based upon the necessity for active interpretation. This is the trait that informs the detective's and the modern subject's shared ability to analyse discursive systems, be they cultural, juridical, political, or military. Whether in the first Wimsey novel, *Whose Body?* (1923); in the last, *Busman's Honeymoon* (1937); in the fulcrum text, *Strong Poison* (1930); or in *The Wimsey Papers*, a set of articles published serially in *The Spectator* during the early months of the Second World War, Sayers's characters navigate social structures through critical approaches to cultural dogma and are thereby able to engage with hegemonic systems analytically and according to local and communal connections. The network of allusions in her texts is thus analogous to the network of social relations that Sayers presents, as both require contextualized interpretation: that is, interpretation informed by the socio-economic contexts of specific characters, the intersubjectivity of the spaces and societies they inhabit, and the cultural knowledges that inform a reader-citizen's reception of narrative. It is a relational model of modernity that, while derived from traditional forms of class interdependence and depicted through genre fiction, is grounded in the lived, intertwined experiences of modern subjects.

Down the Rabbit Hole: Intertextuality and Interpretative Agency

The *Alice* novels play a significant role in this larger literary project and are a source for allusions throughout the Wimsey series. Sayers writes that, as a child growing up in Oxford, she 'knew "Alice" before [she] was four-and-a-half',[1] the age at which her father, the Headmaster of the Cathedral Choir School, relocated the family to Bluntisham. Though certainly known in Oxford, Carroll was not a connection of the family; however, according to Sayers's nurse, 'when the elderly don with the mane of wavy gray hair met them walking, he always smiled at her in her buggy'.[2] For Sayers, Carroll's literature is what matters – as she puts it, the 'entrancing sounds' and 'rhyme and rhythm' of the poetry and the prose, since 'the philosophical beauties of the Looking-Glass world were not fully clear to me till a very late period'.[3] Her references to Carroll's writings are nonetheless wide and varied, as indicated by the *Lord Peter Wimsey Companion*, in which dozens have been identified by Stephan P. Clarke and Donald K. Stephens.

Critics have found structural echoes between the authors, too. Nancy-Lou Patterson, for example, perceives a parallel between the opening of *Alice's Adventures in Wonderland* and Harriet Vane's descent into the Rabbit Hole of a murder investigation in *Have His Carcase* from 1932.[4] That said, the ways in which allusions to Carroll's work signify within her socially engaged modernism have not been explored to the same extent. On one level, Lewis Carroll represents a form of cultural capital that is accessible to author and reader alike, and references to his texts invoke and reiterate a sense of community and common value. Indeed, Carroll's social currency is foregrounded by Sayers herself in 1933's *Murder Must Advertise*, where *Alice in Wonderland* occupies a prominent place on the bookshelf in the office Wimsey takes at Pym's Publicity. A source text for the firm's advertisements – along with 'Bartlett's *Familiar Quotations*, the *Globe* edition of the *Works of Wm. Shakespeare*, and five odd numbers of the *Children's Encyclopedia*'[5] – *Alice* becomes Sayers's self-reflexive gesture to the mobilization of Carroll's aura in commercial contexts, including her own stories. In this sense, allusions to his texts legitimate Sayers's position within the field of British literary production and within the socio-political structures of early twentieth-century Britain. Both educated at Oxford, the authors and their choice of focal characters – white, upper-middle-class, educated Britons – reflect the cultural and economic norms that inform their texts' appeal. In this sense, the traditional function of children's literature – and of nonsense specifically, if viewed in its position as a correlative of 'common sense by providing a residual category for storing disorder'[6] – corresponds to the function of Sayers's detective fiction. As her protagonist asserts in *Strong Poison*, after his sister-in-law has dismissed the moral character of Harriet Vane on the basis of her literary profession: '"Damn it, she writes detective stories, and in detective stories virtue is always triumphant. They're the purest literature we have."'[7] In Valentine Cunningham's approach, such a claim marks the genre's significance for modernism, since, in 'determining order and significance amidst the seeming randomness' of the age, the fiction can be seen as working 'to build and uphold a firm structure of social and moral values'.[8] Thus both the mystery and the children's book provide social lessons that can operate to reaffirm a conservative worldview.

The mode of that perceived pedagogical impulse, however, provides grounds for resistant interpretation, especially given the satirical treatment of conventional morality on the part of both Sayers and Carroll. The latter's wordplay and parodies disrupt an instructional dynamic, as he critiques the foundations of the late-Victorian educational project by undermining its form and content. As Maryn Brown points out, Alice's improper recitations of moral Victorian verse in *Alice's Adventures in Wonderland* end up ridiculing both 'the poems and the rote teaching techniques they represent'.[9] In a passage that is later quoted by Sayers's Lord Peter in *Gaudy Night* (1935) to characterize his time at Balliol, school subjects are satirized through the Mock Turtle's listing of his own curriculum: "'Reeling and Writhing, of course, to begin with [...] and then the different branches of Arithmetic – Ambition, Distraction, Uglification, and Derision'".[10] For Carroll, according to Lisa Sainsbury, education 'requires active engagement and a scrutiny of authority'.[11] She observes the same philosophy in Sayers's satirical references to '"edifying literature" for children' in the stories comprising *Even the Parrot: Exemplary Conversations for Enlightened Children* from 1944.[12] The text's 'investment in reason' and in the dialectical application of thought,[13] rather than rote learning, echoes the intentions of Carroll and, to a lesser extent, his methods. Here, Carroll's use of wordplay would seem to be more of an influence on Sayers's detective fiction, particularly where her main character manipulates language in the company of other adults.

Wimsey is the character in Sayers's oeuvre who most often implements the challenging dynamics of Carroll's riddles, pastiches, and puns. As Alice comes to learn, wordplay works to estrange usage from habitual meaning and unreflective interpretation. When asked how to make bread, Alice responds, "'You take some flour – '", but is interrupted by the White Queen: "'Where do you pick the flower?'"[14] Carroll's disruptions of 'linguistic certainty'[15] often stem from literalizations of language that are otherwise taken at face value: the dry recitation of English history that does nothing to make Alice less wet,[16] a political party's caucus race enacted physically as a pointless sport,[17] the Mouse's tale being imagined and presented visually as a tail.[18] In such instances, 'meaning is often made material, factual, and consistent at the expense of the understanding that makes up common sense'.[19] Alice's application of reason against 'adult silliness'[20] is thus echoed by her author's playful language games, which undermine conventional modes of comprehension. Such methods are enacted by Sayers's detective protagonist, who critiques in order to correct the dubious and often received logic of police officers, judges, lawyers, doctors, members of the aristocracy, artists, advertisers, reporters, men and women of business, etc. Wimsey's approach to detection expresses itself through parody, too, a linguistic tactic that demands 'complex attention'.[21] The result is a challenge to the 'power imbalance' of dominating discursive structures, where inequity 'is worked out at the level of language',[22] not just by Alice but also by Wimsey. Such interrogations of the spaces, roles, and rules, according to which bodies are read, connect the child's experience of the adult world to the citizen's experience of modernist Britain, whether in its most avant-garde or most reactionary expressions.

More than 'literary glibness',[23] then, intertextuality is a technique that compares to the feminist textual strategy Katherine Saunders Nash has identified in her analysis of the 'implied readerly experiences' of Sayers's novels.[24] Nash sees Sayers's narrative ethics as stemming from the point of view through which readers are 'asked to inhabit the separately competent judgements of both male and female focalizers and to adopt a feminist ideology through, and occasionally in spite of, Harriet's viewpoint'.[25] I argue that a similar interpretative agency is called upon in Sayers's references to Carroll. The inferred relationships between source text and citation may be read through Harriet Vane's well-educated, mystery novelist's eyes or from Lord Peter Wimsey's aristocratic perspective, thus enabling a reader's 'vicarious assumption of social privilege',[26] particularly where Wimsey 'solves his cases by detecting the smallest faults in taste and etiquette'.[27] In other words, through an implied alignment with the reading skills and status of her characters, Sayers reaffirms the 'bourgeois fantasy' implicit in the fiction of the autonomous subject.[28] However, at the same time that Wimsey represents 'a qualified model of the modern self' that is impossible to achieve,[29] the interpretative gaze that he and Vane enact speaks also to a '*methodology*' that can be emulated[30] – particularly in their application of reason against rhetoric. In this sense, Aoife Leahy's view of Sayers's realism as 'an attempt to educate the readers of detective fiction' about 'modernist themes'[31] may overlook the other stakes of her middlebrow project, including its presentation of a politics of critical interpretation. Just as the detective must be 'adept at negotiating a mass-mediated modernity',[32] so Sayers's readers are presented with a model for both analysing cultural narratives and thinking differently and for themselves. It is significant, then, that like Alice's journeys, Sayers's attempts to reinterpret, rather than merely reproduce, discursive structures meet materialized limits. Alice's assertion of voice in Wonderland is ended by her sister's conclusive identification of a future domesticity; Sayers's representations of a politically engaged wartime citizenry are contained by a similarly powerful narrative: the Second World War. The year 1940 marks the last of the Wimsey series published by Sayers herself,[33] as she shifts from prose realism to overtly Christian explorations of the individual's relationship to art, society, and morality.

Sayers's religious writings – the plays she created for the Canterbury Festival, her somewhat-controversial twelve-part radio serial on the life of Christ, her scholarly translation of *The Divine Comedy* left unfinished at her death in 1957 – are not difficult to connect to the apparent conservatism of her middlebrow detective fiction. Written by the daughter of the Reverend Henry Sayers, MA[34] and featuring an idealized representation of the landed English gentry, novels such as *Busman's Honeymoon* can be read through the nostalgia for a 'world' that is 'self-contained and never changing',[35] popular in the Golden Age of Detective Fiction. The changes to social roles and structures that Sayers does address have been glossed according to the author's 'unthinking acceptance' of her own classed and raced position,[36] especially where Sayers's feminism privileges, and indeed valorizes, 'the upper-middle-class woman typically pursuing intellectual and professional independence' at the expense of working-class or lower-middle-class experiences.[37] Her '[u]nconscious anti-semitism' suggests her embeddedness in a cultural moment and milieu: in evoking racist and classist stereotypes, she clearly 'mirrored her world'.[38] Of course, by replicating it in print, she thereby reaffirmed and reiterated its norms. Sayers's use of foreign 'types' and stock characters are particularly problematic in this regard. Like her idealized depictions of village churches, country seats, a transcendent Oxford, and an often-benevolent aristocracy, such characters, settings, and plot points work to place her as a writer of, one might say, 'the normalizing functions of tradition'.[39]

The 'politically conservative' author can thus be linked to the commercial writer,[40] whose texts legitimate dominant social and economic structures, particularly through her deliberate recirculation of common cultural touchstones, including, but not limited to, Carroll. Nicola Humble has pointed out that Sayers 'annexes aristocratic identities and values' to create her characters,[41] and Sean Latham has explored how, through Lord Peter especially, the author trades on 'the mass-mediated allure of aristocratic distinction'.[42] That said, Sayers indicates as much in her self-reflexive references to Wimsey's popular origins, as when a character in *Murder Must Advertise* notes that Wimsey (in a rather thin disguise) is a combination of Bertie Wooster and the popular film actor, Ralph Lynn,[43] both associated with the 'silly ass about town' type.[44] Such metafictional allusions to the literary and cinematic conventions from which Sayers borrows are not atypical in her work: Wimsey and his wife are mistaken for '"Film-actors, by the look of yer"'[45] in another nod to the popularity of the image, and Lord Peter names his own literary precursor by calling himself Sherlock Holmes.[46] On one level, these self-aware gestures rupture the illusions of a mimetic reality even as, on another level, they facilitate a suspension of disbelief according to the fictional characters' embodiment of a contemporary cultural scene. A similar dynamic is evident in Sayers's choice of a female detective fiction writer as a key character. Drawing attention to Sayers's own knowledge of and play with the genre, Harriet Vane in *Gaudy Night* researches the nineteenth-century mystery novelist Sheridan LeFanu and argues his distinction from Wilkie Collins.[47] Such gestures generate a believable though fictional mise-en-scène, a culture-world, which is further layered by Sayers's references to canonical novelists, dramatists, and poets: Shakespeare, Donne, Browne, Tennyson, Brontë, T. S. Eliot, and, of course, Carroll. Where Harriet 'gains status in the eyes of others through her connection with Lord Peter Wimsey',[48] Sayers gains status through her deployment of cultural capital. Indeed, it is the cultural currency of her allusions to highbrow and popular art alike that forms the target of Q. D. Leavis's 1937 review of *Gaudy Night* and the final Wimsey novel, *Busman's Honeymoon*. The degree to which 'Miss Sayers is valued', her 'good standing with the respectable'[49] and her 'reputation as a literary figure' comprise the backbone of the criticism, for, despite Sayers's MA in Modern Languages, the Cambridge scrutineer argues that education has neither 'refine[d] the perceptions' of the author nor formed 'decent taste'.[50] Rather, Sayers is a writer who represents 'an average taste which is at best negative',[51] and whose value is not just questioned but illegitimated.

In the context of Carroll and the cultural role of children's and middlebrow literature, however, 'average' may have leverage, especially in terms of the vision of community that arises from Sayers's allusions. Here, leverage stems from the status of 'middlebrow' and 'modernism' as categories that are 'shifting, overlapping, and open to intervention',[52] both are forms of cultural production that, in their day, did not reduce to a rhetorically convenient 'zero-sum game' of cultural hierarchies and divisions.[53] In representing common ground rather than either avant-garde or stolidly refined taste, Sayers's texts do not easily equate to any one half of a great divide that would radically transform cultural landscapes or militantly reaffirm existing literary and social traditions. As Nash has noted, within 'a political climate marked by partisan statements' regarding such issues as women's rights,[54] Sayers's work avoids a revolutionary tone. Indeed, revolutionaries in politics and in art are often the objects of parody for Sayers, be they small-minded communists, champagne socialists, or absurdly flamboyant bohemians. Similarly critiqued are the hollow men of the status quo: cynically commercial novelists, empty-headed aristocrats, or – with much less humour – authority figures who embrace fascistic and eugenical discourses to pursue power, and the citizens who unreflectively reiterate those views. In her critique of 'the social elites' as well as the middle classes,[55] the professional classes, and the workers of the world, Sayers's satire, like Carroll's, is less focused on a specific object or political agenda, and more concerned with modes of social behaviour.

Strikingly, the behaviour that is the focus of Sayers's condemnation is hypocrisy. Hypocrisy crosses classed and cultural lines, particularly in detective fiction plots that depict interpersonal conflict and the local, human consequences of larger economic, political, or ethical systems. Perhaps for this reason, though murder is common in Sayers's stories, blackmail is immoral. It is itself hypocrisy: a sin that deploys sin and that, in many of her texts, levels the unjust or outdated norms of a society against an individual without accounting for human context. As a crime that cites the language of the righteous and enacts the received, unilateral morality of the ruling class, it exploits individual vulnerability. Blackmail refuses history; it refuses to recognize the complexity, diversity, changeability, and especially the interconnected nature of community. Sayers's texts stand in contrast to such solipsism, whether in terms of the varied perspectives of different focal characters,[56] the range of social landscapes Wimsey traverses, or the perceptive, empathetic interpretations of those settings and citizens by the detective who views himself as part of their world. From the first Wimsey novel, class distinctions are crossed physically, as by Lord Peter's cab ride from Piccadilly to Battersea Park. They are crossed socially by the middle- and lower-middle class characters, such as Detective Inspector Charles Parker and Wimsey's manservant, Bunter, who are both able and willing to critique Lord Peter's attitudes and actions. Boundaries are also crossed culturally by the detective himself, as the aristocratic sleuth relies consistently upon a range of different citizens and social circles for the knowledge necessary to solve his cases.[57]

Literary references hold together this vision of an interdependent society, in part because of the interactive dynamic that Wimsey's own speech entails. As Craig

Mattson notes, through 'parodies' and 'paradoxes', Wimsey's wordplay necessitates a 'shared awareness' that makes 'his detective practice constantly affiliative', as he 'draws others into detective conversations'.[58] Allusions to commonly known works and writers mark such moments of connection within Wimsey's world. In his first conversation with Parker, for example, Lord Peter presents a parody of Gilbert and Sullivan to express his excitement at the case. He then deliberately mangles 'Comin' thro' the Rye' in order to criticize the limitations of Inspector Sugg, assigned to the case, and then adapts verse spoken by Lewis Carroll's Mock Turtle. In his nonsensical reference to '"Sugg of the evening, beautiful Sugg!"',[59] Wimsey signals the police officer's nonsensical approach: that is, his reliance on the trope of the usual suspect and irrational decision to take into custody a woman who could not have committed the murder in question. Parker meets Wimsey's stream of literary allusions by recognizing their connotations, where the tone matters more than the content, as evidenced by his '"Ah"' and summary in plainer language of Wimsey's implications. His interpretation of the intention behind the citation speaks to the men's common cultural knowledge. So, too, Sayers implies, can her reader interpret the significance of the reference, particularly where Carroll is concerned. Indeed, the range of characters in the Wimsey series who demonstrate their familiarity with Lewis Carroll's *Alice* books may be one of the more realistic elements of Sayers's genre detective fiction. While the imagery of chessboards and playing cards in both authors' work stems from common diversions in both the golden age of children's literature and the golden age of detective fiction, by the time of the first Lord Peter novel, Carroll is an inescapable part of the cultural landscape.

'Striding Folly' (1939) exemplifies several of the methods through which Sayers alludes to Carroll. The plot of the short story focuses upon a chess player, and as in *Alice Through the Looking-Glass*, chess is the basis for the text's wordplay and its imagery. The surreal experiences depicted in the text draw upon Alice's disorientation in her topsy-turvy worlds: Wimsey notes the dream-vision of the suspect and comments that Mr. Mellilow's '"memory works both ways [...] like the White Queen's"'.[60] While the Chief Constable is not particularly impressed by the reference – '"Time's getting on, Wimsey"'[61] – other collaborators in Wimsey's work share his literary tastes. In 1928's *The Unpleasantness at the Bellona Club*, Sir James Lubbock, a materials analyst, observes that one of Lord Peter's requests makes a situation '"Curiouser and curiouser"'[62] – a phrase that reappears in *The Nine Tailors* (1934) as part of Wimsey's own line of thought.[63] Charles Parker borrows the Mad Hatter's defence from *Alice's Adventures in Wonderland* when Wimsey wants to bet on the outcome of a case: '"I'm a poor man, your Majesty," he temporised.'[64] In the short story 'The Queen's Square' from 1933, guests at a fancy-dress party wear costumes representing various board and card games, but have taken care not to '"make themselves too Lewis Carroll"'.[65] In 'Absolutely Elsewhere', a witness describes his blustering uncle as being '"like the Queen of Hearts in *Alice* – he never executed nobody, you know"',[66] a phrase that is used almost verbatim to describe another character in *Five Red Herrings* (1931).[67] In *Murder Must Advertise*, Carroll is the basis for the copywriters' banter when they develop a last-minute illustration for an incomplete ad: '"I should think it would be rather like a muchness", suggested Bredon. "Lewis Carroll, you know. Did you ever see a drawing of a muchness?"[68] In *Gaudy Night*, Miss De Vine acknowledges Harriet's help by noting to another character that "'Miss Vane has been acting as hair-dresser to the White Queen'"[69] – the same metaphor Wimsey uses when he finds some of Miss De Vine's hairpins in a later chapter. Harriet sees Wimsey brushing soot off the local vicar and is 'reminded of Alice dusting the White King';[70] he uses Carroll to describe her previous reluctance to marry him, noting "'You ran like the Red Queen'",[71] and when a potential suspect is overheard 'chirping agitatedly to herself', Harriet thinks of her as 'the White Rabbit'.[72]

References to the *Alice* books thus take the place of detailed explanations. They act as a kind of shorthand for shared ideas and attitudes, both for the reader and within the culture-world of the texts. Wimsey's nephew demonstrates the dynamic in a scene from *Gaudy Night*. Having been injured in a serious car accident, he asks Harriet to read out a letter from his uncle, a response to the Viscount Saint-George's request for money to pay his creditors:

He looked so ill that Harriet said, rather anxiously:

'Hadn't we better leave it till to-morrow?'
'No. I must know where I stand. Carry on. Speak gently to your little boy. Sing it to me. I'll need it.'[73]

Saint-George is quoting not just David Bates's 1849 poem 'Speak Gently' and its exhortation to spare the rod since children are only mortal, but also the 'far more famous' version from *Alice's Adventures in Wonderland*.[74] Specifically, when Alice describes the Duchess's adaptation of the Bates poem as 'a sort of lullaby', albeit one sung to a child (later, pig) who is given 'a violent shake at the end of every line'.[75] Bates's original is turned on its head in Carroll's parody – '*Speak roughly to your little boy, / And beat him when he sneezes: / He only does it to annoy, / Because he knows it teases*'[76] – and Saint-George anticipates the latter attitude from Wimsey, even as he signals his desire for the former. In an echo of the operation of both irony and intertextuality, Wimsey's response to his nephew delivers both.

As well as marking common knowledge and points of connection, then, the allusions play with the necessity for active interpretation, especially on the part of the detective. References to the arbitrary nature of Wonderland and the Looking-Glass world are often used to emphasize the confusion that Wimsey must work through in his cases. No wonder Sayers quotes the 'Begin at the beginning' approach to testimony in at least eight of the Wimsey stories.[77] Unlike the King of Hearts, however, Lord Peter takes the role of an intelligent listener rather than an unreasonable authority figure, and thus the arbitrariness of the command – "'Begin at the beginning", the King said, very gravely, "and go on till you come to the end: then stop'"[78] – becomes an opportunity for individuals, be it Harriet Vane,[79] or a stranger in a restaurant,[80] to start their stories where their stories start. His desire for witness statements that stem from local, personal, concrete circumstances is prompted by a common sense of disorder. For example, Lord Peter mentions that a suspect keeps "'vanishing and reappearing like the Cheshire

Cat'" at key moments in one of his investigations.[81] Similarly, in *The Nine Tailors*, his dissatisfaction with a case leads him to remark to Superintendent Blundell that "'It's like Looking-Glass Country. Takes all the running we can do to stay in the same place.'"[82] Then, as Blundell is driving away with Wimsey, he looks over the countryside and recognizes the aptness of the comparison: 'Flat as a chessboard, and squared like a chess-board with intersecting dyke and hedge, the fen went flashing past them.'[83]

When Lord Peter is 'depressed' in *Strong Poison* by his lack of progress on Harriet Vane's behalf, he attempts to move the case forward over tea with a kindly employee, Miss Climpson:

'Have a sandwich,' said Miss Climpson.

'Thank you,' said Wimsey, 'or some hay. There is nothing like it when you are feeling faint, as the White King truly remarked. Well, that more or less disposes of the money motive.'[84]

Beyond his sense of futility and absurdity, Wimsey's citation of the White King's "'there's nothing like eating hay when you're faint'",[85] suggests the place of the *Alice* books as a kind of anodyne, though it is, of course, an ironic reference: just as Alice points out that "'throwing cold water over you would be better'" than eating hay, so Wimsey knows that sandwiches will do little to save Harriet from hanging.

Even so, the *Alice* books represent a refuge, particularly where they are coded as gestures to which readers can relate. This narrative strategy ends the opening section of *Busman's Honeymoon*, in which Sayers presents letters and journal entries from various characters as they work through the social implications of Wimsey's marriage to Harriet. 'Excerpts' from Wimsey's mother's diary come last, and hers is positioned as one of the most reliable perspectives. After recounting the difficulties of the previous months and the wedding day itself, the Dowager Duchess finishes her final entry by writing that *The Stars Look Down* – A. J. Cronin's 1935 novel on the British mining industry – is 'not quite soothing enough for a bed-book' and that she 'will fall back on *Through the Looking-Glass*'.[86] Carroll equates to comfort here, both for Honoria Lucasta Denver and for the sympathetic reader, as the Dowager Duchess's retreat from modernist upheaval to Victorian tradition affirms the underlying comic structure of the final Wimsey novel. Indeed, her escape to Carroll is placed immediately before the Wimseys' removal to a village in which, in Harriet's view, 'they were all immutably themselves; parson, organist, sweep, duke's son and doctor's daughter, moving like chessmen upon their allotted squares'.[87] Both moves seem to signal a desire for a 'mythic prewar security'.[88] But *Busman's Honeymoon* remains haunted by the irreconcilable trauma of the war that has been and the war that is to be. The powerful impulses of tradition are thus situated beside ideological and aesthetic challenges that are embodied by Cronin and also by allusions to T. S. Eliot's 'The Hollow Men' in later chapters.[89] Modernism here is a socially relevant and applicable, as well as applied, form of expression rather than elitist or alienated from wider use. The same intertextual possibilities are signalled by the presence of Cronin's novel on the Dowager Duchess's bedside table, even as her turn to Carroll affirms the local or private circumstances that affect the individual's reception (or rejection) of texts.

This Way and That: Making Sense in Modernist Contexts

The conditions and the contingencies of such interpretation are flagged by the epigraphs that Sayers uses from Carroll at the beginning of several of her chapters. On a thematic level, the quotations revolve around the attempt to distinguish between nonsense and sense, and thus they emphasize the tension between chaos and order that is at the heart of the modernist mystery novel. In *Busman's Honeymoon*, for example, the section in which Wimsey and Vane brainstorm conflicting possibilities of who might have committed a crime is titled 'This Way and That Way',[90] and the epigraph ends on Alice's rather short response to the Pigeon's mistaken assumption that the girl is a serpent: "'I haven't the least idea what you're talking about.'"[91]

The need for rereading and overcoming misunderstanding is also signalled, particularly by Sayers's modified version of a repeated line from chapter IX of *Alice's Adventures in Wonderland*: "'and the moral of that is – " said the Duchess'.[92] It is used as an epigraph by Sayers at least twice. Rather ironically, it first heads a chapter in *Clouds of Witness* (1926), in which the Dowager Duchess prompts Wimsey's sister to realize, not without resentment, that she has been misled by the rhetoric of the man to whom she is secretly engaged. The second use appears in one of the final chapters of *Busman's Honeymoon*, and it frames Wimsey's actions according to larger questions of morality and social responsibility. Having sought peace at Duke's Denver after solving a difficult case, Lord Peter is asked to take his older brother's place and 'read the Lessons' as part of the local church service.[93] Sections of his readings from Jeremiah are represented and interspersed with Harriet's thoughts as she applies the words and images to the case, to the upcoming trial, and to the probable hanging of the man who has been arrested. As well as passages that resonate with the detective novel as a moral genre – i.e. 'Run ye to and fro through the streets of Jerusalem, and see now, and know, and seek in the broad places thereof, if there be any that executeth judgement'[94] – Sayers draws attention to Wimsey's self-reflection regarding the execution of his own judgement:

> For among my people are found wicked men: they lay wait, as he that setteth snares; they set a trap, they catch men [...]
> (Harriet looked up. Had she fancied that slight check in the voice? Peter's eyes were steadily fixed on the page.)
> ' [...] and my people love to have it so: and what will ye do in the end thereof?
> 'Here endeth the First Lesson.'[95]

It is a moment in which Sayers foregrounds Wimsey's own fear of hypocrisy, of power and wealth achieved through deceit and levelled for personal gain. The moral here is the danger of a hollow morality, which moves beyond the mere confusion caused by the Duchess's quest for a questionable kind of sense, for it speaks to Wimsey's doubts regarding his role. He states as much in an earlier exchange with Harriet regarding his decision to aid in the investigation: "'How often am I 'called in,' I wonder," he demanded, rather bitterly. "I call myself in, half the time, out of sheer mischief and inquisitiveness. Lord Peter Wimsey the aristocratic sleuth – my god! The idle rich gentleman who dabbles in detection. That's what they say – isn't it?'"[96] Harriet reminds him in the scene that his decision to call himself into her case saved her life, but the layers here – Sayers's awareness of her protagonist's cultural status, the character's recognition of his class privilege, the social and human consequences of analytical thinking – speak to the (self-)critical positioning that is a consistent feature in Sayers's work.

The conversation between Harriet and Wimsey refers back to the events and themes of the fulcrum Wimsey text *Strong Poison*, especially where Sayers foregrounds the tension between the discursive authority of church, state, and the landed gentry, and the individual's agency in the context of interwar Britain's shifting norms. The trial scene from *Alice's Adventures in Wonderland* becomes a key intertext in this light, as it informs the naturalized power structures that are at play when Harriet Vane is charged with the murder of her former lover who has died of arsenic poisoning. In Sayers's novel, Judge Crossley's hostility to Harriet based on her decision to live with her lover outside of marriage is compounded by a press that takes the case at face value: "'They won't be long, I shouldn't think'", said Waffles Newton; "it's pretty damned obvious.'"[97] Members of the public do the same – "'Of course she did it. You could see it by her face. Hard, that's what I call it, and she never once cried or anything'"[98] – as has Charles Parker of Scotland Yard, who has handled the case. Their common view of Harriet is based upon hegemonic conventions of womanly conduct. In agreeing "'to live on terms of intimacy'" with Philip Boyes, she has sinned, a judgement that Crossley emphasizes when projecting his own sense of outrage onto the jury:

> Now you may feel, and quite properly, that this was a very wrong thing to do. You may, after making all allowances for this young woman's unprotected position, still feel that she was a person of unstable moral character. You will not be led away by the false glamour which certain writers contrive to throw about 'free love' into thinking that this was anything but an ordinary, vulgar act of misbehaviour.[99]

His assumptions of proper gendered conduct also inform his summation of the motive, which arises from a situation he does not comprehend: "According to her statement – and on this point her evidence is confirmed by a letter which Philip Boyes wrote to his father – Boyes did at length offer her legal marriage, and this was the cause of the quarrel. You may think this is a very remarkable statement to make, but that is the prisoner's evidence on oath."[100] Where Harriet feels that she has been "'made a fool'" by Boyes – "'I couldn't stand being put on probation like an office-boy, to see if I was good enough to be condescended to. I quite thought he was honest when he said he didn't believe in marriage – and then it turned out that it was a test, to see whether my devotion was abject enough"'[101] – Crossley sees her not as an individual, but as a type. As he informs the jury: "'if Harriet Vane had not become to a certain extent corrupted by the unwholesome influences among which she lived, she would have shown a truer heroism by dismissing Philip Boyes from her society."'[102] The figure of the 'fallen' woman,[103] conveyed through the diction and syntax of an earlier era, reiterates a Victorian trope. Interestingly, Harriet's barrister, Sir Impey Biggs, draws upon the same discourse in her defence, arguing "'that this marriage-offer completely does away with any pretext for enmity on her part"'.[104] By playing to the convention of the fallen-made-honest woman, rather than acknowledging, as Harriet does, her anger at Boyes's hollow vision of "'matrimony offered as a bad-conduct prize"',[105] Biggs signals the power of the norm and anticipates the jury's participation in the judge's mode of thinking.

While Crossley presents 'value judgements that the careful reader – feminist or not – recognizes as unfair',[106] one of the cues that may prompt that recognition is Sayers's alignment of this authority figure with the King of Hearts. In addition to having come to his own conclusions regarding the case, the judge unconsciously echoes the King of Hearts as he presides over the trial of the Knave of Hearts: "'I will now begin at the beginning and try to place the story that we have heard, as clearly as possible before you."'[107] In *Alice*, the King's authoritative commands and comments in the courtroom are 'eagerly' written down by the Wonderland jurists:

> 'Take off your hat,' the King said to the Hatter.
> 'It isn't mine,' said the Hatter.
> '*Stolen!*' the King exclaimed, turning to the jury, who instantly made a memorandum of the fact.[108]

The hegemony of the authority figure is, of course, countered by Alice, who calls the jurists "'Stupid things!"'[109] and who challenges their ability to make sense of the verses that would apparently condemn the Knave of Hearts: "'If any one of them can explain it, […] I'll give him sixpence. *I* don't believe there's an atom of meaning in it."'[110] Her assumption of agency results in the climax of the text, where she squares off against the absolute monarchy of the Queen of Hearts[111]:

> 'No, no!' said the Queen. 'Sentence first – verdict afterwards.'
> 'Stuff and nonsense!' said Alice loudly. 'The idea of having the sentence first!'
> 'Hold your tongue!' said the Queen, turning purple.
> 'I wo'n't!' said Alice.
> 'Off with her head!' the Queen shouted at the top of her voice. Nobody moved.
> 'Who cares for *you*?' said Alice (she had grown to her full size by this time).
> 'You're nothing but a pack of cards!'[112]

The Alice to Judge Crossley's King of Hearts in *Strong Poison* is, it would seem, Wimsey. Indeed, his reading of both Harriet's innocence and the justice system takes the form of an intertextual response to one of Crossley's more pedantic summations of testimony:

> 'I particularly want you to remember those dates – I will give them to you again – the 10th of April and the 5th of May.' (The jury wrote them down. Lord Peter Wimsey murmured: 'They all wrote down on their slates, "She doesn't believe there's an atom of meaning in it." The Hon. Freddy said, 'What? what?' and the judge turned over another page of his notes.)[113]

Significantly, Wimsey's critique is echoed by other characters in the text (though not, it would seem, the rather clueless Freddy Arbuthnot). The Dowager Duchess, attending the trial to support her son, enunciates the disjunct Alice experiences in Wonderland: namely the tension between 'justice and logic'.[114] As she comments, following Crossley's summation and the jury's withdrawal, '"Well I suppose we shall soon know now, not the truth, necessarily, but what the jury have made of it."'[115] The ability to think outside convention is also reflected by three jurists who break with the judge's narrative. Their reasons for doing so lie in their personal interpretations of both the prisoner and her context as based on their own lived experiences. One '"couldn't lay a finger on any real weakness in the chain of evidence, but she said that the prisoner's demeanour was part of the evidence and that she was entitled to take that into consideration"'.[116] Another woman feels that '"it was perfectly possible that Boyes had taken the stuff himself, or that his cousin had given it to him"' – the latter being the actual solution to the case – and distrusts '"expert evidence"' as a kind of masculine sham.[117] A third jurist is an '"artist, and the only person who really understood the kind of life these people were leading"',[118] as well as the only one familiar with the writing and reputation of Philip Boyes who, '"from what he had heard, was a conceited prig"'.[119] The rest of the jury is willing to be guided by the judge, even to the extent of the foreman attempting to assert '"his male authority"' over the two dissenting women,[120] but the three outliers prompt a retrial. These figures on the social margins – an older spinster, a thrice-widowed owner of a sweet shop, a bohemian painter – enact their ability to approach the discursive structure of the trial critically, thus enabling Wimsey to establish a more considered and socially aware understanding of the crime.

Significantly, Wimsey and Alice are not 'simply trying to impose some kind of order on a rule-less and illogical society with no systems of its own'; rather, as Catherine Siemann states in her reading of Alice, they demonstrate 'how close to irrationality the prized rationality' of socially normative structures turns out to be.[121] In part, that inconsistency or lack of logic stems from the emotional dimensions of power as embodied by the representatives of the legal system. It is the very linguistic status of that power, however, that enables language-based challenges. Thus, when Alice recognizes that the 'hierarchy' symbolized by the King and Queen, and suits and numbers is 'nothing', the system loses its effect: 'reduced to squares of pasteboard, the cards are not only harmless, but also equal'.[122] The prose realism of *Strong Poison* presents a more complex experience. In choosing to live with Philip Boyes, Harriet has not rejected the hollow mores of a self-righteous society as much as accepted the worldview of an ultimately self-serving lover. His hypocrisy in offering marriage "'made both himself and me ridiculous'", Harriet tells Wimsey, "'and the minute I saw that – well, the whole thing simply shut down – flop!'"[123] The irony that Sayers emphasizes through Harriet's deflation of the authority of Boyes is that the left-leaning poet proves to be as sexist as the right-leaning judge. Tellingly, both place blame upon Harriet by asserting a traditional masculine privilege and the double standard.

Indeed, Boyes's citation of the norm of matrimony in a letter to his father amounts to the same typology of feminine virtue that is behind the judge's condemnation of Harriet's actions: 'My young woman is a good little soul, and I have made up my mind to do the thing properly. She really deserves it, and I hope that when everything is made respectable, you will extend your paternal recognition to her.'[124] Whether it is the judge's hypocrisy, where the language of order and objectivity masks personal prejudice, or Boyes's, where traditional thinking is masked by the trappings of modernist rebellion, the same discursive convention is wielded by both men. It is imperative, then, that Wimsey does not act alone in *Strong Poison*, but instead draws upon the different kinds of knowledge that characters from other classes, social circles, and genders possess. Nash points out the range of experiences involved: 'Katherine Climpson, Miss Murchison, Marjorie Phelps, Eiluned Price, Sylvia Marriott, Mrs. Pettican, Hannah Westlock, and a female manicurist all have access to valuable information, access that is a direct product of their vocations.'[125] Their collaboration prevents Lord Peter from being tempted "'to do the King Cophetua stunt'",[126] as one character calls it when Harriet is looking for the carefully absent Wimsey once she is acquitted. It represents Sayers's sense of how a society works best: through individuals who think critically according to their own positions, as well as through relationships formed across cultural lines.

Shaking and Waking: Social Engagement and the Second World War

That social vision becomes particularly important for Sayers in war time, when government-dominated discourses of patriotism threaten to prevent the individual's active, critical engagement in the running of the country. The concept of agency is thus central to the series of weekly columns she published in *The Spectator* from 17 November 1939 through 26 January 1940: *The Wimsey Papers*. These fictionalized extracts from letters and diary entries of various characters in the Lord Peter stories reflect an underlying element of Sayers's texts, where 'the full effect' often 'relies on one's first having read one or more other novels in the series'.[127] The familiarity of the voices and attitudes creates a similar sense of community, and echoes the function of her allusions to Carroll, just as the characters' represented experiences of the Phony War may be familiar to and shared by readers of *The Spectator*. What emerges is not merely 'an expression of patriotism'[128] in line with the nationalist sentiments she published elsewhere,[129] but also a layered critique of British and other leaders, a sustained criticism of propaganda as a mode of communication, and a call for individuals to engage with and resist the complacency encouraged by authoritative political structures.

It is striking how many characters express their dissatisfaction with the government in *The Wimsey Papers*. As Miss Climpson puts it, 'They seem (the Government, I mean) to have thought out the *beginning* of everything very well, and then to have rather *stopped thinking!*'[130] A lack of imagination is what Harriet criticizes by pointing out the flaws of politicians who have been elected for their stolid practicality rather than their creativity: 'Trying to get people to *see* and *act* with imagination is like trying to hack one's way through a jungle with a penknife. But if you give up trying – well, there's Germany to look at.'[131] The fact that Sayers places the least sympathetic Wimsey character – his sister-in-law – in 'the Ministry of Instruction and Morale' corresponds to the consistent sense of antipathy expressed towards leaders who underestimate the population's abilities.[132] Lord Haw-Haw is addressed in a number of the articles in order to demonstrate that his performances are not just ineffective but dismissed by citizens who know better, and who are neither ignorant nor helpless. While such views are presented by Sayers as a potentially edifying model of how her readers can resist the perils of German propaganda, the other aim is to critique her own government's clumsy attempts to sway the populace. Sayers thus encourages her audience to recognize and critique any instance of hollow rhetoric. As one character vents: 'All this righteous indignation poured out in the name of the Gallant Troops or the Great British People whenever there's a hint of Government interference with the sacred rights of Branded Goods! I daresay the public ought to keep their eyes skinned.'[133]

The seventh instalment of the *Wimsey Papers* (29 December 1939) engages directly with the effects of such discursive governmental power as experienced and managed by individuals. In a retrospective narration of the British response to the Battle of the River Plate – and the fall of the German Captain Hans Langsdorff of the pocket-battleship *Admiral Graf Spee*[134] – Sayers points to arbitrariness of the rules and practices of war that leave soldiers and citizens in impossible situations. Letitia Martin, Dean of Shrewsbury College, writes a two-part letter to Harriet. The first section, dated 18 December, addresses 'the fight off Montevideo', where the British victory over Germany is seen to possess 'the unmistakable heroic quality that links it up to all our naval history back to the Armada.'[135] The letter-writer then invokes the rather Carrollian image of 'two people playing chess' to describe the war at sea:

you only see one piece after another swept off the board and accounted for – a destroyer here, a merchantman there, a black knight exchanged for a white bishop – all queerly impersonal and worked out in terms of *things* – pieces – so many taken and so many left. And then, suddenly, the combination gets into action, and you see what it was all about, right away from the original gambit – a knight comes dancing across, two little pawns you'd scarcely noticed trip forward hand in hand, the black queen is forced into a corner, the knight hops away and unmasks the waiting rook, and plonk! the black queen's gone and the king in check.[136]

While acknowledging casualties, Letitia Martin contextualizes those deaths using platitudes – 'the job they were doing is done and done well' – and then turns her attention to the captain who, rather than engage in what he viewed as an unwinnable sea battle,[137] decided to destroy the damaged *Graf Spee*: 'I am most dreadfully sorry for poor Langsdorf [*sic*]. He seemed to have had a very good chit from our people – "a very great gentleman," they said, and he must have simply hated having to scuttle his ship.'[138] While she criticizes Lord Haw-Haw for suggesting that the British have labelled Langsdorff 'a coward for running into Montevideo', Sayers's very reference to cowardice speaks to popular British sentiment, just as the letter-writer's commitment to a sense of fair play – 'I'm damned if anybody shall call us bad winners' – speaks to a bygone view of warfare.[139]

Such conventional views of military conflict are then applied in the next part of the letter, dated 19 December. Having taken 'it for granted that the captain had gone down with his ship', Letitia Martin finds it distasteful to see a photo in the newspaper 'of him and his men grinning all over the place', and while she acknowledges that it is Hitler's doing, she observes that 'it's a shock that Nazi cynicism could get as far as their Navy'.[140] Hitler has 'force[d] a decent sea-captain to do a dishonourable thing', which is 'really what we are fighting about – the utter submission of the individual conscience to an ugly system in the hands of one unscrupulous gangster'.[141] The letter is ostensibly sent to Harriet, presenting the binary of honourable naval traditions (going down with the ship and dying for one's country) as preferable to dishonourable modern warfare (listening to Hitler and staying alive to serve the Third Reich). And then Sayers adds a telegram sent from Selfridges the next afternoon: 'Take back anything harsh I said about poor Langsdorf [*sic*] sorry I spoke – Martin'.[142] On 19 December, Langsdorff had committed suicide, penning a note in which he attempts to reconcile the competing discourses in which he was caught: 'I am fully content to pay with my life for any possible discredit on the honour of the flag.'[143] Not merely a game of chess, this moment in the Battle of the Atlantic is Looking-Glass country, where the political leader – like the Kings, the Queens, the adult figures in the *Alice* novels – 'governs and oversees the struggle to generate meaning',[144] and defines the rules to which figures such as Langsdorff lack full access and control. What Sayers presents in this series of recontextualizations is a British citizen's evolving recognition of the individual's place in, and their need to actively make sense of, the contradictory and destructive discourses of modern nationalism.

The shifts in attitude depicted through Sayers's staging of an historical moment suggest the challenges of navigating a world according to social and narrative conventions that do not necessarily apply. That sentiment is addressed in the final instalment of *The Wimsey Papers* by Lord Peter in a warning against domestic fascism: 'The new kind of leaders are not like the old, and the common people are not protected from *them* as they were from *us*.'[145] Against this changing society, in which writers have a responsibility and duty to the citizenry, Wimsey asks Harriet to 'express' to the population the need for action. He asks her to tell 'the people' that '[t]hey must not continually ask for leadership – they must lead themselves. This is a war against submission to leadership and we might easily win it in the field and yet lose it in our own country'.[146] According to his implied distinction between an outdated feudal order and a threatening totalitarianism, the people's 'salvation is in themselves and in each separate man and woman among them', and those individuals 'must not look to the State for guidance – they must learn to guide the State'.[147] It is a vision of self-determination that is integrally linked to local, collective action – community building through gestures of interpersonal connection. Even if, in Wimsey's words, it is 'only a local committee or amateur theatricals',[148] Sayers thereby identifies a Britain that politicians cannot achieve through unilateral assertions of policy or cynical uses of propaganda.

Such a stance may have marked the end of *The Wimsey Papers*, as the eleventh instalment is accompanied by the editorial line '*[Miss Sayers' articles will in future appear not as a weekly series, but at less regular intervals]*'.[149] In fact, they did not appear again, perhaps because of backlash from 'either the public or the editorial board, or just possibly the government'.[150] It would be, perhaps, an understandable intervention, given Sayers's short-lived and rather antagonistic participation in the Authors' Planning Committee of the Ministry of Information.[151] More generally, Roger Kuhn McGregor and Ethan Lewis point out that a 'combination of national and international events signalled the end of the era' that defined Wimsey and the Wimsey series.[152] Like Alice, who 'ceases when the narrative ends',[153] the stories are checked not just by their author but also by the literary and social discourses in operation within and beyond the texts. With the next and more violent phases of the war, Sayers turns to Christian themes through which to express her vision.

Her commitment to critical interpretation as an everyday strategy becomes, increasingly, a scholarly as well as artistic enterprise, and one in which she invokes different and contemporary media, including pamphlets, broadcasts, essays, lectures, staged dramas, translations, and radio plays. Like her citations of the *Alice* novels, such public intellectual activities speak of and to a community of readers and citizens. By invoking and indeed relying upon a mode of reading that requires active participation and relational understanding, such work reflects Sayers's focus on social and political engagement rather than a specific political platform. Even so, the ethics of her method suggest the writerly potential for change towards a more accurate and a more contextualized sense of the world and of individual, lived experiences. In her critique of unreflective leadership and emphasis on the importance of the citizen, Sayers thus indicates the potential of the interpretative agency called upon by Carroll's writing, wordplay, imagery, and irony, and modelled by Alice – practices stretched over time, text, and place. The very expansion of Carroll's work through Sayers's intertextuality and the layers of parody, critique, and interaction upon which it rests signals the continuing influence and impact of the Victorian writer, particularly in modernity, as questions of morality, duty, and community arise as perhaps never before.

Notes

1   Dorothy L. Sayers, 'My Edwardian Childhood', in *Dorothy L. Sayers: Child and Woman of Her Time*, ed. Barbara Reynolds (Cambridge: Dorothy L. Sayers Society, 2002), 9.

2   Alzina Stone Dale, *Maker and Craftsman: The Story of Dorothy L. Sayers* (Grand Rapids, MI: Eerdmans, 1978), 3.

3   Sayers, 'Edwardian', 14.

4   Nancy-Lou Patterson, *Detecting Wimsey: Papers on Dorothy L. Sayers's Detective Fiction*, ed. Emily E. Auger and Janet Brennan Croft (n.p.: Valleyhome Books, 2017), 33. See also Dorothy L. Sayers, *Have His Carcase* (London: New English Library, 1975).

5   Dorothy L. Sayers, *Murder Must Advertise* (London: New English Library, 1978), 16.

6   Susan Stewart, *Nonsense: Aspects of Intertextuality in Folklore and Literature* (Baltimore: Johns Hopkins University Press, 1979), 6.

7   Dorothy L. Sayers, *Strong Poison* (London: New English Library, 2003), 143.

8   Valentine Cunningham, *British Writers of the Thirties* (Oxford: Oxford University Press, 1988), 75.

9   Maryn Brown, 'Making Sense of Nonsense: An Examination of Lewis Carroll's *Alice's Adventures in Wonderland* and Norton Juster's *The Phantom Tollbooth* as Allegories of Children's Learning', *The Looking Glass: New Perspectives on Children's Literature* 9, no. 1 (2005): para. 8.

10 Lewis Carroll, *Alice's Adventures in Wonderland* and *Through the Looking-Glass*, ed. Hugh Haughton (London: Penguin Classics, 1998), 85.

11 Lisa Sainsbury, '"But the Soldier's Remains Were Gone": Thought Experiments in Children's Literature', *Children's Literature in Education* 48 (2017): 153.

12 Ibid., 161.

13 Ibid., 160.

14 Carroll, *Alice*, 223.

15 James R. Kincaid, 'Alice's Invasion of Wonderland', *PMLA* 88, no. 1 (1973): 96.

16 Carroll, *Alice*, 25.

17 Ibid., 26.

18 Ibid., 28.

19 Stewart, *Nonsense*, 78.

20 Kincaid, 'Alice's Invasion', 93.

21 Craig E. Mattson, 'From Wimsey to *The Wire*: Distracting Discourse and Attentional Practice', *Quarterly Journal of Speech* 100, no. 1 (2014): 39.

22 Beatrice Turner, '"Which is to be master?": Language as Power in *Alice in Wonderland* and *Through the Looking-Glass*', *Children's Literature Association Quarterly* 35, no. 3 (fall 2010): 246.

23 Q. D. Leavis, 'The Case of Miss Dorothy Sayers', *Scrutiny* (December 1937): 338.

24 Katherine Saunders Nash, *Feminist Narrative Ethics: Tacit Persuasion in Modernist Form* (Columbus: Ohio University Press, 2014), 3.

25 Ibid., 65.

26 Ibid., 64.

27 Sean Latham, *'Am I a Snob?' Modernism and the Novel* (Ithaca: Cornell University Press, 2003), 172.

28 Janet Montefiore, *Men and Women Writers of the 1930s: The Dangerous Flood of History* (London: Routledge, 1996), 153.

29 Celia Marshik, *At the Mercy of Their Clothes: Modernism, the Middlebrow, and British Garment Culture* (New York: Columbia University Press, 2016), 141.

30 Nash, *Feminist*, 62 (emphasis in original).

31 Aoife Leahy, *The Victorian Approach to Modernism in the Fiction of Dorothy L. Sayers* (Newcastle-upon-Tyne: Cambridge Scholars, 2009), 29.

32 Latham, *Am I a Snob?*, 185.

33 The short story 'Talboys' was written in 1942 but not published until James Sandoe's edited collection *Lord Peter: A Collection of All the Lord Peter Wimsey Stories* (New York: Harper & Row, 1987) in 1972. *Thrones, Dominations* (1998) was based upon Jill Paton Walsh's reconstruction of Sayers's notes for a novel regarding the Wimseys' marriage; *A Presumption of Death* (2002) was also written by Walsh with citations from *The Wimsey Papers*, and was followed by *The Attenbury Emeralds* (2010) and *The Late Scholar* (2013).

34 James Brabazon, *Dorothy L. Sayers* (Don Mills, ON: General Publishing, 1981), 2.

35 Colin Watson, *Snobbery with Violence: Crime Stories and Their Audience* (London: Eyre & Spottiswode, 1971), 102.

36 Carolyn Heilbrun, *Hamlet's Mother and Other Women* (New York: Columbia University Press, 1990), 241.

37 Nicola Humble, *The Feminine Middlebrow Novel 1920s to 1950s: Class, Domesticity, and Bohemianism* (Oxford: Oxford University Press, 2001), 78.

38 Robert Kuhn McGregor with Ethan Lewis, *Conundrums for the Long Week-End: England, Dorothy L. Sayers, and Lord Peter Wimsey* (Kent: Kent State University Press, 2000), 31.

39 Jürgen Habermas, 'Modernity versus Postmodernity', *New German Critique* 22 (1981): 5.

40 Montefiore, *Men and Women*, 1.

41 Humble, *Feminine Middlebrow*, 65.

42 Latham, *Am I a Snob?*, 187.

43 Sayers, *Murder*, 8.

44 Watson, *Snobbery*, 186.

45 Dorothy L. Sayers, *Busman's Honeymoon* (London: New English Library, 1974), 42.

46 Dorothy L. Sayers, *Whose Body?* (1923; Mineola, NY: Dover, 2009), 4.

47 Dorothy L. Sayers, *Gaudy Night* (London: New English Library, 1978), 182.

48 Humble, *Feminine Middlebrow*, 65.

49 Leavis, 'The Case', 335.

50 Ibid., 339–40.

51 Ibid., 339.

52 Marshik, *Garment Culture*, 5.

53 Leonard Diepeveen. *The Difficulties of Modernism* (New York: Routledge, 2003), 2. Nathan Waddell points out the varied ways in which 'popular and modernist culture in the inter-war period' intersected, including 'personal relationships between popular writers and their modernist counterparts; side-by-side placement of modernist and popular writings in journals and magazines; institutional and publication linkages [...]; formal imitation and literary pastiche [...]; and critical questionings of modernist culture by popular writers (and vice-versa) in books, novels, essays and lectures' (Nathan Waddell, 'John Buchan's Amicable Anti-Modernism', *Journal of Modern Literature* 35, no. 2 [2012]: 67).

54 Nash, *Feminist*, 55.

55 Latham, *Am I a Snob?* 171.

56 Nash, *Feminist*, 73.
57 As Robert Kuhn McGregor and Ethan Lewis note, Wimsey is surrounded by 'a community of support players – a police detective, a forensic analyst, a solicitor, a barrister, a financial expert, a Bohemian artist, several family members, a Bunter, and a Miss Climpson' as well as subsequent 'alternative communities, including an artists' colony and an isolated church parish, to assist his endeavours' (McGregor and Lewis, *Conundrums*, 202–3). While these characters are often character types, they suggest the range of lived experiences that Sayers's detective requires and relies upon.
58 Mattson, 'Distracting Discourse', 38–9.
59 Sayers, *Whose Body*, 12.
60 Dorothy L. Sayers, 'Striding Folly', in *Lord Peter: A Collection of All the Lord Peter Wimsey Stories*, ed. James Sandoe (New York: Harper & Row, 1987), 405; Carroll, *Alice*, 171.
61 Sayers, 'Striding', 405.
62 Dorothy L. Sayers, *The Unpleasantness at the Bellona Club* (London: New English Library, 1985), 51; Carroll, *Alice*, 16.
63 Dorothy L. Sayers, *The Nine Tailors* (London: Coronet, 1992), 195.
64 Dorothy L. Sayers, *Unnatural Death* (London: New English Library, 2003), 55; Carroll, *Alice*, 99.
65 Dorothy L. Sayers, 'The Queen's Square', in *Lord Peter: A Collection of All the Lord Peter Wimsey Stories*, ed. James Sandoe (New York: Harper & Row, 1987), 331.
66 Dorothy L. Sayers, 'Absolutely Elsewhere', in *Lord Peter: A Collection of All the Lord Peter Wimsey Stories*, ed. James Sandoe (New York: Harper & Row, 1987), 385.
67 Dorothy L. Sayers, *Five Red Herrings* (London: Gollancz, 1970).
68 Sayers, *Murder*, 47; Carroll, *Alice*, 67.
69 Sayers, *Gaudy Night*, 25; Carroll, *Alice*, 170–1.
70 Sayers, *Busman*, 104; Carroll, *Alice*, 129.
71 Sayers, *Busman*, 318; Carroll, *Alice*, 141–2.
72 Sayers, *Busman*, 348.
73 Sayers, *Gaudy Night*, 175–6.
74 Stephan P. Clarke and Donald K. Stephens, 'Speak gently to your little boy [...]', in *The Lord Peter Wimsey Companion* (Cambridge: The Dorothy L. Sayers Society, 2015), https://lpwc.sayers.org.uk/Speak_gently_to_your_little_boy%E2%80%A6.
75 Carroll, *Alice*, 54.
76 Ibid.
77 Clarke and Stephens, 'Begin at the Beginning', *Wimsey Companion*, https://lpwc.sayers.org.uk/Begin_at_the_beginning.
78 Carroll, *Alice*, 105.
79 Sayers, *Have His Carcase*, 240.
80 Sayers, *Unnatural*, 6.
81 Sayers, *Unpleasantness*, 104.
82 Sayers, Nine Tailors, 186.
83 Ibid.
84 Sayers, *Strong Poison*, 59.
85 Carroll, *Alice,* 196–7.
86 Sayers, *Busman*, 32.
87 Ibid., 98.
88 Stacy Gillis, 'Consoling Fictions: Mourning, World War One, and Dorothy L. Sayers', in *Modernism and Mourning*, ed. Patricia Rae (Lewisburg, PA: Bucknell University Press, 2007), 192.

89   Sayers, *Busman*, 321.

90   Ibid., 226.

91   Ibid., 226; Carroll, *Alice*, 47.

92   Carroll, *Alice*, 79.

93   Dorothy L. Sayers, *Clouds of Witness* (London: New English Library, 1990), 381.

94   Sayers, *Clouds*, 382.

95   Ibid., 382.

96   Sayers, *Busman*, 128.

97   Sayers, *Strong Poison*, 32.

98   Ibid., 35.

99   Ibid., 5.

100 Ibid., 7.

101 Ibid., 48.

102 Ibid., 5.

103 Catherine Kenney, 'Detecting a Novel Use for Spinsters in Sayers's Fiction', in *Old Maids to Radical Spinsters: Unmarried Women in the Twentieth-Century Novel*, ed. Laura L. Doan (Urbana: Illinois University Press, 1991), 132.

104 Sayers, *Strong Poison*, 7.

105 Ibid., 48.

106 Nash, *Feminist*, 67.

107 Sayers, *Strong Poison*, 3.

108 Carroll, *Alice*, 97.

109 Ibid., 96.

110 Ibid., 106.

111 Catherine Siemann, 'Curiouser and Curiouser: Law in the Alice Books', *Law and Literature* 24, no. 3 (2012): 435.

112 Carroll, *Alice*, 107–8.

113 Sayers, *Strong Poison*, 10.

114 Siemann, 'Curiouser', 432.

115 Sayers, *Strong Poison*, 34.

116 Ibid., 41.

117 Ibid., 42.

118 Ibid.

119 Ibid., 43.

120 Ibid., 42.

121 Siemann, 'Curiouser', 434.

122 Ibid., 435.

123 Sayers, *Strong Poison*, 49.

124 Ibid., 68.

125 Nash, *Feminist*, 75–6.

126 Sayers, *Strong Poison*, 281.

127 Nash, *Feminist*, 68.

128 McGregor and Lewis, *Conundrums*, 201.

129 Angus Calder, *The Myth of the Blitz* (London: Pimlico, 2008), 149.

130 Dorothy L. Sayers, 'The Wimsey Papers – III', *The Spectator* (1 December 1939): 770.

131 Dorothy L. Sayers, 'The Wimsey Papers – X', *The Spectator* (19 January 1940): 71.

132 Dorothy L. Sayers, 'The Wimsey Papers – I', *The Spectator* (17 November 1939): 672.

133 Dorothy L. Sayers, 'The Wimsey Papers – X', *The Spectator* (19 January 1940): 70.

134 Britain and countries around the world followed the battle closely, and, as Dan van der Vat writes, 'The response in Britain to the loss of the *Graf Spee* […] was one of

near-hysterical rapture' (Dan van der Vat with Christine van der Vat, *The Atlantic Campaign: World War II's Great Struggle at Sea* [New York: Harper & Row, 1988], 96).

135　Dorothy L. Sayers, 'The Wimsey Papers – VII', *The Spectator* (29 December 1939): 925.

136　Ibid., 925.

137　S. W. Roskill, *The War at Sea, 1939–45*, vol. 1 (London: Her Majesty's Stationary Office, 1976), 120–1.

138　Sayers, 'The Wimsey Papers – VII', 925. Sayers uses Hans Langsdorff's reputation deliberately, I would argue, to contextualize the situation. Though he was responsible for the destruction of nine British ships, it was known that 'not one British life was lost through his ship's action against defenceless merchantmen' (Roskill, *War at Sea*, 121). As significantly, during the funeral in Montevideo for the men killed during the Battle of the River Plate, the Germans who were present 'gave the Nazi salute' but 'Captain Langsdorff gave his dead the old naval salute, in full view of the world's press photographers' (Edward P. Von der Porten, *The German Navy in World War II* [New York: Corwell, 1969], 54).

139　Sayers, 'The Wimsey Papers – VII', 926.

140　Ibid.

141　Ibid.

142　Ibid.

143　van der Vat, *Atlantic*, 96.

144　Turner, 'Language as Power', 248.

145　Dorothy L. Sayers, 'The Wimsey Papers – XI', *The Spectator* (26 January 1940): 105.

146　Ibid.

147　Ibid.

148　Ibid.

149　Ibid., 104.

150　Dale, *Maker*, 117.

151　Brabazon, *Sayers*, 175–6.

152　McGregor and Lewis, *Conundrums*, 194.

153　Turner, 'Language as Power', 244.

Chapter 13

'THE MIME OF MICK, NICK AND THE MAGGIES'; OR, '"ALICE" ON THE STAGE'

James Williams

In a letter of May 1927, James Joyce complained to his friend and patron Harriet Shaw Weaver about some of the critical responses to the early published sections of 'Work in Progress', the book that would become *Finnegans Wake*:

> Another (or rather many) says he is imitating Lewis Carroll. I never read him until Mrs Nutting gave me a book, not *Alice*, a few weeks ago – though, of course, I heard bits and scraps. But then I never read Rabelais either though nobody will believe this.[1]

Joyce's phrase 'bits and scraps' may be a touch defensive, even disingenuous,[2] although by the following March he was, by his own account, absorbed in Carroll and Carrollian biography.[3] The debt Joyce owed to Carroll in the final version of *Finnegans Wake* (1939) goes much further and deeper than 'bits and scraps', and over the decades this literary relationship – a mix of influence and affinity – has garnered a correspondingly expansive critical bibliography, much of it focusing on the structural analogies and intellectual sympathies between the two writers' formal and generic experiments with sense, logic, language, and the psychology of dreaming.[4] To read *Finnegans Wake* 'under the sign of Carroll'[5] is often to feel that Joyce is treading a path of formal and stylistic development continuous, in some significant way, with that of the great Victorian nonsensifier. Often, but not always: we can also detect Carroll's presence in the *Wake* in ways that are as bizarre, episodic, fleeting, or contingent as Alice's own adventures, directed towards ends that are eccentric and unforeseen, quixotic, and unsystematic. In this chapter I want to consider how, in one section of the *Wake* in particular, Carroll becomes tangled up in an unexpected way in the book's engagement with drama, both personal and public.

Joyce and Carroll were both self-dramatizing, even self-mythologizing, artists: one indication of this is their shared propensity to heap significance on autobiographically important dates as if they were Feast Days in a private liturgical calendar. For Joyce, the days were 2 February (Candlemas, Groundhog Day, his own birthday, on which he took pains to have the first copies of *Ulysses* and *Finnegans Wake* arrive), and 16 June (his first meeting with Nora, and later Bloomsday). For Carroll, the supreme day was 4 July 1862, 'the golden afternoon' of the prefatory poem to *Alice's Adventures in Wonderland* when, still enjoying the favour of the Liddell family, he and Canon Duckworth of Trinity College took Alice and her sisters on a boat trip from Oxford to Godstow.[6] It was on this trip that Carroll began the story that would become 'Alice's Adventures Underground', then *Alice's Adventures in Wonderland*. According to the (probably misremembered[7]) accounts of the day-trippers, the weather was blazing hot.

Carroll's diary records that it was only on 13 November that he '[b]egan writing the fairy-tale for Alice, which I told them July 4, going to Godstow',[8] though Duckworth remembered differently: 'he sat up nearly the whole night [of 4 July], committing to a MS book his recollections of the drolleries with which he had enlivened the afternoon'.[9] From the beginning Carroll felt a need to regard the Golden Afternoon as perfect and spontaneous, to hold it apart from the mundane realities of literary composition. The myth of the genesis of *Wonderland* on a single day in July gained the patina of fame and, over time, something of the slickness of a performance. In his essay '"Alice" on the Stage', published in *The Theatre* in April 1887, Carroll used the occasion of Henry Savile Clarke's theatrical adaptation of *Alice's Adventures in Wonderland* to reflect on the performative and improvisational genesis of his work.[10] In it, we find him performing his hallowed conjuring trick with professional aplomb:

> Stand forth, then, from the shadowy past, 'Alice', the child of my dreams. Full many a year has slipped by, since that 'golden afternoon' that gave thee birth, but I can call it up almost as clearly as if it were yesterday – the cloudless blue above, the watery mirror below, the boat drifting idly on its way, the tinkle of the drops that fell from the oars, as they waved sleepily to and fro [....][11]

It is an unrepeatable moment that is endlessly repeated, turned into a piece of consummate story-telling and, at the same time, a disturbing act of necromancy ('Stand forth, then, from the shadowy past [...] I can call it up') in which what is recovered is not what was lost: 'Alice' is not Alice. For Carroll, the gathering 'fame' of this afternoon became increasingly like a haunting: remembering its 'sunny sky' in the lyric poem that ends *Through the Looking-Glass*, he recalls the phrase ten lines later in the mocking phantasm of 'Alice moving under skies'.[12] The other participants in the scene fell in step with this mix of eerie reverence and queasy glamour, this insistent fame: 'the *famous* Long Vacation voyage to Godstow',[13] wrote Duckworth; Alice Hargreaves (née Liddell) remembered 'the *famous* trip up the river',[14] and on each of her retellings it seemed to get sunnier.[15]

The memory, the fame, and the spectre of 4 July 1862 came to spread beyond the cultural enclosure of Carrollian biography. Richard Ellmann accords Joyce the generosity that he 'remembered his friends' birthdays and anniversaries as faithfully as he required they remember his'.[16] He extended that courtesy across literary friendships as well. One passage in part I.8 of *Finnegans Wake*, the chapter known as 'Anna Livia Plurabelle', is alive with the memory of the Golden Afternoon that was the birthday of *Wonderland*. Like much literary allusion it is at the same time a homage and a séance, a ventriloquist's act and the summoning-up of a ghost. In a chapter full of rivers, it marks a point of confluence between the Isis and the Liffey, mingling Alice Liddell's trip along the river with Anna Livia's 'riverrun' towards the sea:

> Well, there once dwelt a local heremite, Michael Arklow was his riverend name, (with many a sigh I aspersed his lavabibs!) and one venersderg in junojuly, oso sweet and so cool and so limber she looked, Nance the Nixie, Nanon L'Escaut, in the silence, of the sycomores, all listening, the kindling curves you simply can't stop feeling, he plunged both of his newly anointed hands, the core of his cushlas, in her singimari saffron strumans of hair, parting them and soothing her and mingling it, that was deepdark and ample like this red bog at sundown. By that Vale Vowclose's lucydlac, the reignbeau's heavenarches arronged orranged her. Afrothdizzying galbs, her enamelled eyes indergoading him on to vierge violetian. Wish a wish! Why a why? Mavro! Letty Lerck's lafing light throw those laurals now on her daphdaph teasesong petrock. Maass! But the majik wavus has elfun anon meshes. And Simba the Slayer of his Oga is slewd. He cuddle not help himself, thurso that hot on him, he had to forget the monk in the man so, rubbing her up and smoothing her down, he baised his lippes in smiling mood, kiss akiss after kisokushk (as he warned her niver to, niver to, nevar) on Anna-na-Poghue's of the freckled forehead.[17]

The passage is replete with Carrollian clues. '[V]enersderg' rhymes in the ear with 'Wednesday', but to the eye with Latin *dies Veneris*, Friday, Venus's day (cf. French *vendredi*, Italian *venerdì*). Joyce could have worked out that 4 July 1862 was in fact a Friday,[18] and 'Junojuly' suggests 'June or July', a vaguely remembered date somewhere around the end of one or the beginning of the other.[19] Carroll appears incognito, as the hermit-scholar ('heremite') 'Michael Arklow', suggesting St Michael the Archangel (and 'Arklow', an Irish town, perhaps suggesting Carroll by anagram as 'Karowl'). His 'riverend name' nods to Carroll the 'Reverend' who plunges into the river and onto, or into, the female body, his 'newly anointed hands': on 4 July 1862, he had been ordained deacon less than a year. Joyce's writing hints that he would forgo religious scruples, 'forget the monk in the man so', to gain the kind of intimacy which, according to Joyce, he desired with Alice.

'Venus' and 'Juno', coming so close together, signal the presence of two goddesses, older and younger: Joyce is conflating Alice Pleasance Liddell, APL (as Carroll's erotic muse, a goddess of love) with the *Wake's* heroine Anna Livia Plurabelle, ALP (Juno, mother and queen, and the figure of the River Liffey). In 'limber' we can hear, I think, a tongue-in-cheek echo of 'limper' in an earlier passage in the *Wake*, where the characters are clearly identifiable as Lewis Carroll and Alice: 'that exposure of him by old Tom Quad, a flashback in which he sits sated [...] a globule of maugdleness about to corrugitate his mild dewed cheek and the tata of a tiny victorienne, Alys, pressed by his limper looser'.[20] The erotic impulse represented by the innocent Alice pressing Dodgson's 'cheek' with a poignant goodbye kiss ('tata') resurfaces now in a 'limber' nixie,[21] a nubile water sprite. 'In the silence [...] all listening' imagines the hushed reception of Carroll's tale by the four other passengers of the boat while whispering, in that silence, Alice's name: 'Alicening'. 'He baised his lips' suggests a more lustful kiss than that in the earlier passage: the French *baiser*, out of which Joyce coins his verb, flickers between chaste and erotic, since the noun *un baiser* means 'a kiss', while the verb *baiser* means 'to fuck'. The 'vierge violetian' towards which he seems to see 'her enamelled eyes indergoading him on', likewise hovers between propriety and infamy: the fickle sexual appetite – 'A violet in the youth of primy nature / Forward not permanent, sweet not lasting'[22] – seeming, to an ungoverned, libidinous, heterosexual male ego, to desire 'violation'.

Violets are conventionally chaste flowers, viewed, in Catherine Maxwell's words, 'as a symbol for an endearingly shy and modest maidenliness'.[23] At the same time, they are also associated with beds, banks, and other sites of flowering and deflowering: Maxwell notes how 'Edith Cooper's lyric "Great violets in the weedy tangle" uses the image of violets visited by nectar-seeking bees as an analogy for youth's receptivity to sexual love'.[24] In Shakespeare, violets often grow at the edge of the innocent and the sexual[25]: the 'verge' in Joyce's 'vierge violetian' is both trespass onto a verge, or bank, of violets, and onto the sexual verge that is virginity (French *vièrge*), imperilled by the male member (*verge*). It is appropriate, in this light, that violet is a liminal colour, the boundary of the visible rainbow. Plays on 'violet', 'viola', 'violent', 'violate' recur in *Finnegans Wake*, as for example 'violer d'amores',[26] 'Violet's dyed!',[27] and 'violast lustres'.[28] The colour has a Carrollian sheen, since violet was the preferred colour of ink for his correspondence with child-friends,[29] a detail that caught Joyce's eye: in a series of notes on Isa Bowman's *The Story of Lewis Carroll*, he recorded simply 'violet ink'.[30] In Joyce's highly sexualized view of these relations, the colour appeared a lure to young girls. Carroll's use of violet ink is referred to directly in the phrase 'indecked o' voylets',[31] which manages also to gesture at 'voyeur'.[32]

One more detail comes into view before the stream of 'Anna Livia Plurabelle' flows off into pastures new, the warnings that are whispered in those parentheses like cupped hands: '(as he warned her niver to, niver to, nevar)' or never, perhaps, to be taken in by questionable old men like himself. 'Niver' echoes 'river'; but 'nevar' is pure Carroll. In a preface to a new edition of *Alice's Adventures in Wonderland* in 1896, Carroll wrote:

> Enquiries have been so often addressed to me, as to whether any answer to the Hatter's riddle can be imagined, that I may as well put on record here what seems to me to be a fairly appropriate answer, viz. 'Because it can produce a few notes, though they are *very* flat; and it is never put with the wrong end in front!'[33]

The riddle is 'why is a raven like a writing-desk?' and, like the Prankquean's riddle in *Finnegans Wake*, it is left unanswered.[34] Carroll offers the *post facto* suggestion that, like a writing-desk, a raven is 'never' put with the wrong end in front: that is, with a pinch of salt, 'raven'. Joyce corrects the solution: 'nevar'. These Carrollean allusions were added to the manuscript of 'Anna Livia Plurabelle' late in its composition;[35] they belong to the period of writing in which the drafts of the chapters were revised with a view to establishing linking motifs that would give an overarching structure to what started out as discrete sketches. This passage, towards the end of I.8, works as a prologue to the chapter that follows, II.1, the 'Mime of Mick, Nick and the Maggies', and it is here that Joyce gives one of the *Wake*'s most extended performances of Carrollian mythos and Carrollian biography.[36]

The 'Mime' is, of all the chapters of the *Wake*, the most explicitly dramatic, and it is shot through with various kinds of stage-fright: anxieties about repetition, textual mutation, comic absurdity, and grotesquerie. Lewis Carroll is an important presence throughout *Finnegans Wake*, but the 'Mime' is, to borrow Carroll's phrase, '"Alice" on the Stage'. First, the *dramatis personae*: the 'Mick' and 'Nick' of the title are Shaun and Shem, the quarrelling sons of the *Wake*'s governing patriarch HCE. The 'Maggies' are 'the two girls who tempted HCE to his fall by the Magazine wall in Phoenix Park'[37]: they are, on one reading, Issy, his daughter, and her mirror reflection as a Carrollian 'linkingclass girl';[38] but more broadly they represent 'all the temptresses in *Finnegans Wake*'[39] and, in the 'Mime' especially, the designation 'Maggies' refers to Issy's entourage, the twenty-nine 'leap-year girls', admirers of Shaun, also known as 'THE FLORAS (Girl Scouts from St Bride's Finishing Establishment [...])',[40] in which guise they reappear as the audience for Shaun's sermon in III.2.[41] The show is, in other words, a domestic comedy anxiously inflected with suggestions of incest and paedophilia, the submerged sins which Joyce – correctly or not, but he was hardly alone in his suspicions – read between the lines of the story of Lewis Carroll and Alice.[42] Finn Fordham notes in his introduction that 'Incestuous desire for Issy becomes an explanation for the idea that the deformed language of the *Wake* is deformed because it's always trying to shove something out of sight.'[43]

On this understanding, Joyce's appropriation of the Carrollian mythos is inseparable from the entire linguistic project of his late work. For his dramatic structure for the chapter Joyce again reaches back towards childhood, to a familiar game. 'The scheme of the piece I sent you,' he wrote to his patron Harriet Shaw Weaver on 22 November 1930,

is the game we used to call Angels and Devils or colours. The Angels, girls, are grouped behind the Angel, Shawn, and the Devil has to come over three times and ask for a colour. If the colour he asks for has been chosen by any girl she has to run and he tries to catch her. As far as I have written he has come twice and been twice baffled. The piece is full of rhythms taken from English singing games.[44]

What Joyce calls 'the Angel' is called 'the Minder' in Alice B. Gomme's monumental collection of British and Irish games; the figure Joyce calls 'the Devil' Gomme calls 'the Angel' (the Devil's only role in Gomme's version is to chase the child whose colour is guessed) and she gives the form of the dialogue as follows:

> Minder: 'Who's there?'
> Answer: 'Angel.'
> Minder: 'What do you want?'
> Angel: 'Ribbons.'
> Minder: 'What colour?'
> Angel: 'Red.'[45]

From Gomme's account of the game we can see more clearly that one of the rhythms of children's games that Joyce gathered up into the 'Mime' was the rhythm of call and response, patterned dialogue: a literary structure flexible and blank enough to be played as solemn ritual or as low flirtation, and the basic form of most drama.

The Angel(s) and the Devil converse four times,[46] but the dialogic shape is found throughout the chapter in different guises, resurfacing for example at the end, in the form of liturgical versicle and response, as the children's games shade into bed-time prayers: 'Loud hear us! / Loud graciously hear us!'[47] This exchange, a spoof of the conventional conclusion to intercessory or 'bidding' prayers ('Lord hear us'), also recalls other liturgical versicle and response pairs: the opening of litanies in the Roman Rite, '*Christe audi nos / Christe exaudi nos*'; the vocative 'Lord' of the *Kyrie*; and the responses to the Ten Commandments following the Collect in the Book of Common Prayer communion, 'Lord, have mercy upon us, and incline our hearts to keep this law.'[48] This dialogic motif, at both a structural and a localized level in the chapter, helps us see its title in a clearer light.[49] The choice of 'Mime', from Greek *mîmos*, meaning 'actor', establishes the chapter as a drama, one 'characterized by mimicry and the ludicrous representation of familiar types of character',[50] as is clear from the opening line: 'Every evening at lighting up o'clock sharp and until further notice in Feenichts Playhouse.'[51] These two structural devices, then – dramatic performance and children's game – are not really separate conceits but fundamentally one and the same. The prominent word here, 'Playhouse', is sensitive to the overlap between 'to play' and 'a play',[52] and it is from this overlap that the chapter takes its characteristic quality. Drama is manifested fundamentally as exuberant, comic, and ludic; by the same token, children's games are recognized as a highly structured form of theatre, often involving set roles, rules, choruses, and rote-learned lines.

We find ourselves both in a Playhouse, then, and a children's playroom: 'play' gestures widely towards the style of the chapter and of the book as a whole, to language 'games' and 'plays' on words, the 'play' of senses or associations, the holding of various meanings simultaneously 'in play'. Also at work is the kind of playful free-association found in dreams: so, for example, when Joyce's eye fell on 'Colours', the name for 'Angels and Devils' in Norman Douglas's *London Street Games*, he would have seen immediately before it on the page 'Full-Stop',[53] which finds its way into the chapter in the description of the Angel: 'An argument follows. / Chuffy was a nangel then and his soard fleshed light like likening. Fools top! Singty, sangty, meekly loose, defendy nous from prowlabouts.'[54]

The two paragraphs that follow are among the many passages in the *Wake* that become suddenly acutely conscious of their printed form, their textual texture: 'Punct'[55] is followed by 'Sammy, call on'.[56] The children's play has become here the play of the text itself, its words and letters and even its dots and dashes ('Now a dash to her dot!'[57]) toys in a children's game, like marbles, or the 'top' of 'Fools top!'[58]

Elizabeth Sewell influentially suggested that nonsense writing sets words into motion according to the rules of 'Play',[59] and Joyce's words, spinning like tops or colliding like marbles, quickly call into being the arch-heroine of English nonsense. We have met her already in the *Wake*, of course, but increasingly we find her moving towards centre stage. The 'tiny victorienne',[60] in the musical and theatrical setting of the 'Mime', is recast in a Wagnerian idiom[61]: in the roll-call of characters we are told that 'THE FLORAS [...] form with valkyrienne licence the guard for / IZOD [...] who [...] is approached in loveliness only by her grateful sister reflection in a mirror'.[62] The echo of 'victorienne' in 'valkyrienne' links the Floras back to that early description of Dodgson and Alice: as Izod's 'guard' of Floras becomes, by association, all Dodgson's 'child friends', Alice is recalled again more directly as Izod herself (a form of Isolde) and the looking-glass girl. The Wagnerian 'guard', the Valkyries, prepare the ground for another Wagnerian retinue, the Rhine Maidens, who are introduced in a complex passage thick with interconnected allusions:

Hymnumber twentynine. O, the singing! Happy little girlycums to have adolphted such an Adelphus! O, the swinginging hopops so goholden! They've come to chant en chor. They say their salat, the madiens' prayer to the messiager of His Nabis, prostitating their selfs eachwise and combinedly. Fateha, fold the hands. Be it honoured, bow the head. May thine evings e'en be blossful! Even of bliss! As so we hope for ablution. For the sake of the farbung and of the scent and of the holiodrops. Amems.

A pause. Their orison arises misquewhite as Osman glory, ebbing wasteward, leaves to the soul of light its fading silence (allahlah lahlah lah!), a turquewashed sky.[63]

The Quranic[64] and Wagnerian overtones of this passage might suggest that Joyce has parted company with the world of Lewis Carroll, but in fact this angelic choir is embedded within and shaped by two references to *The Story of Lewis Carroll* by Isa Bowman, the actor who, as a child, played Alice in the dramatic adaptation of *Wonderland* which occasioned Carroll's essay '"Alice" on the Stage'. 'Happy little girlycums to have adolphted such an Adelphus!' remembers Bowman's remark, of a group of schoolgirls to whom Dodgson volunteered to teach mathematics, 'happy the little girls to have such a master!'[65] Lewis Carroll, who has been foregrounded a little earlier as 'loosicurrals',[66] emerges here as the central figure around whom the little girls flock and sing. He is perhaps a model of God the Father, surrounded by praising cherubim and seraphim: or an apostle or a prophet, since 'adolphted'

and 'Adelphus' both recall *adelphós* 'brother', the normal mode of description for
a man in the early church (the *adelphótēs* or 'brotherhood' of believers). Carroll
is remembered again fleetingly in '[b]e it honoured, bow the head', which Roland
McHugh connects to a line from *The Story of Lewis Carroll* recorded in Joyce's
notebooks: '[f]or ever that voice is still; be it mine to revive some memories of
it'.[67] This passage, too, revives some memories: Carroll half-appears as the focus
of the Angels' adoration and one of the archetypes of their overprotective, always
potentially abusive guardian. He is the writer of letters, 'his nibs' or 'His Nabis', the
'messiager'.

Against and alongside this 'soppy-stern'[68] patriarchal presence, Joyce's 'Mime'
brings forward the Floras, imagined as voices, as colours, and (as their name
suggests) as flowers. Among the arts of the pantomime is a repertoire of ways to
balance sentimentality and satire, and Joyce's manner in the 'feminine' passages
of the 'Mime' becomes increasingly comic and parodic, averting and subverting
the more naïve connotations of the girls-as-flowers motif with a judicious dose
of cattiness and vanity: 'Just so stylled with the nattes are their flowerheads
now and each of all has a lovestalk onto herself and the tot of all the tits of their
understamens is as open as he can posably she and is tournesoled straightcut or
sidewaist, accourdant to the coursets of things feminite.'[69] With the rhythm of a
song title, 'Stille wie die Nacht',[70] the Floras' styles, botanically speaking 'narrowed
prolongation[s] of the ovary',[71] are presented as fashionably 'styled', 'with the nattes'
recalling a 'natty' dresser. The diction of 'tournesoled straightcut or sidewaist,
accourdant to the coursets of things feminite' is archly *au fait* with the shifting
courses (and, in a fine and anxious portmanteau, changing corsets) of women's
fashion. The voice here is that of the flowers themselves, preening and comparing
their foliage, and if the chapter opened at front of house, at 'lighting up o'clock',
here we seem to be in the competitive world of the chorus girls' dressing-room.
Joyce draws directly on the episode of the 'Garden of Live Flowers' in *Through
the Looking-Glass*, in which the flowers, depicted as sharp-tongued, judgemental
Society ladies, make unkind remarks about Alice's appearance couched in
botanical terms:

> 'It isn't manners for us to begin, you know,' said the Rose. [...] 'Still, you're the
> right colour, and that goes a long way.'
> 'I don't care about the colour,' the Tiger-lily remarked. 'If only her petals curled up
> a little more, she'd be all right.' [...]
> [']There's one other flower in the garden that can move about like you,' said the
> Rose '[...] she has the same awkward shape as you [...] but she's redder – and her
> petals are shorter, I think.'
> 'They're done up close, like a dahlia,' said the Tiger-lily: 'not tumbled about, like
> yours.'[72]

Alice's reaction – she 'didn't like being criticised'[73] – foreshadows the scrutinies of
adolescence, the acquisition of what Darwin, in his fine discussion of blushing,
called 'self-attention',[74] that will take her into the performative world of Victorian

womanhood.[75] *Through the Looking-Glass* is a work painfully and sorrowfully conscious of the fleeting nature of childhood: '[y]ou're beginning to fade, you know' says the Rose to Alice.[76] This remark certainly hints at a broader sense of encroaching mortality, but death and the death of childhood are inseparable in the 'the shadow of a sigh' that according to the dedicatory verse, 'tremble[s] through the story'.[77] William Empson wrote of the lines in that same verse – 'Come, hearken then, ere voice of dread, / With bitter tidings laden, / Shall summon to unwelcome bed / A melancholy maiden'[78] – that 'the marriage-bed was more likely to be an end of the maiden than the grave, and the metaphor firmly implied treats them as identical'.[79] In the 'Garden of Live Flowers,' another point of traditional analogy between young women and flowers, their transience and fragility, is woven into the dialogue.

This is a notion with a literary pedigree. In my discussion above, of the boat trip passage that serves as a prologue to the 'Mime', I noted the motifs of flowering and deflowering clustered around Joyce's 'vierge violetian'[80] and quoted the Shakespearean lines 'A violet in the youth of primy nature, / Forward not permanent, sweet not lasting'.[81] So Laertes counsels Ophelia to regard Hamlet's love for her: and when Ophelia is mad with grief, both at Hamlet's desertion and his murder of her father, she seems to recall her brother's words: 'I would give you some violets, but they withered all when my father died.'[82] Passing the word 'violets' back and forth between them through the play, Laertes recalls his sister's words as he grieves in his turn for her: 'Lay her i' th' earth, / And from her fair and unpolluted flesh / May violets spring! I tell thee, churlish priest, / A minist'ring angel shall my sister be / When thou liest howling'.[83] Ophelia, on whose grave flowers are strewn,[84] and who herself scatters flowers, is the most culturally pervasive English literary heroine to be associated with the fleeting beauty of flowers. Her watery death amid her 'fantastic garlands'[85] – remembered in the 'Mime' in 'waters the fleurettes of novembrence'[86] – links Ophelia both with Alice in the Garden of Live Flowers and with Alice the river-nixie, and in that latter category, with the Rhine Maidens and all the related water-spirits – creatures 'native and indued / To that element'[87] – who keep the streams of 'Anna Livia Plurabelle' discernibly flowing amid the landscape of the 'Mime'.

The 'Mime' is comic pantomime – it takes Anna Livia's vast pageant of rivers and makes it into the scenery for its chorus-girls – but it is a show with its tear-jerking moments as well. Ophelia is valuable to Joyce in this regard as a model for his tragic heroine, Issy, seen as a forsaken, jilted lover. Her entrance onstage is concurrent with Ophelia's:

> Poor Isa sits a glooming so gleaming in the gloaming; the tincelles a touch tarnished wind no lovelinoise awound her swan's. Hey, lass! Woefear gleam she so glooming, this pooripathete I solde? Her beauman's gone of a cool. Be good enough to symperise. If he's at anywhere she's therefor to join him. If it's to nowhere she's going to too. But if he'll go to be a son to France's she'll stay daughter of Clare. Bring tansy, throw myrtle, strew rue, rue, rue. She is fading out like Journee's clothes so you can't see her now.[88]

The verbs 'bring', 'throw', 'strew' suggest both Ophelia's distribution of flowers in *Hamlet* Act IV Scene v and the decoration of her grave, 'her virgin crants, / Her maiden strewments'.[89] The girl under description appears to be Alice: the sighing 'Hey, lass!' plays on the 'Alice'/'alas!' pun that originates in Carroll: 'Alas for poor Alice!'[90] and 'poor Isa' recalls the favourite epithet 'poor Alice'.[91] But Issy here – as 'Isa', who in combination with 'Beauman' signals Isa Bowman – is not the Alice of the book so much as Isa Bowman's dramatization of Alice, the 'Alice' of '"Alice" on the Stage'. Bowman's account of Carroll is once again decisively embedded into the scenery of the passage: the aside '[b]e good enough to symperise' recalls a note of Lewis Carroll's to Bowman in 1890 in which he chastises her for forgetting to add the correct postage to her previous letter: 'Oh, you naughty, naughty, bad wicked little girl! You forgot to put a stamp on your letter, and your poor old uncle had to pay *TWOPENCE!* His *last* Twopence! Think of that. I shall punish you severely for this when once I get you here. So *tremble!* Do you hear? Be good enough to tremble!'[92] This letter, recorded by Bowman in her *Story of Lewis Carroll*, exudes a mock fury which is a kind of stage emotion, a camped-up parody of adult annoyance,[93] and its suppressed suggestion of spanking could hardly have escaped Joyce's notice.[94] But it is just as likely that it is the teasing pantomime humour that caught his eye. In the 'poor Isa' passage, this is dampened, shorn of its exclamation mark, 'tremble' turned into both 'simper' and 'sympathize', two parallel child's responses to a character in a play.

The 'Poor Isa sits a glooming' passage displays in miniature the depth of the Carrollian debt in the 'Mime'. Here more than anywhere, the writing is a complex portmanteau of Carroll and Joyce, full of both homage and interrogation. 'Poor Isa' is a reworking of one of the earliest repeated tropes in Joyce's work: the deserted, dejected, or merely pensive woman pictured in gathering dusk. It finds expression in *Chamber Music*, which features a woman sitting at a piano, her head inclined, as 'The twilight turns from amethyst / To deep and deeper blue'.[95] It recurs again at the beginning of 'Eveline', creating the setting for the story: 'She sat at the window, watching the evening invade the avenue'.[96] In the 'Mime', unlike in 'Eveline', the girl's misery is not that she is unable to leave home, but that she has been left behind by a lover: '[h]er beauman's gone of a cool'. By contrast with Eveline, Isa would follow her lover wherever he chose – in the words of the song: 'and if he goes nowhere, I'll go there as well'[97] – but she has no choice in the matter. He is gone, and although 'she'll meet anew fiancy',[98] which hovers with tragicomic indecision between 'fiancé' and 'fancy-man', she is now left 'unmerried'.[99] At the same time, though, as Joyce returns to one of his own old tunes, we find him catching with an eerie emotional precision the haunted vision, the 'shadowy past' of '"Alice" on the Stage': 'What wert thou, dream-Alice, in thy foster-father's eyes? How shall he picture thee?'[100]

As we trace and retrace Joyce's adventures in Wonderland, the temptation is always to read Carroll as, in James Atherton's words, a 'Precursor' – a forerunner on a shared formal trajectory – and *Finnegans Wake* as 'the logical development, or the working out on a larger scale, of ideas that first occurred to Lewis Carroll'.[101] Atherton and others are not wrong to see Joyce's debt to Carroll in terms of 'logic', 'development', and 'ideas', but what close readings of specific chapters and passages of the *Wake* can show us is that Carroll's presence in this *ne plus ultra* of Anglophone modernism can also be found governing a far wider and more random assortment of tastes, allusions, and concerns. Carroll was a recurring thread in the tapestry of Joyce's thinking on, and semiconscious dramatizing of, matters as various as liturgy, children's games, Wagner, mythology, *Hamlet*, flowers, and sentimental pantomime. If, as I have argued, 'The Mime of Mick, Nick and the Maggies' connects Carroll with theatrical performance, we can think also of Carroll as a role Joyce performs, and in whom, like a method actor, he might almost lose himself.

Notes

1   *Letters of James Joyce*, vol. 1, ed. Stuart Gilbert (London: Faber and Faber, 1957), 255.

2   Several of the critics listed in note 4, below, have cast doubt on Joyce's claim not to have had much acquaintance with Carroll before 1927. Hugh Kenner discovered the tantalizing titbit that one of Joyce's college nicknames was 'the Mad Hatter' (according to *A Page of Irish History: Story of University College, Dublin, 1883–1909. Compiled by Fathers of the Society of Jesus* [Dublin and Cork: Talbot Press, 1930], 286) and, more recently, Viviana Braslasu has given a very helpful account of the evidence in Joyce's notebooks (for both references see note 4 below). I would add that it is highly suggestive that the phrase 'bits and scraps' itself appears in Lewis Carroll's essay '"Alice" on the Stage': '"Alice" and the "Looking-Glass" are made up almost wholly of bits and scraps, single ideas which came of themselves' (Lewis Carroll, '"Alice" on the Stage' [*The Theatre*, April, 1887], in *Alice's Adventures in Wonderland* and *Through the Looking-Glass*, ed. Hugh Haughton [London: Penguin, 1998], 294).

3   *Letters of James Joyce*, vol. 3, ed. Richard Ellmann (London: Faber and Faber, 1966), 174.

4   A selective list of the scholarship on Carroll and Joyce would include the following published works (listed chronologically): Stuart Gilbert, 'Prolegomena to Work in Progress', in Samuel Beckett et al., *Our Exagmination Round His Factification for Incamination of 'Work in Progress'* (London: Faber and Faber, [1929] 1972), 58–9; Hugh Kenner, *Dublin's Joyce* (Bloomington: Indiana University Press, 1956), 276–300; James Atherton, *The Books at the Wake: A Study of Literary Allusion in James Joyce's Finnegans Wake* (London: Faber and Faber, 1959), 124–36; Adaline Glasheen, *A Third Census of* Finnegans Wake: *An Index of the Characters and Their Roles* (Berkeley: University of California Press, 1977); John A. Rea, 'A Bit of Lewis Carroll in *Ulysses*', *James Joyce Quarterly* 15 (1977): 86–8; Robert M. Polhemus, *Comic Faith: The Great Tradition from Austen to Joyce* (Chicago: Chicago University Press, 1980), 245–337; Ann McGarrity Buki, 'Lewis Carroll in *Finnegans Wake*', in *Lewis Carroll: A Celebration*, ed. Edward Guiliano (New York: Clarkson N. Potter, 1982), 154–66; Hugh Haughton, 'Introduction', in *The Chatto Book of Nonsense Poetry* (London: Chatto & Windus, 1988), 1–32; Edvige Giunta, 'Dear Reverend: Lewis Carroll and the Boston Girls', *James Joyce Quarterly* 30, no. 3 (1993): 488–92; Roberto Baronti Marchiò, '"All Old Dadgerson's Dodges": Language and Meaning in Lewis Carroll and James Joyce', in *Joyce's Victorians*, ed. Franca Ruggieri (Rome: Bulzoni, 2006),

25–53; Viviana Mirela Braslasu, "'Why, Mr J. and his God alone know!'": Joyce and Lewis Carroll', *Dublin James Joyce Journal* 8 (2015): 114–21. The subject has been treated in a number of doctoral dissertations, including Edvige Giunta, 'A Raven like a Writing-Desk: Lewis Carroll through James Joyce's Looking-Glass' (PhD Diss., University of Miami, 1992), Daphne Marie Shafer, 'Wanderlad beyond the Looking-Glass: the Dream Worlds of Lewis Carroll and James Joyce' (PhD Diss., University of Louisiana at Lafayette, 2001); John David Fielding, 'New Words for New Worlds: The Neologizing Revolutions of Lewis Carroll and James Joyce' (PhD Diss., University of California at Berkeley, 2003); James Williams, 'Nineteenth-Century Nonsense Writing and the Later Work of James Joyce' (PhD Diss., University of Cambridge, 2009); Aingeal Clare, "'Wonderland's wanderlad'": James Joyce's Debt to Victorian Nonsense Literature' (PhD Diss., University of York, 2011).

5   I borrow this turn of phrase from T. S. Eliot's description of four of his early poems as being correctly placed 'under the sign of Laforgue', in a letter of 18 October 1939 to the Canadian scholar E. J. H. Greene: see *The Letters of T. S. Eliot*, vol. 9: 1939–1941, ed. Valerie Eliot and John Haffenden (London: Faber and Faber, 2021), 298.

6   Carroll, *Alice*, 5.

7   See the note on this line in *The Annotated Alice. Definitive Edition*, ed. Martin Gardner (London: Penguin, 2000), 9–10.

8   *Lewis Carroll's Diaries*, ed. Edward Wakeling, vol. 1 (Luton: the Lewis Carroll Society, 1993–2007), 188.

9   Stuart Dodgson Collingwood, *The Lewis Carroll Picture Book* (London: T. Fisher Unwin, 1899), 358–60.

10 Henry Savile Clarke, *Alice in Wonderland: A Dream Play for Children in Two Acts; founded upon Mr. Lewis Carroll's "Alice's Adventures in Wonderland" and "Through the Looking-Glass" with the Express Sanction of the Author* (London: "Court Circular" Office, 1886).

11 Carroll, '"Alice" on the Stage', 295.

12 Carroll, *Alice*, 241.

13 Collingwood, *Picture Book,* 358 (my emphasis).

14 Alice Hargreaves, 'The Friendship that Sparked *Alice's Adventures*', in *Lewis Carroll: Interviews and Recollections*, ed. Morton N. Cohen (Basingstoke and London: Macmillan, 1989), 84 (my emphasis).

15 '[One] summer afternoon', as told to Collingwood (*Picture Book,* 96); 'that blazing summer afternoon' in 'Alice's Recollections of Carrollian Days, as Told to her Son', *Cornhill Magazine* 73, July 1932 (reproduced in Cohen, *Interviews and Recollections*, 86).

16 Richard Ellmann, *James Joyce*, revised edition (New York: Oxford University Press, 2000), 699.

17 James Joyce, *Finnegans Wake*, ed. Robbert-Jan Henkes, Erik Bindervoet, and Finn Fordham (Oxford: Oxford University Press, 2012), 203.17–204.1. Hereafter cited using the standard abbreviation *FW* and referencing convention of page and line number. Editions of *Finnegans Wake* standardly have identical pagination: I cite this one for its editorial matter, especially Fordham's 'Introduction' and 'Chapter by Chapter Outline', which are highly recommended to any newcomer bewildered by the *Wake*.

18 4 July 1931, the date on which James and Nora Joyce married in London, was, alas, a Saturday.

19 The draft goes 'July **June**' before settling on 'Junojuly'. See *A First-Draft Version of Finnegans Wake*, ed. David Hayman (Austin: University of Texas Press, 1963), 125.

20 Joyce, *FW*, 57.24–29.

21 The word 'limber' was added, a considered afterthought: see Hayman, *First-Draft Version*, 125. 'Nixie' is defined more specifically as having the physical form of a mermaid (*OED*, 'nixie', *n.* 1).

22 William Shakespeare, *Hamlet, The Riverside Shakespeare*, ed. G. Blakemore Evans et al., second edition (Boston and New York: Houghton Mifflin, 1997), I. iii. 7–8. Subsequent references to Shakespeare are to this edition.

23 Catherine Maxwell, *Scents and Sensibility: Perfume in Victorian Literary Culture* (Oxford: Oxford University Press, 2017), 68. The whole chapter 'Perfumed Melodies, Violet Memories', 66–84, is essential reading on the cultural history of the flower.

24 Maxwell, *Scents*, 81. Maxwell's account of violets can be usefully supplemented, with respect to matters of gender and sexuality, by Kasia Boddy's remarks in *Blooming Flowers* (New Haven and London: Yale University Press, 2020), 168–75.

25 As in 'a bank of violets', *Twelfth Night*, I. i. 6; 'the violets now / That *strew the green lap of the new come spring*', *Richard II*, V. ii. 46–47 (my emphasis); 'a bank where the wild thyme blows, / Where […] the nodding violet grows', *A Midsummer Night's Dream*, II. i. 250.

26 Joyce, *FW*, 3.4.

27 Ibid., 143.26.

28 Ibid., 231.20.

29 See Isa Bowman, *The Story of Lewis Carroll* (London: J. M. Dent, 1899), 24–5. Violet was also the name of one of the two younger Liddell sisters, the other being Rhoda. They make a cameo appearance as the Rose and the Violet in *Through the Looking-Glass*.

30 *The Finnegans Wake Notebooks at Buffalo*, eds. Vincent Deane et al., vol. 6 (Tournhout: Brepols, 2001–4), VI.B.33.186, 162.

31 Joyce, *FW*, 261.2.

32 Carroll kept an index, or 'record' of letters, and indexed his photographs in violet ink. See, for example, 'Eight or Nine Wise Words about Letter Writing', in *Complete Works of Lewis Carroll*, ed. Alexander Woolcott (Harmondsworth: Penguin, 1988), 1098; *Lewis Carroll, Photographer: The Princeton University Library Albums*, ed. Roger Taylor and Edward Wakeling (Princeton and Oxford: Princeton University Press and Princeton University Library, 2002), 122, 127. Joyce is also known to have used violet ink on occasion: Stanislaus Joyce wrote that 'I had seen the manuscript [of Joyce's early play *A Brilliant Career*] on his desk in his neat, firm handwriting with the stage directions in violet ink and – symptomatic of his power of concentration – hardly a correction in the whole manuscript' (*My Brother's Keeper* [London: Faber and Faber, (1958) 1982], 129). Sam Slote confirms that, while the mature Joyce seldom strayed from a sober black, he used violet ink in notebook VI.B.46 from the late 30s (in an email to the editors of this volume: for which, my thanks).

33 Lewis Carroll, 'Appendix I: Preface to the Eighty-Sixth Thousand of the 6/ – Edition of *Alice's Adventures in Wonderland*', 356.

34 Carroll, *Alice*, 60. Carroll continues the above 'Preface' by saying the solution 'is merely an after-thought: the Riddle, as originally invented, had no answer at all' (Carroll, 'Preface', 256).

35 They are absent from the passage as it appears in the early draft in the British Library MS, as printed in Hayman, *First-Draft Version*, 125.

36 There are briefer echoes of the 'golden afternoon' elsewhere in *Finnegans Wake*: for example '"I feel a fine lady […] floating on a stillstream of isisglass"' (486.23–24). This is often glossed in relation to Joyce's interest in Ancient Egyptian deities (e.g. by Roland

McHugh in *The Sigla of* Finnegans Wake [Austin, TX: University of Texas Press, 1976], 52) but the River Thames at Oxford is known as the River Isis.

37   Adaline Glasheen, *A Census of* Finnegans Wake (London: Faber and Faber, 1956), 80.

38   Joyce, *FW*, 459.4.

39   Glasheen, *Census*, 80.

40   Joyce, *FW*, 220.3–4.

41   Ibid., 430.1–2.

42   Not *literal* incest: I have in mind the line of interpretation advanced by Hugh Kenner: 'Joyce transferred Dodgson's ambivalent relations with Isa [Bowman] to the *Wake* almost unaltered, as HCE's incestuous infatuation with his daughter Iseult. It was, in fact, a relationship of symbolic incest: Dodgson saw in Isa an incarnation of Alice, and Alice was his creation' (Kenner, *Dublin's Joyce*, 288).

43   Fordham, 'Introduction', xx.

44   Joyce, *Letters 1*, 295.

45   Alice B. Gomme, *The Traditional Games of England, Scotland and Ireland* (London: Thames and Hudson, 1984), 8. Joyce did not mention ribbons to Weaver, but we can infer that the version he knew in Dublin included this motif from the exchange ' – Willest thou rossy banders havind? / He simules to be tight in ribbings' (Joyce, *FW*, 250.3–4).

46   Joyce, *FW*, 225.22–27, 233.21–27, 250.3–7, and 252.7–13.

47   Ibid., 258.25–26.

48   This is also parodied: 'Loud heap miseries upon us yet entwine our arts with laughters low!' (ibid., 259.7–8).

49   Like *Ulysses*, *Finnegans Wake* is not printed with chapter titles. I follow the common practice of referring to chapters by the unprinted titles which Joyce himself used. The fact that this chapter was published separately as *The Mime of Mick, Nick and the Maggies: A Fragment from 'Work in Progress'* (The Hague: The Servire Press, 1934) gives me confidence to speak of this as its 'title', though it is often referred to as, e.g., 'Nightgames' (see Fordham, 'Chapter by Chapter Outline', xxxvii).

50   *OED*, 'Mime', *n.* 1a.

51   Joyce, *FW*, 219.1–2.

52   For example, compare this use of 'play' to the German 'Schauspiel'. For a useful survey of theories of play see Thomas Karshan, *Vladimir Nabokov and the Art of Play* (Oxford: Oxford University Press, 2011), 8–15.

53   Norman Douglas, *London Street Games* (London: Chatto and Windus, 1931), 26.

54   Joyce, *FW*, 222.21–24.

55   Ibid., 222.26.

56   Ibid., 222.36–223.1.

57   Ibid., 232.27.

58   Douglas writes that 'Full-Stop and Comma' is a game that is played with marbles and similar collectable stones called 'gobs' or 'cobs' which are 'shaped like dice, or ought to be' (Douglas, *London Street Games*, 69–70). These 'gobs' and 'cobs' crop up in *FW* 453.7 – where Joyce's 'lemoncholic gobs' suggest the kind of marble 'you got out of lemonade bottles' (ibid., 62) – and *FW* 613.6–7.

59   Elizabeth Sewell, *The Field of Nonsense* (London: Chatto & Windus, 1952), 25.

60   Joyce, *FW*, 57.28.

61   On the Wagnerian stratum of the *Wake*, see Timothy Martin, *Joyce and Wagner: A Study of Influence* (Cambridge: Cambridge University Press, 1991), 185–221, and Alex Ross, *Wagnerism: Art and Politics in the Shadow of Music* (London: 4th Estate, 2020),

508–11. Wagner is put into play from the first sentence of the 'Mime', with 'Feenichts Playhouse' containing the title of the composer's earliest opera, *Die Feen* (1833).

62 Joyce, *FW*, 220.3–9.

63 Ibid., 234.34–235.8.

64 See Atherton, *The Books at the Wake*, 202–3, and Joyce's notes in *The Finnegans Wake Notebooks,* VI.B.33.180–81, 155–7.

65 Bowman, *Story of Lewis Carroll*, 5.

66 Joyce, *FW*, 234.15.

67 Bowman, *Story of Lewis Carroll*, 4, as recorded by Joyce in *The Finnegans Wake Notebooks*, VI.B.33.183, 160, pointed out in Roland McHugh, *Annotations to Finnegans Wake* (Baltimore and London: Johns Hopkins University Press, 1991), 235.

68 Philip Larkin's phrase in 'This Be the Verse', in *The Complete Poems*, ed. Archie Burnett (London: Faber and Faber, 2012), 88.

69 Joyce, *FW*, 236.33–237.1.

70 McHugh, *Annotations*, 236.

71 *OED*, 'Style', *n.* 8.

72 Carroll, *Alice*, 136–8.

73 Ibid., 137.

74 Charles Darwin, *The Expression of the Emotions in Man and Animals*, ed. Paul Ekman (Oxford: Oxford University Press, 2009), 324.

75 Signalled in *Through the Looking-Glass* by the word 'awkward' (Carroll, *Alice*, 138): in the late nineteenth century 'the awkward age' comes to refer to adolescence, to the stage of life when one is 'too old to cry and too young to swear', as the *Daily Mirror* put it in 1928 (*OED*, 'Awkward', 7c). Its earliest citation in print (1895) is in a British periodical, the *Windsor Magazine* (ibid.).

76 Carroll, *Alice*, 138.

77 Ibid., 118.

78 Ibid., 117.

79 William Empson, 'Alice in Wonderland: The Child as Swain', in *Some Versions of Pastoral* (Harmondsworth: Penguin, [1935] 1966), 215.

80 Joyce, *FW*, 203.29.

81 Shakespeare, *Hamlet*, I.iii.7–8.

82 *Hamlet*, IV.v.184–85.

83 *Hamlet*, V.i.238–42.

84 *Hamlet*, V.i.245: 'I thought thy bride-bed to have deck'd, sweet maid / And not have strew'd thy grave', remarks the Queen, lines which are almost certainly in Empson's mind in the passage cited above.

85 *Hamlet*, V.i.168.

86 Joyce, *FW*, 226.32–33.

87 Shakespeare, *Hamlet*, V.i.179–80.

88 Joyce, *FW*, 226.4–12.

89 *Hamlet*, V.i.232–33.

90 Carroll, *Alice*, 14.

91 Used eleven times in *Wonderland* and three times in *Through the Looking-Glass*.

92 Lewis Carroll, *The Letters of Lewis Carroll*, ed. Morton N. Cohen with Roger Lancelyn Green, vol. 2 (New York: Oxford University Press, 1979), 803.

93 I am thinking of Susan Sontag's remark that '[t]o perceive Camp in objects and persons is to understand Being-as-Playing-a-Role. It is the farthest extension, in

sensibility, of the metaphor of life as theater' (Susan Sontag, 'Notes on "Camp"', in *Against Interpretation* [London: Vintage, 1994], 280).

94 On spanking as a particularly English kink, compare the overtones of the discussion of British naval discipline in *Ulysses*, ed. Hans Walter Gabler et al. (New York: Vintage, 1986), 12.1333–59.

95 Joyce, *Poems and Shorter Writings*, ed. Richard Ellmann, A. Walton-Litz, and John Whittier-Fergusson (London: Faber and Faber, 1991), 14.

96 Joyce, *Dubliners*, ed. John Kelly (London: Everyman, 1991), 37.

97 From 'Still I Love Him, Can't Deny It'. See McHugh, *Annotations*, 226.

98 Joyce, *FW*, 226.14.

99 Ibid., 226.18.

100 Carroll, '"Alice" on the Stage', 295.

101 Atherton, *The Books at the Wake*, 124.

Chapter 14

WASTING TIMELESSNESS: LEWIS CARROLL, FLANN O'BRIEN, AND MODERNIST TEMPORALITY

Paul Fagan

This chapter explores the influence of Lewis Carroll's Wonderland on modernist representations of time and timelessness through the test cases of Flann O'Brien's 1940 novel *The Third Policeman* and his *Irish Times* newspaper column *Cruiskeen Lawn*, published under the pseudonym Myles na gCopaleen from 1940 to 1966.[1] The importance of Carroll's legacy to both O'Brien's writing and its reception is foregrounded in numerous scholarly titles, from Wim Tigges's 1989 article, 'Ireland in Wonderland: Flann O'Brien's *The Third Policeman* as a Nonsense Novel' to Carol Taaffe's 2008 monograph, *Ireland Through the Looking-Glass: Flann O'Brien, Myles na gCopaleen and Irish Cultural Debate*.[2] To date, comparative analyses have focused on Carroll and O'Brien's shared employment of nonsense towards satirical ends, their mutual practice of writing under pseudonyms,[3] and their common interests in science writing, absurd logic games, the philosophy of language, and fantastic body transformations.[4] Despite this exemplary critical work, a key aspect of the implicit conversation between these writers that remains under-scrutinized is their by turns comic and political interrogation of the increasingly blurred boundaries of temporal and atemporal realms under modernity. My wager is that a reflective comparison of Carroll and O'Brien's 'comic timing' will reveal new dimensions of the role of timelessness in modernist poetics.

Indeed, this juxtaposition of authors is not only comparative but also intertextual: the Hatter's claim that 'It's always six o'clock' in Wonderland is explicitly evoked in the description of *The Third Policeman*'s uncanny jurisdiction as a place 'where it was always five o'clock in the afternoon'.[5] I want to take up the invitation implicit in this echo to read the impossible temporal forms and comic reversals staged in *Cruiskeen Lawn* and *The Third Policeman* as direct engagements with Wonderland's nonsensically wasteful timelessness. To further narrow my focus in relation to this potentially expansive theme, I will concentrate on Carroll and O'Brien's performances and reversals of distinct temporal logics in their representations of timeless eternities that are, impossibly, characterized by change and becoming. To my thinking, this recurrent comic confusion of the stasis and timeless duration of 'eternity' with the regulations of labour and consumption at the heart of modern industrial 'clock time' is the deeper affinity that makes these texts worthy of comparative contemplation, and which informs their evocative surface play with logic (and illogical play with surfaces). It is also the aspect that gives itself most fully to the central modernist concern with what Jacques Derrida characterizes, after Hamlet's well-worn phrase, as learning to live in a time that is 'out of joint'.[6]

My argument proceeds in three interrelated movements. In the first part, I explain the theoretical framework of my argument and foreground the influence of Carroll's play with temporality (the progression of past, present, and future) on a specific strand of twentieth-century literature that explores the status of timelessness (eternity, stasis, duration without change) in modernity. Here, I draw on Derrida's writing on *limitrophy* to argue for an expanded conception of modernist temporality, in which Carroll's comic depiction of an impossibly productive eternity plays a pivotal role, before sketching out a genealogy of the time and timelessness topos and its place in the modernist literary imaginary. In the second part, I show that Myles na gCopaleen's writing about Carroll in his *Cruiskeen Lawn* newspaper column explores Wonderland's confusion of temporal categories of time and timelessness as a durable comic, philosophical, and political template that can be profitably augmented and redrawn to address concerns pertinent to both modernist aesthetics and twentieth-century experiences of mass industry and war. In the final part, I claim that the comic handling of themes of timelessness and eternity in key scenes of *The Third Policeman*, O'Brien's posthumously published masterpiece, are directly influenced by Wonderland time. This claim, and my overall argument, rests upon three interrelated presuppositions:

1. that the time and timelessness topos inherited from classical and medieval thought is given new life in modernist writing;
2. that Carroll and O'Brien, positioned at (and beyond) the outer limits of the modernist era, likewise engage with this topos; however, they turn it on its head in a comic reversal, staging a modern timelessness characterized by measurable fluctuations of excess and waste;
3. that each writer's employment of such atemporal 'nonsense' constitutes a satirical mirror of the rhetorics of never-ending progress, industry, and crisis that prevailed, with distinct forms and stakes, in Victorian Britain and Second World War-era Ireland.

A Brief History of Timelessness: Beating Time in Dante, Carroll, Joyce, Beckett, O'Brien

In his posthumously published lecture, *The Animal That Therefore I Am*, Jacques Derrida acknowledges the debt that his thinking on 'the logic of the limit'[7] owes to Wonderland: 'Although I don't have time to do so, I would of course have liked to inscribe my whole talk within a reading of Lewis Carroll. In fact, you can't be certain that I am not doing that, for better or for worse, silently, unconsciously, or without your knowing'.[8] The aside suggests a deeper conversation about the comic limit transgressions that are an unmistakeable quality of Carroll's writing and legacy, which Derrida must decline owing to temporal constraints. And yet – conspiring to have his cake and eat it, too – he acknowledges the impossibility of situating his address within such a broader discussion of Carroll, while *at the same time* fostering a suspicion that he might be doing so anyway. With a sly sense of Carrollian play, Derrida hints that in the course of his address, he will both fall subject to and surpass the lecture's temporal limits. In her foreword to *The Animal That Therefore I Am*, Marie-Luise Malle draws our attention to the talk's recurrent 'motif of the time one doesn't have' and encourages us to consider its significance, beyond 'circumstantial reasons', to Derrida's deconstruction of the limit.[9] Indeed, Derrida's suggestive insistence that it is clock time that prevents such a productive reading, that renders it impossible, in itself mirrors a key characteristic of Carroll's comic art. If only we could step outside of time's limits, Derrida seems to imply, with its regulatory and disciplinary injunctions, then we might really get somewhere.

The seeming aporia of a temporal stasis offset by the fantasy of a productive eternity is succinctly captured in Carroll's 'The Two Clocks'. This short puzzle proves that a clock that 'doesn't go *at all*' is more accurate than one that 'loses a minute a day', as the stopped clock will tell the correct time twice a day, whereas the slow clock will tell the correct time only once every two years.[10] The counter-intuitive solution provides the opportunity to slip, playfully, into logical irony:

> You *might* go on to ask, 'How am I to know when eight o'clock *does* come? My clock will not tell me.' Be patient: you know that when eight o'clock comes your clock is right, very good; then your rule is this: keep your eyes fixed on your clock, and the *very moment it is right* it will be eight o'clock.
> 'But – –,' you say.
> There, that'll do; the more you argue the farther you get from the point, so it will be as well to stop.[11]

The puzzle's wry implication is that a stopped time will be more productive than a mechanical regulation of time, which will ultimately overwhelm and defeat its own purpose of increasing accuracy and eliminating waste.

This comic confusion at the limits of time and timelessness – amplified by the suggestive choice of the figure 8 as a symbol of infinity – is turned to good account at the Mad Tea-Party in Wonderland, where 'It's always six o'clock' and yet the Hatter's watch is 'Two days wrong'[12]:

> 'What a funny watch!' [Alice] remarked. 'It tells the day of the month and doesn't tell what o'clock it is!'
> 'Why should it?' muttered the Hatter. 'Does *your* watch tell you what year it is?'

'Of course not,' Alice replied very readily: 'but that's because it stays the same year for such a long time together.'
'Which is just the case with *mine*,' said the Hatter.
Alice felt dreadfully puzzled.[13]

As Gillian Beer underlines, the scene depicts a strange version of timeless duration, as 'the participants at the tea party can continue their own lives and conversations within the arrested time'.[14] However, the stayed time of Wonderland is shot through, almost paradoxically, with incompatible temporal coordinates of time's passage:

'Now, if you only kept on good terms with [Time], he'd do almost anything you liked with the clock. For instance, suppose it were nine o'clock in the morning, just time to begin lessons: you'd only have to whisper a hint to Time, and round goes the clock in a twinkling! Half-past one, time for dinner!' [...]
'That would be grand, certainly,' said Alice thoughtfully: 'but then – I shouldn't be hungry for it, you know.'
'Not at first, perhaps,' said the Hatter: 'but you could keep it to half-past one as long as you liked.' [...]
'Is that the reason so many tea-things are put out here?' she asked.
'Yes, that's it, [...] it's always tea-time, and we've no time to wash the things between the whiles.'
'Then you keep moving round, I suppose?' said Alice.
'Exactly so, [...] as the things get used up.'
'But what happens when you come to the beginning again?' Alice ventured to ask.
'Suppose we change the subject,' the March Hare interrupted, yawning. 'I'm getting tired of this.'[15]

The exchange confirms Wonderland to be an impossible temporal sphere marked simultaneously by stasis and change, in which one can both declare 'It's always six o'clock' and earnestly proclaim 'Half-past one, time for dinner!'[16]

The Mad Tea-Party plays out the charged relationship between an impossible temporality and the surpassed limit that is the subject, in part, of Derrida's remarks on *limitrophy*, which he defines as a 'strategy' for 'complicating, thickening, delinearizing, folding, and dividing' the limit 'by making it increase and multiply'.[17] Certainly, the comic energy of Carroll's scene is produced through impossible transgressions and multiplications of the limits of distinct temporal logics. Yet, we can more precisely identify the drives behind these border transgressions (which, like other aspects of Wonderland's strange ontology, place the Victorian categorization of meaning that Alice has learned from her lessons under a considerable stress) when we read the scene through Derrida's relation of the '*transgressal* [...] experience of *limitrophy*' to 'the semantics of *trephō*, *trophē*, or *trophos*' that pertain to food and nourishment.[18] Thus, we observe that the limits of timelessness are surpassed at the Tea-Party through figures of simultaneously unquenched and sated hunger, conservation and waste, excess and want, production and consumption, energy and exhaustion. Such a timeless duration where, nevertheless, 'things get used up' – resulting in both endless labour and, impossibly, 'no time' for productivity 'between the whiles' – resonates with a certain mode of modernist temporality that I mean to explicate in detail here, before turning to its manifestation in O'Brien's writing. Taking up Derrida's implicit invitation to read Wonderland as a site in which temporal limits are neither fixed nor effaced, but rather recurrently augmented, multiplied, and transgressed, I argue that modernism's debt to Carroll's Wonderland rests upon its comic confusion of the classical and medieval time and timelessness topos with a modern temporal register that measures time's passing against the coordinates and fluctuations of production, consumption, conservation, waste, labour, exhaustion, austerity, and excess.

The time and timelessness topos is notably expressed in Plato's definition of time as 'a moving likeness of eternity'.[19] This classification establishes eternity as a real but distinct realm outside of and unaffected by time; an unbounded timeless duration without reference to past or future, not subject to change and becoming. In this paradigm, 'the meaningful distinctions depend upon the contrast between time and eternity and not between past and present'.[20] Such a scheme organizes the thought of medieval Christian thinkers (Augustine, Boethius, Aquinas), who endeavour to capture the tension between an earthly temporal mode that is determined by its position in a series and a divine atemporal mode that is independent of this series. The changes wrought to the time and timelessness topos by Enlightenment ideas of time and the individual are oft-rehearsed: 'Modern temporality', Steven Connor summarizes, 'begins with the replacement, during the late medieval period in Europe, of the cyclical, recurrent or sacred time of religion, with the form of linear, progressive and secular time centred not on God but on the State.'[21] This discursive shift necessitated the identification of uniform motions to aid in time's correct measure, but also resulted in a new conceptualization of timelessness. Ronald Schleifer observes that 'Enlightenment definitions, such as Newton's, homogenize time so that the opposite of time is not another species of time, "eternity," but the (logical) absence of time, an "atemporal" essence.'[22]

Concomitantly, the dominant literary temporal order shifted away from encounters between mutually distinguishing temporal and atemporal realms (staged in dreams, visions, divine pilgrimages, as in Dante's *Divina Commedia*) and towards a linear mode of past-tense narration that 'unifies time and rationalizes consciousness' by foregrounding the 'mutually informative' distinction 'between past and present' within the temporal realm.[23] The homogenizing linearity of this form, which labours to forge consensus among partial perspectives, culminates in the objective historical 'clock time' of the nineteenth-century realist novel that is the foil to Carroll's nonsense time. Recurrently, the Wonderland books unhinge realism's supposedly informative distinctions and connections between past and present, emphasizing multi-temporality over linearity, relativity over uniformity, discontinuity over continuity, diversity over consensus. The key instances are well-known: the 'effect of living backwards' on the White Queen leads her to plaster her finger, then cry out in pain, then finally prick it; the King's Messenger is imprisoned prior to judgement for a crime he is yet to commit; the Unicorn advises Alice that the way to divide a Looking-Glass cake is to '[h]and it round first, and cut it afterwards' (note again the *limitrophic* testing and disruption of temporal borders through indices of food, consumption, labour, division, hunger).[24]

Calvin R. Petersen, Tamsin Lorraine, Caroline Garcia de Souza, Gillian Beer, and others have historicized and theorized Wonderland's strange temporality at the nexus of nineteenth-century scientific, technological, and social transformations.[25] The belated White Rabbit is read as figuring the stressed Victorian 'under the cosh' of an increasingly 'time-regulated society' (and a societally regulated temporality).[26] Wonderland's uncanny transforming bodies and temporal anomalies are interpreted, in turn, as indices of a culturally unstable moment, in which the human's relation to spatial and temporal coordinates was being altered by scientific observations 'that newly suggested that our view of space and time within the Euclidean order was local, not universal'.[27] Both readings are united by a sense that the text as a whole 'engages in a reflection upon the nature of time',[28] and that Wonderland functions as an index of 'a split time' in which 'human experience [is] increasingly divorced from the increasingly autonomous regime of technological modernity'.[29]

I do not wish to take issue with the coordinates of these readings or their findings: indeed, the resonance of the rhetoric of 'a split time'[30] with the critical understanding of modernism as a response to the experience of living in a time-out-of-joint is pivotal to my argument. However, I do want to suggest that such a purely synchronic view conceals Carroll's place in, and comic engagement with, the broader historical, philosophical, and literary traditions of the time and timelessness topos. Beer points to such a reading with her insight that 'industrial, scientific, and technological changes are not the only markers of temporality in [the *Alice*] books: sundials, solar time, dreams, and tenses each add their diverse processes'.[31] If Alice finds herself in a time-out-of-joint, then it is not as a consequence of the smooth erasure of divine timelessness in favour of human linearity, finitude, and consensus, but rather by virtue of the jarring ways in which these emergent, dominant, and residual temporalities continued to compete for space in scientific and literary spheres, applying pressure to and transgressing each other's boundaries. Wonderland nonsense not only travesties the experience of a new discursive, social, and technological regulation of time, but is 'ultimately derived from the existence of two fundamentally divergent temporalities'[32] – the temporal and the eternal – which no longer conform to their traditional meanings. It is precisely Carroll's introduction of this comic twist into the history of time and timelessness that is pivotal for understanding his legacy to a certain strand of twentieth-century writing.

Literary modernism rejects the consensus of *external-objective-time* for an a-linear, refracted, and pluralistic *internal-subjective-time*. A key element of this temporal aesthetic explores the potential of reviving the time and timelessness topos to capture obliquely, but more faithfully, the secular, fragmented, industrialized experience of twentieth-century life. Examples are legion, but perhaps the pre-eminent instance is Eliot's argument in 'Tradition and the Individual Talent' that the modern poet should acquire a 'sense of the timeless as well as of the temporal and of the timeless and of the temporal together'.[33] This idea that the past is both behind us (thus historical and temporal) and yet still with us in its continued, spectral influence on the present (thus, timeless) underpins the characterization of history in Eliot's *Four Quartets* as 'a pattern / Of timeless moments', as well as that poem's declaration that 'to apprehend / The point of intersection of the timeless / With time, is an occupation for the saint' – or, Eliot implies, for the modernist writer.[34] The modernist drive to innovate a form of literary expression that escapes the clock's control over human life is also found in D. H. Lawrence's aesthetic project to secularize Augustine's concept of 'the sublimity of an eternity which is always in the present'.[35] Ricardo J. Quinones identifies this dynamic in 'Ursula's quest to find a new sense of eternity *within* the flux of time' in *The Rainbow*,[36] and it is borne out also in *Kangaroo*'s declaration that it is only in 'the great pause between' the ceaseless 'tic-tac' of the clock that one 'finds the [...] reality of timelessness'.[37] Elsewhere, Teresa Prudente demonstrates Woolf's diverse representations of an experience of a-linear time, which variously allows the subject to enter a timeless temporal dimension (as in *Orlando* and *To the Lighthouse*) or tragically separates the subject from consensus 'reality' (as in *Mrs Dalloway*).[38]

For each of these modernist writers, *La Divina Commedia* is the point of reference par excellence; yet, I propose that Carroll is a key if under-acknowledged intermediator between Dante and a number of modernist authors who undertake a comic, even absurdist approach to reviving the sacred ideas of timelessness and eternity in the secular age of mass culture. Dante's epic presents timeless eternity and human finitude as 'two divine empires, each embodying the authority of God, and each truly divided from the other' by virtue of their distinct laws of stasis and change.[39] The impossibility that the finite mind could comprehend or represent the eternal is figured in Dante's dictum 'Trasumanar significar *per verba* / non si poria' (The passing beyond humanity may not be set forth in words).[40] Barbara Newman emphasizes that Dante's creative response to this aporia is to express his impossible experience of eternity through neologisms.[41] As the neologistic impulse arises, in part, from the encounter with incompatible, inexpressible temporalities, so Dante's poetics finds its modernist culmination in the extreme wordplay of Joyce's simultaneously cyclical and progressive *Finnegans Wake*. Yet, such a liminal encounter between incompatible temporal realms also informs and necessitates Carroll's Wonderland portmanteaus.

Jorge Luis Borges confirms the debt that modernist writing owes to Wonderland time in his insistence that it was not Faulkner or Priestley who taught modern writers 'to play' with the possibilities of 'reversible time' and 'delayed time', but Carroll.[42] Similarly, Marshall McLuhan argues that into the 'uniform Euclidean world of continuous space-and-time, Carroll drove a fantasia of discontinuous space-and-time that anticipated Kafka, Joyce, and Eliot'.[43] In each case, a key inspiration is the model that Wonderland offers for thinking an impossible time.

I agree, but contend that Carroll is more specifically still a key coordinate for a certain strand of modernist writing, exemplified by Beckett, Joyce, and O'Brien, which revives the pre-Enlightenment conception of timelessness and eternity to offer a darkly comic twist on the experience of living in a time-out-of-joint, amid the fluctuations of unchecked austerity and excess in the secular age of mass culture. While Eliot asks us to delineate clearly and observe the interplay between time and timelessness, for Joyce, Beckett, and O'Brien it is rather the banal but comic *confusion* between these ideas that characterizes the twentieth century. In other words, what Carroll's play with time offers these writers is not just a reorganisation of linear clock time – stopping it, reversing it, and so on – but a picture of timelessness which is *nevertheless and at the same time* characterized by the modern coordinates and measurements of time's passing: production, consumption, conservation, waste, labour, exhaustion, austerity, excess.

Schleifer contends that in twentieth-century modernism, the *topoi* of eternity, timelessness, and timeless duration are set in a dialectic relationship with the era's defining crisis of abundance.[44] Tim Armstrong relates this crisis specifically to economies of mass production and consumption 'driven by desire rather than need', and insists that any 'economics in which waste, excess and mass consumption are central terms has important consequences for the arts'[45] and their temporal aesthetics. However, for a late modernist such as Beckett or O'Brien, this 'strict opposition between the immanent and the transcendental, between the noisy clamor of our world and […] the harmonious silence of heaven'[46] is no longer tenable, as the sense of proliferating abundance identified by Schleifer and Armstrong is shot through, simultaneously, with the effects of wartime austerity and deprivation. This contradictory set of concurrent drives towards austerity (conceived as a time of stasis) and excess (marked by radical, exponential change) account, in part, for a modernism that 'itself is shot through with contradictory associations'[47] with maximalism and minimalism, extravagant spectacle and a severe economy of expression.

In Beckett and Joyce, we observe variants of a modernist temporal aesthetic that is stimulated and sustained by the Dantean vision of time and the eternal, but which also engage with the Mad Tea-Party paradigm of a comic *confusion* of distinct temporal logics. Recalling Nietzsche's dictum that 'moderns' distinguish themselves 'by filling [themselves] to *overflowing*' with 'a chaotic and overburdening' inherited culture, Jean-Michel Rabaté pinpoints the recurring modernist impulse 'to conjure up the figure of a ghostly writer who imagines himself posthumous' as the only atemporal vantage 'available from which to take stock of this *cumbersome mass*'.[48] The quintessential example is the Beckettian subject, '[s]uspended between death and the inability to finish dying'.[49] In Beckett's writing 'time itself becomes timeless',[50] as in Vladimir's declaration in *Waiting for Godot* that '[t]ime has stopped',[51] or the narrator's desire, in *From an Abandoned Work*, for 'a long unbroken time without before or after'.[52] Crucially, however, Beckett's figuration of timeless duration distinguishes itself from that of Eliot, Lawrence, or Woolf by depicting a time stayed by excess: 'the question may be asked, off the record, why time doesn't pass, from you, why it piles up all about you, instant on instant, on all sides, deeper and deeper, thicker and thicker, your time, other's time, the time of the ancient dead and the dead yet unborn'.[53] If Beckett's writing presents a paradigm in which '[t]ime is stayed but trickles pointlessly', this is a quality that Beer explicitly traces back to the comically incompatible rhetorics of timeless duration, abundance, and waste staged at the Mad Tea-Party in Wonderland.[54]

This modernist engagement with the Carrollian temporal model is exemplified in Joyce's cyclical dreamwork *Finnegans Wake*, which Stuart Gilbert characterizes as offering a 'new vision of a timeless world'.[55] Borg identifies the 'most recognisable stylistic gesture' of Joyce's *Wake* as a 'surpassing of the limit [that] is reflected in a logic of waste and unmasterable semiotic excess' tied to contesting temporal economies, in which 'the passing of time can only be figured as waste or excess'.[56] These competing logics are staged most explicitly in the *Wake*'s parable of 'The Ondt and the Gracehoper', in which 'the Ondt promotes a productive understanding of temporality marked by industry, accumulation and memory' while 'the Gracehoper embodies an economy of waste in which the Ondt's productivity is refused and cancelled'.[57] For Borg, this tension informs the *Wake*'s neologistic excess, as the portmanteau 'produces a hesitation between meaning and non-meaning, between work and waste'.[58] The language of the *Wake* draws on the history of neologistic writing as a creative response to the impossibility of expressing incompatible temporalities, a tradition inherited from Dante but given a comic twist through Carroll. As such, it is telling that Joyce's parable ends with an explicit allusion to the Mad Tea-Party, as the Gracehoper's final charge to the Ondt – '*why can't you beat time?*'[59]– refashions the pun that the Mad Hatter wrings out of Alice's statement that she has to 'beat time when [she] learn[s] music'.[60] This intertextual allusion signals that Wonderland's significance to modernist thought is its complex logic of a timelessness distinguished, impossibly, by excessive productivity and senseless waste.

Yet it is Flann O'Brien, I propose, who tests and applies the Wonderland paradigm most explicitly and thoroughly in a modernist context, by engaging Carroll directly in a conversation about temporality and modernity. Indeed, O'Brien's recurrent comic play with interrupting, halting, and reversing time's flow constitutes a revealing participation in, and reflection on, these interrelated temporal arcs: on the one hand, from medieval Christian thought through Newtonian mechanics to special relativity, and, on the other, from Dante's divine poetry through Carrollian nonsense to Joycean or Beckettian modernism. O'Brien reportedly described the temporal design of his 1939 debut novel *At Swim-Two-Birds* as one in which '[c]onventional notions of Time would be scorned. Past, present and future would be abolished, and the work would exist in a supra-Bergsonian continuum'.[61] And he explained his final completed novel, 1964's *The Dalkey Archive*, via Einstein and J. W. Dunne's theories on the 'simultaneity of time':

The idea is that time is as a great flat motionless sea. Time does not pass; it is we who pass. With this concept as basic, fantastic but coherent situations can easily be devised, and in effect the whole universe torn up in a monstrous comic debauch.[62]

O'Brien's proposition that 'Time does not pass; it is we who pass' resonates with diverse theological, philosophical, and scientific positions throughout the history of the philosophy of time.[63] However, his intuition of the potential to recast such a temporal paradigm – in all its jarring incompatibilities with certain modern consensuses – as 'a monstrous comic debauch' is manifested in his work's explicit and implicit dialogues with Carroll's Wonderland time.

Carroll Marx: Wonderland *and* Cruiskeen Lawn

In his *Irish Times* column of 8 March 1954, titled 'March Hare', Myles na gCopaleen affects to present himself as a serious critic of the works of Lewis Carroll. Myles promises his readers an 'astonishing thesis' in which he will reveal 'a serious, sinister discovery' regarding Carroll, once the requisite 'research, documentation, concordance' has been undertaken.[64] He writes:

> ON THURSDAY EVENING I was sitting in the library of my house in Santry. Believe me when I aver that I was reading 'Alice in Wonderland,' having also read a biographical preface about 'Lewis Carroll,' otherwise Charles Lutwidge Dodgson. Some hours before, I had been reading the biography of Karl Marx. Several familiar things in 'Alice' had a new impact on me, and I soon discovered that this was due to an extraordinary coincidence of dates, time and work as between Marx and Carroll. 'Alice,' like many another work, was written for children but intended for adults; it is saturated with the Hegelian dialectic upon which Marx superimposed his own philosophy of economics and the classes. 'Alice' is a pro-Communist parable. I believe I can demonstrate that, with exhaustive annotation.[65]

Myles's exhaustive study, however, is interrupted by a loudspeaker announcing what appears to be an air raid but turns out to be an earthquake caused by 'violent political tremors' – men shaking in their boots, no doubt in anticipation of Myles's paradigm-shifting reading of *Alice* – and the promised comparative analysis of Carroll and Marx is not taken up again.[66] While acknowledging the central irony to Myles's parable – that his reading of Carroll, like Derrida's in *The Animal That Therefore I Am*, is infinitely delayed by the immediacy of events in the now – I am interested, in part, in retrieving Myles's unstated theories on Alice, labour, and politics and tracing their influence on his reworking of Carroll's strange temporalities.

If we entertain the idea that Myles means his claim that '"Alice" is a pro-Communist parable' semi-seriously (and not only as a groanworthy play on the name 'Carroll Marx'), then the key scene for Myles's Marxist reading would seem to be the Mad Tea-Party, in which Time is personified as a frustrated, overworked labourer. Alice's charge that the Hatter is wasting time is met with the rebuttal: 'If you knew Time as well as I do [...] you wouldn't talk about wasting *it*. It's *him*.'[67] The Hatter relates that this anthropomorphized Time stopped working for him owing to a quarrel in which the Queen of Hearts accused the Hatter of 'murdering the time' when singing '*Twinkle, twinkle, little bat*': 'ever since that', he tells Alice mournfully, 'he won't do a thing I ask!'[68] It seems likely to me that Myles notes Carroll's punning rhetoric of time not only as an abstraction that may be saved, spent, or wasted, as in the modern idiom, but also as a worker who is beaten, murdered, and exhausted. The comic image that Myles inherits from the Mad Tea-Party is of a timeless eternity in which Time still works, yet where his productivity is always potentially interrupted by a labour dispute.

This reading is bolstered by an earlier, more overt reworking of the Mad Tea-Party in the 7 August 1946 column, in which Myles reflects that 'maturing is not solely a matter of time, but the time factor is important and it happens *I know him well*'.[69] Myles relates the 'time factor's' involvement in a strike on the Dublin docks when 'there was a lot of extra time being imported for building contracts':

> Do you know what happened? It went bad. *The mairrchints* [merchants], of course – the usual thing – wanted to blame it on the time factor. The time factor washed his hands of the whole thing, said his contract ended at Dublin quay, said he'd have to be paid. The mairrchints said it would have to go to arbitration. The time factor invoked the war clause. Well, to cut along Storey's heart, he got his money. But [...] he's done himself a lot of hairrm [harm] with the mairrchints.[70]

Myles's punning on the idiom 'to cut a long story short' ('to cut along Storey's heart') amid this confusion of temporal logics signals an engagement with the lineage of Dante-Carroll-Joyce. However, the allusion to the 'war clause' demonstrates that here in the national paper, he engages the mad timelessness of the Tea-Party more specifically as a satirical critique of immediate labour and political conditions.

While not explicitly alluding to Carroll, the 26 October 1942 instalment of *Cruiskeen Lawn*, subtitled 'The Future', demonstrates the resonance between the logic of the Mad Tea-Party and Myles's view of wartime Europe as an absurd conflation of progress and stasis, excess and austerity:

> I read somewhere the other day [...] that the great motor car manufacturers are continuing for the duration of the war to design 'phantom' models of their vehicles, one new one every year, each improving on its predecessor, but that the public is to be kept in ignorance of all this. After the war (if that means anything) the first model to be (launched) will be as much an improvement on 1939's model as 1939 was on 1910 [...]. This is awful nonsense. By 1978 – not that I suppose your men will have laid off their scrapping by then – I'll certainly have forgotten how to drive the 1939 model.[71]

The key point to be underlined here is that from Myles's vantage, there is no reason to believe that the world will ever advance beyond this state of perpetual war. He continues to develop the conceit in increasingly over-the-top Carrollian terms, through an image of wasteful invention beyond all good measure:

> Supposing this strictly private progress is also carried on in (other spheres)? What then? Suppose Montague Burton in his secret laboratory turns out each year a phantom lounge suit, gradually stream-lining it, knocking off a pocket here, a lapel there, changing the trousers, taking them off, turning the waist-coat back to front, sewing the buttons on inside, coming out with two spare sleeves as well as the usual two, eventually throwing aside all accepted dress theories in favour of some mad invention (in shark-skin probably) buttoning down the back with a pair of stainless steel elastic breeches, hollow glass-tiled shoes and a hat with a periscope and a radiogram that turns records over and plays them upside-down and pours out drink for you and your pals every time you press the button on the zip fastener at the back of your neck. What decent Irishman would be seen in that rig-out matther [*sic*] a damn what year it is in it? Sure it's nonsense.[72]

The speculated 'mad invention' of the extravagantly embellished 'phantom lounge suit' provides a figurative image of the absurdity of exponential production, growth, and technological innovation amid the simultaneous crisis and stasis of never-ending war. The image captures, comically, the Beckettian and Joycean sense of a modernity defined simultaneously by coordinates of abundance and austerity; yet it also demonstrates how Myles draws on the Carrollian 'nonsense' of confusions of time and timelessness to advance a socio-political critique of the Fordist modernization of Ireland.[73] This image of modernity as a suspended time in which commodities are endlessly produced without the necessity of their consumption builds on a central image of *The Third Policeman*. This novel, which was hanging in its own unpublished limbo (as it was composed in 1939–40, but first published posthumously in 1967) as Myles was writing these absurdist wartime columns, comprises O'Brien's most sustained and multifaceted engagement with the stakes of the comic temporal scheme of the Mad Tea-Party.

An Astonishing Parade of Nullity: Wonderland and The Third Policeman

The Third Policeman tells the story of a rural Irish scholar and his co-conspirator John Divney, who rob and murder a retired cattle trader named Mathers. When the nameless narrator-protagonist returns to Mathers's house three years later to retrieve the cash box, he feels something strange pass over him: the box has disappeared, and he finds himself engaged in a conversation with his murder victim. The next morning, he sets off to the local police barracks to enquire about the return of his black box, where he encounters Policeman MacCruiskeen and

Sergeant Pluck. Working from inside a barracks that appears from the outside to be two-dimensional, these bicycle-obsessed policemen introduce the most explicitly Carrollian level of absurdity to the text. MacCruiskeen presents the narrator with a series of mind-boggling inventions, such as an apparatus for wrangling sound out of light, a spear so sharp that the point is invisible for the last seven inches of it, and a Russian-doll style series of boxes-in-boxes that go all the way down to the invisible nano-atomic level. Pluck informs the narrator of the principle of the atomic theory that is at work in the parish, transforming cyclists into their bicycles and vice versa. Clues are laid for the policemen's connection to Wonderland, such as the detail that Policeman Fox 'is as mad as a hare'.[74] Indeed, Tigges emphasizes the 'Carrollian logic' of the policemen's strange jurisdiction as a place in which 'time, space and language change' constantly as the reader is inundated with 'logical impossibilities', and concludes that 'to anyone familiar with the Alice books the resemblances in technique are striking'.[75]

O'Brien's narrator is driven to the murder in order to fund the publication of his autodidactic scholarship on the eccentric philosopher de Selby, whose unusual theories are detailed in the book's footnotes: such as that the earth is sausage-shaped or that sleep is a consequence of light asphyxiation due to an accumulation of 'black air'.[76] Time is a key concern of the philosophy of de Selby, who, we are told, 'would question the most obvious realities and object even to things scientifically demonstrated',[77] as in his assertion that human existence is 'a succession of static experiences each infinitely brief'.[78] From this presupposition, which he determines from examining cinematograph films frame by frame, de Selby

discounts the reality or truth of any progression or serialism in life, denies that time can pass as such in the accepted sense and attributes to hallucinations the commonly experienced sensation of progression as, for instance, in journeying from one place to another or even 'living'.[79]

The assertion that linear time is an illusion which conceals an underlying stasis is manifested throughout the policemen's realm, where, in an echo of Wonderland time, it is 'always five o'clock in the afternoon'[80] and where Sergeant Pluck declares, 'This is not today, this is yesterday'.[81]

Both the *Alice* novels and *The Third Policeman* treat the fall-out of a radical event: Alice's descent through the Rabbit Hole or journey through the looking-glass; the nameless de Selby scholar's encounter with the mysterious black box. In each case, the event thrusts Alice and the de Selby scholar into realms in which 'reality' is in constant flux and experience thereof unaccountable. Wonderland and O'Brien's parish are each characterized by the simultaneous functioning of fundamentally irreconcilable temporalities, the incompatibilities of which engender not only comic misunderstandings but also a range of ontological impossibilities. The experience of living in such a disrupted time cannot but place the coherence of the self under stress, and in each novel, the protagonist is 'pushed against the limits of ordinary temporality', in the process becoming 'a subject able to live in a time out of time' or 'the dispersed self of a time out of joint'.[82] Each figure loses their sense of self as a consequence, with Alice asking 'Who in the world am I?'[83] and the de Selby scholar confessing: 'I was shocked to realise that [...] I did not know my name, did not remember who I was. [...] I had no name'.[84]

The narrator's loss of identity drives *The Third Policeman* towards both wasted exertion and excessive semiotic openness, as staged in the scene in which Sergeant Pluck attempts to guess his name:

'Would it be Mick Barry?'
'No.'
'Charlemagne O'Keeffe?'
'No.'
'Sir Justin Spens?'
'Not that.'
'Kimberley?'
'No.'
'Bernard Farm?'
'No.'
'Joseph Poe or Nolan?'
'No.'
'One of the Garvins or the Moynihans?'
'Not them.'
'Rosencranz O'Dowd?'
'No.'
'Would it be O'Benson?'
'Not O'Benson.'
'The Quigleys, The Mulrooneys or the Hounimen?'
'No.'
'The Hardimen or the Merrimen?'
'Not them.'
'Peter Dundy?'
'No.'
'Scratch?'
'No.'
'Lord Brad?'
'Not him.'
'The O'Growneys, the O'Roartys or the Finnehys?'
'No.'
'That is an amazing piece of denial and denunciation,' he said. '[...] An astonishing parade of nullity.'[85]

This disappointment of scripts of answer-and-response echoes the Mad Tea-Party. When the attendees admit they do not know the answer to the Hatter's riddle 'Why is a raven like a writing-desk?', Alice becomes frustrated: 'I think you might do something better with the time [...] than waste it in asking riddles that have no answers.'[86] For Beer, the unanswered riddle mocks a temporal ideology of productivity which is undone by wasted effort: 'The lack of an answer infringes all the rules of game time, so dear to Victorian middle-class culture: riddles rely on the pleasurable disappointment when the ingenious (but usually inadequate) answer is reached among the universe of possibilities.'[87] Beer's conclusion that the riddle of the raven and the writing desk, 'nullity is all that occurs'[88] resonates with the 'astonishing parade of nullity' that O'Brien's protagonist offers under interrogation. The refusal to provide an answer to either the Hatter's riddle or the mystery of the de Selby scholar's name establishes a dual move towards both the wasted exertion of attempting to make nonsense mean, and the excessive semiotic productivity of a riddle whose meaning is never closed.

O'Brien's play with the ironies of Carrollian conventions of naming and riddling – which produce waste, exhaustion, and nullity, rather than (self-)knowledge – culminates in a depiction of eternity that bolsters Myles's Marxist reading of Wonderland time. A 'map of the parish, complete, reliable and astonishing' is found in the cracks of the ceiling of the police barracks, and Sergeant Pluck informs the narrator that it 'was always there and MacCruiskeen is certain that it was there even before that.'[89] The map leads the policemen to the discovery, after seven years of study, of the fact that this eternal parish is the location of another, even more timeless eternity, the entrance to which is to be found beside 'Jarvis's outhouse' (again, aligning the coordinates of eternity and waste), accessible by means of a mechanical lift.[90] The protagonist's descent into this subterranean eternity-within-eternity via this mechanical means is an iteration of Alice's fall down the Rabbit Hole; but crucially it is a repetition with a difference. In *Alice* we read:

> Either the well was very deep, or she fell very slowly, for she had plenty of time as she went down to look about her, and to wonder what was going to happen next. [...] Down, down, down. Would the fall *never* come to an end? [...] [W]hen suddenly, thump! thump! down she came upon a heap of sticks and dry leaves, and the fall was over.[91]

For the de Selby scholar's mise-en-abyme-like descent, O'Brien inverts the slow drop and sudden landing of Alice's fall:

> With no noise or warning at all, the floor was giving way beneath us. [...] The floor was falling so fast beneath us that it seemed once or twice to fall faster than I could fall myself [...]. I swore and groaned and closed my eyes and wished for a happy death [...], falling appallingly for ever [...]. Almost at once the falling changed, either stopping altogether or becoming a much slower falling. 'Yes,' said the Sergeant brightly, 'we are there now.'[92]

The parish's eternity-within-eternity into which O'Brien's protagonist falls is, like the Wonderland into which Alice tumbles, strangely governable by the demands of earthly temporality, figured in the policemen's obsessive maintenance of 'daily readings' from infernal clock-faces that purport to measure eternity's fluctuating mechanical levels.[93] These intertextual echoes signal O'Brien's intention both to map his eternity-within-eternity onto Wonderland and to signpost the accelerated confusion of progress and stasis with which his twentieth-century fantasy grapples.

The absence of time in O'Brien's eternity-within-eternity is demonstrated in the 'eight-day clock' there that 'never goes'.[94] This timelessness is also 'measured in the stasis of the observer's body' which does not 'grow old',[95] as demonstrated by the endless but empty consumption that is enabled in this limitrophic space:

> The beard does not grow and if you are fed you do not get hungry and if you are hungry you don't get hungrier. Your pipe will smoke all day and will still be full and a glass of whiskey will still be there no matter how much of it you drink and it does not matter in any case because it will not make you drunker than your own sobriety.[96]

Here we must note a distinction from the timeless Mad Tea-Party where nevertheless 'things get used up'[97]: in so far as O'Brien's eternity-within-eternity is a place where commodities are never expended, it is superficially closer to a classical or medieval understanding of timeless duration. Yet, the essential contradiction remains of a timeless after-world organized around the limitrophic coordinates of hunger, consumption, and desire: as Maebh Long makes clear, this eternity is both 'a place wholly outside of time' and 'a place of wish fulfilment', an 'eternity of the bodily or the corporeal'.[98] In O'Brien's novel, the forges of eternity are refigured as factories of industry: this is a timeless eternity lined with walls 'made with bolted sheets of pig-iron in which were set rows of small doors like ovens or furnace-doors or safe-deposits such as banks have'.[99] It is a sterile space characterized by 'the coldness of the iron interior, the functionality of the door-lined corridors, the artificiality of the tangle of wires and pipes overhead' and 'the constant sound of grinding cogwheels' that, as Long observes, 'measure out not progressive time but time in a loop and the changelessness of infinite repetitions'.[100]

Having witnessed the infernal production of 'a bicycle that would cost at least eight pounds ten to buy' in one of these immortal furnaces, the narrator announces: 'I now found myself taking an interest in the commercial possibilities of eternity'.[101] As Jennika Baines underlines, 'the narrator visits an Eternity filled with useless commodities, obtaining things there in time that does not pass'.[102] However, he is frustrated by the fact that while the forges of this eternity-within-eternity can produce anything he wants – a solid block of gold weighing half a tonne, a bottle of whiskey, a serge suit of blue with silk linings – he cannot take his spoils back with him overground as he must be the same weight going up in the lift as he was coming down. Realizing that his plans for wealth 'were vanquished and [his] visit to eternity unavailing and calamitous', the narrator breaks 'down completely and crie[s] loudly like a baby'.[103] The sequence is a repetition with a difference of the paradigmatic Carrollian scene: while the Mad Tea-Party is a timeless event where 'things get used up' – as it occurs in a place where time has stopped yet trickles on regardless – the eternity into which O'Brien's protagonist falls is 'a place wholly outside of time' in which commodities are endlessly produced in superabundance without the possibility of their consumption.

Towards the novel's close, Policeman Fox continues this theme when he describes the productive power of omnium (the substance which, we learn, is 'the driving force or power behind eternity'[104]) by virtue of a thought experiment: if your wish is for strawberry jam, then with access to the black box's contents 'you could have a house packed full of strawberry jam, every room so full that you could not open the door'.[105] Keith Hopper notes that the 'bizarre analogy' constitutes an intertextual allusion to the White Queen's *Looking-Glass* injunction, 'jam to-morrow and jam yesterday – but never jam to-day'.[106] While Hopper persuasively unpacks the metafictional operations of this intertextual allusion, I should like to emphasize its functions at and across the diversified limits of temporal experience and measurement that have been developed throughout this chapter. In the White Queen's rhetoric of 'jam to-morrow and jam yesterday – but never jam to-day', Carroll deploys a pun to capture the impossible point of encounter between incompatible temporal logics as he 'plays on the Latin word *iam* (*i* and *j* are interchangeable in classical Latin), which means now [...] in the past and future tenses, but in the present tense the word for now is *nunc*'.[107] If the eternal 'now' of the classical Christian eternity compels us to think an eternal duration without reference to past or future, Carroll turns this concept on its head, obliging us to think a modern timeless duration voided of the eternal 'now', with reference *only* to past or future 'nows'. This temporal impossibility adds further potential dimensions to Myles's suggested but withheld Marxist reading of the *Alice* novels through its rhetoric of eternal exploitation (the White Queen offers Alice 'jam every other day' as an inducement to work for her as a lady's-maid, with the implication being that payment for this labour will be eternally deferred) and of infinitely delayed consumption (Alice doesn't 'want any [jam] *to-day*', to which the Queen responds she 'couldn't have it if [she] *did* want it'[108]). *The Third Policeman*'s Marxist reading of Wonderland time, then, presents industrialized modernity not only as a time-out-of-joint, but as a static time disrupted, limitrophically, by an unquenchable hunger, a kind of eternal production line creating desires which are themselves frustrated through overabundance (as figured in the policeman's reference to 'a house packed [...] so full' with strawberry jam 'that you could not open the door'[109]). The promise of 'jam every other day' informs the excessive eternal production of intangible commodities in O'Brien's Irish eternity, but it also underpins its broader depiction of time's never-fulfilled promise of presence, captured elsewhere in Sergeant Pluck's declaration 'This is not today, this is yesterday', or more economically still in the temporal case of the narrator's dream utterance 'I was dead'.[110]

Posthumous Conclusions

This final quote recalls the irony that *The Third Policeman* – like Derrida's lecture that also invites us to deconstruct the logic of temporal limits through Carroll's Wonderland – was published posthumously. This coincidence only furthers the novel's strange, comic staging of a modern temporal rhetoric of production, labour, and commodification that surpasses even the limit of death. This is a temporal scheme which, I have argued, is stimulated and sustained by Carroll's modes of 'complicating, thickening, delinearizing, folding, and dividing' temporal limits 'by making [them] increase and multiply'.[111] Yet, while the confusion of temporal realms in *Alice's Adventures in Wonderland* is ultimately disclosed to have been the manifestation of a dream, in *The Third Policeman* it is revealed, in the closing pages, to have been the consequence of the protagonist suddenly finding himself living posthumously, in an uncanny afterlife governed and regulated by the arbitrary justice of the local policemen. As Long underlines, the narrator's death – which occurs in the second chapter but is withheld from the reader until the book's final twist – 'is marked by a sudden metamorphosis in time and space [...] after life and beyond time'[112] in which the de Selby scholar becomes 'a sempiternal man',[113] who 'exists in a place indifferent to a measured movement of time'.[114] This shift from dreams, in Carroll's Wonderland, to the afterlife, in O'Brien's parish, as the *topos* through which an atemporal vantage on the present is leveraged, renders *The Third Policeman* more thoroughly modernist than *Alice's Adventures in Wonderland*, at least in terms of Rabaté's identification of literary modernism's attempts to assume a ghostly vantage that 'constantly projects, anticipates, and returns to mythical origins, but [...] also teaches us more about the "present" which it historicizes'.[115] However, such clear distinctions between dream visions and posthumous vantages are themselves frustrated in O'Brien's novel by virtue of the fact that the dead de Selby scholar regularly sleeps and dreams in this not-quite-timeless afterlife, where he even dreams of his own death.[116] The temporal limits of life, death, and sleep are surpassed through the transgressal movement of 'an undead waking marked by recurring sinking into deathly sleep'.[117]

As Hopper explains, 'the semiotic significance' of Sergeant Pluck's list of the narrator's potential names 'is its infinite range – the fact that it can go on forever and still be incomplete proclaims its open-endedness and essential emptiness'.[118] This figure of the simultaneously closed and unclosed riddle is indexical of *The Third Policeman*'s 'Möbius strip-like narrative structure',[119] which itself resonates with Gilles Deleuze's assertion that Carroll's recurrent folding of surface into depth works like a Möbius strip that reveals to us 'the "Radiance" of pure events, entities that never finish either happening or withdrawing'.[120] O'Brien's novel closes with the unanswered riddle 'Is it about a bicycle?',[121] which takes the reader back to the first instance of that question in a circular movement that renders pointless the narrator's attempts to escape the policemen's eternal punishment for his crimes. This is a movement that O'Brien characterizes as 'the re-experience of the already suffered, the fresh-forgetting of the unremembered',[122] and which evokes certain Christian moralities and philosophies of time. Maciej Ruczaj contends that the de Selby scholar's trip to eternity 'abounds in ironic play with the motifs [...] from Dante';[123] however, Long insists that O'Brien's 'inferno' is a specifically 'modernist hell of nauseous uncertainty, alienation and defamiliarization, where identity, agency and control are eroded but not destroyed'.[124] If, as Long insists, '[t]he cycles of this hell are not those of Dante',[125] I would argue that we gain a greater vantage on both its comic and modernist qualities by pursing the text's own indications that its hellish circularity is indebted to the legacy of the timeless yet impossibly productive and wasteful eternity of Carroll's Mad Tea-Party, at which the attendees are stuck perpetually 'moving round' the table, using everything up, so that they cannot respond, with any words or logic known to the language of linearity, to Alice's question: 'But what happens when you come to the beginning again?'[126]

Notes

1   Versions of this chapter were presented at *Metamorphoses: III International Flann O'Brien Conference* at the Charles University, Prague (2015), the CEMS *Borders of Modernism* conference at the University of Perugia (2016), the AAUTE Conference Salzburg (2018), and as an invited address to the Lewis Carroll Society (2021). As well as the invaluable feedback from the present volume's editors and readers, I am grateful for the insightful comments offered during and after these sessions by Ruben Borg, Maebh Long, Joseph Brooker, Katherine Ebury, Onno Kosters, Erika Mihálycsa, Radvan Markus, Giulia Falistocco, Joseph LaBine, Markus Oppolzer, Sarah Heinz, Michaela Borzaga, Jane Skelly, Stephen Folan, and Kiera Vaclavik, among others.

2   Wim Tigges, 'Ireland in Wonderland: Flann O'Brien's *The Third Policeman* as a Nonsense Novel', in *The Clash of Ireland: Literary Contrasts and Connections*, ed. C. C. Barfoot and Theo D'Haen (Amsterdam: Rodopi, 1989), 204–6; Carol Taaffe, *Ireland Through the Looking-Glass: Flann O'Brien, Myles na gCopaleen and Irish Cultural Debate* (Cork: Cork University Press, 2008).

3   Both 'Flann O'Brien' and 'Myles na gCopaleen' are pseudonyms of the Irish author Brian O'Nolan. While the standard critical practice over recent years has been to refer to the author by his biographical name (O'Nolan), to avoid inconsistencies with Carroll studies – in which the pseudonym 'Lewis Carroll' is standardly used over Charles Dodgson – in this chapter I refer to the author by his most famous pseudonym 'Flann O'Brien' except in instances where I am directly discussing his columns published under the 'Myles na gCopaleen' name.

4   As well as Tigges, 'Ireland in Wonderland', and Taaffe, *Ireland Through the Looking-Glass*, see Keith Hopper, *Flann O'Brien: A Portrait of the Artist as a Young Post-Modernist*, second edition (Cork: Cork University Press, 2009), 215–18; John Attridge, 'Nonsense, Ordinary Language Philosophy, and Flann O'Brien's *The Third Policeman*', *Modern Fiction Studies* 60, no. 2 (summer 2014): 308; Katherine Ebury, 'Physical Comedy and the Comedy of Physics in *The Third Policeman, The Dalkey Archive* and *Cruiskeen Lawn*', in *Flann O'Brien: Problems with Authority*, ed. Ruben Borg, Paul Fagan, and John McCourt (Cork: Cork University Press, 2017), 88, 92, 95–6.

5   Lewis Carroll, *Alice's Adventures in Wonderland* and *Through the Looking-Glass*, ed. Hugh Haughton (London: Penguin, 1998), 64; Flann O'Brien, *The Complete Novels* (New York: Everyman's Library, 2007), 291.

6   Jacques Derrida, *Specters of Marx: The State of the Debt, the Work of Mourning and the New International*, trans. Peggy Kamuf (London: Routledge, 2011), 3, and *passim*.

7   Jacques Derrida, *The Animal That Therefore I Am*, trans. David Wills, ed. and intro. Marie-Luise Malle (New York: Fordham University Press, 2008), 29.

8   Ibid., 7.

9   Ibid., xii. Malle catalogues the following instances of the motif throughout Derrida's talk: 'If I had time and if we had the time together. […] we don't have time. […] if I had time I would try to show how. […] we won't have time to go very far. […] if we have the time to get there. […] one should spend a long time on this. […] I won't have time to do it. […] if I had time, I would have liked to do justice. […] I would have liked to insist on the moments of vertigo and circularity in this text. That's what would take time. […] This exclamation mark is something I would have liked to follow throughout this enormous discourse, I'll do it, I hope, if I have the time and the strength. I'd like to do justice to this text' (ibid.).

10 Lewis Carroll, 'The Two Clocks', in *The Works of Lewis Carroll*, ed. Roger Lancelyn Green (London: Paul Hamlyn, 1965), 1056.

11 Ibid., 1056–7.

12 Carroll, *Alice*, 62, 64.

13 Ibid., 62.

14 Gillian Beer, *Alice in Space: The Sideways Victorian World of Lewis Carroll* (Chicago: Chicago University Press, 2016), 39.

15 Carroll, *Alice*, 63–4.

16 Ibid., 63.

17 Derrida, *Animal*, 29.

18 Ibid.

19 Plato, *Plato's Cosmology: The Timaeus of Plato*, trans. Francis MacDonald Cornford (London: Routledge, 2001), 98.

20 Elizabeth Deeds Ermarth, *Realism and Consensus in the English Novel* (Princeton: Princeton University Press, 1983), 24–5.

21 Steven Connor, 'The Impossibility of the Present: or, from the Contemporary to the Contemporal', in *Literature and the Contemporary: Fictions and Theories of the Present*, ed. Roger Luckhurst and Peter Marks (New York: Longman, 1999), 16.

22 Ronald Schleifer, *Modernism and Time: The Logic of Abundance in Literature, Science, and Culture 1880–1930* (Cambridge: Cambridge University Press, 2000), 37–8.

23 Ermarth, *Realism*, 24–5.

24 Carroll, *Alice*, 171–3, 203.

25 See Calvin R. Petersen, 'Time and Stress: *Alice in Wonderland*', *Journal of the History of Ideas* 46, no. 3 (July–September 1985): 427–33; Tamsin Lorraine, 'Living a Time Out of Joint', in *Between Deleuze and Derrida*, ed. Paul Patton and John Protevi (New York: Continuum, 2003), 30–45; Caroline Garcia de Souza, '*But when the Rabbit actually took a watch out of its waistcoat-pocket […]*': *Alice's Adventures in Wonderland* and Time (Ph.D. diss., UFRGS, Instituto de Letras, 2014); and Beer, *Alice in Space*, *passim*.

26 Beer, *Alice in Space*, 29.

27 Ibid.

28 Garcia de Souza, *Wonderland and Time*, 11.

29 Tim Armstrong, *Modernism: A Cultural History* (Cambridge: Polity, 2005), 7.

30 Ibid.

31 Beer, *Alice in Space,* 31.

32 Garcia de Souza, *Wonderland and Time*, 18.

33 T. S. Eliot, 'Tradition and the Individual Talent', in *The Sacred Wood and Major Early Essays* (Mineola: Dover, 1998), 28.

34 T. S. Eliot, *Four Quartets* (Orlando, FL: Harcourt, 1977), 58, 44. See Kenneth Paul Kramer, *Redeeming Time: T.S. Eliot's Four Quartets* (Lanham: Cowley, 2007), 5, 20, and *passim*.

35 Augustine, *The Confessions*, trans. Henry Chadwick (Oxford: Oxford University Press, 1991), 16.

36 Ricardo J. Quinones, *Mapping Literary Modernism: Time and Development* (Princeton: Princeton University Press, 1985), 61.

37 D. H. Lawrence, *The Cambridge Edition of the Works of D. H. Lawrence: Kangaroo*, ed. Bruce Steele (Cambridge: Cambridge University Press, 2002), 333–4.

38 Teresa Prudente, *A Specially Tender Piece of Eternity: Virginia Woolf and the Experience of Time* (Plymouth: Lexington Books, 2009).

39 Thomas J. J. Altizer, 'The Self-Saving of God', in *The Blackwell Companion to Postmodern Theology*, ed. Graham Ward (Malden, MA: Blackwell, 2005), 433.

40 Dante Alighieri, *The Divine Comedy, Paradiso 1: Text*, trans. Charles S. Singleton (Princeton: Princeton University Press, 1991), Canto 1, Lines 70–1.

41 Barbara Newman, 'The Artifice of Eternity: Speaking of Heaven in Three Medieval Poems', *Religion and Literature* 37, no. 1 (2005): 8–9.

42 Jorge Luis Borges, *Prólogos, con un prólogo de Prólogos* (Buenos Aires: Editorial Torres Agüero, 1975), 110. Translation: https://juandahlmann.wordpress.com/2010/07/22/borges-month-borges-on-lewis-carroll/.

43 Marshall McLuhan, *Understanding Media: The Extension of Man* (New York: McGraw-Hill, 1965), 162.

44 Schleifer, *Modernism and Time*, 27.

45 Armstrong, *Modernism,* 2–3.

46 Schleifer, *Modernism and Time*, 27.

47 Rónán McDonald and Julian Murphet, 'Introduction', in *Flann O'Brien and Modernism*, ed. Julian Murphet, Rónán McDonald, and Sascha Morrell (London: Bloomsbury, 2014), 3.

48 Jean-Michel Rabaté, *The Ghosts of Modernity* (Gainesville: University Press of Florida, 1996), 188.

49 Ruben Borg, 'Putting the Impossible to Work: Beckettian Afterlife and the Posthuman Future of Humanity', *Journal of Modern Literature* 35, no. 4 (summer 2012): 177.

50 Eric Levy, 'The Beckettian Mimesis of Time', *University of Toronto Quarterly* 80, no. 1 (2011): 89, 97.

51 Samuel Beckett, *Waiting for Godot* (New York: Grove Press, 1954), 24.

52 Samuel Beckett, *First Love, and Other Shorts* (New York: Grove Press, 1974), 48.

53 Samuel Beckett, *Three Novels: Molloy, Malone Dies, The Unnamable* (New York: Grove Press, 2009), 382–3.

54 Beer, *Alice in Space*, 38.

55 Stuart Gilbert, 'Prolegomena to *Work in Progress*', *Transition* 13 (summer 1928): 70.

56 Ruben Borg, *The Measureless Time of Joyce, Deleuze and Derrida* (London: Continuum, 2007), 53.

57 Andrew Gaedtke, 'James Joyce as Philosopher and Theologian of Time: Review of Ruben Borg *The Measureless Time of Joyce, Deleuze and Derrida*' (London: Continuum, 2007)', *Journal of Modern Literature* 34, no. 2 (winter 2011): 193.

58 Borg, *Measureless Time*, 99.

59 James Joyce, *Finnegans Wake* (New York: Viking Press, 1939), 419.

60 Carroll, *Alice*, 61.

61 Quoted in Niall Sheridan, 'Brian, Flann and Myles', in *Myles: Portraits of Brian O'Nolan*, ed. Timothy O'Keeffe (London: Martin, Brian and O'Keeffe, 1973), 44.

62 Brian O'Nolan writes this in a letter to Timothy O'Keeffe, dated 21 September 1962 (Flann O'Brien, *The Collected Letters of Flann O'Brien*, ed. Maebh Long [Victoria, TX: Dalkey Archive Press, 2018], 324).

63 For a discussion of Dunne's influence on O'Brien's by turns comic and modernist rendering of serialism and timeless duration, see Hopper, *Flann O'Brien*, 206–15; Mark O'Connell, 'How to Handle Eternity: Infinity and the Theories of J. W. Dunne in the Fiction of Jorge Luis Borges and Flann O'Brien's *The Third Policeman*', *Irish Studies Review* 17, no. 2 (summer 2009): 223–7; Jack Fennell, 'Irelands Enough and Time: Brian O'Brien's Science Fiction', in *Flann O'Brien: Contesting Legacies*, ed. Ruben Borg, Paul Fagan, and Werner Huber (Cork: Cork University Press, 2014), 33, 38–9; and Maebh Long, *Assembling Flann O'Brien* (London: Bloomsbury, 2014), 73–4. Fennell also discusses the importance of Aquinas to O'Brien's temporal aesthetics (Fennell, 'Irelands Enough', 39–40). For the importance of the new physics and relative cosmology to the author's vision of time and space, see Katherine Ebury, *Modernism and Cosmology: Absurd Lights* (Basingstoke: Palgrave Macmillan, 2014), 24; and Ebury, 'Physical Comedy', *passim*.

64 Myles na gCopaleen, 'March Hare', *Cruiskeen Lawn*, *The Irish Times* (8 March 1954): 4.

65 Ibid., 4.

66 Ibid.

67 Carroll, *Alice*, 63.

68 Ibid., 64.

69 Myles na gCopaleen, *Cruiskeen Lawn*, *The Irish Times* (7 August 1946): 3. Emphasis mine.

70 Ibid., 3.

71 Myles na gCopaleen, 'The Future', *Cruiskeen Lawn*, *The Irish Times* (26 October 1942): 3.

72 Ibid., 3.

73 Andrew McFeaters, 'Reassembling Ford: Time Is Money in Brian O'Nolan's Brave New Ireland', *The Parish Review: Journal of Flann O'Brien Studies* 3, no. 1 (fall 2014): 35.

74 O'Brien, *The Complete Novels*, 288.

75 Wim Tigges, *An Anatomy of Literary Nonsense* (Amsterdam: Rodopi, 1988), 208.

76 O'Brien, *Complete Novels*, 246.

77 Ibid., 265.

78 Ibid., 263.

79 Ibid.

80 Ibid., 291.

81 Ibid., 273.

82 Lorraine, 'Living a Time', 30, 32.

83 Carroll, *Alice*, 17–18.

84 O'Brien, *Complete Novels*, 245.

85 Ibid., 310.

86 Carroll, *Alice*, 62–3.

87 Beer, *Alice in Space*, 37–8.

88 Ibid.

89 O'Brien, *Complete Novels*, 332.

90 Ibid., 332.

91 Carroll, *Alice*, 10–11.

92 O'Brien, *Complete Novels*, 338.

93 Ibid., 346.

94 Ibid., 341.

95 Ebury, 'Physical Comedy', 99.

96 O'Brien, *Complete Novels*, 341.

97 Carroll, *Alice*, 63–4.

98 Long, *Assembling*, 71.

99 O'Brien, *Complete Novels*, 339.

100 Long, *Assembling*, 71.

101 O'Brien, *Complete Novels*, 343.

102 Jennika Baines, '"Un-Understandable Mystery": Catholic Faith and Revelation in *The Third Policeman*', *The Review of Contemporary Fiction* 31, no. 3 (fall 2011): 85.

103 O'Brien, *Complete Novels*, 348.

104 Long, *Assembling*, 72.

105 O'Brien, *Complete Novels*, 392.

106 Hopper, *Flann O'Brien*, 126; Carroll, *Alice*, 170.

107 Lewis Carroll, *The Annotated Alice: The Definitive Edition*, ed. Martin Gardner (New York: Forum Books, 2000), 206, note 3.

108 Carroll, *Alice*, 171.

109 O'Brien, *Complete Novels*, 392.

110 Ibid., 273, 328.

111 Derrida, *Animal*, 29.

112 Long, *Assembling*, 69–70.

113 O'Brien, *Complete Novels*, 278.

114 Long, *Assembling*, 69–70.

115 Rabaté, *The Ghosts of Modernity*, 3.

116 Ibid., 328–9.

117 Long, *Assembling*, 71.

118 Hopper, *Flann O'Brien*, 137.

119 Tamara Radak, '"walking forever on falling ground": Closure, Hypertext, and the Textures of Possibility in *The Third Policeman*', in *Flann O'Brien: Problems with Authority*, ed. Ruben Borg, Paul Fagan, and John McCourt (Cork: Cork University Press, 2017), 243.

120 Gilles Deleuze, 'Lewis Carroll', in *Essays Critical and Clinical*, trans. Daniel W. Smith and Michael A. Greco (London: Verso, 1998), 22.

121 O'Brien, *Complete Novels*, 404, 267.

122 Ibid., 406.

123 Maciej Ruczaj, 'Infernal Poetics/Infernal Ethics: Flann O'Brien's *The Third Policeman* Between Medieval and Modern Netherworlds', *The Review of Contemporary Fiction* 31, no. 3 (fall 2011): 92.

124 Long, *Assembling*, 57. The fuller thesis that Long develops is that *The Third Policeman*'s 'repetitions and temporal confusions do not (simply) stem from divine punishment, but can be seen as manifesting from the timelessness of the unconscious, and the repetitions of the death drive' (ibid., 69). While we approach the text through different theoretical frameworks, I believe that our analyses complement each other, and it is worth pointing out that Long's chapter is the first to explore the crucial function of timelessness in O'Brien's text in any systematic way.

125 Ibid., 57.

126 Carroll, *Alice*, 64.

SELECT BIBLIOGRAPHY

Abate, Michelle Ann. "'The Queen Had Only One Way of Settling All Difficulties […]'" "Off with His Head!": *Alice's Adventures in Wonderland* and the Anti-Gallows Movement'. *Papers: Explorations into Children's Literature* 21, no. 1 (2011): 33–56.

Aizenberg, Edna. 'Borges, Postcolonial Precursor'. *World Literature Today* 66, no. 1 (winter 1992): 21–6.

'Alice's Adventures in the New Wonderland [brochure]'. *National Park Service Website*, National Park Service, 18 January 2012. https://www.nps.gov/yell/blogs/Alices-Adventures-in-the-New-Wonderland-brochure.htm.

Armstrong, Tim. *Modernism: A Cultural History*. Cambridge: Polity, 2005.

Atherton, J. S. *The Books at the Wake: A Study of Literary Allusion in James Joyce's* Finnegans Wake. London: Faber and Faber, 1959.

Atherton, J. S. 'Carroll: The Unforeseen Precursor'. In *The Books at the Wake: A Study of Literary Allusions in James Joyce's* Finnegans Wake, 124–35. New York: Viking, 1960.

Auden, W. H. *The Complete Works of W. H. Auden, Volume II: Prose, 1939–1948*. Edited by Edward Mendelson. Princeton: Princeton University Press, 2002.

Auden, W. H. *The Complete Works of W. H. Auden, Volume III: Prose, 1949–1952*. Edited by Edward Mendelson. Princeton: Princeton University Press, 2008.

Auden, W. H. *The Complete Works of W. H. Auden, Volume IV: Prose, 1956–1962*. Edited by Edward Mendelson. Princeton: Princeton University Press, 1996.

Auden, W. H. *The English Auden: Poems, Essays and Dramatic Writings, 1927–1939*. Edited by Edward Mendelson. New York: Random House, 1977.

Auden, W. H. *Forewords and Afterwords*. Edited by Edward Mendelson. New York: Random House, 1973.

Auden, W. H. *Juvenilia: Poems, 1922–1928*. Edited by Katherine Bucknell. Princeton: Princeton University Press, 1994.

Auden, W. H. *Selected Poems: New Edition*. Edited by Edward Mendelson. New York: Vintage, 1979.

Auden, W. H. 'Today's "Wonder-World" Needs Alice'. In *Aspects of Alice: Lewis Carroll's Dreamchild as Seen through the Critics' Looking Glasses, 1865–1971*. Edited by Robert Phillips, 3–12. New York: Vanguard, 1971.

Auerbach, Nina. 'Alice and Wonderland: A Curious Child'. *Victorian Studies* 17, no. 1 (September 1973): 31–47.

Avery, Gillian. 'Fairy Tales with a Purpose; Fairy Tales for Pleasure'. In *Alice in Wonderland, Norton Critical Edition*. Edited by Donald J. Gray, 321–7. New York: W. W. Norton & Company, 1992.

Axelrod, Steven Gould. 'The Poetry of Sylvia Plath'. In *The Cambridge Companion to Sylvia Plath*. Edited by Jo Gill, 73–89. Cambridge: Cambridge University Press, 2006.

Banfield, Ann. *The Phantom Table: Woolf, Fry, Russell, and the Epistemology of Modernism*. Cambridge: Cambridge University Press, 2000.

Beer, Gillian. *Alice in Space: The Sideways Victorian World of Lewis Carroll*. Chicago: Chicago University Press, 2018.

Benjamin, Walter. *The Arcades Project*. Translated by Howard Eiland and Kevin
    McLaughlin. Edited by Rolf Tiedemann (German edition). Cambridge, MA: Harvard
    University Press, 1999.

Benjamin, Walter. *The Origin of German Tragic Drama*. Translated by John Osbourne.
    London: Verso, 1998.

Benjamin, Walter. *Selected Writings*, 4 vols. Translated by Marcus Bullock et al.
    Cambridge, MA: Harvard University Press, 1996–2003.

Benjamin, Walter, and Gretel Adorno. *Correspondence 1930–1040*. Translated by Wieland
    Hoban. Edited by Henri Lonitz and Christoph Gödde. Cambridge: Polity, 2008.

Bishop, Elizabeth. *The Collected Prose*. Edited by Robert Giroux. New York:
    Noonday, 1984.

Bishop, Elizabeth. *The Complete Poems: 1927–1979*. New York: Farrar, Straus and
    Giroux, 1983.

Bivona, Daniel. 'Alice the Child-Imperialist and the Games of Wonderland'. *Nineteenth-
    Century Literature* 41, no. 2 (September 1986): 143–71.

Borg, Ruben. *The Measureless Time of Joyce, Deleuze and Derrida*. London:
    Continuum, 2007.

Borges, Jorge Luis. *Collected Fictions*. London: Penguin, 1999.

Borges, Jorge Luis. *Selected Non-Fictions*. London: Penguin, 1999.

Bowman, Isa. *The Story of Lewis Carroll*. London: J. M. Dent, 1899.

Bozorth, Richard R. *Auden's Games of Knowledge*. New York: Columbia University
    Press, 2001.

Breton, André. *Manifestoes of Surrealism*. Ann Arbor: Michigan University Press, 1972.

Breton, André. 'Preface to Pierre Mabille'. In *Le Miroir du merveilleux* (1962). Paris:
    Éditions de Minuit, 1977.

Breton, André. 'Qu'est-ce que le surréalisme?' In *Œuvres complètes*, vol. II, 223–62. Paris:
    Gallimard, 1992.

Buck-Morss, Susan. *The Dialectics of Seeing: Walter Benjamin and the Arcades Project*.
    Cambridge, MA: MIT Press, 1991.

Buki, Ann McGarrity. 'Lewis Carroll in *Finnegans Wake*'. In *Lewis Carroll: A Celebration,
    Essays on the Occasion of the 150th Anniversary of the Birth of Charles Lutwidge
    Dodgson*. Edited by Edward Guiliano, 154–66. New York: Clarkson N. Potter, 1982.

Carpenter, Humphrey. *Secret Gardens: A Study of the Golden Age of Literature*. London:
    George Allen and Unwin, 1985.

Carroll, Lewis. *Alice's Adventures in Wonderland* and *Through the Looking-Glass*. Edited by
    Hugh Haughton. London: Penguin, 1998.

Carroll, Lewis. *The Annotated Alice: The Definitive Edition, Alice's Adventures in
    Wonderland and Through the Looking-Glass*. Edited by Martin Gardner. New York:
    Penguin, 2001.

Carroll, Lewis. 'Christmas-Greetings [from a Fairy to a Child]'. In *Alice in Wonderland,
    Norton Critical Edition*. Edited by Donald J. Gray, 5. New York: W. W. Norton &
    Company, 1992.

Carroll, Lewis. *Symbolic Logic* and *The Game of Logic*. New York: Dover
    Publications, 1958.

Chesterton, G. K. 'A Defence of Nonsense'. In *A Defence of Nonsense and Other Essays*,
    1–11. New York: Dodd, Mead and Co., 1911.

Childs, Peter. *Modernism and the Post-Colonial: Literature and Empire 1885–1930*.
    London: Continuum, 2007.

Chopin, Kate. *The Awakening*. Edited by Margaret Culley. New York: W. W. Norton, 1976.

Ciolkowski, Laura E. 'Visions of Life on the Border: Wonderland Women, Imperial Travelers, and Bourgeois Womanhood in the Nineteenth Century'. *Genders* 27 (1998). https://www.colorado.edu/gendersarchive1998-2013/1998/02/01/visions-life-border-wonderland-women-imperial-travelers-and-bourgeois-womanhood.

Clarke, Stephan P. and Donald K. Stephens. *The Lord Peter Wimsey Companion*. Cambridge: The Dorothy L. Sayers Society, 2015.

Cohen, Margaret. *Profane Illumination: Walter Benjamin and the Paris of Surrealist Revolution*. Berkeley: University of California Press, 1993.

Connolly, Julian W. 'Ania V Strane Chudes'. In *The Garland Companion to Vladimir Nabokov*. Edited by Vladimir E. Alexandrov, 18–25. London: Routledge, 2014.

Connolly, Julian W. 'Cincinnatus and *Différance*: Subversive Discourse in *Invitation to a Beheading*'. *Cyncos* 12, no. 2 (1995): 73–82.

Crawford, Robert. *Young Eliot: From St. Louis to* The Waste Land. London: Jonathan Cape, 2015.

Dayton, Gail H. 'Elizabeth Bishop: Child of Past, Child of Present in "The Country Mouse."' In '*In Worcester, Massachusetts*': *Essays on Elizabeth Bishop from the 1997 Elizabeth Bishop Conference at WPI*. Edited by Laura Jehn Menides and Angela G. Dorenkamp. WPI Studies, 35–41. New York: Peter Lang, 1999.

Deleuze, Gilles. *Capitalism and Schizophrenia: A Thousand Plateaus*. Translated by Brian Massumi. London: Continuum Books, 2004.

Deleuze, Gilles. *Cinema 2: The Time Image*. Translated by Hugh Tomlinson and Robert Galeta. London: The Athlone Press, 1989.

Deleuze, Gilles. *The Logic of Sense*. Translated by Mark Lester and Charles Stivale. Edited by Constantin V. Boundas. London: The Athlone Press, 1990.

de Souza, Caroline Garcia. '"*But when the Rabbit actually took a watch out of its waistcoat-pocket ...*"': *Alice's Adventures in Wonderland and Time*. Dissertation: UFRGS, Instituto de Letras, 2014.

Despotopoulou, Anna. '"Running on Lines": Women and the Railway in Victorian and Early Modernist Culture'. In *Women in Transit through Literary Liminal Spaces*. Edited by Teresa Gomez Reus and Terry Gifford, 47–60. London: Palgrave Macmillan, 2013.

Derrida, Jacques. *The Animal That Therefore I Am*. Translated by David Wills. Edited and introduced by Marie-Luise Malle. New York: Fordham University Press, 2008.

Dickey, Frances. 'The Musical World of Eliot's *Inventions*'. In *The Edinburgh Companion to T. S. Eliot and the Arts*. Edited by Frances Dickey and John D. Morgenstern, 103–20. Edinburgh: Edinburgh University Press, 2016.

Dodgson, Charles. *The Political Pamphlets and Letters of Charles Lutwidge Dodgson and Related Pieces: A Mathematical Approach*. Edited by Francine F. Abeles. Charlottesville: Virginia University Press, 2001.

Douglas-Fairhurst, Robert. *The Story of Alice: Lewis Carroll and the Secret History of Wonderland*. Boston: Harvard University Press, 2015.

Driscoll, Catherine. *Girls: Feminine Adolescence in Popular Culture and Cultural Theory*. New York: Columbia University Press, 2002.

Dupree, Robert. 'The White Knight's Whiskers and the Wasp's Wig in *Through the Looking-Glass*'. In *Lewis Carroll: A Celebration, Essays on the Occasion of the 150th Anniversary of the Birth of Charles Lutwidge Dodgson*. Edited by Edward Guiliano, 112–22. New York: Clarkson N. Potter, 1982.

Dusinberre, Juliet. *Alice to the Lighthouse: Children's Books and Radical Experiments in Art*. Basingstoke and London: Macmillan and New York: St. Martin's, 1999.

Ebury, Katherine. 'Physical Comedy and the Comedy of Physics in *The Third Policeman, The Dalkey Archive* and *Cruiskeen Lawn*'. In *Flann O'Brien: Problems with Authority.* Edited by Ruben Borg, Paul Fagan, and John McCourt, 87–102. Cork: Cork University Press, 2017.

Eliot, T. S. *Fireside*, MS Am 1635.5. Houghton Library, Harvard University.

Eliot, T. S. *The Poems of T. S. Eliot*, vol. 1. Edited by Christopher Ricks and Jim McCue, Baltimore: Johns Hopkins University Press, 2015.

Ermarth, Elizabeth Deeds. *Realism and Consensus in the English Novel.* Princeton: Princeton University Press, 1983.

Fet, Victor. 'Beheading First: On Nabokov's Translation of Lewis Carroll'. *The Nabokovian* 63 (2009): 52–63.

Fiddian, Robin W. *Postcolonial Borges: Argument and Artistry.* Oxford: Oxford University Press, 2017.

Garland, Carina. 'Curious Appetites: Food, Desire, Gender, and Subjectivity in Lewis Carroll's Alice Texts'. *The Lion and Unicorn* 32, no. 1 (January 2008): 22–39.

Geist, Anthony L. and José B. Monleón, eds. *Modernism and Its Margins: Reinscribing Cultural Modernity from Spain and Latin America.* New York: Garland Publishing, 1999.

Gilbert, Stuart. 'Prolegomena to Work in Progress'. In *Our Exagmination Round His Factification for Incamination of 'Work in Progress.'* Edited by Samuel Beckett et al., 58–9. London: Faber and Faber, 1972.

Gilmore, Lois. '"Where Childhood's Dreams Are Twined": Virginia Woolf and the Literary Heritage of Lewis Carroll'. In *Virginia Woolf and Heritage.* Edition by Jane deGay, Tom Breckin, and Anne Reus, 121–6. Clemson: Clemson University Press, 2018.

Giunta, Edvige. 'Dear Reverend: Lewis Carroll and the Boston girls'. *James Joyce Quarterly* 30, no. 3 (1993): 488–92.

Graner, Emma D. 'Dangerous Alice: Travel Narrative, Empire, and *Alice's Adventures in Wonderland*'. *CEA Critic* 76, no. 3 (November 2014): 252–8.

Guiliano, Edward, ed. *Lewis Carroll: A Celebration, Essays on the Occasion of the 150th Anniversary of the Birth of Charles Lutwidge Dodgson.* New York: Clarkson N. Potter, 1982.

Haas, Andrew W. *Auden's O: The Loss of Sovereignty in the Making of Nothing.* Albany: SUNY Press, 2013.

Hancher, Michael. '*Punch* and *Alice*: Through Tenniel's Looking-Glass'. In *Lewis Carroll: A Celebration, Essays on the Occasion of the 150th Anniversary of the Birth of Charles Lutwidge Dodgson.* Edition by Edward Guiliano, 26–49. New York: Clarkson N. Potter, 1982.

Hancher, Michael. *Tenniel's Illustrations to the Alice Books.* Columbus: Ohio University Press, 1985.

Haughton, Hugh. 'Introduction'. In *Alice's Adventures in Wonderland* and *Through the Looking-Glass.* Edition by Hugh Haughton, ix–lxiv. London: Penguin, 1998.

Haughton, Hugh. 'Introduction'. In *The Chatto Book of Nonsense Poetry*, 1–32. London: Chatto & Windus, 1988.

Hayman, David, ed. *A First-Draft Version of* Finnegans Wake. Austin: University of Texas Press, 1963.

Heidegger, Martin. *Poetry, Language, Thought.* Translated by Albert Hofstadter. New York: Harper Perennial, 1971.

Henkle, Roger B. 'Carroll's Narratives Underground: 'Modernism and Form'. In *Lewis Carroll: A Celebration, Essays on the Occasion of the 150th Anniversary of the Birth of Charles Lutwidge Dodgson.* Edited by Edward Guiliano, 89–100. New York: Clarkson N. Potter, 1982.

Holquist, Michael. 'What Is a Boojum? Nonsense and Modernism'. *Yale French Studies* 43 (1969), reproduced in *Yale French Studies: 50 Years of Yale French Studies, A Commemorative Anthology* 96 (1999): 100–17.

Humble, Nicola. *The Feminine Middlebrow Novel 1920s to 1950s: Class, Domesticity, and Bohemianism*. Oxford: Oxford University Press, 2001.

Irwin, John T. *The Mystery to a Solution: Poe, Borges, and the Analytic Detective Story*. Baltimore: Johns Hopkins University Press, 1996.

Johnson, Barton D. 'The Alpha and Omega of Nabokov's *Invitation to a Beheading*'. In *Nabokov's Invitation to a Beheading: A Critical Companion*. Edited by Julian W. Connolly, 119–38. Evanston: Northwestern University Press, 1997.

Jolas, Eugene et al., eds. *transition*. Paris, 1927–38.

Joyce, James. *Finnegans Wake*. Edited by Robbert-Jan Henkes, Erik Bindervoet, and Finn Fordham. Oxford: Oxford University Press, 2012.

Joyce, James. *The Mime of Mick, Nick and the Maggies: A Fragment from 'Work in Progress'*. The Hague: The Servire Press, 1934.

Kelly, Richard. '"If You Don't Know What a Gryphon Is": Text and Illustration in *Alice's Adventures in Wonderland*'. In *Lewis Carroll: A Celebration, Essays on the Occasion of the 150th Anniversary of the Birth of Charles Lutwidge Dodgson*. Edited by Edward Guiliano, 62–74. New York: Clarkson N. Potter, 1982.

Kent, Kathryn R. *Making Girls into Women: American Women's Writing and the Rise of Lesbian Identity*. Durham: Duke University Press, 2003.

Kerchy, Anna. *Alice in Transmedia Wonderland: Curiouser and Curiouser New Forms of a Children's Classic*. Jefferson: McFarland, 2016.

Kerchy, Anna. 'Alice's Non-Anthropocentric Ethics: Lewis Carroll as a Defender of Animal Rights'. *Cahiers victoriens et édouardiens* 88 (fall 2018): http://journals.openedition.org/cve/3909.

Kincaid, James R. 'Alice's Inversion of Wonderland'. *PMLA* 88, no. 1 (1973): 92–9.

Knowles, Murray, and Kirsten Malmkjaer. *Language and Control in Children's Literature*. London: Routledge, 1996.

Lacan, Jacques. *The Four Fundamental Concepts of Psychoanalysis*. Translated by Alan Sheridan. New York: W. W. Norton, 1981.

Lakoff Robin, T. 'Lewis Carroll Subversive Pragmaticist'. *Pragmatics* 3, no. 4 (1993): 367–85.

Latham, Sean. *'Am I a Snob?' Modernism and the Novel*. Ithaca: Cornell University Press, 2003.

Lecercle, Jean-Jacques. 'Modalities of Translating Nonsense'. *Translation Studies* 12, no. 1 (2019): 15–23.

Lecercle, Jean-Jacques. *Philosophy of Nonsense: The Intuitions of Victorian Nonsense Literature*. London: Routledge, 1994.

Lecercle, Jean-Jacques. 'Translate It, Translate It Not'. *Translation Studies* 1, no. 1 (2008): 90–102.

Leslie, Esther. *Walter Benjamin: Overpowering Conformism*. London: Pluto Press, 2000.

Levine, Robert S. 'Circadian Rhythms and Rebellion in Kate Chopin's *The Awakening*'. *Studies in American Fiction* 10, no. 1 (spring 1982): 71–81.

Little, Judith. 'Liberated Alice: Dodgson's Female Hero as Domestic Rebel'. *Women's Studies* 3 (1976): 195–205.

Lorraine, Tamsin. 'Living a Time Out of Joint'. In *Between Deleuze and Derrida*. Edited by Paul Patton and John Protevi, 30–45. New York: Continuum, 2003.

Lucas, Ann Lawson. 'Enquiring Mind, Rebellious Spirit: Alice and Pinocchio as Nonmodel Children'. *Children's Literature in Education* 30, no. 3 (1999): 157–69.

Lukes, Alexandra. 'Dictionary and Divination: Mallarmé Translating, Back-Translating, and Not Translating'. *MLN* 134, no. 4 (2019): 745–63.

Lukes, Alexandra. 'Mallarmé's Madness: Poetry, Pedagogy, and Translation'. *Modernism/modernity* 24, no. 1 (2017): 141–60.

Lull, Janis. 'The Appliances of Art: the Carroll-Tenniel Collaboration in *Through the Looking-Glass*'. In *Lewis Carroll: A Celebration, Essays on the Occasion of the 150th Anniversary of the Birth of Charles Lutwidge Dodgson*. Edited by Edward Guiliano, 101–11. New York: Clarkson N. Potter, 1982.

Mallarmé, Stéphane. *Œuvres complètes*, vol. I. Paris: Gallimard, 1998.

Mallarmé, Stéphane. *Œuvres complètes*, vol. II. Paris: Gallimard, 2003.

Mallarmé, Stéphane. *Thèmes anglais pour toutes les grammaires*. Paris: Gallimard, 1937.

Mansanti, Céline. *La Revue transition (1927–1938): Le modernisme historique en devenir*. Rennes: Presses Universitaires de Rennes, 2009. 215–49.

Mansanti, Céline and Anne Reynes-Delobel, eds. 'Early American Surrealisms, 1920–1940'. Special Issue. *Miranda* 14 (2017). https://journals.openedition.org/miranda/9754.

Marchal, Bertrand, and Marie-Pierre Pouly. *Mallarmé et L'Anglais récréatif. Le Poète pédagogue*. Paris: Cohen & Cohen, 2014.

Marchiò, Roberto Baronti. '"All Old Dadgerson's Dodges": Language and Meaning in Lewis Carroll and James Joyce'. In *Joyce's Victorians*. Edited by Franca Ruggieri, 25–53. Rome: Bulzoni, 2006.

Marshik, Celia. *At the Mercy of Their Clothes: Modernism, the Middlebrow, and British Garment Culture*. New York: Columbia University Press, 2016.

Mattson, Craig E. 'From Wimsey to The Wire: Distracting Discourse and Attentional Practice'. *Quarterly Journal of Speech* 100, no. 1 (2014): 31–52.

McAra, Catriona, 'Surrealism's Curiosity: Lewis Carroll and the Femme-Enfant'. *Papers of Surrealism* 9 (summer 2011): 1–25.

McCarthy, Mary. 'A Bolt from the Blue'. In *Pale Fire*, v–xxii. London: Penguin, 1962.

McGarrity Buki, Ann. 'Lewis Carroll in *Finnegans Wake*'. In *Lewis Carroll: A Celebration, Essays on the Occasion of the 150th Anniversary of the Birth of Charles Lutwidge Dodgson*. Edited by Edward Guiliano, 154–66. New York: Clarkson N. Potter, 1982.

McLoughlin, Kate. 'Prufrock, Party-Goer: Tongue-Tied at Tea'. In *The Modernist Party*. Edited by Kate Mcloughlin, 45–63. Edinburgh: Edinburgh University Press, 2013.

Michon, Jacques. *Mallarmé et Les Mots anglais*. Montréal: Les Presses de l'Université de Montréal, 1978.

Mignolo, Walter D. *The Idea of Latin America*. Oxford: Blackwell, 2005.

Nabokov, Vladimir. *Invitation to a Beheading*. Translated by Dmitri Nabokov. London: Penguin, 2010.

Nabokov, Vladimir. *Pale Fire*. London: Penguin, 2000.

Nabokov, Vladimir. *Vladimir Nabokov: Selected Letters, 1940–1977*. Edited by Dmitri Nabokov and Matthew J. Bruccoli. San Diego: Harcourt Brace Jovanovich, 1989.

Nash, Katherine Saunders. *Feminist Narrative Ethics: Tacit Persuasion in Modernist Form*. Columbus: Ohio University Press, 2014.

Oates, Joyce Carol. '"First Loves: From "Jabberwocky" to "After Apple-Picking"'. In *The Faith of a Writer: Life, Craft, Art*, 13–22. New York: Plume, 2003.

O'Brien, Flann. *The Complete Novels*. New York: Everyman's Library, 2007.

Petersen, Calvin R. 'Time and Stress: Alice in Wonderland'. *Journal of the History of Ideas* 46, no. 3 (July–September 1985): 427–33.

Plath, Sylvia. *The Collected Poems*. Edited by Ted Hughes. New York: Harper Perennial, 1992.

Plath, Sylvia. *The Unabridged Journals of Sylvia Plath*. Edited by Karen V. Kukil. New York: Anchor, 2000.

Polhemus, Robert M. *Comic Faith: The Great Tradition from Austen to Joyce*. Chicago: Chicago University Press, 1980.

Ren, Aihong. 'Power Struggle between the Adult and Child in *Alice's Adventures in Wonderland*'. *Theory and Practice in Language Studies* 5, no. 8 (2015): 1659–63.

Reynes-Delobel, Anne and Céline Mansanti. 'Americanizing Surrealism: Cultural Challenges in the Magnetic Fields'. *Miranda* 14 (2017).

Richter, Amy G. *Home on the Rails: Women, the Railroad, and the Rise of Public Domesticity*. Chapel Hill and London: University of North Carolina Press, 2005.

Roth, Christine. 'Looking through the Spyglass: Lewis Carroll, James Barrie, and the Empire of Childhood'. In *Alice Beyond Wonderland: Essays for the Twenty-first Century*. Edited by Cristopher Hollingsworth, 23–36. Iowa City: University of Iowa Press, 2009.

Sarzano, Frances. *Sir John Tenniel*. London: Art and Technics, 1948.

Sayers, Dorothy L. *Busman's Honeymoon*. London: New English Library, 1974.

Sayers, Dorothy L. *Lord Peter: A Collection of All the Lord Peter Wimsey Stories*. Edited by James Sandoe. New York: Harper & Row, 1987.

Sayers, Dorothy L. *Strong Poison*, London: New English Library, 2003.

Schleifer, Ronald. *Modernism and Time: The Logic of Abundance in Literature, Science, and Culture 1880–1930*. Cambridge: Cambridge University Press, 2000.

Sewell, Elizabeth. *The Field of Nonsense*. London: Chatto and Windus, 1952.

Sewell, Elizabeth. 'Lewis Carroll and T. S. Eliot as Nonsense Poets'. In *T. S. Eliot, A Symposium for His Seventieth Birthday*. Edited by Neville Braybrooke, 49–56. London: Rupert Hart-Davis Ltd., 1959.

Sewell, Elizabeth. *Lewis Carroll: Voices from France*. New York: The Lewis Carroll Society of North America, 2008.

Sigler, Carolyn, ed. *Alternative Alices: Visions and Revisions of Lewis Carroll's Alice Books*. Lexington: The University Press of Kentucky, 1997.

Sigler, Carolyn. *Lewis Carroll's Alice's Adventures in Wonderland: A Documentary Volume, Dictionary of Literary Biography*, vol. 375. Detroit: Gale Research, 2014.

Smith, Grover. *T. S. Eliot's Poetry and Plays: A Study in Sources and Meaning*. Chicago: Chicago University Press, 1956.

Soldo, John T. 'Jovial Juvenilia: T. S. Eliot's First Magazine'. *Biography* 5, no. 1 (1982): 25–37.

Stephenson, Sarah Kate. 'The Disquieting Muse: Childhood and the Work of Sylvia Plath'. Dissertation. University of Virginia, 2001.

Stern, Jeffrey. 'Lewis Carroll the Surrealist'. In *Lewis Carroll: A Celebration, Essays on the Occasion of the 150th Anniversary of the Birth of Charles Lutwidge Dodgson*. Edited by Edward Guiliano, 132–53. New York: Clarkson N. Potter, 1982.

Struve, Gleb. 'Notes on Nabokov as a Russian Writer'. *Wisconsin Studies in Contemporary Literature* 8, no. 2 (1967): 153–64.

Süner, Ahmet. 'On the Contribution of Tenniel's Illustrations to the Reading of the Alice Books'. *Children's Literature in Education*, 51, no. 1 (2020): 41–62.

Sword, Helen. *Ghostwriting Modernism*. Ithaca: Cornell University Press, 2002.

Toker, Leona. *Nabokov: The Mystery of Literary Structures*. Ithaca: Cornell University Press, 1989.

Taaffe, Carol. *Ireland Through the Looking-Glass: Flann O'Brien, Myles na gCopaleen and Irish Cultural Debate*. Cork: Cork University Press, 2008.

Tigges, Wim. *An Anatomy of Literary Nonsense*. Amsterdam: Rodopi, 1988.

Tigges, Wim. 'Ireland in Wonderland: Flann O'Brien's *The Third Policeman* as a Nonsense Novel'. In *The Clash of Ireland: Literary Contrasts and Connections*. Edited by C. C. Barfoot and Theo D'Haen, 195–208. Amsterdam: Rodopi, 1989.

Trubikhina, Julia. 'Nabokov's Beginnings: "Ania" in Wonderland or "Does Asparagus Grow in a Pile of Manure?"'. In *The Translator's Doubts*, 38–85. Boston: Academic Studies Press, 2017.

Turner, Beatrice. '"Which Is to Be Master?": Language as Power in *Alice in Wonderland* and *Through the Looking-Glass*'. *Children's Literature Association Quarterly* 35, no. 3 (fall 2010): 243–54.

Veitch, Jonathan. *American Superrealism, Nathanael West and the Politics of Representation in the 1930s*. Madison: University of Wisconsin Press, 1997.

Williams, James. 'Lewis Carroll and the Private Life of Words'. *The Review of English Studies* 64, no. 266 (2013): 651–71.

Woolf, Virginia, 'Lewis Carroll'. In *Collected Essays*, vol. 1, 254–55. London: The Hogarth Press, 1966.

Woolf, Virginia. 'A Sketch of the Past'. In *Moments of Being: Unpublished Autobiographical Writings*, 61–160. London: The Hogarth Press, 1978.

Woolf, Virginia. *The Waves*. Oxford: Oxford University Press, 1992.

Zirker, Angelika. '"All about Fishes?" The Riddle of Humpty Dumpty's Song and Recursive Understanding in Lewis Carroll's *Through the Looking-Glass and What Alice Found There*'. *Victorian Poetry* 56, no. 1 (spring 2018): 81–102.

INDEX

Milton Keynes UK
Ingram Content Group UK Ltd.
UKHW022237290324
440229UK00004B/63

9 781350 248717